Women, Technology and Entrepreneurship
Global Case Studies

Women, Technology and Entrepreneurship

Global Case Studies

Editors

Vinnie Jauhari, Ph.D.

Charla Griffy Brown, Ph.D.

Reference Press

4831/24, Ansari Road, Darya Ganj,
New Delhi-110002
Tel. : 23260807, 41563444
Fax : 011-41563334
E-mail: info@essessreference.com
url:http://www.essessreference.com

REFERENCE PRESS
4831/24, Ansari Road,
Darya Ganj,
New Delhi-110 002.

Tel.: 23260807, 41563444
Fax: 41563334
E-mail: info@essessreference.com
www.essessreference.com

Rs.1225/-

First Published - 2009

ISBN: 978-81-8405-042-4

Cover Design by Patch Creative Unit

Published By Reference Press and printed at Salasar Imaging Systems

PRINTED IN INDIA

Contents

Preface

This book contributes to a global understanding of entrepreneurial issues related to women entrepreneurs and their use of technology. The strong management underpinning makes it a valuable resource both for entrepreneurs and academics. This volume was put together to explore the dynamics of entrepreneurship initiated by women and to assess the role technology plays in creating and sustaining these initiatives. Through global case studies, this book analyzes the growth of successful entrepreneurial initiatives by women. Included are businesses developed by women from India, Singapore, the United Kingdom, the Middle East, the United States, Thailand, Chile, and Slovenia among others. The cases give insight into the socio-economic contexts of the firms created as well as how these initiatives were positioned to survive and thrive in their given industries.

The cases featured in the book give insights into the trials, tribulations and successes of women entrepreneurs in diverse sectors and show how these women have leveraged technology to achieve their goals. Lessons learned across 10 different cultures are presented.

According to the Global Entrepreneurship Monitor (GEM), women entrepreneurs create jobs, wealth and innovations across the 37 GEM countries surveyed. In many of these countries the rate of growth of women creating new businesses is greater than the rate of growth for men entrepreneurs. All over the globe, there have been instances where women have started and grown businesses using very elementary technologies as well as very sophisticated technologies. However, surveys of research indicate that very few publications look at the use of technology in women's entrepreneurial activity and less than 10% of academic publications explore women and entrepreneurship at all (Gatewood, et. al, 2003; Brush and Edelman, 2000). In addition, most publications tend to be targeted primarily for academicians. Given the important and changing role of women entrepreneurs in the social, political and economic fabric of global commerce, it is essential that we document such experiences in different countries providing both common parameters for assessment and insight for women who are interested in leveraging technology to create wealth. This book helps us better understand how women can succeeded in creating new enterprises across cultures and even in emerging economies.

Though each case presents a unique "voice" from a specific culture, all cases have been well referenced and well researched. In addition, all manuscripts have been through a blind peer review process. This volume is a valuable resource for academics, entrepreneurs, venture capitalists, business schools, entrepreneurship research centers and consultants. Furthermore, this book is unique in that it reflects real situations providing great insight both for potential entrepreneurs as well as class room discussions. It is our hope that these cases will be an invaluable resource for faculty teaching entrepreneurship courses at business schools and teaching notes are available for some cases upon request to the editors.

Acknowledgements

For any outcome, there is a lot of work behind the scenes. The authors would like to gratefully acknowledge the contribution of numerous people who supported the development of this work.

We would like to extend heartfelt thanks to all the contributing authors who put in tireless efforts in working on the case studies as well as going through multiple rounds of revision. In addition, we are grateful for all of the reviewers who provided insight for the case authors and played such a key role in the selection and revision process.

My very sincere thanks to Prof. Chihiro Watanabe for his mentorship and support for my research interests. I would like to express my gratitude to Dr. Kamlesh Misra, Dr. Umashankar Venkatesh, Mr. K.B. Kachru, Dr. Ramesh Kapur for providing an opportunity for working on this research project. My grateful thanks go to Dr. Michel Benard and Mr. Rob Bouzon at Hewlett-Packard Company for providing inspiration and support.

My sincere gratitude to my parents – Krishan and Krishna Verma who have always stood by me and have always been an inspiration for achievement. My gratitude to my family- Sunil , my husband and my son Shaurya, brother Shallen who have been so supportive and let me work for long hours at work. My very special thanks to my in-laws Krishan and Usha Jauhari, my brother in law Prabhat for his inspirational messages everyday.

I would like to thank my co-author and a very dear friend Charla for her strong support for this project throughout.

We would also like to sincerely acknowledge the support from Amit Saxena and Ashok Sahu at IIMT who have contributed immensely to the development of this work

Vinnie Jauhari

I personally wish to thank you, the reader, for taking the time to learn more about women who are changing the world one small business at a time. Reading even this far proves that you are interested and dedicated to a brighter future for women everywhere.

I am grateful to my colleagues Associate Professor Linnea McCord, Dr. Terry Young, Dr. Sandra Moore, Dr. Maggie Phillips and Dr. Frieda Gehlen for supporting and encouraging me in my own career. I would like to thank Dr. Ian Lowe, Dr. Greg Hope, Dr. Chihiro Watanabe, and Dr. Richard Dasher for constantly being wonderful advocates and mentors. I'm grateful beyond words to Vinnie, my co-editor, co-author and friend, whose presence in my life is a divine gift.

I am deeply indebted to my parents - Charles and Felicia Griffy whose grace and selfless support constantly inspire me. I am extremely grateful to my husband Glen, my daughter, Sienna, and my son, Adam, who are the motivation behind everything I do.

Finally, I want to dedicate my contributions to this volume to my grandparents, Walter and Aldeena Southern. "Deenie", your spirited refusal to accept anything but the greatest of opportunities and possibilities for your daughters, even against social and cultural norms, lives and breaths through your granddaughter.

Charla Griffy-Brown

List of Tables

List of Figures

About the Contributors

Vinnie Jauhari, is M.Sc. (Hons.) in Electronics from Panjab University, Chandigarh and MBA (Gold Medalist) (Marketing). She received her Ph.D. on Corporate Entrepreneurship from Indian Institute of Technology, Delhi and her Post-Doc from the United Nations University, Tokyo in the area of Technology and Society. She is a researcher currently working on numerous international projects on technology and sustainable development. She has delivered lectures at Japan, Netherlands, Australia, UK and Spain among other countries. Dr. Jauhari manages the HP Labs Open Innovation Office India, HP India and also an Adjunct Professor at School of Management and Entrepreneurship at IIMT. She is also the founding editor of the Journal of Services Research, which features in the EBSCO, PROQUEST databases. She has over seventy publications in National and International Journals and has also authored books such as *Business Strategy, Services Management, Readings in Services Management, Global Case Studies on Hospitality Industry*. Her area of expertise is Corporate Entrepreneurship, Strategic Management and Technology issues.

Charla Griffy-Brown Ph.D., an Associate Professor of Information Systems at Pepperdine

University's Graziadio School of Business and Management, is currently part of an international research team examining technology and development issues. In 2004, she received a research award from the International Association for the Management of Technology in which she was recognized as one of the most active and prolific researchers in the Technology Management and Innovation field. A former researcher at the Foundation for Advanced Studies on International Development, Tokyo, Dr. Griffy-Brown has also served as associate professor at the Tokyo Institute of Technology. Dr. Griffy-Brown graduated from Harvard University, is a former Fulbright Scholar, and holds a Ph.D. in Technology Management from Griffith University in Queensland, Australia. She has worked for NASA at the Kennedy Space Center and has taught innovation/technology management courses in Australia, Singapore, Indonesia, Malaysia, and Japan. Dr. Griffy-Brown has also served as a consultant for the United Nation's Global Environmental Facility and the European Commission. Dr. Griffy-Brown's publications include more than 40 articles as well as books in the areas of technology management, information systems, and techno-economic development. Some of her publications are written in Japanese. She has also conducted information systems research at large enterprises such as American Honda Motor Corporation, as well as in more than 100 small and medium sized enterprises in Japan, the U.S., and China. Dr. Griffy-Brown's research is currently funded by an SAP University Alliance Grant, and she also has funding from the Pepperdine Voyager/ Lilly Foundation, and the Rothschild Research Endowment as well as the Graziadio School of

Business Funds for Excellence.

Kirti Dutta is B.Sc. and MBA (Institute of Management Studies and Research, Rohtak) Kirti Dutta is a hardcore marketing professional with thirteen years of work experience in the industry and academia. She has been actively involved in marketing and project management in different parts of the country in the field of lubricants, textiles and dyeing. She has been responsible for framing and successful implementation of marketing strategies especially in the field of concept and product marketing. She has also been involved in logistics, purchase and inventory management. Her areas of interest are marketing and consumer behavior. Kirti Dutta is currently Lecturer of Institute for International Management and Technology, Gurgaon. Currently she is in the process of pursuing her Ph.D.

Gunjan M. Sanjeev, is an Associate Professor at Indus World School of Business, India. She has earlier been teaching at IILM for last ten years. Her research interests include The Commercial Banking system, Microfinance and Corporate Finance. She teaches courses in Financial Management of Banks and Insurance Companies, Financial Services and Corporate Finance. She has a number of refered publications to her credit. She has presented her research work in national and international forums. She was given the Best Paper award at a conference organized by IIM, Lucknow, India in March, 2005. Her other research paper presented at an international conference at Indian Institute of Science, Bangalore, India in September 2005, was amongst the five papers in the finance area considered for the award.

Kakoli Sen is an Assistant Professor at Institute for Integrated Learning in Management, New Delhi. She has corporate and teaching experience of over fifteen years. She holds her postgraduate qualification in Journalism and Mass communication and Human Resource Management. She is a keen researcher in the area of Organization Behaviour. She is currently the associate dean at the Undergraduate Business school –IILM.

Himani Kaul, Open Innovation Office, Hewlett–Packard Company, India. She supports capacity building efforts in engineering education.

Shivangi Gupta, Open Innovation Office, Hewlett–Packard Company, India. She support capacity building efforts in engineering education.

Smitu Malhotra, Ph.D. is Assistant Professor (Marketing) at XLRI Jamshedpur. Her thesis' studied the impact of globalization on competitive practices of Indian firms. Prior to her Ph. D. she has worked in the industry in the marketing area. Her other areas of interest include social entrepreneurship and marketing communications.

Madhukar Shukla, Ph.D., is a professor (OB and Strategic Management) at XLRI Jamshedpur. He has worked with the National Productivity Council and Administrative Staff College of India, Hyderabad and was a Visiting Professor at ESADE (Barcelona), Spain, during 1993-94. His fields of special interest include Organizational Design, Organizational Change and Development, Learning Organizations and Management of Creativity. Authored two books: *Designing Organizations* and *Competing through Knowledge*, and about 30 papers in professional journals. Consultancy with many public and private organizations.

Ghee Soon LIM, National University of Singapore, NUS Business School Department of Management & Organization, 1 Business Link, BIZ 2 Building, Singapore.

Carla C.J.M. Millar, is Professor and Chair of International Marketing and Management at the University of Twenty and of Groningen in the Netherlands.

Mirjana Mladic, is Managing Director of Atlanta, a consultancy firm in Maribor, Slovenia. Specialising in Marketing, Communication and Strategy Advice and Training.

Linzi J Kemp, PhD, MBA, BEd (Business), DipMkt, Academic Area Coordinator (Business, Management and Economics), Empire State College, Center for Distance Learning, State University of New York (SUNY). This role involves coordination of an online business program. As a member of faculty with the Center for International Programs, Empire State College, Linzi teaches and mentors students online and in Lebanon. Previous experience as an educator has been in schools, colleges and universities in the areas of management; organizational theory and behavior; marketing. In Dubai (United Arab Emirates), Linzi taught, and was professional development coordinator. In the Kingdom of Saudi Arabia, she coordinated the information technology curriculum at a Junior High School. At a teacher training college in the People's Republic of China, she was involved with training teachers to teach English. Originally from the UK, Linzi has worked there in private and public organizations within the fields of education, retail and the health service.

Janet Rovenpor, PhD, is Professor of Management and Marketing Department, School of Business, Manhattan College, Manhattan College Parkway, Riverdale, New York.

Rebecca White is an Associate Professor of Management and the Founding Director of the Fifth Third Bank Entrepreneurship Institute at Northern Kentucky University. She received her Ph.D. from Virginia Tech University. Her teaching and research interests are in the areas of Strategic Choice and Strategy Formulation and Implementation in entrepreneurial and growing firms.

Fred Beasley is an Associate Professor of Marketing at Northern Kentucky University. He received his Ph.D. from the University of Maryland. He teaches principles of marketing, marketing research, and marketing strategy, and his research interests are in the areas of consumer price promotions and marketing education.

Steven F. Freeman PhD, is Visiting Scholar and Affiliated Faculty in the Center for Organizational Dynamics. Since 1998, he has been Professor of Management at INCAE (Central American Institute of Business Administration), Alajuela, Costa Rica, an international MBA program established by Harvard University. During 2002, he was Karel Steuer Chaired Professor in Entrepreneurship at Universidad de San Andreas, Buenos Aires, Argentina. His research interests include strategy, entrepreneurship, loss, change, and resilience. A recent paper (with Maltz and Hirschorn), "Moral Purpose and Organizational Resilience: Sandler O'Neill & Partners, L.P. in the Aftermath of September 11th" has been chosen by the Academy of Management as 2003 Best Paper on Organizational Change and Development. He received his Ph.D. in Organization Studies from the MIT Sloan School of Management.

Fredy Valenzuela is a Ph.D. candidate at New England Business School, University of New England, Australia and an Assistant Marketing Professor at University of Talca, Chile. He also has an MBA degree at University of Ottawa, Canada. His area of research is marketing and in particular topics related with service recovery, customer satisfaction management and relationship marketing. His work has been published in several international refereed journals, such as Journal of Travel Research, Journal of Contemporary Management Research and Journal of Services Research, among others. He has also participated in several international conferences in México, Puerto Rico, Chile, India, Hong Kong and Australia. In the International Conference on Business and Information held in Hong Kong, 2005 he got the best paper award.

Víctor Nocetti has an MBA degree at University of Dallas, USA and is a Lecturer at University of Talca, Chile. He teaches, since its inception in 1994, Management, Human Resources, Negotiation and other courses related to business management. He is also owner and CEO of ZONA 5, an Internet Center located in Talca's downtown, which has 7 years in business. Besides his work at UTALCA and ZONA 5, Mr. Nocetti does consulting for some companies in Chile in subjects such as Mission and Strategy, Service Quality, Planning, Collective Bargaining, and so on. One of his cases, CCU: Sed o no sed, was published in the last Spanish edition of Koontz & Weihrich, 2003, "Management: A Global Perspective", 12a. Edition, McGraw Hill, pgs. 180-186.

1
Women, Technology and Entrepreneurship: An Introduction

Vinnie Jauhari
Charla Griffy-Brown

WOMEN AND GLOBAL ENTREPRENEURSHIP

According to the Global Entrepreneurship Monitor (GEM), women entrepreneurs create jobs, wealth and innovations across the 34 GEM countries surveyed. In many of these countries the rate of growth attributed to new businesses created by women is greater than the rate of growth for men entrepreneurs. Throughout the world women are increasingly starting and growing businesses using very elementary as well as very sophisticated technologies. However, surveys of research indicate that very few publications have examined the use of technology in women's entrepreneurial activity, and less than 10% of academic publications explore women's roles in entrepreneurship at all. Those publications that do explore women's roles have created a discourse that inherently compares women's entrepreneurship to that of men (Ahl, 2004). By its very nature, this research construction creates a gendered concept of women's entrepreneurship with some intrinsic assumptions that are hard to test quantitatively without getting caught up in the very discourse that creates this bias. In other words, by putting gender as a dependent and independent variable, most surveys and statistical researches assume that there are intrinsic differences among women and men as entrepreneurs. This case book, constructed entirely on qualitative rather than quantitative methods, provides a departure from this methodology and an opportunity to not only explore the role of technology in the area of women and entrepreneurship, but to test some of the most fundamental assumptions about women and entrepreneurship in the process.

1. Given the important and changing role of women entrepreneurs in the social, political and economic fabric of global commerce, it is essential that we document women's entrepreneurship in those significant economies in which it is occurring. Such acknowledgement not only serves to document the trend, but also to provide both standardized parameters for assessment and insight that will benefit women who are interested in and capable of leveraging technology to create wealth. This book helps us to a better understanding of how women have succeeded in creating new enterprises across cultures and even in emerging economies. The goal has been to do so without comparing women entrepreneurs to men, but rather comparing them to women entrepreneurs to each other across cultures. By exploring the social, cultural and institutional basis for successful ventures started by women, it is possible to draw conclusions regarding common themes as well as identify whether or not gender plays a role in these ventures as well as how these ventures are using technology. The

cases featured in this book throw light on the following aspects:

1. How technology has been deployed by firms,
2. The motivation behind setting up the ventures,
3. Gender as a factor influencing the setting up and operation of the firm,
4. Growth strategies adopted by businesses,
5. Major challenges encountered by the entrepreneur and how they were overcome,
6. Competitive analysis for the firm and challenges therein,
7. Financial analysis and viability of the business wherever it was possible. This also included perspective on how initial start up happened,
8. Any cultural factors which were impediments or responsible for success of the venture,
9. Sustainability of business in long run.

Statistics on Global Women Entreprenuers

In order for this book and its cases to move beyond statistics and quantitative data regarding women entrepreneurs, we must first understand the quantitative realities of this group globally. Data from Global Entrepreneurship Monitor's (GEM) 2004 Report on Women and Entrepreneurship estimate that about 73 million people are active entrepreneurs in the 34 nations that have participated in the survey. Of that total, 30 million are women. The GEM Report documents that 71.4% of the women entrepreneurs report choosing entrepreneurship for exploiting an opportunity, while 28.4% of such entrepreneurs choose entrepreneurial activity out of necessity. The choice for this career arises especially in the case of low income countries.

The profile of women entrepreneurs globally can be summarized as follows: In low and middle income countries, the peak years for women to become involved in entrepreneurial activities are ages 25 to 34. In high income countries, the peak years to become involved in entrepreneurial activities for women are ages 35 to 44. In low income countries the majority of entrepreneurially active women (54%) have not completed a secondary degree. For example, in Peru and Uganda, more than 80% of the entrepreneurially active women have only *some* secondary education. In high income countries, it is typically women who have some *graduate* experience who are most likely to start new businesses. The GEM data also reveal a negative correlation between female entrepreneurial activity and both current and long-term levels of female unemployment. Furthermore, a high level of unemployment within a country for both men and women is most likely associated with a reduction in the demand for goods and services, a consequence that stifles that country's economic growth. Therefore, entrepreneurial activity among women is important because it additively creates economic opportunity and encourages economic development.

In Asia, 35% of the SME's are already headed by women (APEC). In China, women account for substantial new business starts. In Japan, the percentage is much higher. Women entrepreneurs in Asia are significant engines of economic growth. Technology access and usage could have an impact on the cost savings. Brisco (2000) postulates that Asian women constitute a huge potential market as consumers of products and services. Yet this market is not tapped fully. In Japan, women account for less than 17% of transactions on e-commerce websites in a recent study (Nikkei Market Accesses August, 2000). Brisco (2000) in her study points that since smaller companies are contributing up to 60% of GDP and 35% of these smaller companies in Asia are owned by women, corporations should facilitate low cost computers with small charge for internet access in order to tap into this burgeoning market.

Jalbert (2000) has given an insight into ownership by women entrepreneurs across various countries:

> Women in advanced market economies own more than 25 percent of all business. Across various nations, the ownership establishments by women are as follows: Russia – 64%, Japan – 23%, China – founded 25% of the businesses since 1978.
>
> In Hungary, women started more than 40% of all businesses since 1990.
>
> In Poland, women own 38% of all businesses.
>
> In France, women head one in every four firms. In Great Britain, women are one-fourth of the self-employed sector.
>
> In the EU, one-third of new businesses are started by women.

Source: Estes, 1999; NFWBO, 1998; Women in Business – Lesotho, 1998; Jalbert, 1999c; Carter and Cannon, 1992

Entrepreneurship has always been used as tool for economic development. It has been related with dimensions of innovation, risk-taking and proactiveness (Miller, 1983; Jauhari, 2004). The analysis of the birth of enterprises across the globe gives some interesting insights into the dynamics of entrepreneurship. Entrepreneurship by women is a sub-set of entrepreneurial efforts initiated by the general population. The issues are also somewhat similar. However, the role of women and status issues vary across different cultures and these differences therefore create challenges for women entrepreneurs. The Global Entrepreneurship Monitor (GEM) offers some interesting insights into the dynamics of entrepreneurship spanning 34 countries in the GEM 2004 cycle. The study covered 784 million people covering the age group of 18-64 year old population. The Gem Conceptual Model is very comprehensive in its approach and reflects on the various social, political, and cultural context factors which have a bearing on the entrepreneurship in a particular country. It also relates these factors with national growth.

The Global Entrepreneurship Monitor, 2004 study revealed the following:

1. The study points out that the entrepreneurial activities could be classified in the following four sectors:

   (a) Extractive sector, (b) transforming sector, (c) business services, (d) consumer oriented sector.

   Across various countries, consumer oriented sector is the dominant sector for entrepreneurial activities.

2. In terms of jobs creation, regardless of the income level, about two-third's of the new ventures expect to employ no more than two people. In high and low income countries, about 30% expect to create 3 to 10 jobs. Middle income countries expect to create least jobs.

3. Start-ups that are focused on growth are more prevalent in high income countries.

4. There are almost twice as many men who are active entrepreneurs than women. In middle

income countries, men are 75% more likely than women to be active entrepreneurs. In high income countries men are 33% more likely than women to be active entrepreneurs. In low income countries, men are 41% more likely than women to be active entrepreneurs.

5. Gender differences are consistent across age groups and across most countries. In no country, there are more women who are active entrepreneurs than men, but there is a wide variation between nations. The gender gap is narrower for necessity entrepreneurship than for opportunity entrepreneurship. This has some interesting ramifications. If majority of entrepreneurship happening is necessity entrepreneurship, then chances of failure are high as it leads to setting up of "me too" category of entrepreneurship ventures. Even at a global level opportunity entrepreneurship is low, therefore when women get involved with high-tech ventures, it makes an important reason to look at the motivations and reasons for such entrepreneurship happening.
6. The relationship between education and entrepreneurship is complex. The high income categories need to emphasize R&D, technology, commercialization and scientific education. Low income categories need a strong commitment to education and training in order to develop an environment more conducive to entrepreneurship.
7. Regardless of the level of the income in their countries, 25-34 olds are most active in entrepreneurship. Women are less likely than men to start businesses. Most people who start

businesses work elsewhere. In low income countries, those with lower levels of education start businesses. In high income countries, those with higher levels of education start businesses. Unemployment and necessity entrepreneurship are highest in the low income countries.

Women in the years to come will have a larger role in national economies. Women are an economic force that policy makers will not be able to ignore. In fact, fostering women's entrepreneurship was adopted by the member states as one of the strategic directions for economic action in the economic area at the UNECE Regional Meeting on the 2000 Review of the Implementation of the Beijing Platform for Action held in January 2000, Geneva.

Developing Women Entrepreneurs in Asia

Women's entrepreneurship has a tremendous potential in empowering women and transforming society. Yet this potential remains largely untapped with less than 10% of entrepreneurs in South Asian countries being women (Sinha, 2005).

According to the White Paper presented by Brisco(2000) at the World Economic Forum, women represent nearly 50% of the labour force in Asia (Statistics on Women in Asia and the Pacific, United Nations, 1999) and 75% in China alone –higher than any other Asian nation"(Sharma, 1999). (See figure 1). SMEs make up 95% of all enterprises in Asia Pacific, employing upto 84% of the work force and contributing 30-60% of GDP of each APEC economy. In Asia, 35% of SMEs are already headed by women. In China, women account for 25% of all new business starts (Sharma, 1999). The use of technology specially the web can allow them to start a successful home based enterprise more easily. In many cases a successfully deployed home-based business that relies on technology spells the difference between meager living and a profitable enterprise. The ability of women to earn income at home "the E-commerce site technology to efficiently market goods and services, process orders and perform accounting tasks–," is adding attraction of the internet for women. In Asia, women represent only 22% of internet users (Brisco, 2000). There is a need to reduce this digital divide in the population.

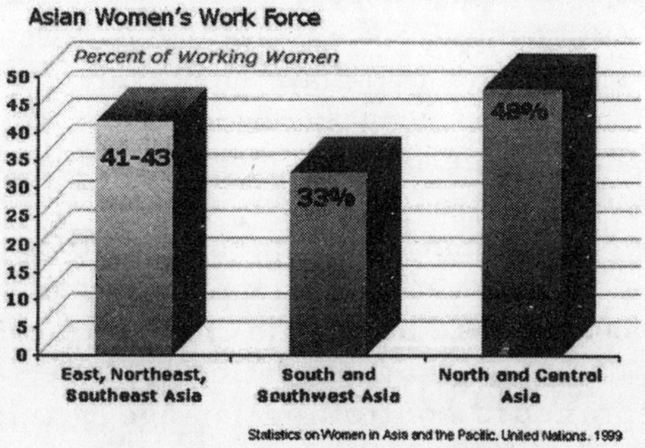

Fig. 1. Asian Women's Work Force

The entrepreneurial experiences of women vary across various nations. One can see from the chart that women have diverse backgrounds and their economic activities may be undertaken at home, may be seasonal or may change frequently. We can classify most enterprises into three categories based on the kind or scale of activity and income (Entrepreneurship Development for Women, 1996 SIDO ILO and SIDA, Sourced from http://www.ilo.org/public/english/region/asro/bangkok/ paper/ manu_tra.htm.)

* Survival enterprise, (mostly for poor and low income women) generally involved in traditional business activities at the survival level; these

could include handicrafts, food-processing, tailoring, vending, etc. For this reason some people do not consider these women to be 'entrepreneurial';

* Micro enterprise, (mostly for poor, low and middle income women);
* Small enterprise, (mostly for middle and higher-middle income women).

Djankov et. al. (2006) have compared the entrepreneurship practices in China and Russia. In their study they have reported that Russian and Chinese entrepreneurs have more entrepreneurs in their family and among childhood friends, value work more than leisure and have higher wealth ambitions. Russian entrepreneurs have a better educational background. Chinese entrepreneurs are more risk-taking and have more entrepreneurs among their childhood friends. Russian and Chinese entrepreneurs have common characteristics relative to non-entrepreneurs controlling for age, gender and education.

The World Bank (2006) data on Gender variables across the various Asian countries are indicated in Table 1.

If we look at the Gender Development Index, we find that the scores vary across different countries. The scores are higher in the case of China, Singapore, Malaysia and even Sri Lanka as compared to India. The scores on Gender Development Index also provide insight into the empowerment of women and the opportunities for them in the society. In terms of governance and participation in the government, China, the Philippines and Pakistan have higher scores as compared to India. Korea, Japan, Malaysia have a

Table 1: World Bank Indicators on Gender

	China	India	Japan	UAE	Philippines	Taiwan	Korea	Singapore	Malaysia	Nepal	Sri Lanka	Pakistan
Gender												
Gender Development Index	0.75	0.59	0.94	0.8	0.75	0	0.9	0.88	0.79	0.51	0.75	0.51
Seats in Parliament Held by Women (as % of total)	20.2	9.3	9.3	0	15.4	0	13	16	13.1	6.4	4.9	20.6
School Enrollment, Tertiary, Female (% gross)	0	9.3	45.5	52.8	35.1	0	63.6	0	28.1	3.2	0	2.8
Females in Labor Force (% of total labor force)	45	32.7	41.9	14.5	38.5	0	40.5	38.6	38.6	40.5	30.4	27
School Enrollment, Secondary, Female (% gross)	62.3	42.5	102.9	80	85.9	0	89.9	0	73.1	37	82.6	22.9

Source: World Bank (2006)

higher degree of female enrollment in tertiary schools. This is also true for secondary school enrollment as well. These parameters also influence the nature of entrepreneurship in a nation and the ability to maneuver them successfully.

There are distinct differences in the economic accomplishments and supporting infrastructure for innovation and growth across various nations. The biggest challenges for economies like India and China are investments in infrastructure, education investments and innovation. The opportunities for women are also dependent on the broad socio-economic milieu of the country. Table 2 gives an indication of the entrepreneurial activities ranked by various countries. Some of the South American countries have higher entrepreneurial activity as compared to the developed countries.

Table 2: Total Entrepreneurial Activity (TEA) Ranked by Country

Country	2004 TEA
Peru	40.3%
Uganda	31.6%
Venezuela	
Ecuador	27.2%
Thailand	
Jordan	18.3%
India	
Chile	
New Zealand	14.7%
South Korea	
Iceland	13.6%
Brazil	13.5%
Australia	13.4%
Argentina	12.8%
Mexico	

China	
United States	11.3%
Canada	8.9%
Poland	8.8%
Ireland	7.7%
Switzerland	
Norway	7.0%
Israel	6.6%
United Kingdom	6.3%
France	6.0%
Greece	5.8%
Singapore	5.7%
South Africa	5.4%
Denmark	5.3%
Spain	5.2%
Netherlands	5.1%
Germany	4.5%
Finland	4.4%
Italy	4.3%
Hungary	4.3%
Taiwan	
Portugal	4.0%
Croatia	3.7%
Sweden	3.7%
Belgium	3.5%
Hong Kong	3.0%
Slovenia	2.6%
Russia	
Japan	1.5%

Source: GEM Consortium http://www.gemconsortium.org/default.asp

Table 2 indicates that South American and some of the Asian countries have a higher degree of entrepreneurial activity than countries such as Japan and US.

In Soundarapandian (1999), a study of the women entrepreneurs and enterprises by the Centre for Entrepreneur Development, Chennai reveals that a few

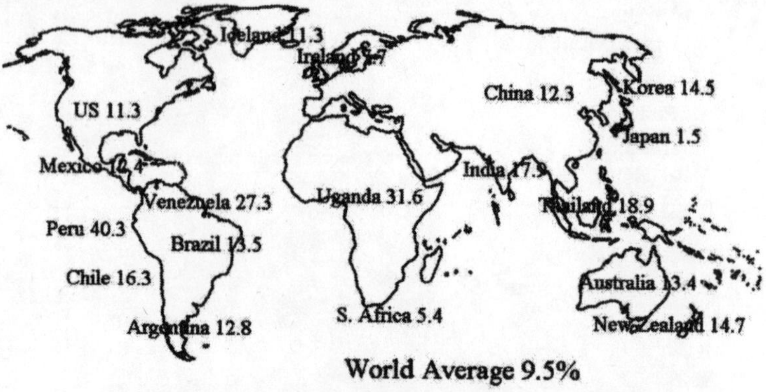

***Source* : http://www.gemconsortium.org/**

Fig. 2. Total Entrepreneurial Activity across various countries

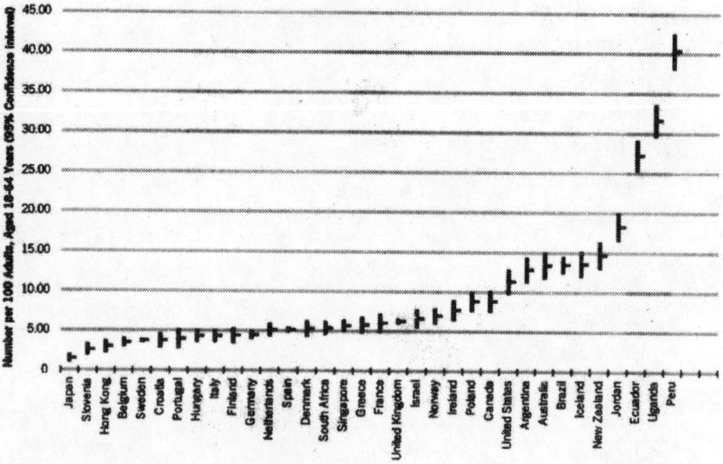

***Source*: GEM Consortium http://www.gemconsortium.org/default.asp**

Fig. 3. Total Entrepreneurial Activity (TEA Prevalence) 2004: By Country

issues in social status play an important role in women owned business in India in particular and other Asian economies as well. These issues were:

* Psychological dependency of the business women on their family members in decision-making,
* To share family responsibility also, simultaneously along with their entrepreneurial responsibility,
* The personality traits of the women in communicating with others,
* Lack of interest and proper exposure to the things leading to enterprises run with binomial name of women,
* Lack of proper training before entering into the business,
* Interested in routine matters only and not involving in innovative ventures,
* Lack of marketing orientation in entrepreneurship,
* Inability to distinguish entrepreneurial functions from other functions like management, production and speculation.

PROFESSIONAL CHALLENGES FOR WOMEN

Women managers face a range of issues in their work life. For instance, Cheng and Liao (1994) have elaborated on the challenges faced by women managers in Taiwan. The study points out that women face resistance to their leadership and need to overcome stereotypes about women in positions of authority. The report concluded that after marriage, women civil servants are only capable of routine work and not of taking major responsibilities. Women managers emphasize principles of upright and proper conduct and guard their reputation more carefully than their male counterparts. Only 61% of women managers report feeling satisfied with their work, the lowest proportion, after social work, among ten occupations studied.

Siengthai and Leelakulthanjit (1994) have discussed the role of women in management in Thailand. There is a clear trend of women moving selectively into government and men into private business. Thai women are still expected to be supportive of men, dependent on them, subservient to them, to yield to the wishes of the others, care for others' needs before their own. Many firms believe that women employees are more obedient, less rebellious, more willing to work for lesser pay than men. They regard men as having higher social status and greater authority. Men traditionally gained power through monkhood, political positions, military and government service, all of which are closed to women. The study points out that women have fewer opportunities for career advancement than men. These attitudes discourage women from developing stronger achievement motivation and from working towards achieving higher work status. There are also indications in legal inequalities between men and women (pg. 169).

Chan and Lee (1994) have discussed numerous factors, internally perceived or externally fostered, which inhibit women's career advancement in management. These include gender stereotyping, work discrimination and inadequate networking. Though there is a gradual increase in women managers in all sectors of the economy due to women's increasing enrolment in university and colleges. More women administrators are being recruited into the public and the sunrise sectors. A disproportionate number of women managers would continue to be single. Mansor (1994) has reflected on women's participation in management which started in Malaysia in the 1970s.

Some of the obstacles faced by Malaysian women have been conflict between career and family responsibilities, employer's stereotypical attitudes, lack of strategic career planning, etc.

Korabik (1994) suggests that in spite of the factors hindering advancement, women managers in China appear to have ample access to women's networks and role models. Though they still manage the bulk of domestic responsibilities, most have the support of their families and many government provided services and workplace protections. Many women managers are acquiring advanced education and training. As more women become educated and highly trained, it will be harder for the people to sustain negative attitudes about women's competence.

LIMITATIONS ON WOMEN'S ECONOMIC ACTIVITIES

Research indicates that women's employment is not only important for economic growth but also for the well being of families. However, restricted access to education and vocational training, heavy workloads at home and in non-paid domestic and market activities and labour market discrimination often limit women's participation in paid economic activities. Women entrepreneurs are fewer as compared to men since few women have access to credit markets, capital, land, training and the education that may be required to start up a business. Cultural norms may also prevent women from working on their own or from supervising other people. In addition, women face more time constraints as compared to their male counterparts due to women's traditional family responsibilities. Women are also vastly underrepresented in decision making positions in government, although there is some evidence of recent improvement (World Development Indicators, 2006).

With the exceptions of Italy and Sweden, worldwide the average number of people willing to share the ownership of an entrepreneurial venture with women tends to be fewer than five. Very few women-owned businesses are expected to provide more than 25 jobs within five years, specifically about 1% of such businesses in both low and middle income countries and 1.6% in high income countries. Furthermore, in the vast majority of countries, regardless of per capita income, women's early stage businesses have substantial competition. Female entrepreneurs also tend to have smaller amounts of venture capital and of equity and a higher proportion of bank loans. The issue of external financing is particularly relevant for high income countries where increasing numbers of women are beginning to move towards technological and hence more capital intensive businesses. The 2004 Global Entrepreneurship Monitor (GEM) report on financing indicates that entrepreneurs themselves provide 65.8% of the start-up capital for their new ventures. For all the GEM nations combined, the average amount needed to start a business is US $53,673. Across all countries, except in Ireland, a high income country, the largest portion of women entrepreneurs (almost 40%) provides only up to 10% of their own start-up money and obtains the remaining 90% from external sources.

SEVEN MYTHS THAT CHALLENGE WOMEN ENTREPRENEURS

The data from GEM indicate that there are many challenges faced by women entrepreneurs globally. The US Diana Project (Brush, Carter, Gatewood, Greene &

Hart, 2001) examined and repudiated following seven myths relating to women entrepreneurs: 1) Women do not want to own high growth businesses; 2) they do not have the right education or experience to lead high growth businesses; 3) they lack suitable networks; 4) they are not financially savvy; 5) they do not submit to business plans; 6) they are not in industries that venture capitalists find attractive, and, 7) they are not a force in the venture capital arena. All of these assumptions were found to be false. In addition, the use of technology is a factor which in and of itself negates many of these assumptions (Griffy-Brown and Whitfield, 2006).

Countering false assumptions such as those above is the reality that the participation by women in building enterprises opens doors of opportunity for other women as well as for members of their families. Studies of women entrepreneurs are mainly divided among the following five thematic areas (Brush 1992; Ahl, 2002; Monaci, 1997):

1. Breeding grounds of female entrepreneurship,
2. Patterns of female entrepreneurship,
3. Barriers against female entrepreneurship,
4. Motivations of women entrepreneurs,
5. Organizational and managerial methods (the "enterprise culture" of women entrepreneurs).

With regard to the first area of "breeding grounds", researchers have found that the *service sector* provides many opportunities for women entrepreneurs. In fact, women entrepreneurship has primarily been witnessed in the service sector because of women's typical lack of specific technical skills and their difficulties in obtaining financial support for business startups and ongoing business efforts.

PATTERNS OF FEMALE ENTREPRENEURSHIP

In terms of the patterns of female entrepreneurship, these have been classified (Goffee and Scase, 1985; Cromie and Hayes, 1988; Monaci, 1997) in the following categories (Bruni et al., 2004):

a. "**Aimless**" - Young women who set up business as an alternative to unemployment;

b. "**Success-oriented**" - Women for whom entrepreneurship is not an obligation, but a long term strategy;

c. "**Strong success-oriented women**" - Women without children who view entrepreneurial activity as an opportunity for greater professional fulfillment;

d. "**Dualists-women**" - Who must reconcile work and family responsibilities;

e. "**The return worker**" - Women who have quit their previous jobs to look after their family responsibilities and are motivated mainly by economic considerations or by desire to create space for self-fulfillment outside the family sphere;

f. "**Traditionalists**" - Women with family backgrounds in which owning and running a business is a long-standing tradition;

g. "**Radicals**" - Women motivated by a culture antagonistic to conventional values who set up initiatives intended to promote the interests of women in society.

BARRIERS TO WOMEN ENTREPRENEURS

Studies in a majority of Western countries indicate that the main barriers to women entrepreneurship are similar to those described in Asia.

They are, firstly, the socio-cultural status of women that identifies the primary role of women with family and domestic responsibilities and reduces the credibility of women intent on setting up businesses in a variety of ways (Bruni et al., 2004). The access to information networks and assistance are also sources of possible gender exclusion (Aldrich, et al., 1989). Lack of access to venture capital is also among other obstacles.

Motivations among women for initiating enterprises have been found to range from compulsions to exploitation of opportunity in the market. The compulsion factor results many times in smaller ventures, and entrepreneurial success can sometimes be immensely challenging in such cases.

Finally, researchers exploring the "enterprise culture" of women entrepreneurs have found that female entrepreneurship is different from that of men largely because the socialization processes within business are typically unique for women. The leadership styles are also different among women, often following more of a transformational style as compared to that of men. This transformational style seeks to foster positive interactions and trust relations among and with subordinates with regard to sharing power and information and encouraging employees to subordinate their personal aims and interests to collective ends (Rosener, 1990).

Impediments for Women Entrepreneurship in Asia

There are lot of impediments for entrepreneurship for women in Asia.. Some of these are indicated below (Sinha, 2005):

1. Access to finance,
2. Access to markets,

3. Access to training,
4. Access to networks,
5. Access to policy makers.

In the Indian context, there are a range of institutions which provide the initial and subsequent support to entrepreneurs. However, there is an overlap of support offered. Post- venture creation is offered by smaller number of firms. Initial hurdles such as feasibility studies, techno-economic feasibility, access to venture capital, requisite training in management areas are all areas of challenge for women entrepreneurs. There should be opportunities for single window clearance for women entrepreneurs. The challenges are quite similar across various Asian countries.

Finding Commonalities Across National Boundaries

The challenges facing women entrepreneurs have a number of elements in common. Some of the challenges faced by them relate to the difficulties encountered due to traditional roles ascribed to them. There are the challenges of family support, work-life balance, access to credit, lack of awareness and skill sets, lack of support systems, lack of exposure to technology related issues. Most entrepreneurship which happens falls in the domain of necessity based entrepreneurship which again increases the risk of survival for the firm.

Similarly, there are support mechanisms available for women entrepreneurs in other countries. Some of the following interventions be initiated to attract, support and nurture entrepreneurs in the mainstream economy:

1. Access to credit: There is a need to minimize the barriers to access the credit. Given the literacy rates that exist in some of the South Asian countries, credit access is essential to the sustenance of the firm. For example, Mohammad Yunus was awarded the Nobel Peace Prize for the year 2005-2006 for his work on micro-credit in Bangladesh which has mobilized entrepreneurship to the weakest level in the society. There is a need for thinking through the realities of various societies which are not at the same level of development.

2. Initial training and support: Most entrepreneurs as indicated through the Global Entrepreneurship Monitor study have not been educated beyond the school level. Their exposure to various facets of management is limited. This becomes a high risk situation as the ability to forecast market trends and demand is limited. There is a need to identify training strategies for the larger community which could be attached to the entrepreneurship stream.

3. Traditional Role of women in the society: Asian societies have typical roles for women and they are accepted as being confined to their homes. However, the Chinese women and the women in Thailand have demonstrated that they are at ease with technology and more and more women are joining the work force. However, at work place women confront challenges of biases and harassment.

There is a need for empowerment of women and facilitating access to information. A lot of good work can be done by engaging the communities and also offering support mechanisms which reduce the obstacles for women entrepreneurs. This can be seen in interventions initiated by SEWA in a subsequent chapter. External consultants can never provide solutions as they are external to the communities and are not living with the day to day challenges faced by the communities. The initiatives undertaken by Barefoot College in Tilonia are noteworthy and have been replicated at numerous places in India. These are the initiatives which apply to the local context in rural India and generate employment opportunities and empower the communities by initiating interventions which could go a long way after the consultant and foreign workers have departed.

4. Networks: A lot of work can be initiated on different government bodies, NGOs, firms working together towards achievement of networks and offering complementary services. Globally, the best practices could be shared and similar interventions could be initiated in different parts of the world. The successful cases in one country could be replicated across others through the creation of networks. These networks could also be fostered for providing support at various stages of entrepreneurship. There could be mentors who could guide the entrepreneurs at various stages of their venture creation and sustenance.

5. Managing Information Networks: The biggest challenge today is to let the prospective entrepreneur know that support exists. There is a sea of information which is available. An entrepreneur does not know where to start or which source to tap on account of numerous sources which exist. The government needs to facilitate online portals or user friendly services which could offer single window solutions to prospective entrepreneurs depending on the level of investment that could be made by them. This could truly have a transformational effect. Setting up deadlines for the services provided would go a long way in paving way for a clean, transparent system devoid of corruption and bureaucracy.

QUALITATIVE RESEARCH USING CASE STUDIES

We propose an approach which extends the quantitative work described above by exploring the role of technology and testing some of the fundamental assumptions embedded in the current research discourse on women entrepreneurs. Firstly, by focusing on qualitative research using case studies, this book provides practical, real-world insight into global entrepreneurship among women that is easily readable and accessible for scholars and practitioners. In this regard, the methodology used in developing these peer reviewed cases and teaching notes utilizes established qualitative research methodologies (Miles & Huberman, 1994; Strauss & Corbin, 1998, Lee, 1989, Yin 1994). Use of this methodology for these cases offers very personal insight into the practice as well as theory regarding entrepreneurship among women. It enables us to explore globally the social, cultural and institutional realities of female entrepreneurs to see if gender plays a role in successful business ventures. This book explores in particular the use of technology in female entrepreneurship. It is envisioned that this approach will provide entrepreneurs, policy makers and academics a rich array of global insight into the barriers, challenges, opportunities and successes that women face in the rapidly changing technology enabled business world.

CASE STUDIES IN THE BOOK

The book on Women, Technology and Entrepreneurship provides insight into the dynamics of women-initiated entrepreneurial ventures across various countries. It documents cases of successful women entrepreneurs across countries such as India,

China, Doha, Thailand, Singapore, Great Britain, the United States, Canada, Chile, Slovenia, among others. With regard to use of technology, the case studies range in their coverage from deployment of primitive technology to the establishment of sophisticated online businesses. The book provides insights into the unique socio-economic systems in which each of these women function. The types of enterprises in the cases cover a diverse entrepreneurial range: bio-technology, software, real-estate, on-line education, food processing, natural products, manufacturing, retailing, restaurants, water purifier systems to Non Governmental Organization (NGO) entrepreneurship. This wide spectrum of businesses offers useful insights into important aspects of female entrepreneurship as well as the role of technology in this growing phenomenon.

The brief summaries of each of the cases are provided below.

The Biotech Industry: The Case of Kiran Mazumdar Shaw

Vinnie Jauhari and Kirti Dutta discuss the case of Biocon which is today recognized as India's pioneering bio-tech enterprise primarily due to the founder, Kiran Mazumdar Shaw. Starting from a garage in 1978 she came a long way when in 2004 she became the richest self-made businesswoman with a worth of $440 million. And in 2005 she entered the Fortune's list of 50 most powerful women in international business (Elliott, 2005). The case traces the socio-economic context and also analyses the value drivers in the biotechnology industry. The firm is compared with competition and factors responsible for its success are enumerated.

The Case of Shahnaz Hussain: A Perspective of Global Products from India

Kirti Dutta explores the case of Shahnaz Husain, a quintessential entrepreneur. Shahnaz Husain came from a conservative Muslim family, surmounted social, economical and personal barriers to win more accolades, awards and mentions in the international press than any other Indian woman. The Esprit magazine of Germany has dubbed her as Asia's Helena Rubenstein, Good Housekeeping calls her Estee Lauder and Daily Telegraph has named her "The uncrowned queen of Indian Beauty Therapy". Today, she heads the largest organization of its kind in the world, with more than 400 franchise salons worldwide and ranges of natural formulations for skin, hair and body care. The case study traces the period of growth along with challenges encountered during the growth of the organization. The case study also traces the business environment and its effect on the growth of the firm.

Women Entrepreneurship in India—A Case of Lijjat Papad

Gunjan M. Sanjeev and Kakoli Sen examine Shri Mahila Grih Udyog Lijjat Papad, or Lijjat Papad, an organisation set up in 1959 by a group of women who started with rolling papads, with borrowings of eighty rupees. These women also called *Bens* or sisters had no formal education but felt that they could do something with the free time that they had on hands after finishing their family chores. Their commitment and perseverance has helped them to achieve success. Today they are a large and successful organisation. Lijjat is not only helping the members contribute to the family income but also empowering them. Valuing people and understanding their problems has created for Lijjat a sound and sustainable business model. It is also noteworthy for its commitment to improving the quality of the lives of its members.

A Case Study of Divya Thangadurai

Himani Kaul and Shivangi Gupta traces the entrepreneurial initiative of Divya Thangadurai , also called Sandhi.

SEWA: Creating Women Entrepreneurs

Smitu Malhotra and Madhukar Shukla discuss the case of an NGO led by women entrepreneurs. Self-Employed Women's Association (SEWA) is an all-women "membership organization" which was founded in 1972 in Ahmedabad, India at the initiative of Ela Ramesh Bhatt. The guiding purpose of SEWA is to empower women who work in unorganized/ informal business sectors. From modest beginnings as a small group of poor illiterate women, its membership has grown to around 700,000 throughout India. SEWA is based on Gandhian principles of self-reliance and full employment and functions as a democratic institution. Through its innovative practices and initiatives it has helped its members become fully self-employed and self-reliant. Often been described as a trade union or a confederation of cooperatives, SEWA is more accurately a movement for social change. Its greatest achievement has been in not only publicizing the issues of self-employed workers, but also in influencing policies to give legal/political visibility to such workers' status and contributions. Moreover, it also provides a scalable and sustainable model for harnessing the entrepreneurial potential in developing societies. This case describes the story of the growth of this unique example of social entrepreneurship, which in turn, transforms illiterate, poor and marginalized women into entrepreneurs and leaders.

Women Entrepreneurship in Asia: A Singaporean Case Study

The Ghee Soon LIM case documents the success story of water treatment specialist Hyflux, a young and growing technology company based in Singapore. Founded by female entrepreneur Olivia Lum in June 1989 on a shoestring budget of S$20,000 (US$1 = about S$1.70), Hyflux gradually and painstakingly built its clientele from scratch over a period of more than a decade. The case study is the entrepreneurial story of Lum, who initiated a venture in Singapore. She saw an opportunity in the area of treatment of water and traveled across Indonesia, Maldives, and China for business. On January 17, 2001, Hyflux was listed on Singapore's SESDAQ, the country's stock market for smaller firms. Within three years after the listing, Hyflux chalked up impressive growth results: revenues quadrupled from the prelisting level of S$20.8 million in 2000 to S$81 million and S$89 million in 2003 and 2004, respectively. In April 2003, Lum was elected to the council of Singapore Institute of Management. She was also awarded the 2003 Entrepreneur of the Year Award given by Ernst and Young. This entrepreneurial venture is an example of technology led innovation that targeted the gap in the market. Lum's success is an illustration of a woman's organizational capability in doing business which spans countries and yields respect for her company's concern for stakeholders.

Pioneering Private Education: An Entrepreneurship Challenge in an Economy in Transition —A Case Study of DOBA, Voted the Best and "Coolest" Private Educational Institution in Slovenia

Carla C. J. M. Millar and Mirjana Mladic in their case study of DOBA, the largest private education and training provider for youths and adults in **Slovenia,** have focused on entrepreneurship in the education sector of Slovenia.. This case study traces the growth of DOBA and explores the reasons for its growth. It traces the challenges faced by the founding entrepreneur and DOBA's subsequent challenges for future growth. The case study also brings in the industry context and the socio-cultural milieu in which the entrepreneurial venture has flourished. This case study traces the entrepreneurial journey of Mrs. Jasna Dominko-Baloh, the founder of DOBA. The organization team that Dominko-Baloh created was vibrant and had permanent teams that managed functions such as quality control, education and training, marketing, customer satisfaction, IT, projects and business satisfaction. The case discusses initiatives on creating the right work culture, traces the company's competitive dynamics and evaluates the vision of the institution, which has the potential of becoming one of the best schools in Europe.

Tejari.com – 'The Middle East Online Marketplace' under the leadership of Sheika Lubna Al Qasimi

This case study is embedded in a socio-cultural milieu where women have traditionally not been working. **Linzi J. Kemp** traces the growth of Tejari, under the leadership of Sheikha Lubna Al Qasimi, from the company's inception in 2000 to its becoming known as the "The Middle East Online Marketplace" (Tejari, 2005). The organization is the premier online business to business (B2B) environment facilitating procurement in the Middle East. In 2001, Sheikha Lubna was appointed to head the Dubai e-government executive team for the public sector. This appointment served as the seedbed for creation of Tejari. The case study explores the reasons behind this initiative. Tejari has widened its scope from being a United Arab Emirates (UAE) operation to include other areas in the Middle East. The case study shows the capacity of women in the Middle East to be recognized globally as entrepreneurs and leaders. The case study traces the trajectory of growth of the on-line business and provides insight into the work culture and an analysis of Tejari's consumer and employee dynamics.

Sustainable Entrepreneurship-The Case of the Body Shop

Vinnie Jauhari discusses **The Body Shop International (a UK based entrepreneurial initiative)** and the unique entrepreneurial initiatives of Anita Roddick. The Body Shop was a unique entrepreneurial initiative of an entrepreneur with Italian origin who set up this enterprise in UK. **The Body Shop International** is a high quality skin and body care retailer operating in 52 markets with 2045 stores, spanning 25 languages and 12 time zones. The Body Shop has retail sales amounting to 708.7 million pounds in 2004/2005. The Body Shop business consists of a combination of company owned and franchised markets and developing multi- channel service with direct selling organization - the Body Shop at Home and on-line retail in the US. The enterprise was borne out of a desire to find a suitable work opportunity. This case study traces the route of growth adopted by the enterprise, the journey from a standalone unit to a firm having 2045 stores in which 25 languages are spoken. The case study provides insights into how genuine PR can transform the face of the organization. The entrepreneurial initiative also has important lessons including the concept of incorporation and dealing with stakeholders.

Barbara Corcoran's Successful Career in Real Estate: A Story of Resourcefulness, Marketing Prowess and Creativity

In her case study on **Barbara Corcoran**, **Janet Rovenpor** gives insight into and traces the growth of her successful real estate business in New York City. Climbing to the top of the residential real estate market in New York City is no easy feat. Rents and sale prices for apartments in the borough of Manhattan have been the highest in the United States for decades. The Corcoran Group has survived and prospered within this competitive residential real-estate market. As founder of the firm, Corcoran has been its source of inspiration and the creator of its prestigious public image. Corcoran established her first realty in 1973 with $1,000 from a partner, then ultimately took her share of the assets of the business and opened her own agency. Over a period of 30 years, the firm grew steadily under her stewardship from renting cooperative apartments, to selling condominiums, townhouses and lofts. Corcoran's advice on up-and-coming neighborhoods was widely sought. In 2001, she sold her firm for approximately $70 million, though she retains the position of chairwoman. This case study traces the growth of the Corcoran Group over time and discusses Corcoran's personal characteristics and background. With limited resources, Corcoran created brand name recognition for her firm and introduced several technological innovations that changed the nature of the real estate business. Today her namesake firm has grown domestically and internationally.

Vickie Buyniski Gluckman and United Medical Resources, Inc.

Rebecca J. White and Fred M. Beasley explore Vickie Buyniski Gluckman's business, United Medical Resources (UMR), from its initial conception to its current state, highlighting the important problems and opportunities faced by Ms. Gluckman along the way. In addition to a focus on how technology is used in the business, the case study also discusses how the company's business model can be transferred outside of the U.S. to any country having privatized health care. UMR also provides an example of the role of technology in a company with a high tech, customer service strategy based on customized products and services. The case provides insight into the work culture and the way in which excellence is sustained. The case raises questions about expansion both in the U.S. and outside of the country and illustrates that while the need for more customized health care benefits may be present in other countries, global expansion also offers many challenges.

Costa Rica: The Two Vecosa Cases

The two **Vecosa** cases by **Steve F. Freeman** focus on two broad marketing strategy decisions for a young Costa Rican woman trying to establish a vegetable processing business in her home country. In Vecosa (A), students and business practitioners reading the case are asked to decide which market segment to initially pursue, retail or institutional sales. However, the case is rich in content dealing with an interesting, easy-to-understand new venture that can be used to illustrate six actions crucial to developing a business:

(1) Evaluating a new venture opportunity,

(2) Researching a new venture,

(3) Analyzing a marketing problem,

(4) Making entrepreneurial decisions, and

(5) Determining the ways in which an entrepreneurial decision making differs from that of a large, established firm.

The case study Vecosa (B) centers on ways in which to deal with an anticipated powerful competitor. The case study traces the growth of an entrepreneurial venture in an emerging industry. It assesses the opportunity in an emerging area of consumer products in food processing and examines various factors influencing the enterprise. The case study also provides insight into the personal effort required to balance the work and the challenges of starting a new enterprise.

MOKKA: 20 Years of Tradition

Fredy Valenzuela and Victor Nocetti in her entrepreneurial story about Marta Pfeil discusses the establishment of Café Mokka, in Santiago, Chile. Despite the difficulties of balancing her personal and business lives and of implementing new technologies, Marta ran her sandwich shop for more than 20 years and sustained the business through positive word of mouth. This case study traces the growth of the business, evaluates Pfeil's management style at various stages as well as her leadership approach to the competitive dynamics of converting Café Mokka into one of the leading businesses in the industry. The study also provides ample insight into operational aspects of the business, people related issues, the role of technology and the competitive dynamics of creating a successful business.

This book documents case studies which are evidence of some firms which become successful as start up firms, expanded internationally and created global impact. These firms are examples of determination and success in highly competitive environment. The cases provide insight into how these ventures succeeded despite challenges. The context of business environment in all cases gives an overview of the dynamics of various industry segments and how the start-ups created trajectories of growth in the different socio-economic environments in which they began.

Common variables that are examined in all the cases include: 1) Tracing the growth of business from inception; 2) exploring reasons for business creation; 3) environmental and governmental support networks; 4) supporting institutions and firms; 5) key obstacles encountered and how these were overcome; 6) the current state of women in business; 7) future growth scenarios 8) strategies deployed for growth; 9) role of technology; and 10) role of gender. The case studies also include conclusions and lessons learned as well as questions for review so that can be used in a classroom setting. Some of the cases also include indications of whether or not these endeavors can be replicated in other national contexts.

Importantly, the Concluding chapter brings together an analysis of all of the cases in order to draw conclusions about the role of technology and the fundamental assumptions in research regarding women and entrepreneurship. This chapter analyzes the content and commonalities among all of the cases in terms of what drove success and the role technology played in the endeavors. The chapter also points out at lessons learnt in areas such as strategies deployed for growth, overcoming obstacles in setting up a business, Also it is sums up aspects related with individual entrepreneur characteristics, motivation behind setting up the venture and also gender aspects along with cultural factors influencing the setting up of these firms. It is envisaged that in addition to the rich insight provided by the cases themselves, this final analysis will contribute to the growing study of women and entrepreneurship by drawing insight from these stories of women who have succeeded in new business ventures around the world.

REFERENCES

Ahl, H. (2002). *The making of the female entrepreneur: A discourse analysis of research texts on women's entrepreneurship*, Dissertation Series, No. 15, Jonkoping, Sweden: Jonkoping International Business School.

Alderich, H., Reese, P. and Dubini, P. (1989). Women on the verge of a breakthrough: Networking among entrepreneurs in the United States and in Italy, *Entrepreneurship and Regional Development,* 1(4): 339-56.

Brisco, R. (2000). Turning Analog Women into A Digital Work Force, While Paper presented at World Economic Forum, Asia Pacific Economic Summit, September. Retrieved from <www.ToTheWeb.com> January 2001.

Bruni, A., Gherardi, S. and Poggio, B. (2004). Entrepreneur-mentality: Gender and the study of women entrepreneurs, *Journal of Organizational Change Management, 17, 3.*

Brush, C., Carter, N., Gatewood, E., Green, P. and Hart, M. (2001). *The Diana project - Women business owners and equity capital: The myths dispelled,* Kansas City, MO: Kauffman Center for Entrepreneurial Leadership.

Brush, C.G. (1992). Research on women business owners: Past trends, a new perspective and future directions, *Entrepreneurship Theory and Practice,* 16(4): 5-30.

Carter, S. and Cannon, T. (1992). *Women as entrepreneurs*, London: Academic Press Limited.

Chan, A. and Lee, J. (1994). Women Executives in Newly Industrialized Economy: The Singapore Scenario, in Nancy J. Adler and Dafna, N. Izraeli (ed.), *Competitive Frontiers: Women Managers in a Global Economy*, Massachusetts: 'Blackwell, Cambridge.

Charantimath, P.M. (2006). *Entrepreneurship Development Small Business Enterprises*, New Delhi: Pearson.

Cheng, W. and Liao, L. (1994). Women Managers in Taiwan, in Nancy J. Adler and Dafna, N. Izraeli (ed.), *Competitive Frontiers: Women Managers in a Global Economy*, Massachusetts: Blackwell, Cambridge.

Djankov, S. Qian, Y., Roland, G. & Zhuravskaya, E. 2006 Entrepreneurship in China and Russia Compared, Retrieved from <www.elsa.berkeley.edu>

Estes, V. (1999). *Women and business development: Promoting economic growth and job creation*, USAID/Europe and Eurasia Bureau: author, November 18.

Griffy-Brown, C. and Whitfield, G. (2006). Women Technology and Entrepreneurship: An Analysis of Small Office/Home Office Development in Japan, *Proceedings of the Global Information Technology Management Conference, Orlando, Florida*, June 11-13, 2006.

Jalbert, S.E (1999c). *Report on the Zimbabwe and Malawi focus group outcomes*, Washington, DC: Center for International Private Enterprise.

Jalbert, S.E. (2000). Women Entrepreneurs in the Global Economy, March 17.

Jauhari, V. (2004). *Corporate Entrepreneurship: An Insight from Indian Electronics and Electrical Sector*, International Engineering Management Conference, Singapore, Pan-Pacific, October 18-21.

Korabik, K. Peoples Republic of China, in Nancy J. Adler and Dafna, N. Izraeli (ed.), *Competitive Frontiers: Women Managers in a Global Economy*, Massachusetts: Blackwell, Cambridge.

Lee, A. (1989). A scientific methodology for MIS case studies. *MIS Quarterly*, 13(1): 33-50.

Mansor, N. "Women Managers in Malaysia: Their Mobility and Challenges," in Nancy J. Adler and Dafna, N. Izraeli (ed.),

Competitive Frontiers: Women Managers in a Global Economy, Massachusetts: Blackwell, Cambridge.

Menzies, T.V., Diochon, M. and Gasse, Y. (2004). Examining Venture—Related Myths Concerning Women Entrepreneurs, *Journal of Development*, Vol. 9 No. 2, August 2004.

Miles, M. and Huberman, A. (1994). *Qualitative Data Analysis*, Second Edition. Thousand Oaks, CA: Sage Publications, Inc.

Miller, D. (1983). The Correlates of Entrepreneurship in Three Types of Firm, *Management Science*, Vol. 29, Vol. 7, July.

Monaci, M. (1997). Genere e organizzazione. Milan: Guerini e Associati.

National Foundation for Women Business Owners (1999). *Women business owner in Sao Paulo Brazil: A summary of key issues*, Washington, DC: Author.

Planning Commission (2006). Indian Planning Experience: A Statistical Profile, Government of India, New Delhi. Retrieved from <www.developmentfirst.org/India/planning_commission/statiscalprofile.pdf>

Rosener, J.B. (1990). Ways women lead. *Harvard Business Review*, 68, November/December, 119-20.

Sen, Kalyani Menon and Kumar, A.K. Shiva (2001). *Women in India, How Free? How Equal?*, United Nations, New Delhi.

Sharma, R. (1999). Executive Director, *Women's Edge*, Remarks at Asia Society, December.

SIDO, ILO and SIDA (1996). Entrepreneurship Development for Women, Retrieved from <http://www.ilo.org/public/english>

Siengthai, Sand Leelakuthanjit, O. (1994). Women in Management in Thailand, in Nancy J. Adler and Dafna, N. Izraeli (ed.), *Competitive Frontiers: Women Managers in a Global Economy*, Massachusetts: Blackwell, Cambridge.

Sinha, S. (2005). Developing Women Entrepreneurs in South Asia : Issues, Initiatives and Experiences, Women in Global Economies, Economic and Social Commission for Asia and the Pacific, United Nations.(www. Cipe.org/pdf).

Soundarapandian, M. (1999). *Women Entrepreneurship Issues and Strategies*, New Delhi: Kanishka Publishers.

Strauss, A. and Corbin, J. (1998). *Basics of Qualitative Research: Techniques and Procedures for Developing Grounded Theory* (2nd ed.), Thousand Oaks: Sage Publications, Inc.

Vinita Pandey (2005). Empowering Women in India Changing Horizons — The Kalanjiam Experience, *Journal of South Asia Women Studies*, Vol. 10, No. 1, March 3. <www.asiatica.org>

World Bank (2006). Knowledge Assessment Methodology, Basic Indicators, *World Bank*. Retrieved from <http://www.worldbank.org/kam>

Yin, R.K. (1994). *Case Study Research: Design and Methods*, Thousand Oaks, CA: Sage Publications, Inc.

2
The Biotech Industry: The Case of Kiran Mazumdar Shaw

Vinnie Jauhari
Kirti Dutta

ABSTRACT

Biocon is today recognized as India's pioneering biotech enterprise thanks to the tireless and assiduous efforts of the person responsible for setting it up – Kiran Mazumdar Shaw. Referred to as "India's Mother of Invention" by the New York Times she has steered Biocon's transition from an industrial enzyme company to an integrated biopharmaceutical company with strategic research initiatives. Even today no other Indian biotech company is as committed to or as advanced in drug discovery as Biocon. Starting from a garage in 1978, she became the richest self-made businesswoman in 2004 with a worth of $440 million. In 2005 she entered the Fortune's list of 50 most powerful women in international business (Elliott, 2005).This case documents the growth trajectory of the firm and identifies the value drivers for this growth. It also brings out the major achievements and challenges encountered in the process of growth. It brings an insight into the management style as well as the broad economic and competitive scenario in which the firm came up. The financial data and comparative insight into other firms in this domain give rich insights into the unique place which Biocon has been able to create for itself.

INTRODUCTION

Dr Kiran Mazumdar-Shaw's is a successful technocrat with global standing. Her pioneering efforts in biotechnology have drawn global recognition not only for Biocon but for the Indian industry as well. Ms. Shaw is highly respected in the corporate world and has been referred to as "India's Biotech Queen" by The Economist, (*Biocon*, 2006) and as "as a pioneering enterprising scientist who brought global recognition for Indian Biotechnological industry, and said that "she represents the spirit of innovation Indians are capable of" by Governor of Maharashtra S. M. Krishna (Indian Express, 2006). Not one to be deterred when she did not get many opportunities after becoming the first woman brew master in India, she channelized her fermenting knowledge to start the first Indian Biotechnology company. Thus gaining a first mover advantage in the biotechnology industry when many people in India were not even aware of the term, she started with two people in a small shed and converted it into the multi-million dollar industry that it is today.

Her Early Life

Kiran was born in Bangalore in 1946. Her father was a master brewer at United Breweries. She was educated in Bishop Cotton Girls School and then studied in Mount Carmel College. She received a graduate honors degree in Zoology from Bangalore University in 1973. She then went on to Ballarat College, Melbourne, Australia, specializing in Malting and Brewing Technology, to become India's first woman brew master in 1975. At Ballarat, she was the only woman in an all-male class but she still managed to top. (http://nrcw.nic.in, Biocon, 2006). She wanted to get into the business but ran into excuses about how its remote locations and often violent labor unions were unsuitable for women. So she used her knowledge of fermentation to set up what is now India's largest Biotech company. (Elliot, 2005) In recognition of her preeminent contributions to the field of biotechnology Kiran also received an honorary Doctorate of Science, from her alma mater, Ballarat University. She also received an honorary Doctorate from the Manipal Academy of Higher Education (MAHE) and the Indian Institute of Technology, Roorkee in recognition of her outstanding achievements in biotechnology and industrial enzymes. (Biocon, 2006)

Initial Struggle

Kiran thought of doing many things but she had never thought of starting her own business. It was a chance meeting with the founder of Biocon Biochemicals in Ireland, Leslie Auchinclaus that marked the start of Biocon India. Leslie wanted her to start a firm to manufacture enzymes in India which were a rich source of raw materials. So in 1978 when Kiran was only 25 years old she turned entrepreneur using her microbiological training to start Biocon India Ltd. But it was never smooth going. Banks and financial institutions had not heard of biotechnology in the 1970's and shied away from her proposals. Thus Biocon India started in a small garage in Koramangala on the outskirts of Bangalore. An added reason was also that she was a woman. This was a problem when she started recruiting, because people were wary of working for a woman. But it did not take long for Kiran to dispel those myths. (Virtual Bangalore 2006, Hari, 2002, Elliott, 2005)

Today Biocon Industries is a pioneer in the field of biotechnology. In the beginning Biocon manufactured simple enzymes extracted from sources such as raw papaya and tropical fish. Kiran realised the potential of research outsourcing in the 1990's, and launched Syngene, a contract research company in 1994. Syngene today earns revenues of Rs. 40 crores annually, partnering some of the world's biggest drug companies including GlaxoSmithKline Beecham, Bristols Myers Squibb and AstraZeneca on research projects. She has coined the term "Research Process Outsourcing (RPO)" and aggressively promoted it overseas. In August 2000, Clinigene was launched to focus on clinical trials of oral insulin on diabetes patients. (http://nrcw.nic.in)

Biocon

Major challenges

Biocon is India's leading biotechnology enterprise. Over the past 28 years, it has evolved from an enzyme manufacturing company to a fully integrated biopharmaceutical enterprise focused on healthcare. Biocon applies proprietary fermentation technologies to develop innovative and effective biomolecules in diabetology, oncology, cardiology and other therapeutic segments. Biocon's success lies in its ability to develop innovative technologies and products and to rapidly leverage them to adjacent domains. This unique "integrated innovation" approach has yielded a host of patented products and technologies that have enabled multi-level relationships with their global clientele.

Biocon Limited has three subsidiary companies:

Syngene International Private Limited provides chemistry and molecular-based custom research services in early stage drug discovery and development. Kiran formed Syngene in 1994 when some foreign visitor told her about the opportunities of contract research. She floated Syngene as a separate business and Biocon was not expected to chip in funds frequently. Kiran pauses before entering another space, testing the waters first and expanding only when she is sure of its potential. Hence for four years Syngene progressed at a slow pace and took off in 1998.

Clinigene International Private Limited conducts longitudinal research in diabetes and offers a wide range of comprehensive services in drug development and clinical trials. In the late 1990s Gordon Ringold, a former business associate who had formed a company, Surromed, in the US told Kiran about the exciting possibilities of clinical research and Clinigene was formed in the year 2000 (Biocon, 2006 and Hari, 2002)

Biocon Biopharmaceuticals Pvt. Ltd (BBPL) was set up on 17th April, 2006 in collaboration with CIMAB, representing the Centre of Molecular Immunology, Cuba. The state-of-the-art cGMP compliant facility is designed to manufacture a broad range of novel and bio-similar therapeutic products through large scale cell-culture fermentation for the treatment of cancer, auto-immune and metabolic diseases. Commercial operations will commence in the second quarter of financial year 2007.(CapitalineDatabase)

In 1978, Biocon had started with extracting two enzymes- papain and singlass from papaya and catfish. She produced low-cost enzymes for the food and beverage industry to increase the translucence of fruit juices, for example, or to lighten the structure of bread. She then moved into pharmaceuticals, supplying generic ingredients used in the manufacture of cholesterol-lowering statins to companies such as Myland in the U.S. and Sandoz in Germany (Elliott, 2005). In the 1980s Biocon started R&D to manufacture enzymes through fermentation. At a time when only the Japanese could handle solid-state fermentation with ease, Biocon also decided to focus on it. The R&D team knew nothing about designing a manufacturing plant, let alone about solid-state fermentation. The first blueprint for a fermenter was ready in 1989 and Biocon commissioned its first commercial plant in 1991(Hari, 2002). Initially Kiran had promoted the company as a joint venture with Ireland-based MNC Biocon Biochemicals. However in 1989 Unilever Plc acquired Biocon Biochemical's Ltd. in Ireland and merged it with its subsidiary Quest International (Biocon, 2006). In 1998 Unilever inked a deal with ICI to sell its speciality chemicals division of which Quest International is a part. This year was crucial for Kiran as it was the year she married John Shaw (then the Managing Director of Madura Coats). Shaw with his wide experience and large savings helped Kiran to buy Unilever's share in the company. Unilever had let Kiran float other companies but did not allow it to veer away from its original business of making and selling enzymes. Thus Biocon became an independent entity.

By the late 1990s Biocon got well entrenched in the fermentation space. It designed a new reactor for solid-state fermentation, which could contain micro-organisms well, and its contents could be mixed while fermentation was going on. Things could be added and removed without disturbing the fermentation process and it was named the PlaFractor. To top it all it consumed less energy than the Japanese model. In 2001, Biocon became the first Indian company to be approved by US FDA for the manufacture of lovastatin, a cholesterol lowering molecule. In the same year it also received the US2001 and world-wide patent for its PlaFractor™.

In 2004, Biocon announced a strategic partnership with Vaccinex Inc. to discover and co-develop at least four therapeutic antibody products. In the same year Biocon created a buzz in the stock market with its hugely successful IPO. Biocon closed day one of the listing with a market value of $1.11 billion. It became the second Indian company to cross the $1 billion mark on the day of listing. After this success Biocon announced research collaboration with North Carolina's Nobex Corporation to jointly develop oral insulin for the treatment of diabetes on a global scale. It then launced INSUGEN ™, the new generation bio-insulin, manufactured in Asia's largest human insulin plant. Currently, 75% of insulin sales come from overseas markets such as Latin America, the Middle East and Southeast Asia. Biocon is also planning to finalize marketing tie-ups to sell insulin in US and Europe by the fiscal year ending March 2007. In April, 2006 Biocon invested Rs 1 billion in a new facility in Bangalore to make monoclonal antibodies for cancer and autoimmune diseases (Financial Express, 2006). Table 1 shows Biocon's Drug Discovery Pipeline. In June 2006 Kiran set up the Biocon Park, which is India's largest biotech hub comprising of an integrated cluster of research labs and manufacturing facilities on a 90-acre expanse in Karnataka Area Industrial Board in Bommasandra Industrial Estate Phase IV on the outskirts of Bangalore. The park was built with an investment of Rs. 600 crore and is the single largest capital investment made by Biocon in its 27 years of history. The multi-product facilities cater to the cardiovascular cholesterol reduction, immunosuppressant in organ transplants, diabetes and cancer. (Pharmabiz, 2006).

Table 1 : Biocon's Drug Discovery Pipeline

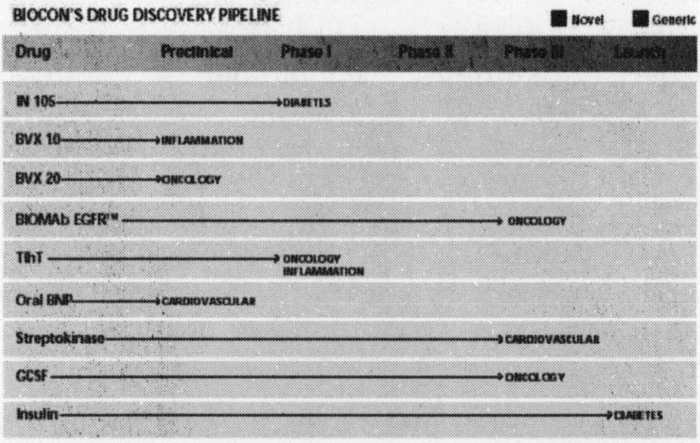

***Source*: Biocon Financial Report, 2006**

THE PEOPLE

Biocon has a flat management structure. Kiran realized that for such a structure to work she had to adopt a "networking management" style wherein there is high level of networking and communication thus helping people to make their own decisions. This has inspired her employees as is evident from their long tenures at Biocon and the less than 1% attrition rate (Elliott, 2005, Biocon, 2006). Most of the top executives at Biocon have been working there since the beginning. Kiran started the R&D division with Shrikumar Suryanarayan from IIT-Madras whom she had met in the early 1980's when he was a student and wanted enzymes for his project which Kiran gave him for free. When Suryanaranyan completed M.Tech and had a number of offers for Ph.D Programs he wanted Kiran to help him choose but she instead offered him an opportunity to start an R&D Division for her and he heads the same today. Murali Krishnan is another example. He was helping Biocon in 1981 while studying to be a Chartered Accountant. He joined the company soon without completing his CA and is the president of Biocon Group Finance. Biocon, Syngene and Clinigene together employ approximately 2000 qualified personnel - from biologists, chemists, IT specialists, medical practitioners, pharmacologists, engineers, finance/legal/marketing analysts to general administrators. 10% of the employees hold a Ph.D degree, 30% have a Masters degree in Science and the remaining are graduates with a Bachelors degree in Science, Commerce or Arts. 30% of Biocon employees are women. The employee attrition rate is less than 1% and the average age of employees in the company is 28. The employees say they enjoy working at Biocon because of the leadership style Kiran has adopted. Her husband, Shaw, who has worked in many countries in the world as a senior manager in Coats Viyella, marvels at the open culture in Biocon. According to ICICI Ventures who have closely studied Biocon, all the senior managers of the company have a say in business.

THE COMPETITION

The Associate Chamber of Commerce and Industry of India estimates that over US$ 4 billion are likely to be invested in Indian Biotech Industry by 2010, primarily in the areas of healthcare, agriculture, environment and food processing industries. It further stated that India would become a global player through export of bio-products particularly to neighboring countries, West Asia, South-East Asia and certain developed countries. In June 2003 a study on Biotechnology by Frost and Sullivan pegged the value of domestic biotechnology market at US$ 2.5 billion in 2002, which would zoom to US$ 6.75 billion by 2010. In 2005 there were 265 domestic Biotech firms of which 131 were in Karnataka out of which 127 were in Bangalore alone giving it the sobriquet of Biotech cluster of India. In 2005, 46 new companies came up in India. The distribution of companies also seems to be evenly spread -- 18% were agri-biotech firms and 17% were biotech firms. Supply companies (those who supply raw materials to the biotech firms) accounted for 30% of the biotech companies, while outsourced Research and Development including clinical development firms, accounted for 14%. The takeover of Lotus Labs by Iceland based Aciavis for 25 million Euro is another development worthy of notice (Economic Times, 2005). According to the latest industry figures the Indian biotechnology industry crossed the $2 billion mark in revenues with Bio-services contributing $ 250 million; Bio-agriculture $ 250 million: Bio-industrial $ 100 million, Bio-informatics $ 32 million and Bio-pharma forming a major part of the biotechnology pie at $ 1400 million (ABLE, 2007). The revenue of the top ten Biotech companies in India is given in Table 2 .

A brief description of the top ten Biotech companies that compete with Biocon is important for understanding the competitive horizon for the company.

Serum Institute of India continues to be a leader in the vaccine market. Amidst stiff competition in vaccine market, Serum Institute of India Ltd. continued its leadership position in the vaccines business with a record sales of Rs 950.95 crore in 2006-07 registering a growth of 35 percent over the previous year's sales revenue of 703 crore. Over 80 percent of its sales are

Table 2 : Top ten Biotech companies in India (2006-07)

Rank	Company	Revenue (Rs. Crore)
1.	Serum Institute of India	950.95
2.	Biocon	823
3.	Panacea Biotec	607.87
4.	Rasi Seeds	340
5.	Nuziveedu	226.42
6.	Novo Nordisk	222
7.	Venkateshwara Hatcheries	190.50
8.	Indian Immunologicals	157.90
9.	Mahyco Morsants Biotech	150.30
10.	Glaxo Smithkline Pharmaceuticals	120

Source: http://www.biospectrumindia.com/

from overseas market with little from the Indian market. Serum Institute supplies vaccines to more than 130 countries across the world and it leads in MMR and Hep B vaccines in India. Its subsidiary company, Serum International, generated Rs 42 crore in 2006-07 against the previous year's sales of Rs 36 crore, registering a growth of over 16 percent. With this, the group turnover of Serum Institute has touched Rs 992.95 crore for 2006-07.

Biocon comes second in the competitive landscape reporting a total sales of Rs 823 crore for the year ending March 2007 from the sale of biopharmaceuticals and enzymes. As a group, the company ended the year at Rs 990 crore. Revenues from the biopharmaceuticals and enzymes business grew 20 percent to Rs 823 crore from Rs 688 crore contributing 83 percent to operating revenues in FY 2007. Revenues from research services and licensing grew 63 percent from Rs 100 crore to Rs 163 crore, contributing 17 percent to operating revenues in FY 2007.

The number 3 competitor Panacea Biotec has added new drugs to its product basket like Siropan, Lower A, Myelogen Forte, Inrica, TOFF Expectorant, Toff DC, Upright SP and Trepro. Rasi Seeds is the number 4 competitor and a leading seed company located at Attur near Salem in Tamil Nadu. The company is committed to serve the needs of farmers across India by supplying quality seeds of various crops. Number 5, Secunderabad-based Nuziveedu Seeds Ltd (NSL), had the commercial release of two Bt hybrid cotton varieties following the approval from the Genetic Engineering Approval Committee (GEAC). The two Bt hybrid cotton varieties, Bt Bunny and Bt Mallika, is being sold in Maharashtra, Gujarat, Madhya Pradesh, Andhra Pradesh, Karnataka and Tamil Nadu. No. 6, Novo Nordisk India is the Indian subsidiary of Novo Nordisk, a focused healthcare company and a world leader in diabetes care. The number 7 competitor Venkateshwara Hatcheries Pvt. Ltd (VHL), a group company of the VH Group, continues to dominate the Indian poultry vaccine market with a market share of over 60 percent. Coming in at number 8 is Indian Immunologicals Ltd (IIL), a wholly owned subsidiary of National Dairy Development Board (NDDB), established in 1983 with the objective of making Foot & Mouth Disease (FMD) vaccine available to farmers at an affordable price. The number 9 competitor, Mahyco Monsanto Biotech (India) Ltd is a 50:50 joint venture with Mahyco and Monsanto Holdings Pvt. Ltd. (MHPL). Mahyco Monsanto Biotech (India) Ltd. (MMB) is not a listed company and was created to bring the benefits of Bollgard cotton technology to farmers in India. In 2002, Bollgard cotton was the first biotech crop to be approved for commercialization in India by the GEAC. MMB registered a fall in its sales revenue to Rs 150.30 crore in 2006-07 over the previous year's sales of Rs 391.25 crore. The sudden fall in the revenue was mainly because of the government intervention in fixing the price for Bt cottonseeds during the 2006 kharif season. In 2005, it has generated revenue of Rs 391.25 crore by transferring the technology to the Indian seed companies. Last, but not least is the number 10 competitor, GlaxoSmithKline Pharmaceuticals. GSK continues to lead the Indian representative vaccine market by registering a growth of over 27 percent with its biotech sales reaching Rs 120 crore for the year 2006-07 against the last's sales revenue of Rs 94 crore.

After examining the top ten Biotech companies we see that Biocon is today a biopharmaceutical company with strong capabilities in statins, immunosuppressants, recombinant insulin and a wide product range across key therapeutic segments including diabetology, cardiology and oncology. Biocon extended its R&D to new domains of knowledge, spanning bioprocess development, gene expression technologies, secondary metabolites, bioconversions and proteomics. Today, it leverages its multiple expertise to leading-edge recombinant biopharmaceuticals and human therapeutics. The invention of the PlaFractor and through it the ability to pioneer novel production processes for therapeutic molecules is testimony to Biocon's path-breaking R&D capabilities and exceptional engineering skills.

Biocon's subsidiary, Syngene, has entered into a research partnership with Bristol Myers Squibb. This is expected to significantly increase the scope of Bristol Myers Squibb's existing relationship with Syngene to further develop integrated capabilities in medicinal chemistry, biology, drug metabolism and pharmaceutical development. Through this symbiotic global partnership, Biocon's Syngene will provide research and development services for discovery and early drug development. Biocon is developing Nasulin, an intra-nasal insulin spray with Bentley Pharmaceuticals. Nasulin is the second non-injectable insulin that Biocon is working on, besides the oral tablet-form insulin IN 105, which is almost on a parallel track at phase 1C. Both the drugs may be 3-4 years from commercial stage.

Biocon and Abu Dhabi's NMC Group signed an MoU to establish a JV to manufacture and market a range of biopharmaceuticals for the GCC region (Gulf Cooperation Council). This landmark agreement between the two companies heralds the region's first foray to develop and market life-saving biopharmaceutical products and will expand Neopharma's (NMC Group) existing portfolio with a range of Biocon's therapeutic products. These products will be in the cardiovascular, diabetes and oncology segments, which represent the fastest growing class of drugs in the $ 5 billion GCC pharmaceutical market. This JV is a key milestone for Biocon's marketing foray in the Gulf.

Biocon launched BIOMAb-EGFR, a therapeutic monoclonal antibody-based drug for treating solid tumors of epithelial origin, such as head and neck cancers. The drug is the first of its kind to be clinically developed in India and is the first anti-EGFR humanized monoclonal antibody for cancer to be made available commercially anywhere in the world. The product has shown consistent positive outcome in clinical trials initiated both in India and globally and is being studied in global clinical trials for Colorectal, Lung Cancer, Glioma and Pancreatic cancers. BIOMAb-

EGFR is produced at Biocon's state-of-the-art manufacturing facility-Biocon Park. Biocon has also granted an exclusive license to Ferozsons Laboratories for marketing BIOMAb-EGFR in Pakistan. Ferozsons Laboratories is a leading oncology company.

Biocon has a pipeline of 12 molecules that could be out-licensed over a period of 12 to 24 months. The company is in an advanced stage of discussion on three molecules. It is keen to out-license an oral insulin molecule called IN105 for type II diabetes and potential drug for congestive heart failure. The others range from a monoclonal antibody for rheumatoid arthritis to a squamous cell antibody for non-Hodgkin's lymphoma.

Biocon launched a comprehensive portfolio of renal therapy products which are priced 35 percent less than those available in the market. Biocon's nephrology division is committed to finding solutions to kidney disorders using the highest standards of biotherapeutics and will simultaneously strive towards reducing the risks of the disease in the future, through progressive research and innovative therapies. The new immunosuppressant drugs for renal therapy include Ranodapt, Tacrograf, Cyclophil ME, Rapacan and Erypro. Immonusuppressants are medicines that inhibit or prevent the activity of the body's immune system. Its newly carved out nephrology division expects to release more drugs in the market which include certain aspects of kidney related eases. To achieve this end, Biocon will continue to increase investments in the R&D division. Biocon expects to double its R&D spend in 2007-08.

"Biocon truly believes that non-injectable insulins will drive the future of diabetes therapy the world over. The company wants to play a big role in the insulin market, currently valued at nearly Rs 300 crore in the country," said Rakesh Bamzai, president, marketing, Biocon.

Biocon's new product pipeline includes therapeutic biomolecules ranging from small molecules (e.g., statins, immunosuppressants) to recombinant proteins (human insulin and monoclonal antibodies) derived from microbial and mammalian cell culture based fermentation technologies. (Biospectrum, 2007). Thus we see that in comparison to other competing firms Biocon's portfolio is wider.

Many firsts...

Biocon is the first Indian company to manufacture and export enzymes to USA and Europe which it started in 1979. In 1989 it became the first Indian biotech company to receive US funding for proprietary technologies. It is the first company to have solid substrate fermentation technology from pilot to plant level. The commercial success of Biocon's proprietary fermentation plant leads to a three folds expansion. In 1993 its R&D and manufacturing facilities received ISO 9001 certificate from RWTUV, Germany. In 2002 Clinigene's laboratory became the first in India to receive CAP accreditation. In 2003 Biocon became the first company worldwide to develop human insulin on a Pichia expression system.

BIOCON'S BUSINESS MODEL

Biocon is India's largest biotech company with a presence in bio-pharmaceuticals, enzymes, customs research and clinical research. It is difficult to say whether it is an enzyme company, a biotech company or a pharmaceutical company. Biocon has a multi-business revenue share model with pharmaceutical products forming 75% of its revenue, research services constituting 13% and enzymes 12%. (see figure 1). Thus we can say Biocon is a biotech-turned pharmaceutical company (Hari, 2002). However Chairman Kiran Mazumdar Shaw says Biocon is rapidly transforming into an innovation-led organization where they have developed a balance between all-round revenue growth and risk mitigation in order to build a strong and sustainable business for the long-term.

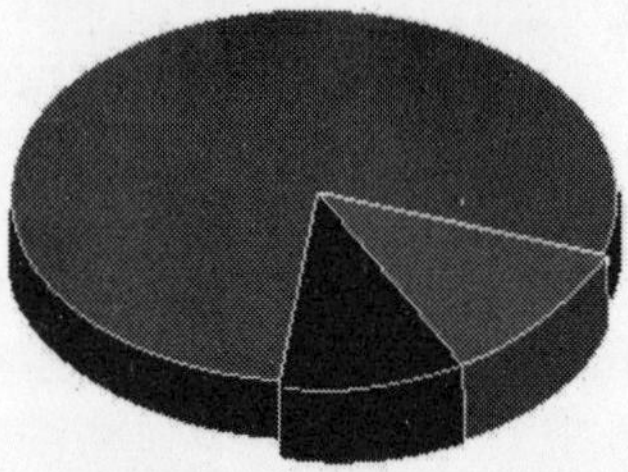

***Source*: Biocon Annual Report, 2006**

Fig. 1. Biocon's Multi-Business Revenue Share

The integrated business approach has enabled Biocon to establish a significant presence in the global biopharmaceutical market. From early stage drug discovery to clinical development and commercialisation, Biocon leverages its collective expertise and resources to provide an innovative range of products and services. This integrated business model allows it to offer its strategic global partners customised, high value solutions at any stage in the lifecycle of a drug - right from discovery to market. The three stages are (Figure 2):

Step 1: Early stage Drug Discovery:

At Syngene, a Biocon subsidiary, Biocon offers outsourced, high value research and development -

from target identification and validation to small molecule and library synthesis. With its reputation for meticulous Intellectual Property Right protection, it provides pharmaceutical and biotechnology majors customized solutions in the areas of synthetic chemistry and molecular biology.

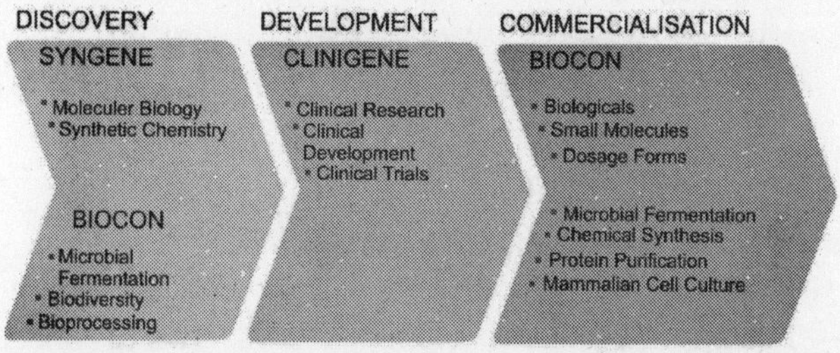

Source **: www.biocon.com**

Fig. 2. Biocon's Business Model

Step 2: Clinical Development:

At Clinigene, another Biocon subsidiary, Biocon specializes in Phase I-IV clinical trials and studies, using well-characterized clinical databases in diabetes, oncology, lipidemia and cardiovascular diseases. It offers its services at its CAP (College of American Pathologists) . (CAP is widely recognised as the "gold standard" and NABL (National Accreditation Board for Testing and Calibration Laboratories) accredited Central Reference Laboratory and a state-of-the-art Bioavailability and Bioequivalence Centre (BA / BE Centre).

Step 3: Commercialization:

Biocon's track record of commercialization has been out-standing. It has commercialized in excess of 25 enzymes over two decades. In the past five years, their chemical synthesis skills have enabled us to leverage their proprietary fermentation expertise to the manufacture of biopharmaceuticals. Biocon's biopharmaceutical foray began with statins and immunosuppressants. Their commercial success is evident in the rapid market share they have gained in the US and Europe. In fact, Biocon continues to be the only Indian company to have US FDA qualification for Lovastatin. FDA has inspected and accepted Biocon's facilities for Simvastatin, Pravastatin, Pioglitazone HCl, Lovastatin (submerged fermentation). Biocon has also commercialized Human Insulin (rDNA) based on Pichia expression system. Biocon has also submitted a Drug Master File for the same to the USFDA. (*www.biocon.com*).

Biopharmaceuticals have been and will continue be the mainstay of the company promising exciting growth opportunities. This segment is involved primarily in manufacture and marketing of Active Pharmaceutical Ingredients (API) that require advanced fermentation and other skills and that offer significant market potential in the regulated markets once the product goes off patent. Within this segment, statins constitute major products. Biocon has received U.S. FDA acceptance for its pravastatin, simvastatin, lovastatin and pioglitazone manufacturing facilities. This acceptance allows Biocon to access the lucrative US$ 6 billion market slated to go off patent in the United States in 2006. Biocon has already established itself as a leading exporter of lovastatin to the U.S. and simvastatin to Europe. Apart from statins, other major Biopharma's APIs are for immunosuppressants and anti-diabetic drugs.

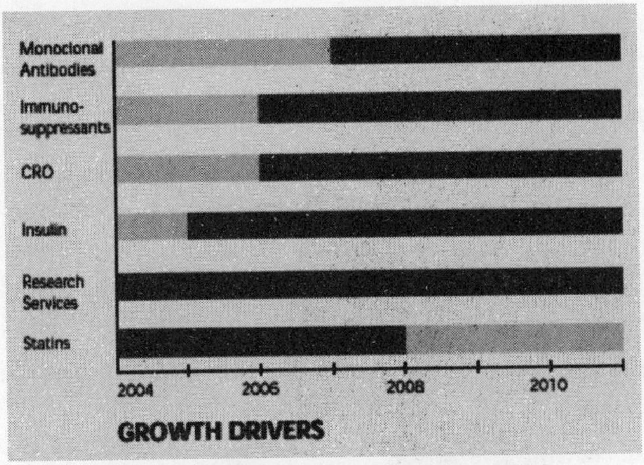

***Source*: Biocon Annual Report, 2006**

Fig. 3. The Growth Drivers

The focus on statins augurs well, as statins are cholesterol lowering agents used to treat / prevent coronary diseases and are amongst the largest selling drugs worldwide. Patent at expiration of pravastatin in Europe will augment statin growth in the year ahead followed by a quantum jump in the US markets in 2006 when both pravastatin and simvastatin go off patent. The recent announcement of simvastatin going OTC is perceived as an additional opportunity by Biocon. Biocon intends to further differentiate its statin strategy through initiating supply arrangements with innovator companies. (see figure 3)

Biocon has also successfully developed recombinant human insulin at a commercial scale, and the success of this technology has been endorsed by its long-term supply agreement with Bristol-Myers Squibb as well as its ability to file a drug master file with US FDA. The company is confident that finished formulation 'Insugen' due to be launched soon will compete very effectively in the market, and it is also addressing global opportunities for generic insulin in the semi and non-regulated markets in the near term and to the regulated markets in the medium term.

FINANCIAL ANALYSIS FOR BIOCON

All these efforts are reflected in Biocon's income statement which in the first quarter of 2007 showed an increase of 22% with total sales standing at Rs 212 crore (Table 4). Biocon's Profit and Loss statement for First quarter of 2007 is indicated below :

Table 4. Profit and Loss Statement for Biocon, 2006.

BIOCON LIMITED (CONSOLIDATED)

PROFIT & LOSS STATEMENT

(Rs. crores)

Particulars	Q1 FY 2007	Q1 FY 2006	Variance Q1 FY 07 vs Q1 FY 06	Full Year ended March 31, 2006
INCOME				
Sales-Biopharmaceuticals	161	135	19%	603
Sales- Enzymes	22	20	10%	85
Contract research	29	19	52%	100
Total Sales	**212**	**174**	**22%**	**788**
Other income	1	2		5
Total Income / Revenues	**213**	**176**	**21%**	**793**

***Source*: Biocon, 2006**

Industry Aggregate Analysis

The aggregate financial figures for Biocon are indicated in Table 5 below. The data has been derived from Capitaline Plus Database and indicates aggregate analysis of Biocon versus select group of companies for which financial data is available.

The financial figures for Biocon are indicated in Table 6. The data is from March 2003 to March 2007. The capital employed has increased at an exponential rate and sales have also increased during the span of last five years by almost 4 times. The profits have also

Table 5. Aggregate Financial Figures for Biocon 1998-2007.

[Rs. in Crs.]

Year	*2007*	*2006*	*2005*	*2004*	*2003*	*2002*	*2001*	*2000*	*1999*	*1998*
No. of Companies	*Biocon*	*8*	*14*	*15*	*15*	*14*	*8*	*6*	*5*	*3*
INCOME :										
Sales Turnover	887.15	1,371.96	1,191.64	929.59	658.97	535.65	286.92	220.62	130.36	104.21
Excise Duty	36.18	49.37	49.5	40.44	36.1	9.39	9.44	7.76	0	0
Net Sales	850.97	1,322.59	1,142.14	889.15	622.87	526.26	277.48	212.86	130.36	104.21
Other Income	23.63	19.24	31.4	24.14	9.96	7.21	7.92	2.27	0.6	0.26
Stock Adjustments	21.9	21.2	43.44	38.62	18.54	1.03	-0.54	5.79	10.87	2.85
Total Income	896.5	1,363.03	1,216.98	951.91	651.37	534.5	284.86	220.92	141.83	107.32
EXPENDITURE :										
Raw Materials	439.31	716.1	599.39	475.76	318.85	279.25	149.6	126.2	69.72	64.15
Power & Fuel Cost	62.07	38.6	33.13	24.25	20.97	13.41	2.14	2.1	0.41	0.18
Employee Cost	49.43	77.74	86.59	79.83	66.38	45.2	15.97	10.17	7.41	4.9
Other Manufacturing Expenses	16.65	18.93	39.04	34.14	23.91	15.75	4.83	7.66	27.51	9.28
Selling and Administration Expenses	88.26	135.62	111.1	82.16	62.32	52.02	33.01	20.19	13.52	10.85
Miscellaneous Expenses	3.95	29.23	17.06	15.7	6.99	4.56	2.53	2.95	0.86	1.42

Less: Pre-operative Expenses Capitalised	0	6.98	10.05	10.45	2.84	0	0	0	0	0
Total Expenditure	659.67	1,009.24	876.26	701.39	496.58	410.19	208.08	169.27	119.43	90.78
Operating Profit	236.83	353.79	340.72	250.52	154.79	124.31	76.78	51.65	22.4	16.54
Interest	8.17	20.28	18.42	21.48	21.9	18.38	13.54	9.92	4.41	3.11
Gross Profit	228.66	333.51	322.3	229.04	132.89	105.93	63.24	41.73	17.99	13.43
Depreciation	57.61	46.63	44.93	33.72	27.11	17.56	6.4	4.29	3.85	1.8
Profit Before Tax	171.05	286.88	277.37	195.32	105.78	88.37	56.84	37.44	14.14	11.63
Tax	0.92	55.09	25.19	26.58	23.87	23.27	21.03	7.52	1.24	0.97
Deferred Tax	11.78	16.68	12.37	5.01	2.67	1.73	0	0	0	0
Reported Net Profit	158.35	215.11	239.81	163.73	79.24	63.37	35.81	29.92	12.9	10.66
Extraordinary Items	0.03	0.31	-0.58	-0.05	0.12	0	1.62	0	0	0
Adjusted Net Profit	158.32	214.8	240.39	163.78	79.12	63.37	34.19	29.92	12.9	10.66
Adjst. below Net Profit	0	0	0	-0.01	-0.11	0	-0.02	-7.68	-0.9	0
P & L Balance brought forward	330.14	315.46	195.16	121.51	57.36	17.91	17.07	11	6.92	3.55
Statutory Appropriations	0	0	0	0	0	0	0	0	0	0
Appropriations	50.93	72.34	79.87	104.03	20.5	23.95	24.48	16.4	7.92	7.25
P & L Balance carried down	437.56	458.23	355.1	181.2	115.99	57.33	28.38	16.84	11	6.96
Dividend	30	32.93	30.55	17.48	7.31	9.83	7.04	5.71	1.71	1.14
Preference Dividend	0	4.07	4.39	0.82	0.66	0.77	0.93	0.82	0.49	0

http://www.capitaline.com

increased exponentially. Select ratios have been indicated in the table below which give insight into the financial health of the firm.

Table 6 : Financial Figures for Biocon March 2003- March 2007

Year End	*2007- Mar*	*2006- Mar*	*2005- Mar*	*2004- Mar*	*2003- Mar*
Equity	50	50	50	50	1.84
Networth	940.53	801.77	694.51	540.04	124.8
Enterprise Value	4,953.64	4,564.04	4,154.92	0	0
Capital Employed	1,047.30	906.81	770.85	604.73	193.36
Gross Block	860.08	314.83	268.77	189.64	153.4
Sales	887.15	725.75	684.35	531.55	275.16
Other Income	23.63	11.7223.41		13.93	3.69
PBIDT	236.83	186.19	209.29	163.79	64.79
PBDT	228.66	183.71	206.6	161.33	59.74
PBIT	179.22	163.34	191.2	149.94	52.77
PBT	171.05	160.86	188.51	147.48	47.72
RPAT	158.35	133.48	174.39	124.67	35.87
APAT	158.32	133.31	174.21	124.62	35.75
CP	215.96	156.33	192.48	138.52	47.89
Rev. Earnings in FE	480.03	358.95	378.04	300.57	108.53
Rev. Expenses in FE	264.14	259.93	237.82	204.62	77.66
Book Value (Rs)	94.05	80.1869.45		54	678.26
EPS (Rs.)	15.33	13	17.16	12.34	194.95
Dividend (%)	60	50	40	20	0
Payout (%)	19.58	19.2411.66		8.1	0
Debt-Equity	0.12	0.12	0.11	0.2	0.64
Current Ratio	1.29	0.97	1.64	2.25	1.18
Invtry Turnover	6.93	8.22	8.82	8.14	7.85
Debtors Turnover	3.69	3.83	4.74	5.6	4.04
Interest Cover	21.94	65.8671.08		60.95	10.45
PBIDTM (%)	26.7	25.6530.58		30.81	23.55
PBDTM (%)	25.77	25.3130.19		30.35	21.71
APATM (%)	17.85	18.3925.48		23.45	13.04
ROCE (%)	18.34	19.4727.8		37.57	30.56
RONW (%)	18.18	17.8428.25		37.5	34.11

EV/EBIDTA	20.92	24.5119.85		0	0
Net Worth	17.31	15.4428.6		332.72	45.93
Sales	22.24	6.05	28.75	93.18	70.27
PAT	18.63	-23.46	39.88	247.56	76.61
M Cap	8.82	9.28	0	0	0

Table 7 Compares Biocon with select competitors on financial ratios.

Table 8 indicates the shareholding pattern for the firm.

Table 9 indicates the R&D expenditures of the biotechnology industry which has increased over the last five years. A key value driver for the biotechnology industry is the investment on R&D.

REASON FOR SUCCESS

Ever since Biocon became the buzzword in the market for the emerging field of biotechnology, Kiran has been a much-quoted personality. According to her, her belief in the field, a magnificent team of people who shared her passion for the subject, determination and urge to succeed have all contributed to Biocon's reputation as the leader in the field.(*http://www.virtualbangalore.com/Ppl/PplKiranM.php*) Another reason is that Biocon extends its friendliness to its customers. They not only provide the customers with a product but also provide information on the market, a strategy, and a future. According to the Managing Director of Delhi based Harvest Gold Foods "Only Biocon works with the customer to reduce costs." (Hari, 2002).

The primary reasons for success of the firm are explored below:

1. The firm had a distinct strategy and focus area. The firm focused on a gap in the market and was

Table 7 : Comparision of Biocon with select competitors

YRC	*Aggregate*	*Biocon*	*Celestial Labs*	*Hind. Bio Science*	*Jupiter Bio.*	*Panacea Biotech*	*Saamya Biotech*
		200603	*200603*	*200603*	*200603*	*200603*	*200603*
Key Ratios							
Debt-Equity Ratio	0.48	0.12	0.01	0.01	0.71	1.6	0
Long Term Debt-Equity Ratio	0.33	0.04	0.01	0.01	0.71	1.15	0
Current Ratio	1.57	0.97	3.1	86.21	2.65	2.25	7.06
Turnover Ratios							
Fixed Assets	2.17	2.48	1.55	0.15	0.84	2.96	0
Inventory	4.52	8.21	0	0	3.71	2.95	0
Debtors	4.63	3.82	2.97	0.68	5.4	7.02	0
Interest Cover Ratio	14.98	65.86	0	-5	6.27	8.51	0
PBIDTM (%)	25.74	25.69	34.93	-3.33	44.15	23.24	0
PBITM (%)	22.33	22.54	32.39	-16.67	32.64	20.7	0
PBDTM (%)	24.25	25.35	34.93	-6.67	38.95	20.81	0
CPM (%)	18.98	21.57	34.64	-6.67	32.95	13.66	0
APATM (%)	15.57	18.42	32.09	-20	21.44	11.12	0
ROCE (%)	18.03	19.47	26.06	-0.5	16.9	18.73	0
RONW (%)	19.47	17.84	26.18	-0.57	16.15	39.87	0

http://www.capitaline.com

Table 8 : Shareholder pattern for Biocon 2007.

Shareholding Pattern

(AS ON Jun 2007)	*Shares*	*[%]*
Foreign	8,950,180.00	8.95
Institutions	7,933,204.00	7.93
Govt Holding	0	0
Non Promoter Corp. Hold.	2,000,356.00	2
Promoters	60,901,573.00	60.9
Public & Others	20,214,687.00	20.22
Totals	100,000,000.00	100

Table 9. Industry :Biotechnology R&D Expenditures

(Rs in Crs)

	200703	*200603*	*200503*	*200403*	*200303*
Capital Expenditure	9.8	21.6	10.34	8.99	3.4
Recurring Expenditure	38.1	18.5	13.75	14.34	8
Total Expenditure	47.9	40.1	24.09	23.33	11.4
Total R&D expenditure as percentage of net turnover(%)	5.5	5.8	3.7	4.6	4.48

http://www.capitaline.com

able to expand its market around the area. It focused on the enzymes and steadily expanded its operations in the area. It sourced technology initially and even acquired the stake from Levers to retain the competitive edge.

2. The business model of the firm is very sound. It offers and maps the entire value chain in the drug development and delivery process. It covers the entire spectrum from discovery, development to commercialization. The focus on diseases such as diabetis and cancer is appropriate as there is a lot of room for development. Over the years the

firm evolved from a firm focused on enzyme manufacturing to fully integrated biopharmaceutical enterprise.It followed an integrated innovation approach to yield patented products and technologies which enabled multi-level partnerships. It also tapped the global market and was not restricted to Indian market. The export orientation of the firm enabled it to prepare itself for a global strategy rather than have a micro perspective. The firm prepared itself for discovery, clinical development and commercialization.

3. The team dynamics and the complementary roles played by team members are critical to the success of any venture. The firm clearly demonstrates that it used the networks of the founding entrepreneur as well as its employees to have a committed team at the top who have stayed with the firm for an extended period thereby lending stability and building and nurturing the R&D culture and a penchant for innovation.

4. Capitalising on the University Linkages, the firm works closely with educational system as well.

Vision for the Future

After achieving this phenomenal success where does Kiran go from here? "My vision is to grow into a global bio-therapeutics company with very innovative and proprietary products and technologies. Two years is a very short time to predict drug discovery but we hope to discover a few new drug molecules in three-four years through a new in-house initiative." (Kiran, cited in Virtual Bangalore, 2006)

THE ENTREPRENEUR'S ACHIEVEMENTS

But there is another face of Kiran, which many Bangaloreans are familiar with, though it has been less visible of late. And that is her passion for Bangalore. She has actively campaigned and raised her voice for things, which she felt were needed - civic amenities, roads, cleanliness, etc. She was the core member of a group of Bangaloreans who used to meet regularly to discuss the problems ailing the city, which included among others former Chief Secretary T.P. Issar and former Union Minister Ramakrishna Hegde. Due to her commitments and added responsibilities, she appears to have discontinued these meetings. But her commitment is solid nevertheless. She was among the first to hail the Bangalore Agenda Task Force (BATF) initiative and added her mite to it by contributing Rupees one crore. Her donations went towards starting the Swachcha Bangalore programme of door-to-door collection of garbage. (*http://www.virtualbangalore.com/Ppl/PplKiranM.php*). Working in the direction of social responsibility Kiran set up the Biocon Foundation in 2004 with the aim of identifying and implementing projects in healthcare that will bring about radical and meaningful social and economic change in the country. The Foundation has identified a strong need to provide lowcost health insurance and health education to all levels of our social structure aimed at providing quality healthcare and improving the health standards of rural India. Arogya Raksha Yojana (ARY) is the first step taken by the foundation in this direction. With India's huge disease burden the pressing necessity of healthcare affordable to the masses is evident.

The Arogya Raksha Yojana Trust comprising Narayana Hrudayalaya and the Biocon Foundation launched ARY in collaboration with ICICI Lombard General Insurance Company Pvt Ltd. ARY is a comprehensive health insurance scheme that offers people of rural India, affordable access to high-quality healthcare provided by a network of hospitals and clinics. Starting at Rs 120 per year per person, the scheme not only covers people against critical illnesses and surgeries, but also entitles them to free medical examinations, free or subsidised hospitalization and low-cost medicines.

The first ARY centre with a clinic, office and biocare pharmacy was set up at Huskur village, Anekal Taluk, Karnataka, in December 2004. The first phase of this launch has touched the lives of over 60,000 people residing in Anekal Taluka. This year, the scheme will be extended to cover the entire Taluk with a population of six lakh, and will further be taken across the state in the months to come. As the scheme is extended across Karnataka, Arogya Raksha Clinics and Biocare Pharmacies will be built to ensure that people can access good healthcare facilities even in the remotest villages, at discounted prices.

Kiran plans to cover many more rural pockets in Karnataka and reach out to other parts of India as well and to look at various other activities in the areas of healthcare, sanitation and hygiene education towards the betterment of Indian societies at all levels. (Shaw, 2006)

Positions held

As Chairperson and Mission Leader of CII's National Task Force on Biotechnology she has led several delegations to USA, Canada, UK, etc. to propel India into the global super league of biotech trailblazers. She chairs Karnataka's Vision Group on Biotechnology and also served on the Board of Science Foundation, Ireland. She presently serves on the Advisory Council of the Government's Department of Biotechnology where she has been instrumental in bringing government, industry and academia together, to chart a clear and progressive growth path for Biotechnology in India. Ms. Shaw is also a Board member of BVGH (Bio-Ventures for Global Health). Most recently, she has been invited to join the Prime Minister's Council on Trade & Industry in India. (*www.biocon.com*). She has held important positions in Industry Councils, including Vice-President, Association of Women Entrepreneurs of Karnataka (AWAKE). (http://nrcw.nic.in)

Awards Received

Ms. Shaw is the recipient of several prestigious awards including the ET Businesswoman of the Year. Best Woman Entrepreneur, Model Employer, Ernst & Young's Entrepreneur of the Year Award for Life Sciences & Healthcare, Leading Exporter, Outstanding Citizen, Technology Pioneer, National award for Best Small Industry and Rotary Award for Best Small Industry. Her most cherished awards are however, the PADMASHRI (1989) and PADMA BHUSHAN (2005) presented to her by the President of India, for her pioneering efforts in Industrial Biotechnology. In 2003, she was awarded the BioSpectrum Person of the Year award. (*www.biocon.com, http://nrcw.nic.in*). In 2005 Kiran was honoured with the Corporate Leadership Award, 2005 of the American India Foundation (AIF). (Business Line, 2005). In 2006 she received the Indian Merchants' Chamber Diamond Jubilee Endowment Trust's Eminent Businessperson of the Year Award (The New Indian Express, 2006). Kiran has also been adjudged the "most influential" person in bio-business outside the US and Europe, according to an international poll conducted by the Nature Biotechnology journal (Business Line, 2006).

Personal values of the founding entrepreneur, dedication, perseverance, and hard-work, along with a vision that did not seek immediate gratification were the hallmark of Kiran's struggle. These concepts present lessons learned for aspiring entrepreneurs.

BIBLIOGRAPHY

Biocon (2006). (online) (cited on 28th September, 2006) available from <URL*http://www.biocon.com*>

Biocon Annual Report (2006) available from Capitaline Database

Biospectrum (2007) (online) (cited on 2nd July, 2007) available from <URLhttp://www.biospectrumindia.com>

Business Line (2005) (online). "Award for Biocon CMD", Business Line, October 11, 2005 cited in <URL*http://www.thehindubusinessline.com*>

Business Line (2006). "Biocon chief tops poll of biotech personalities outside US, Europe", Business Line, March 10, 2006. cited from <URLhttp://www.thehindubusinessline.com/2006/03/10/stories/2006031003290800.htm

Economic Times, (2005), "Biotech turnover could touch $5bn by '10:Shaw", Economic Times, dated April, 23, 2005 available from press releases in www.biocon.com.

Elliot, John (2005). "Biotech Queen", Fortune, November 14, 2005 cited in press releases in www.biocon.com.

Financial Express (2006) (online). "Biocon to sell insulin in US, Europe; up R&D", Financial Express, September 14 cited in press releases from *www.biocon.com*

Hari, P (2002). "The World of Biocon", Business World, 2nd December, 2002

Pharmabiz (2006) (online). "President Kalam dedicates BioMAb EGFR to the nation", June 07, 2006 available from *www.pharmabiz.com*

Shaw, Kiran Mazumdar (2006). "We aim to make healthcare affordable to masses", Financial Express, January 29, 2006.

cited in press releases from *www.biocon.com*

The New Indian Express (2006). "Kiran Mazumdar is 'Eminent Businessperson", The New Indian Express, February 25, 2006 cited in press releases from *www.biocon.com*

Virtual Bangalore: Bangalore on the net, (online) (cited on 25th September, 2006). "Kiran Mazumdar Shaw- Frothing with Enthusiasm", cited from <URL*http://www.virtualbangalore.com/Ppl/PplKiranM.php*>http://nrcw.nic.in/shared/sublinkimages/166.htm

DISCUSSION QUESTIONS

1. What is a value chain for a pharmaceutical company? Using the value chain analysis, what are the value drivers for Biocon as a firm?
2. Please evaluate the financial performance of Biocon for five years until 2007 using the financial data in the case study and correlating it with the achievements and investments made.
3. If a new biotech firm would have to be a successful entrepreneurial initiative, what are the essential preconditions for success? Bring in factors which have been responsible for success for Biocon.
4. Compare and contrast the growth of Biocon as a firm with the nearest competition using data provided in the case study.
5. An entrepreneurial leader leads to emergence of a successful business venture. Please examine this statement critically in light of the Biocon experience.
6. What has been the role of technology in the success of Biocon?

3

Case Study on Shahnaz Hussain

Kirti Dutta

SYNOPSIS

Shahnaz Hussain, a quintessential entrepreneur, who ,coming from a conservative Muslim family, surmounted social, economical and personal barriers to be crowned the pioneer and the undisputed International Herbal Queen. The living legend that created fame and fortune not only for herself but also brought the rich cultural heritage of India in the limelight globally. The lady who created a dreamsville land of eternal beauty and youth and conquered the hysterical cosmetic-crazy west with her Indian herbal remedies. Her vision forced the world to turn their eyes on India for natural cosmetics. She has won more accolades, awards and mentions in the International press than any other Indian women. The Esprit magazine of Germany has dubbed her as Asia's Helena Rubenstein, Good Housekeeping calls her Estee Lauder and Daily Telegraph has named her "The uncrowned queen of Indian Beauty Therapy". Today, she heads the largest organization of its kind in the world, with more than 400 franchise salons worldwide and ranges of natural formulations for skin, hair and bodycare. Indeed, hers is the story of a truly successful entrepreneur who transcends geographical boundaries to reign over the world.

INTRODUCTION

When we talk of women entrepreneurs the study is not complete without taking into consideration the first woman to receive the World's Greatest Entrepreneur Award, 2003, in the 107 years old history of the prestigious US magazine – Success (Rangaraj, 2005) When Success wanted to select an entrepreneur who had worked a strong business, set an example by defying faith and had taken the future into its own hands – from hundreds of successful entrepreneurs across the globe – they unanimously chose Shahnaz Hussain. How Shahnaz Hussain brought the therapeutic values of herbs and flowers out of the mist of antiquity and combined them with the scientific research to build a multimillion-dollar empire is worthy of applause. Hers is the face that launched thousands of beauty products and trained hundreds of housewives in India to set up beauty salons in their own homes just as she had started decades ago. The multimillion-dollar business, which started in 1971 with a capital of Rs. 35000, borrowed from her father, in the first Shahnaz Herbal Salon, a small shop in her veranda, has now spread across 104 countries and has six factories and 4200 employees (Bhardwaj, 2006). Her training schools have created entrepreneurs out of housewives and have given a better life opportunity to the numerous deaf and mute girls who have passed out from her Shamute training school. Apart from being the first to start beauty training schools in India, to Shahnaz also goes the credit of pioneering franchises of Beauty Salons in India and the credit of being the number one beautician in the world as she is currently owning the largest franchise chain in the world. (Rangoonwala, 2001). She has also authored books on beauty (Rediff Books, 2006).

Her early days

Shahnaz Hussain was born in a conservative Muslim family. She belongs to a royal family, who originally came from Samarkhand and later held prominent positions in the royal governments of Bhopal and Hyderabad during the pre-independence days. It is also a family of eminent legal luminaries. Her mother descended from Hyderabad's royal family, who firmly believed in conservative upbringing. Her father Chief Justice N.U. Beg was on the other hand educated in Oxford in Britain and had a highly liberal approach to life. This combined to give Shahnaz a unique childhood – a conservative upbringing along with an exposure to the world of Shakespeare, Milton and Keats. She received her basic education at an Irish convent – Queen Mary's in Allahabad. Her fathers love for poetry mirrored in her. He also imbued in her the right combination of traditional values and progressive ideas and Shahnaz learnt to love and respect the rich heritage of India. However her father had to give in to her mother's wishes and Shahnaz was engaged at fourteen; married at fifteen and for her sixteenth birthday had a two-month-old daughter (Kurian, 2003).

Her educations

When Shahnaz was married she was only an undergraduate. After her marriage when her husband was posted abroad, as the Director of Foreign Trade, she traveled to Tehran, UK, France and Germany. Her father was keen that she should study further. So he kept collecting numerous brochures for various courses ranging from engineering to beauty care. (Kurian, 2003). She picked up beauty care and studied as an herbalist by day and wrote under twenty pen-names by night and doing odd typing jobs and running a magazine in Tehran to earn the surfeit money required for her course as a chemist (Singh, 2002). Initially she went to a school in Tehran to take up the job of an English Teacher. Since she was from a convent school and well into Shakespeare and Keats since she was 14 she thought that teaching Basic English would be no problem. Sure of getting the job she was horrified the next day when she was told that she had been disqualified because the basic qualification for the job was a college degree. (She is not a Graduate till today.) She cried her heart out but this incident only fired her determination to believe in herself and her dreams. Then she started writing articles in the Iran Tribune on various subjects. Initially she was asked to contribute 1000 words per week, but looking at the response she was asked to handle all the features in English and soon she was running the entire English magazine – cover to cover. As her handwriting was bad she had to type and there were only manual typewriters those days. She did not know typing so she used only two fingers and she would be typing furiously to meet the deadlines. "I remember that my fingers became sore and started bleeding. I would tie bandages and continue typing, oblivious to the pain. Finally, I had to seek medical treatment and the Russian doctor told me "If you don't stop typing, I will have to chop off your fingers." I will never forget the emotional upheaval. I knew I could not stop writing. I needed the money for my education. I looked at my fingers and quietly murmured, "Doctor, how much?" – I thought even if he cut off the minced part – I would still have enough left. I was that desperate to continue, so that I could pay the fees for my studies. I needed to earn the money to pay for my education. He was amazed that my first thought or anguish was not about the fingers I would lose! This incident made me believe that in life it is not what you want that is important, but how badly you want it. It made me believe in myself and my own abilities." (Sengupta, 2003, Shahnaz Press folder, 2006)

With the funds she did her first course from Helena Rubinstein in London. Other institutes followed like Arnould Taylor, Swarzkopf, Christine Valmy, Lancome and Lean of Copenhagen (Shahnaz Hussain, 2006). She studied beauty therapy in Germany, London and New York. She took ten years to complete her course in Cosmetic Chemistry and cosmetology and was all set to become a beauty care specialist using chemical products like the rest . However two incidents were to change the course of her life.

REASONS FOR STARTING BUSINESS

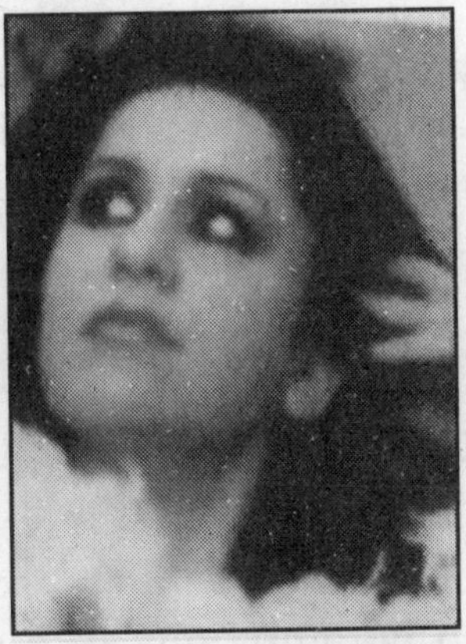

During her stay abroad while Shahnaz was studying cosmetic chemistry, she was horrified to witness the havoc caused by the use of chemical treatment in the West. One of her friend had put a suntan lotion on her neck and burned her skin. The result was that she could no longer model for diamonds and while Shahnaz was away in India her friend committed suicide. Another incident that affected her tremendously was that a model that was modeling mascara that elongated eyelashes and helped them grow became blind from the use of this mascara. She learnt that the chemical ingredients used carry the risk of such dangers. She resolved that if people are committing suicide due to the use of chemicals and their dangerous side effects, she would evolve a treatment which is safe and without risks. Thus her quest began. She began to question the use of chemical ingredients in beauty care. "From my family I had inherited a faith in traditional remedies", she realizing that her mother had used creams and cosmetics made from herbs, Shahnaz rejected the existing salon treatment and upheld the nature principle. She delved deep into the Sanskrit texts studying the wisdom of Indian sages and of other great civilization which have considered flowers for healing ailments. For 25 years she delved deeper into the mysterious and fascinating kingdom of flowers and after researching on thousands of species of flowers and drawing from the ancient literature dating back to 3000 B.C. and studying these age old, time tested Indian herbal remedies she came up with concoctions of herbs and oils of plants which aimed to create a perfect balance of body, mind and spirit. (Cunningham, 2005). Thus her famous quote "I sell civilization in a jar". She hired a chemist to work with her in creating ayurvedic beauty remedies. In 1970 she received her license to practice and opened her first store with a loan taken from her father.

CHALLENGES ENCOUNTERED

It could not have been easy for a girl who from a child bride went on become a successful entrepreneur, to be ambitious in a conservative society, blend her own range of creams and potions and build an empire on it (Singh, 2002). Very early on Shahnaz realized that "a woman's greatest crime is that she dared to dream. And if she believed in the magic of her dreams and does succeed, she has truly sinned!" However she says that the support and understanding of her family helped her to keep her belief in herself and keep trying relentlessly. Her father encouraged her by telling her "Now the fun is over. You must create something for yourself". He extended her a loan of Rs 35,000 with which she turned her verandah into a beauty salon and later pumped all her revenues into research and development and eventually bought a 35 acre flower farm. When she started her own exclusive beauty clinic, skin and hair treatments were relatively unknown in India. Superficial beauty treatments or hair styling were special treats women went in for. Shahnaz showed them that beauty is the outcome of long term and life long care (Lane, 2000). She devised her own clinical treatments for modern demands but combining ancient system with the latest techniques was not the only challenge. Shahnaz also had to create awareness about the goodness of herbs and the dangers of chemical treatments. Thus to popularize this concept she started writing articles for papers and magazines. She attended world beauty congresses, paving her own way to the world congresses and spoke about India's great herbal heritage. Since 1977, Shahnaz has consistently appeared on the BBC Television, London, impressing her belief that India leads the international empire in herbal cosmetics.

Entering the international market against great odds of financial constraints and closed doors did not deter her. In 1980 when Shahnaz participated in the

Festival of India in London, she was given a counter in the Perfumery Section at Selfridges. There rubbing shoulders with the biggest international brand, without financial resources and advertising (compared to the billions of dollars spent on advertising and packaging by the others), and having only her "India and Ayurvedic" image to help her, Shahnaz sold out her consignment in three days – breaking the store's existing cosmetic sales records. The London Daily carried the headline "Herbal Hell Breaks Loose in Selfridges" the next day heralding the arrival of the Diva. (The Times, 2003)

When she participated in the Festival of India in Paris and wanted a permanent counter at Galeries Lafayette, the famous Paris department store, she was informed that in order to have a permanent counter, she had to achieve a certain sales figure. However realizing that she was running short of the sales target, she knew she had to think of an ingenious idea to push the sales up. Nothing was going to deter her from missing the opportunity to get a permanent counter at the Paris store. So she called her Delhi office and asked her secretary to fly to Paris with four Kashmiri carpets. She offered this carpet as a gift for purchases worth 20,000 francs and above. This resulted in a stampede - something the store had never witnessed before. She actually sold products much more than the targeted amount, earning us a permanent counter at Galeries Lafayette, the world's most prestigious cosmetic store (Shahnaz press folder).

Since then there has been no looking back. Shahnaz went on breaking sale record internationally. In the Kuwait Beauty Fair at Mishrif at the world's largest cosmetic bazaar, she sold 37,000 dinars (equal to Rs 37 lakhs) in three days working only 8 hrs a day.

She actually received a letter from Guinness Book of World Records verifying the same (Sinha 2006).

Entry in Japan : More than 40% of Shahnaz sales come from Japan (CNN, 2004). According to Shahnaz, the Japanese are honest, prefer brands but when it comes to cosmetics they prefer natural products. Also, the Japanese women spend 16% of their income on cosmetics. But gaining an entry there was not easy. The country's drug department cleared all the lotions and potions before they could be launched in the country (Singh, 2002).

Shahnaz has used the power of the press to gain entry into other countries. Holding press conferences and talking about the ill effects of chemicals and synthetics gives her a platform to discuss the benefits of her herbal products. She followed this by providing free consultation. Each paper carried her story and not her advertisement along with her address where she could be contacted for free consultation. Till now Shahnaz never advertised. She used her larger than life personality to sell her brand through personal promotion. A rare instance when a woman entrepreneur has become a brand in itself. (Success, 1996). However in 2005 for the first time she planned to advertise extensively both in print and electronic media (Majumdar, 2005).

RANGES OF SPECIALIZED PRODUCTS

As leaders in product innovation, the Shahnaz Husain Group has evolved more than 350 formulations for general care, treatment of skin and scalp disorders, health and fitness. In fact, a characteristic feature of the Group has been its dynamism, introducing unique concepts from time to time and keeping abreast of the latest techniques in Ayurvedic and herbal products cosmetology.

The products have grown out of clinical usage, based on massive client feedback, as an answer to precise and individual needs. Based on "Care and Cure", the product ranges include entire lines of therapeutic formulations, which perform high level multiple tasks and reflect a deep understanding of the demands of protective, preventive and corrective care. They have no exact equivalents in the market. Apart from the legendary Shahnaz Herbal Range, there are ranges for precise needs, as well as those based on specific extracts, like Flower Power (of floral extracts), Neem Range, Honey Health, Himalayan Herb, Sun Range (sun-block products), Man Power, Kids Collection, Colour Magic (range of make-up cosmetics), Aromatherapy bar, Color-magic and Shapet (Ayurvedic formulations for the care of pets). A line of Ayurvedic health tonics, medicinal formulations (like pain relieving balm, blood purifiers, cough syrup, Isabgol), food supplements, herbal drinks, herbal teas, immunity enhancers, medicines, Ayurvedic slimming capsule, Aromatherapy essential oils, as well as the medicines used in the Ayurvedic Centers, have also been launched, along with innovative accessories and gift items (Mahajan). The Group has recently launched some revolutionary products in modern skin-care, which include the 24 Carat Gold Range, Pearl Cream and Mask, Oxygen Cream, Astro-Gem Therapy range, Diamond Collection and a signature Spa Collection. Shahnaz also entered the mass market with Fair One, a natural fairness cream and plans to launch Shahnaz Forever this year, an entire range at affordable prices for all segments of the market (Shahnaz, 2006).

SETTING UP THE EMPIRE, REASONS FOR SUCCESS

The undisputed Queen of world of beauty

presented an exciting new level of botanical energy with her flower power collection. Rejecting the synthetic artificiality of the west, she portrayed the unspoiled cosmetic innocence of nature in her products. She started this herbal crusade single handedly. As the saying goes – imitation is the best form of flattery, the number of other people entering this niche segment was a compliment to her. But still she is a force to reckon with and has earned the sobriquet of "India's Beauty Ambassador" from none other than Barbara Cartland for her tremendous contribution towards popularizing Indian products in the West.

One of the main reasons for success is that since beauty care is an image–based business, she has become the brand ambassador herself. So the clients and consumers have a brand, which is a trained cosmetologist herself, who is answerable for the product. Basing her customized beauty care on the adage that "external body condition is a barometer of internal health", Shahnaz came up with beauty care of the level of paramedical care complete with diagnosis and prescriptions. It was this holistic trend that set the terms for her long innings as the "Herbal Queen" (Bakshi, 2005).

Another reason for her success is that she just did not concentrate only on makeup and doing hair but proposed total skincare. Her company showing an annual growth rate of 19.4% is not finance driven but emotion driven. All the presidential and prime ministerial guests are given Shahnaz Husain hampers as a matter of routine (Singh, 2002).

Shahnaz believes in looking at the larger picture and thinks in the long term. In 1991 when war broke out in Yugoslavia her advisors advised her not to send the $ 300,000 worth of products one of her local partners had ordered as she would never get paid. Realizing that without the order her partner would be ruined, Shahnaz sent the products – and got her full payment in three months. It was these small instances that helped her build her multimillion dollar empire and earn a name of Herbal Empress from the Success Magazine (Success, 1996).

THE BUSINESS SCENARIO

The last decade has seen a significant increase in the use of cosmetics by Indian consumers with more and more women and men taking greater interest in personal grooming. This has been influenced by a number of factors like increasing disposable incomes, changing lifestyles, influence of satellite television and greater product choice and availability. With the demand for cosmetics on the rise and the opening up of the market to foreign companies, many of the world's popular cosmetics brands entered the Indian market in the early and mid-nineties and some more have set their sights on India.

The cosmetics and personal care industry has been growing at an average rate of 20 per cent for the last few years. The turn of the century witnessed a renewed craze for herbal cosmetic and personal care products, especially in the skin care segment with the growing belief that chemical-based cosmetics are harmful. Shehnaz Hussain, Biotique, and Lotus

Herbals are the major players in this segment. The growing popularity for natural products also attracted many primarily health-care companies such as Himalaya Drugs (with its Ayurvedic Concepts range), and Dabur to launch natural-based cosmetic products (Phookan, 2003).

Environment in Context

The beauty services industry in India is largely unorganized but is slowly and steadily taking the organized route to business. The emergence of players such as Marico's Kaya Skin Clinic, Lakme Beauty Salon, VLCC, CavinCare's Limelite and Green Trends, Keune and Jawed Habib Hair & Beauty along with Shahnaz can be attributed to this trend. According to industry estimates, the organized and semi-organized beauty services industry in the country is about Rs 1,500-Rs 1,600 crores (some peg it as high as Rs 6,000 crores). Clearly, the scope for conversion from unorganized to organized (Financial Express, 2006). Kaya Skin Clinic, Lakme Beauty Salon and Limelite, along with Shahnaz, cater to the premium segment while Green Care of CalvinCare's fall in the budget parlor category. Keune which is a hair care brand from Holland, marketed by Brushman, India fall between the two. Pantaloon has also launched its beauty services with its budget parlor Star and Sitara in Bangalore in May, 2006 (Financial Express, 2006). Shahnaz and Biotique both cater to the premium herbal cosmetics segment which is estimated at USD 300 million (Hussain cited in Bakshi, 2005).

The competition and their Modus Operandi

Kaya Skin Clinic, closed the financial year 2005-2006 with a turn-over of Rs 44 crores on the back of 43 company owned outlets in 15 locations in the country. It now plans to increase the overall number to 50 this fiscal. In the Middle East, where it has three clinics in Dubai and Abu Dhabi, the company will add a few more centers. Plans are to achieve a turnover of about Rs 60 crores this fiscal by pitching its flagship skin solutions to customers, though the company does not rule out an entry into the hair care segment too. "We are currently test-marketing a hair-loss treatment in Bangalore," says Rakesh Pandey, chief executive officer, Kaya Skin Clinic.

Close rival Lakme Beauty Salons, in the interim, which has over 85 franchisee-controlled outlets in over 34 cities, is keeping its focus on a select few metros and mini-metros. These include Mumbai, Delhi, Baroda, Kolkata, Jaipur, Ahmedabad and Kochi among others, says a company spokesperson.

CavinCare's Limelite and Green Trends, according to its business head S. Jagdish, will go up to about 100 in the next two-three years from the current 22 properties located at Bangalore, Chennai and Delhi.

The US-based Regis Corp, the dominant group in the international hair salon segment with some 11,000 outlets in North America and allied locations, also has its sights on India. Not surprising then that its entry is being monitored closely by its nearest rival Toni & Guy with some 3,000 salons across the world, is also believed to be studying the Indian marketplace.

The mode of operation is another area critical to a player, with VLCC, for instance, embedding its beauty regimen within its weight loss and fitness programme. Lakme, in contrast, plays on its exclusive beauty and hair services, Kaya boasts of its scientific approach to skin problems, while Green Trends is all about affordable hair and skin solutions using natural products. "Limelite is an upmarket salon-cum-day spa targeting a well-heeled audience," says Jagdish, "Green Trends, however, is your neighbourhood salon," he adds. (Financial Express, 2006)

Modus Operandi: Shahnaz

Compared to the other players in the market Shahnaz has drawn out a detailed plan for the Health and Beauty products, Spas, Beauty training schools, Forever beautiful shops and ayurvedic centers and Franchisee arrangements. She has also invested in rigorous and constant R&D efforts which form the backdrop of all its operations. The details are as follows:

Health and Beauty products

Today Shahnaz is described as Asia's Helena Rubenstein, exporting "Nature Care and Cure" products that are more than 400 in number to 104 countries and having over 650 salons globally (Bhardwaj, 2006).

Shahnaz has 400 formulations for general care and treatment of skin and scalp disorders already on the shelves. She has outlets at prestigious stores like Gallerie Lafayette in Paris, Harrods and Selfridges in London, and Seibu Chain in Japan. Her products also sell at Bloomingdales in New York, La Rinascente in Milan and El Certe Inglis in Spain as well as exclusive outlets and clinics worldwide. In fact, Shahnaz was the first Asian to enter Galeries Lafayette in Paris in herbal care and the first Asian to be featured in the 18-foot shop window of the store. Hers is the first Indian herbal cosmetic company to have featured in Harrods and Selfridges (Shahnaz, 2006). Shahnaz Husain is also carrying out research on ageing in continuation to which she had sent her products to NASA for trials and may be launched around 2008 (Shahnaz, press folder).

Today her products are selling globally from USA to Japan, in Europe, Russia, Middle East, Africa, South East Asia, Australia and even in Iceland. Her empire is estimated to be worth 200 million dollars with a growth rate of 19.4% (CNN, 2004; Choong, 2004)

After creating a presence in the premium product range Shahnaz has entered the mass market in India with "Shahnaz Forever" which she will be marketing with Elder Pharmaceuticals starts from the range of Rs. 150. Realizing that a large portion of consumers in India could not afford her creams, Shahnaz did extensive R & D to launch this range. (Majumdar, 2005).

Spas

Shahnaz Hussain ventured in the spa business by setting up the Medispa in the US island of Saipan, off the Pacific Coast in collaboration with Hyakumata group of Japan to open a spa at their 24 hour Golf Course.. This is now called Shahnaz Hussain Ayurvedic Spa. At the spa she is incorporating holistic healing techniques such as yoga and meditation along with a spa experience. The spa has traditional ayurvedic treatment and soothing massages, anti-stress treatments, aromatherapy, specialized body packs, skin and hair treatments, supervised diets, yoga, meditation, etc. This spa received much success and was followed up by spas in Toronto and Greece. Based on this success Shahnaz is planning to launch a spa collection (Bakshi, 2005). She is planning to set up a health resort at Dhauj (Haryana), just 45 kms from Delhi. It is targeted at foreign tourists and urbanites who wish to get a healthy weekend get-away (Mahajan). Currently, the Group is considering Spa proposals for countries like Saudi Arabia, Spain, Italy and Australia.

Beauty training schools

Shahnaz is also the pioneer of vocational training in beauty in India. More than three decades ago, when only apprenticeship training was available, Shahnaz started her beauty institute, Woman's World International, to provide comprehensive training in beauty. Today, students come from all over the world to acquire training in Ayurvedic treatments and receive the coveted Shahnaz Husain Diploma. In 1993, she started Men's World International, to cater to the demand for trained personnel in Men's Salons. As a philanthropic venture Shahnaz set up "Shamute Beauty School" – a free training center cosmetic therapy for speech and hearing impaired in the year 1984. She has translated her spiritual values in real terms, bringing hope and a sense of purpose in the lives of the students.

All the courses offered at these various institutes are in tune with international standards and students are taught the latest techniques in skin and hair care. These schools were the basis of the franchise-based enterprise (Hindustan Times, 2006).

THE FRANCHISEES

In 1979 Shahnaz started her first franchise clinic in Calcutta. This was the beginning of the worldwide chain. The idea occurred to her "when Threety Irani, a friend, came to me from Calcutta, with a list of products for her friends, worth Rupees one lakh." Shahnaz told her that most of my products were prescriptives and specialized training was needed to advise others on their use. Threety then requested Shahnaz to train her and brought her two daughters along for the training. Once she was trained, she wanted to start her own salon and use Shahnaz treatments and products. So, together they worked out a one line letter by which Shahnaz gave Threety the right to use the Shahnaz Herbal name. This was the beginning of the Shahnaz franchise system and training school. After that Shahnaz began to encourage ordinary housewives to open salons in their own homes. "I had already shown them the way by opening her own very first salon in her house – which finally went International – becoming the largest chain of Herbal Salons in the world!!" Shahnaz trained them and offered the Shahnaz Herbal franchise. "I saw how shy, submissive housewives blossomed into confident entrepreneurs. Within the first year I already had 80 franchise salons." (Rangoonwala, 2001)

Shahnaz also adopted a highly successful method to promote the new franchise salons. She made it a point to attend their opening. She addressed press conferences, where she spoke on the benefits of herbal care and also gave free consultations. This not only attracted crowds to the inauguration of the salons, but gave the new venture a real impetus. It was based on a personal interaction, where she would meet people, listen to their problems and provide beauty solutions. Thus, she was answering a human need, specializing in Care & Cure. Her presence at the openings evoked much media coverage and a fantastic response. This method proved so successful that soon she was attending two openings on the same day, flying to two or three different cities in India like Pune in the morning, Mumbai in the afternoon and Bangalore at night. She did this in 300 cities and towns, spending a few hours in each speaking to the Press and giving free consultations, and flying back a day later. The pace was hectic, but it became a distinctive style. Later, she adopted it for the openings of her franchise clinics and other ventures abroad. During one such trip, she held a press conference in Hawaii in the morning, one at the airport in Tokyo the same afternoon and attended a Press Reception at the residence of the Consul General of India in Hong Kong the same night. Apart from training all the franchisees and therapists, refresher courses are also provided from time to time. An excellent feedback is maintained and all new innovations and techniques are communicated to the franchisees (Shahnaz press folder).

Shahnaz Husain Forever Beautiful Shops and Ayurvedic Centres

The success of the franchise system prompted the opening of Shahnaz Husain Forever Beautiful Shops, based on a concept of lifestyle marketing. The wide and varied ranges, along with accessories, are housed under one roof, with exclusive shop design and efficient customer information system. Specially trained sales staff provides guidance and information regarding products. Shahnaz Husain Ayurvedic Centres, carrying out traditional treatments of Panchkarma, Dhara and Kerala massage have also been set up for the cure of various ailments. The Centre employs Ayurvedic physicians and professionally trained personnel to conduct the various treatments. An individualized approach, along with all necessary facilities have been made available to provide a perfect environment for treatment (The Times, 2003).

RESEARCH & DEVELOPMENT

Research & Development have always received high priority in the Group's two R & D units. To ensure the purity of raw material, a herb and flower farm has also been set up near Delhi. Thus, quality control is exercised right from the raw material stage. This is done through rigorous testing and research. The extraction of essential oils, infusions, decoctions, tinctures and other extracts is carried out by the Group itself. Various methods of soil culture and cultivation are being followed, using superior natural composts and fertilizers, which actually contribute, not only towards the purity and quality of the raw material, but towards actually creating a superior product. From the herbs and flowers, various preparations are obtained for use in the formulations, like infusions, decoctions, distillates, essences, powders, tinctures and so on, in keeping with the Ayurvedic system. These are made under strict supervision, using the latest technology. Stringent quality control tests are carried out for various dilutions. Thus, by exercising control at each stage, high quality is ensured. (Shahnaz press folder).

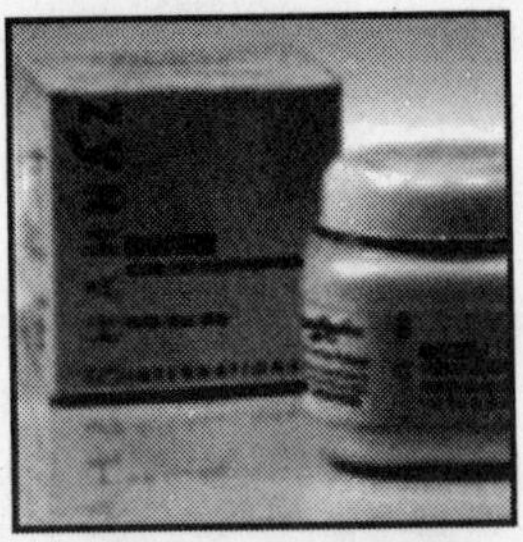

Finally...

Shahnaz Husain Herbal has a large network of over 400 franchise and associate clinics in India and abroad, operating under the Franchise system. The franchise clinics have extended not only to the cities, but even small towns, all over India. Today, a countrywide zonal distribution network exists, with 40 distributors and more than 600 sub-distributors all over India. There are more than 500 outlets in India, which include the franchise clinics, Shahnaz Husain shops, counters in leading stores, shops and Cottage Industries Emporia. Thus, the brand is ideally positioned in the herbal cure and care market as a premium brand. (Shahnaz press folder).

Future vision

In India Cosmetology is an Rs 1800 crores industry having a growth rate of 25%. The Herbal segment alone is worth Rs 300 crores with a growth rate of 40%. Thus there is ample scope for Shahnaz who is taking this opportunity to target the Indian consumers with her premium and mid-ranged beauty products. Shahnaz plans to supplement this with advertising. But according to Shahnaz beauty salons and parlours will be passé in times to come. Consumers are increasingly under stress and pressure and at the same time more diet and health conscious. The focus will not be on better looks and visual improvement but total relaxation. The estimate of spa business in India by 2008 is Rs. 500 crores and the current global market is estimated at $14 billion (Husain, cited in Bakshi, 2005).

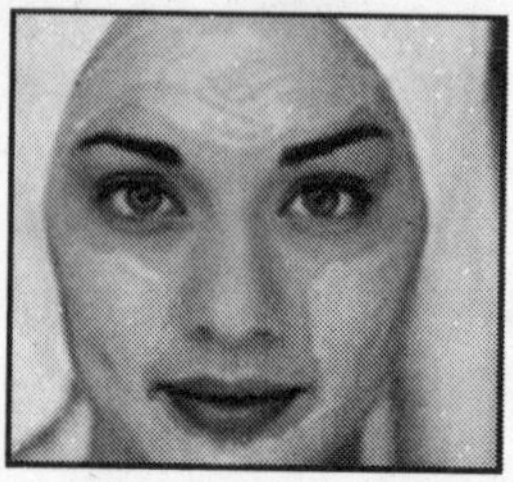

Personality traits that have helped her to succeed...

The phenomenal growth and success of Shahnaz Husain Group is testimony to Shahnaz's rare personal qualities, her dynamism and spirit of enterprise and at the same time have made her a living legend in beauty and personal care. (Global Indian, 2005). Her faith in her abilities, her relentless determination, an iron will and the capacity for hard work is some of the qualities that have brought her so far. Her innovative ideas, foresight and a knack for putting her finger on the pulse of the market demands have made her an entrepreneurial success. For example, in Japan golf is a big hit and so she came up with Shahnaz and the Golf Collection. In Las Vegas, cards and gaming are the prime focus and millions of dollars are spent on cards so there she launched her Casino Collection. She emphasizes that her emotional bonding with her organization and the undercurrent of emotional bonding that she is able to inculcate between the different people within the group is the secret of her success (Shahnaz CD-ROM). Her zest for learning and not resting on past laurels is what drives the living legend even today. She is constantly searching for new frontiers to cross and new mountains to climb so that she can apply her innovative ideas and create new milestones for herself. In spite of all these qualities she is a real and vital person. Through her interaction with others, she leaves a lingering fragrance of her personality.

Balance between personal and professional life

Everything in life comes for a price. Who else but Shahnaz would know it better who had to juggle her personal life and her professional life to reach where she is today. This experience has lead her to conclude that there is a mind boggling price to success and in skimming the waves of success you can miss the finer values of life. Shahnaz accepts that it was very difficult to juggle work, career and social obligations. Though her husband was very supportive she had loads of responsibilities to fulfill as a mother, daughter, wife and sister. To expand her business beyond the Indian skies Shahnaz had to travel a lot. This kept her away from family and home for some stretches of time. Shahnaz is an emotional person at heart and has always cherished family values and shares a close relationship with her children. Her home is her haven of retreat, imparting a sense of peace that she values. She makes it a point to spend quality time with her family on vacations. She also involved her children in her business so that they can discuss ideas and share responsibilities. Her daughter Nilofer is more like a sister than a daughter. Since she was only sixteen when Nilofer was born they both grew up together, sharing clothes and shoes. Once, in London, they were both attending a beauty institute together and "it was fun." Nilofar has schooled at some of the best cosmetic centres in the world. Nilofer is now the president of her company and the only person who shares the formula secrets of the different products Shahnaz has produced for her clients. They both make it a point not to appear together at the same time or travel on the same plane at any point of time just to keep Shahnaz Herbal alive. (Sherman, 1990). It is Nilofer who created the pearl cream. Shahnaz loves beauty and fragrance and loves to surround herself with beautiful things. She has collected artistic and ornate pieces and paintings, which have been used to decorate every room. The all-pervading exotic fragrance is like a signature tune. You cannot miss it. In fact, in many ways it reflects her dreams, her life and the very essence of her being. Shahnaz loves poetry and Keats is her favourite. In fact, right from childhood, she has expressed her innermost feelings in verse. Often, when she has been away from home, she has written poetry for her children. She feels she can express herself better this way, instead of merely telling them how much she misses them. She paints too and her regret is that her demanding career does not allow her to indulge in her favourite pastimes.

Awards and Accolades

Shahnaz has been conferred several national and international awards apart from the Greatest Woman Entrepreneur Award from Success magazine. She has received Arch of Europe International Gold Star in Madrid, Spain, the Quality Excellence Award in Geneva, Cannes and London, Golden America Award in New York, (The Times, 2003), the Outstanding Woman Entrepreneur Award in London, Woman of the Millenium Award in USA, Woman of the Year Award from the Governor of California, USA, and the Outstanding Entrepreneur of the Millennium by Dame Barbara Cartland in London. Shahnaz was the only woman among eighteen leading Indian entrepreneurs, who was invited to attend the recently held Forbes Global CEO Conference in Sydney, Australia. (Shahnaz press folder).

In 2006, she received the Padma Shri Award. The prestigious Padma awards are the highest civilian awards and Shahnaz Husain who single-handedly put India on the world beauty map and kept Indian flag flying high at the cosmetic capitals of the world truly earned it. She has also been awarded the Udyog Ratan Award for Export Excellence (won three times), the Rajiv Gandhi Gold Medal for propagating the Indian herbal heritage and the Export Excellence Award (thrice) from the Delhi Government (Financial Express, 2006). (For a more detailed list of the awards received see Annexure).

CONCLUSION AND LESSONS LEARNT

"What really matters in life is not what you want but how badly you want it. You can achieve any level of success if you want it that much" has been one of the guiding principles of Shahnaz. She also says that "If I am walking towards the goal and if I feel the door is closed, I don't walk away but open my own doors". (CNN, 2004) Thus having a vision, being passionate and focused about it and trying to achieve it with a crusaders zeal, no matter what the obstacles, have been the reasons Shahnaz could find success in spite of coming from a conservative family and trying to sell a new concept to the world. She says "An entrepreneur is someone with independence of spirit, heart, mind and soul. One should be innovative and be willing to try every avenue, with success as the ultimate goal...Believe in yourself implicitly and blindly and you will arrive where you dreamed you would". The 61-year-old entrepreneur says, "You never fail until you stop trying. I never stop, so I never fail." According to her a leader must possess the following qualities:

— Have an overall and detailed view of the entire organization and yet know how to delegate responsibilities.
— Must have the ability to judge people, their abilities and their talents.
— Should be well informed and should be creative and innovative.
— Should have the vision and be a step ahead of the organization.
— Should be a motivational force and show understanding, diplomacy and tact where necessary.
— To evaluate the worth of an idea a leader should be able to understand the market, should be aware of the changing trends and awareness in the target audience. Have the ability to learn, be dynamic and adapt to these changing trends.

— May start in a small way but should think big.

— Relentless determination, courage and the desire to excel complemented with the ability to work hard.

To summarize she says that the secret of being a leader and successful entrepreneur one should be able to seize opportunities and look forward to challenges. It is important to dream and believe in the magic of your own dreams. (Sakhuja, 2005). Having come full circle she now lays much emphasis on the spiritual development of a person. According to her true success is measured in terms of spiritual goodwill –

What is earthly success but a passing flame,
For a time it burns high and bright,
Like Eden glimpsed through a veil of smoke,
Then it is out of sight,
A fleeting dream that comes and goes, the queen of success for a day,
Alas it passes away,
Then why not struggle for spiritual success,
Why not find favor with God,
Instead of struggling for an inky parchment,
That must end in the dust and sod!
(Shahnaz cited in Kurian, 2003)

BIBLIOGRAPHY

Bakshi, Veeshal (2005) "Remaking the Beauty Business" The Financial Express, dated February 5, 2005, pp IV.

Bhardwaj, Manali (2006) "Padma Sundari Shahnaz Husain" City Limits, Issue:15 February, 2006, pp 79.

Business Today, (2006) "The 25 Most Powerful Women in Indian Business", Business Today, March 12, 2006.

Choong, Renee (2004) "Herbal Products to enhance Natural

Beauty" The Star, 10 March 2004.

Cunningham, Jennifer (2005) "Shahnaz Hussain Ayurvedic Cosmetics Manufacturer", The Herald, dated 20 June, 2005, pp19.

Financial Express (2006) (online 1st September, 2006) available from URL : *http://www.financialexpress.com/fe_full_story.php?content_id=115954.*

Financial Express India Inc. (2006*), "Armed for the Beauty Market"* dated May 06, 2006 (online). (cited on 2nd September, 2006) available from *http://www.financialexpress.com/inc/index.html.*

Global Indian (2005), "Estee Lauder of India", Global Indian, Middle East Edition, Vol2, Issue 11, pp 18.

Kurian, Anupa (2003) "A truly beautiful Woman must have Inner Beauty", Gulf News Tabloid, dated May 8, 2003, pp 1-2.

Lane, Winsome (2000) "Secrets of Eternal Beauty", Standard Hong Kong, Issue: February 27, 2000, pp 6-8.

Mahajan, Prarthana, "India is Naaz of Shahnaaz", Inside Fashion, Vol. 2, Issue 7, pp 18.

Majumdar, Pallavi (2005), Shahnaz Hussain goes Mass Market", Business Standard, dated 19 January 2005, pp 22.

Rangaraj, R (2005), "Shahnaz Husain launches Fair One", Chennai Online (online) (cited on 20th September, 2006) Available from URL *http://www.chennaionline.com/fashion-lifestyle/Fashiontips/2005/05elder.asp.*

Rangoonwala, Yousuf (2001), "Herbal Queen", The Telegraph in Schools, 19 July – 1 August, 2001, pp 11.

Rediff Books (2006) (online) (cited on 2nd September, 2006) available from URL: http://books.rediff.com/bookstore/

Sakhuja, Latika (2005), "Herbal Beauty Care Franchising Pioneer", The Franchising World, Issue 6, pp 48-50

Sengupta, Hindol (2003), "From Bloody Fingers to Hands Decked with Diamonds", Delhi Mid Day, May 6.

Shahnaz Husain (online) (cited on 1st September, 2006) available from URL *http://www.shahnaz-husain.com*

Sherman, Elizabeth, (1990) "India's Queen of Beauty", Harpers and Queen, Issue September, 1990, pp 274-277

Singh, Kishore (2002), "In the Parlour of the Diva of Potions", Business Standard, dated 13 february, 2002, pp 14.

Sinha, Vimmy (2006) "Guts and Glory", Delhi Times, The Times of India, 14th April, 2006, pp 11.

Success (1996) "Indias Beauty Queen", Success, Issue June, 1996, pp37-38.

Telegraph, (2001) "Herbal Queen", The Telegraph n Schools, Issue 19 July to 1 August, 2001, pp 11.

The Times (2003), "Amazing Success Story of Shahnaz Husain", The Times, Kuwait, Aug 15-31, 2003,

QUESTIONS FOR DISCUSSION

1. What have been the factors which influenced Shahnaz to start the entrepreneurial venture?
2. Critically examine the growth strategy for the Shahnaz Husain's venture? What have been the major challenges in emergence of a global business?
3. What are the lessons which can be learnt in light of success of Shahnaz Hussain's venture?

4

Women Entrepreneurship in India – A Case of Lijjat Papad

Kakoli Sen
Gunjan M. Sanjeev

ABSTRACT

Lijjat Papad is an organisation set up in 1959 by a group of women who started with rolling papads, with borrowings of eighty rupees. These women, also called Bens or sisters, had no formal education but felt that they could do something with the free time that they had on hands after finishing their family chores. Their commitment and perseverance has helped them to achieve success. Today they are a large and successful organisation. Lijjat is not only helping the members contribute to the family income but also empowering them. Valuing people and understanding their problems has created for Lijjat a sound and sustainable business model. It is also noteworthy for its commitment to improving the quality of the lives of its members.

INTRODUCTION

The Term "entrepreneur" originated in French Economies in the 17th and 18th centuries with French economist Jean-Baptiste Say describing an entrepreneur as one who "shifts economic resources out of an area of lower into an area of higher productivity and greater yield." (Martin & Osberg, 2007) Mort et al.(2003) further suggests that they are innovators, change agents and they move the economy forward by serving new markets or creating new ways of doing things.

The oxford dictionary defines "Entrepreneur" as a person who sets up a business or businesses, taking on greater than normal financial risks in order to do so. Reiss (2000) opines that "Entrepreneurship is the recognition and pursuit of opportunity without regard to the resources you currently control, with confidence that you can succeed, with the flexibility to change course as necessary, and with the will to rebound from setbacks."

According to an estimate (Mishra, 1996), women entrepreneurs presently comprise about 10% of the total number of entrepreneurs in India, with the percentage growing every year. It also predicts that if the prevailing trends continue, it is likely that in another five years, women will comprise 20% of the entrepreneurial force. Today, the Indian government is offering easy loans, micro credit, and special training programs to encourage women entrepreneurs. Few decades ago, when an average Indian woman would aspire to get into a small business run from home to augment the family income or to while away time, she did not have any of these opportunities. Today more and more educated and skilled women are willing to give up on demanding jobs to pursue an enterprise of their own which gives more freedom & provides better work life balance.

Srivastava (2006) suggests that there are three categories of Indian women entrepreneurs, one, namely from big cities, educated, savvy and moneyed, the second type is from smaller cities and towns engaged in low skill jobs like beauty parlours, crèches etc. The third category is of illiterate, rural women who are into agriculture, horticulture, animal husbandry, dairy, fisheries, agro-forestry, handloom, power loom, etc. mainly to augment family income. This case considers the third category. It highlights the entrepreneurial and management skills of seven semi-literate Maharashtrian women who started what is today known the world over as Shri Mahila Grih Udyog Lijjat Papad (SMGULP) or in short Lijjat Papad.

Lijjat Papad's success has become a symbol of women's economic enfranchisement in India (Merchant, 2002). Lijjat papad's success is also a symbol of women's economic empowerment in a male dominated society of India and serves a very good example of how a model of simple and committed governance can command tremendous commercial success. It is also noteworthy for its commitment to improving the quality of the lives of its members. When it was started more than forty years ago, the founding members may have had no idea of the social and economic revolution they were about to start in the form of entrepreneurship.

THE BEGINNING

Shri Mahila Grih Udyog Lijjat Papad (SMGULP) or Lijjat Papad, is an organization set up in 1959 by a group of seven almost illiterate women who in a congested locality of South Bombay (now Mumbai) saw an opportunity in a local loss making papad unit and decided to take over the venture along with its loss of eighty rupees. Buying the needed ingredients, they started rolling out papads and drying them on the residence terrace. These women also called *Bens* or sisters had no formal education but felt that they could do something with the free time that they had on their hands after finishing their family chores. They had no special skills, only some domestic skills handed down to women across generations viz. making pickles, papads, spices, etc. -- household items which are required at every Indian household but with today's demanding lifestyles, no one has the time and inclination to make them at home. Using their own household items, these women started making papads at the residence terrace of one of them. After drying and packing them, they would give them to a known merchant in Bhuleshwar. During the first year they had to stop production during the rainy season, but by the next rains, they had made arrangements for a cot and stove to dry the papads. They tried using coals but it coloured the papads. They would distribute the broken papads to the neighbours (Ramanathan, 2004). In three months, there were about twenty-five women working with them which rose to a hundred and fifty women by two years. The first profit that the group made in six months time was distributed among the women in the form of half a gram of gold. This is a system followed till date.

All these women would get together everyday, knead the dough, roll out the papads, dry them, pack them all at one place under direct supervision. As the numbers grew and the physical space became a constraint, additional rooms were taken on rent and at one point of time the women were rolling papads out of eight rented rooms. The entire production was centralized but by the third year, when there was space constraint again, the *bens* realized that with the growing demand and the additional number of women joining in, renting more and more additional space was not the solution. It would also add to the costs and the prices may not remain attractive enough. They came up with the most innovative production decision by decentralizing the production process completely. The papads were now to be rolled and dried in the members' houses; however the quality checking and packing remained centralized. This decision made sure that the production process continued uninterrupted in small little houses and drove away the heavy cost of manufacturing at one location. To maintain the high quality and standard of Lijjat products and uniformity in taste for the same product from different branches, the central office supplies the raw material – moong and urad flour — to all its branches. This remains the only involvement of the central office in the entire production and marketing exercise of the branch office. (Srivastav,2003)

ORGANIZATION STRUCTURE AND GOVERNANCE

In 1966, the women registered their group under the Bombay Public Trust Act 1950 which proved to be a turning point for Lijjat. The same year it was also registered under Societies Registration Act, 1860 and got stated as a village industry by Khadi and Village Industries Commission (KVIC). The KVIC also granted a working capital of about eight lakhs rupees and tax exemptions. Though initial attempts to start branches in Malad and Sangli were unsuccessful, today Lijjat has metamorphosed into a Rs. 300 crore (1 Crore = 10^7) organization providing employment to about 42,000 women members in 62 branches, 40 divisions across 17 states in India. It is also guided by separate divisions of advertising, marketing, sales promotion and exports. There is great coordination between branch offices (different production and marketing units) and centralised marketing, advertising and exports departments.

Lijjat's membership is open to women only. Men

can be salaried employees but not members. All members are also joint owners. The recruitment process of members is simple. Any woman irrespective of religion, caste or class who pledges to adopt the institution's values and has respect for quality can become a member and co-owner of the organization (Naik, 2005). The women sign a pledge of devotion to the basic tenets of the organization. It is a commitment to earn "legitimate" honest income, through work on cooperative basis. Renouncing of membership is voluntary and no one can be asked to leave unless she has violated the tenets of the organization. (Ramanathan, 2004)

There is a central committee comprising the branch managers or *Sanchalikas* which takes decisions on behalf of all the member sisters. Any decision, major or minor, cannot be taken without the consensus of all its members. Each and every member has the veto power. The 21-member committee including President, Vice President, two secretaries, and two treasurers is elected every three years.

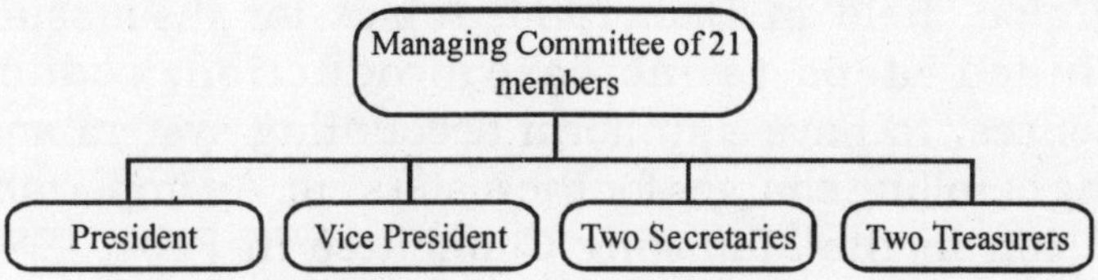

Office bearers are chosen from the existing members on the basis of consensus every three years. All women start by rolling papads and among these members, those who show leadership skills and administrative abilities are given greater responsibilities. Any member-sister can hold an office by expressing her willingness and be selected by due process.

The *Sanchalikas*, or branch supervisors manage the daily affairs of their own branch. To manage its own affairs, each branch has a committee of eleven member sisters chose by consensus. The responsibilities of every office bearer and member–sister are laid down in the constitution and are modified with changing times and increasing growth of the organisation. The branches are run independently, however for any new project or starting a new product, a formal approval from the head office is necessary. The branch is responsible for all activities from production to packaging to collection and distribution of *vanai (rolling charges)* and profit for its particular geographical region.

Branches hold their own coordination meetings and area meetings of the various branches in a region or state. At the All India Level there are Annual General Body meetings attended by member-sisters of the branches and divisions. Issues pertaining to the maintenance of quality, interpersonal and other administrative problems are dealt with in these meetings. For example, at the All India convention held at Valod, held in Dec.,1984, topics for discussion included steps to increase production, reduce expenses, to have a uniform accounting system and fixing of rolling charges for the sisters etc. An important decision in the Managing Committee in Feb., 1988 placed the responsibility of handling all cash amounts, sales proceeds and other receipts only by the sisters and not by accountants or any other staff members at any branch. "One sister in each branch," was "to take the entire responsibility of handling the cash amount and go to the bank to deposit it." This is significant because many among the member-sisters have had very little formal education and they learnt through direct experience. (Ramanathan, 2004)

Every branch is independent in its governance, sharing its profits and losses among its member-sisters, so they are all responsible for the profitable functioning of the branch. If the branch does well, the rolling charges are increased and the profits are shared in terms of cash, gold coins, gold rings, gold chains, etc. In case of mismanagement or loss due to negligence, the concerned Sanchalika or other member sisters could be relieved of their membership if the charges are severe, else they are relieved of the responsibility they mismanaged though they could continue to perform other functions. (Ramanathan, 2004)

OPERATIONS

Every morning women are fetched from their homes by buses or vans along with their prepared papads and are left back in their homes with the kneaded flour to be rolled for that day. When these women come in to collect the dough, they also give in the previous day's production, which is tested for quality. After the quality checks, the papads are packed. Every member gets her share of *vanai* (rolling charge) every day for the work she does. There is a vehicle for every branch, which, at fixed times, brings the *bens* and rolled papads to the branch and also drops them back. This is done for all the *bens* — those who mix the dough, do the *vanai* (rolling), testing, packaging, etc.

All raw materials are purchased in Mumbai and then distributed to the 62 branches to ensure consistent quality of Lijjat Papad, the Urad Dal is imported from Myanmar, asafoetida is imported from Iran and black pepper from Kerela. The grinding of flour is also a centralized process. There are two grinding mills, one in Vashi (Navi Mumbai) and one in

Nashik (in Maharashtra). The head office does the pricing of the products. Lijjat papad all over India costs the same. This price factors in the cost of raw materials, transport, taxes, distributors commission, profit percentage and so on. (Naik, 2005)

Packed papads are sealed into boxes and the production from each centre is transported to the depot for that area. There are about sixteen branches and six depots in Mumbai. Each depot stocks production from the nearby three to four branches. The depots are the storage areas as well as pick up points for distributors. The Lijjat distribution cycle is as under:

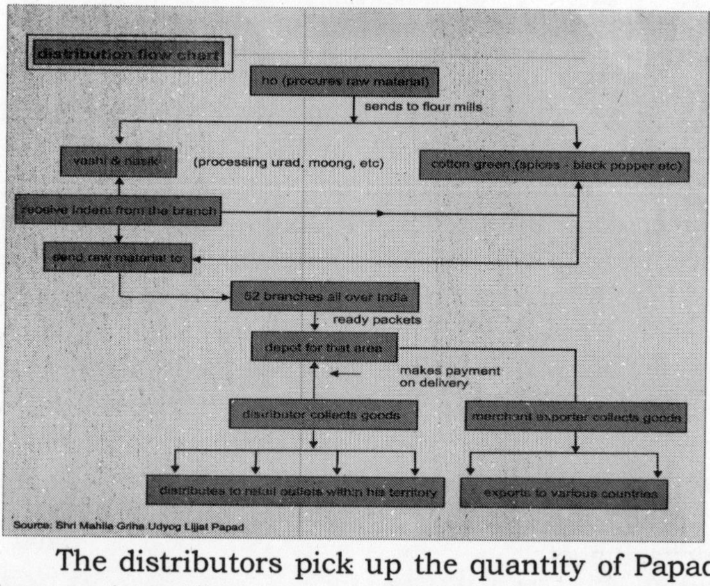

Source: Shri Mahila Griha Udyog Lijjat Papad

The distributors pick up the quantity of Papad they require and pay cash on delivery and the members are paid every day. The production is also according to the estimate of the quantity each distributor takes to ensure that no stock inventory has to be kept.

Lijjat markets its products through a wide network of dealers and distributors all across the country, and has never chosen to sell or push its products directly through the vast network of its offices and sister-members even during the initial years. Rather, over the years, Lijjat has developed cordial and mutually beneficial relationships with its dealers. Sisters claim they believe in doing the business wisely and on sound business ethics. Dealers are given a set commission of seven per cent and retailers' earnings are fixed between Rs 2.25 and Rs 26 on the investment of Rs 14 for 200 grams and Rs 150 for 2.5 kilogram packs respectively.

There are no individual door-to-door salesmen or women selling from homes – sale happens only through the appointed distributor for the area. There are about 32 distributors in Mumbai. Each distributor is earmarked for an area. Distributors are selected after members from the marketing division personally check and approve the godown facilities. A distributor has to pay Rs 150,000 as deposit. This is the system followed through out the country. Irrespective of whether there is a branch or not, the papads can reach every place through appointed distributors. There are monthly meetings with distributors where problems and issues are discussed.

The operating procedures at Lijjat have become standardized and have been followed for the past forty years, without compromising on the core values as well as the commercial benchmarks. It follows a self sustainable model in which a new branch team is completely trained by the experienced members in all the operational areas and hand held till it becomes stable after which the new branch nurtures additional branches in similar manner.

MARKET PRESENCE & EXPORTS

Lijjat Papad can now boast of an annual turnover

of Rs. 315 crores of which Rs. 12 crores comes from its export wing alone (started in 1960). Today, Lijjat Papad is the generic reference for papads. Launched on a shoe-string, the co-operative now exports to countries and regions such as the US, UK and the Middle East, which generates 4 per cent of sales. Lijjat papad is not directly involved in exporting, but recognized professional merchant exporters place an export order.

SMGULP has followed a systematic brand building strategy over the years. The sales rose from a humble Rs. 6196 in 1959 to more than Rs. 3 billion in 1992 (Bhatanagar,2003).Marketing is centralized and done by its advertising division & seven sales offices across the country. Lijjat also participates in various trade fairs and exhibitions held across India to popularize its brand. This participation not only improved sales and promoted the Lijjat brand, it also called for tremendous organizational abilities which proved to be a good training ground for the sisters. The phenomenal growth and expansion of SMGULP into a multi-product company has opened up new employment opportunities for the sister-members; eligible candidates are chosen and trained to work in its modern Polypropylene, Sasa detergent & cake and printing divisions. (Srivastav,2003)

Advertising was undertaken from the initial years through the vernacular newspapers. The institution sponsored programs and gave away gifts for the winners of specific shows on the TV. The cost of advertising was borne by all the branches and divisions of the Lijjat institution through an ingenious method. The money for the advertising was spent by the Propylene division which recovered the same by adding it the price of bags it supplied to all the branches and divisions throughout India. Thus all shared the cost of advertising equitably, according to their individual productive capability (Ramanathan, 2004).

"The final product is well publicized and sold through the network of retailers (Planning Commission, 1981).The advertisement expenses are about 15 % of the selling expenses (Sharma, 2006).

FINANCIAL MODEL

Maintaining proper accounts is high on Lijjat's agenda. Chhagan Bapa, their mentor in the initial days, had advised the founding member sisters on the importance of maintaining updated accounts. Till today, every branch closes the account book every day. The sales and payment record is maintained on a daily basis, and monthly profit and loss statement and balance sheet has to be prepared. On one hand it brings

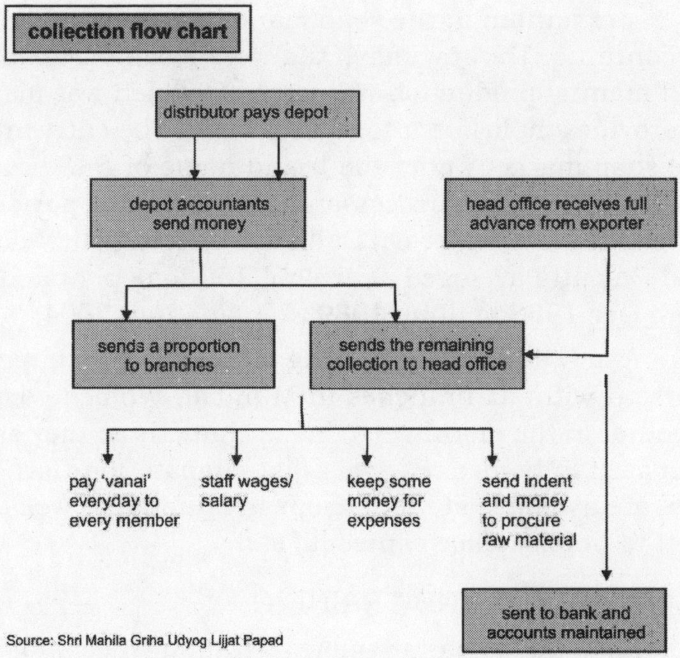

Source: Shri Mahila Griha Udyog Lijjat Papad

in tremendous discipline and regularity, on the other it is absolutely transparent for all its members. It strictly follows cash only sales which results in readily available funds for growth. In addition, it maintains a Sisters Savings Fund to tide over short term cash deficits experienced by branches.

Diversification

Though Lijjat also diversified in other cottage industry like Agarbatti, Leather and Match they had to be closed down. However the processing of those items that were needed to make or sell papads were successful viz. the Khakra Division, the flour mills, the masala division, the printing division and the Propylene division as well as the bakery products.

Lijjat launched the detergent powder division at Dahisar near Bombay as it saw a consistent growth of 15 % per annum in the soap market which was likely to continue. The raw materials were locally available and manual production was possible which was ideal to provide employment to rural women. The entry into the soap market under the brand name of *SASA* met with tremendous success and the detergent powder sold by the five centres in Dahisar,Pune, Rajkot, Valod and Calcutta averaged at around 150 tons per month from Dec 1988 to June 1989 (Ramanathan,2004)

A new and very promising product is the chapati division with six branches in Mumbai. Women come together in the mornings to make chapatis as they are prepared in homes. Packed Lijjat chapati, four for Rs five, are available at retail shops in Mumbai as well as sent to hotels, office canteens, etc.

EMPLOYMENT AND TRAINING

Lijjat papad has an informal training mechanism

to train new members. Each new member is introduced and trained by an existing member before her enrollment. Availability of labor is not a problem as the need or requirement for any new member is that they would operate from their homes and sometimes in the premises of the division (UNIDO report)

In May 1968, the first branch of the institution was founded in Valod, in Gujarat. Initially, a few member-sisters from Girgaum went by turns and stayed at Valod to train the new member-sisters who joined the new branch. Once they had learnt the ropes of running it, they were entrusted with the administration of the branch. The first branch that opened in any state took care of the other branches that opened in the state, especially in their initial stages. Gradually Lijjat opened branches in Bhopal, Madhya Pradesh, Baroda, Gujarat and even Rajgir and Ranchi in Bihar.

Lijjat has created opportunities for those women who are discouraged to move out of their homes. There is a wide range of activities that bens can do: making the masala, pounding the flour, weighing the flour, preparing the dough, rolling papads, receiving papas after weighing, checking the papads, packing the papads, distributing the wages and handling the accounts (Bhatnagar,2003). And bens are allowed to choose any activity.

"As an experiment, Lijjat has insulated its sister-members from joblessness. These women also work from their homes, where help from other family members not only adds up to the income but also makes the work more enjoyable. At the workplace they are self-respecting, hard-working and sisterly to one another. More importantly, besides the strength of womanhood, Lijjat is also an experiment in the restoration of the essence of womanhood. The Lijjat women offer an alternative to the highly competitive and stressful work environment defined and dominated by men in which a woman competes with a man more as a man than a woman," says an elderly Gandhian, TK Sumaiya, of Bombay Sarvodaya Mandal. (Srivastav,2003)

QUALITY CONSCIOUSNESS

Initially the women were making two types of papads. Chhaganlal Karamsi Parekh, a local elder also their guide and philosopher advised them to make one standardized papad and asked them never to compromise on quality (Ramanathan, 2004). The trend continues till date and there is a great deal of quality consciousness for the products that Lijjat manufactures.

The women are trained to prepare papad so that all the papads made by different women conform to the same specifications. If it is found during testing that papads are not up to the required specification, say, spices could be more or less than required, the entire lot of that make is destroyed even if it costs a big sum of money to the organization.

Given the fact that the quality of water varies across different parts of the country, the papads are tested at their own laboratory in Mumbai to avoid any deviation from the specifications.

If a branch repeatedly does not seem to abide by the Organization's philosophy of consistent quality of papads, the wage rate of the members of that particular branch is reduced by a rupee. The committee also makes surprise visits to its various branches to ensure quality and hygiene of the products.

THE VALUES SYSTEM

Shri. Mahila Grih Udyog Lijjat Papad was started with a strong belief in the Gandhian philosophy of self-dignity, respect and simplicity. It is driven by the Sarvodaya Principles. Since its inception, it has followed the principles of cooperation and collective ownership. Self-dignity and respect are held high and any kind of class distinction is not favored. Lijjat would not like to known as an organization for poor or needy women. It would like to describe itself like any other business, only that it would like to help women become self sufficient and progressive. No donations or charity is accepted, even if voluntarily offered. Every member at Lijjat works with a sense of pride in her work and shares her destiny with all others. Every woman is paid according to her labor and output but the profits are shared equally to highlight collective effort. They all work together for a better tomorrow.

By helping these women who are not encouraged to work outside their homes, Lijjat is not only helping them contribute to the family income but also empowering them. Valuing people and under-standing their problems has created for Lijjat, a sound and sustainable business model. It is for the same reason that Lijjat has not adopted modern technology for mass production or used machines for packaging, etc. though it would make much more business sense. If the papad making process is mechanized, the managing committee feels that the very purpose of the organization's existence to provide a source of livelihood and dignity to women through self-employment will be completely defeated.

Communication

The "Lijjat Patrika" published in languages like

English, Hindi, Gujarati and Marathi publishes the significant events of Lijjat throughout India. It also carries articles on topics of interest to the women as well as to promote awareness on different topics.

Social Responsibility

At Lijjat, it was made a policy to return a little of what they had gained, back to the community, as a share of their earnings either in cash or kind. Lijjat offers health care facilities, merit scholarships and literacy campaigns as well as banking facilities etc. to make the lives of their member- sisters better. Apart from this, it also set up at the Valod Centre, an educational and hobby centre that would help the rural women acquire new skills. Orientation courses in typing, cooking, sewing, knitting, toy making, child welfare, first aid, hygiene etc which could make them employable. This contributed to the image of the organization in the society as well. The Valod branch was also to give Valod its first ever *pucca* (tarred) road in 1979. Lijjat has also helped Mother Teresa for Ashadan, a home for the destitute women in Calcutta. The member-sisters also helped rehabilitate Chincholi & Bhujpur, earthquake affected villages in Maharashtra and Kutch. Apart from this, the member- sisters have actively undertook specific activities like planting of trees, distributing nutritious food for children, donating money for community marriages, prize money to spread primary education, blood donation drive, draught relief work, donating money to hospitals, organizing eye camps etc. The member sisters also help each other in times of costly medical services like heart surgery or cancer treatment etc. Thus there is a strong tradition of giving donations, in cash or kind by the member-sisters to social causes (Ramanathan,2004).

Lijjat also started literacy campaigns for their own member-sisters as well as their children especially girl children and sponsored computer education for them as educating their children was understood to be vital for their progress in life. The literacy campaign also equated literacy to prosperity and the call was "Each One, Teach one! Literacy is a gold chain, Lijjat presents to all its bens!" The member sisters were taught everyday for half an hour before work at the branches by the daughters who were educated. Lijjat believes that today a woman can not be independent unless she is literate.

CHALLENGES

Lijjat works on a margin of Re 0.5 between the selling price of a 200 gram papad pack and the production cost of the same (Bhatnagar, 2003). As a business enterprise, the declining sales figure for three consecutive years – Rs 298 crore (1999-2000), Rs 288 crore (2000-2001) and Rs 281 crore (2001-2002) – is a matter of concern for Lijjat management. Some of its home turf in Maharashtra and Gujarat has been captured by a growing competitive local market. Lijjat has also expanded to the North – Delhi, Punjab, Himachal Pradesh and, with the latest branch in Jammu, to the Kashmir market as well. Though Lijjat is the strongest brand in the papad industry, however there are some other big brands too in the market viz. Bikaner, MDH and Shaktibhog who are steadily establishing themselves.

The papad industry is worth about Rs 500 crore and only a minuscule percentage has been tapped so far by the cooperatives. About 95% of the production of papad in the country is prepared at household level or in cottage scale, by traditional method which is time consuming and laborious. According to Ministry of Food Processing Industries, the Central Food Technological Research Institute (CFTRI) has devised a simple inexpensive leg/hand operated press machine which can make about 500 papads/hour. With this machine, the production will be faster and will require less people. Even if Lijjat does not encourage mechanization, it may need to look at this issue as it may affect it in a number of ways, one if it would like to upscale its production; it may need to invest in some machines and get them operational at the branches itself. If operating the machines in the branches is an issue, it may also need to give loans to its member sisters to procure the machines.

Over the years, Lijjat has faced several situations where they have been challenged in various manners. One of the prominent cases is that of 1979 when the general secretary of a trade union made certain demands on behalf of a few sisters who had enrolled as its members. The President, Mrs.Shashikala More issued an appeal to all the member-sisters in Marathi that in case of grievances, they should approach her and solve the issue internally rather than calling an outside agency.

In another example, the Jabalpur branch was being taken over by one Shantilal Shah as his own unit which he ran with the help of a Sanchalika, wife of one of his employees. The organisation went through tremendous pressures and court stay orders to retrieve the situation. The main approach of the institution in similar cases was to disassociate with the concerned branch and file cases for protecting its brand name. This promoted an active participation by the sisters to a better understanding and sense of deeper involvement in the progress of the institution.

As the number of outstation branches have grown, it has been seen that there is a tendency of one or two members- sisters to take initiative in all matters and not involve others. This has been addressed by Lijjat by repeatedly requesting all member sisters to take active interest in all the activities of the branch as a matter of both right and duty. (Ramanathan,2004)

Closing Remarks

Lijjat has come a long way in last 45 years. Lijjat received the "Best Village Industry" Award from Khadi and Village industries commission in 1998-99; 2001-02 & 2003 and was featured by BBC World in the programme "Business bizarre". Jashwantiben Popat, founder of Lijjat Papad received the Economic Times Award for Business woman of the Year 2001-2002 for "Corporate Excellence". She was also awarded by Whirlpool Gr8 Women Awards in the "Social Services" category in 2004. The most recent award has been the PHDCCI AWARDS FOR EXCELLENCE 2005 under the "Brand equity" category.

In the global economy of the 21st century women are emerging as a strong economic force. Not only are they entering the workforce in big numbers, they are also creating jobs for themselves and fellow women; Research shows that women have certain proficiencies like intuition, instinct, sensitivity and values which they bring to their work place and which helps them build and maintain long-term relationships and network, effective communication skills, sensitivity to cultural differences and to the importance of appropriate behavior, organizational abilities, and non-threatening, non-aggressive behavior (Annenkova, 2001). There is a need to encourage these special abilities of women especially in India where there is no dearth of zeal, creativity and enterprise. The Lijjat papad thus represents a case of how the women can enjoy the social and financial independence. This has resulted in a greater empowerment as they are now contributing to their family income or in some cases are the sole earners in their families.

Lijjat makes almost equal money for all its people and makes just enough money. Lijjat's success has definitely fired the imagination of women and rural folks. In many parts of Maharashtra and Gujarat, locally manufactured and marketed eatables are catching on. There is hardly any NGO or voluntary organization nowadays which does not try to create employment and funds, small or big, along Lijjat's line. There are quite a few such micro-enterprises like Craft producers of Sasha in Kolkata, Turmeric Processing in Samanwita Kandhamal, Sujuni Embroidery in Mahila Vikas Sahyog Samiti Muzaffarpur, Bihar, Bharat (Embroidery) Workers of Bajju, Rajasthan and Food processing in Mahila Gruh Udyog Pratishthan, Rajasthan who have been helping with the skills and knowledge to increase and sustain their earning power.

LESSONS FROM THE CASE

— The case is a classic example of how a good eye for business opportunities can help one even with modest means, start an industry. The women in this case were not only illiterate; they also had no money and no special skills with them. All they had was, time on their hands and a skill handed down to all women through generations. They were quick to identify that there was a big market for the papads and that they would be able to make them themselves. The women suffered setbacks, a number of them, they made losses initially but they persisted in their endeavor. The good quality and attractive prices of the product soon caught on. As the women upscaled their production, they made a very innovative production decision by de-centralizing the Production Process which turned out to be a revolutionary business decision.

— Addressing a distinguished gathering on the occasion of the 10th anniversary of business line, Arun Shourie, Union minister for communications and divestment said that Innovation is India's strength. Giving examples of innovations in delivery, he cited the dabbawalas of Mumbai, a world class operation with 5000 semi literate persons distributing 200,000 tiffin boxes every day. Talking about pioneering efforts in decentralised production, centralized collection, centralized/modern marketing, he quoted Amul or Lijjat papad which are completely new ways of transacting business (Business Line,2004)

— A central philosophy practiced by Lijjat from the very beginning, was that the institution would not accept any charity or donation from anybody. This brought in self confidence and sense of independence as well as accountability for one's own work. Though most of them come from the lowest economic sections of the society, yet this philosophy gave them a sense of pride in themselves and their capability to earn their own livelihood (Ramanathan,2004). Lijjat is to a sound example for a high order achievement as they do not seek any external support and is totally self managed.

— Lijjat has from day one followed the Gandhian

principle of equality and practiced equitable distribution of profit/loss among all the member-sisters of the organization. It is a well thought-out Gandhian business strategy, carried forward by late Chhaganlal Karamshi Parekh and Damodar Dattani, who worked tirelessly from behind the scene to create an exclusive women's organization run and managed by them, a quality product that these women had the expertise to make, and, finally, a work environment which is not competition-driven and mechanized but based on pure labor and love for the organization and its people. Lijjat Papad's success has perhaps given rise to the best possible model for the women's economic enfranschisement in India.

— The Lijjat system did not collapse under the weight of its growing number of workers but, on the contrary, gathered strength from them. It's an easily replicable story of teamwork and profit-sharing.(Srivastav,2003) The seven women of Lijjat papad acted as the change agents for societies, seizing opportunities, inventing new approaches, and creating solutions to change society for the better.

LIJJAT AND SOCIAL ENTREPRENEURSHIP

According to Klaus Schwab, executive chairman and founder of the World Economic Forum (WEF), India is a key country to look for leading social entrepreneurs. (Katz,2006). There is a historical example of leading Social Entrepreneurs like Vinoba Bhave: Founder and leader of the Land Gift Movement, making possible the redistribution of more than 7,000,000 acres of land to aid India's untouchables and landless.

Some of the present day leading entrepreneurs

in India are Dr.A.R.K.Pillai, founder of the Indian Development Foundation that works for leprosy, Dr.Verghese Kurien, The George Foundation etc. The George Foundation's women empowerment program empowers women by providing education, cooperative farming, vocational training, savings plan and business development.

India has not been very open with women education and advancement in general for the past many years. As a result the women, especially in the lower socio economic bracket continue to be completely financially dependent on the male members of the family. To quite an extent, Lijjat is a Social enterprise as it started with innovative solutions to the Indian society's one of the most pressing social problems. The member sisters of Lijjat have acted as change agents; have been ambitious and persistent, offering new ideas for wide-scale change.

Today there are many such organizations that specialize in providing direct support to social entrepreneurs viz. Skill foundation, Global giving, Ashoka, the Schwab foundation, Kauffman foundation etc. Some of the best universities are also actively promoting advancement of social entrepreneurship worldwide. Oxford university, Stanford university and Harvard university have centers dedicated to social enterprise related research, teaching and activities.

REFERENCES

1. Annenkova, V. (2001), *"Global Approach to Fostering Development of Women Entrepreneurship", FSA Contemporary Issues, IREX,* University of Pittsburgh, Pittsburgh.
2. Bhagat, R(2004),"Innovation is India's strength", Business Line, Mar 25
3. Bhatnagar, D. & Rathore, A. (2003), "Empowering women in Urban India: Shri Mahila Griha Udyog Lijjat Papad", *World*

Bank case studies.

4. Horsnell, A & Pepin J. (2002), "*How your nonprofit can enhance capacity, impact and sustainability*", Front & Centre,9(4), pgs*1,6,7,8,*
5. Katz, R.(2006)," India has most innovative social entrepreneurs", Hindustan Times, November 2
6. Martin, R.,& Osberg S(2007),"Social Entrepreneurship : The case for definition", Stanford Social Innovation Review
7. Merchant, K. (2002), "*A recipe for Job creation in India*", Financial Times, Dec 29.
8. Mishra, S.P. (1996), "Factors Affecting Women Entrepreneurship in Small and Cottage Industries in India", *International labour Organization publication*, November.
9. Mort,G.S. Weerawardena,J.,Carngie K. (2003), "*Social Entrepreneurship : Towards conceptualization*", International Journal of Non Profit and Voluntary Sector Marketing, 8(1),76-88
10. Naik, J.(2005), "*The incredible story of Lijjat Papad*", *www.rediff.com*, April 15.
11. Planning Commission report on *National committee on the development of Backward areas*, 1981.
12. Reiss,B. and Cruikshank, J.L. (2000), "Low-Risk, High-Reward: Starting and Growing Your Small Business With Minimal Risk", NY: Free Press, New York
13. Roper J., Cheney G., "*The meanings of Social Entrepreneurship Today*", Corporate Governance,5(13),95-104
14. Sharma, P. (2006), "Supporting Sustainable Livelihoods: Lessons from Five Case Studies", Report, *Joint Initiative of World Food Programme and International Fund for Agricultural Development.*
15. Srivastava, A. (2003),"*Dignity through papad making*", India Together, February
16. Srivastava, M. (2006), "***Women Entrepreneurship in India; Problem and Prospects" paper presented at seminar organized by Australia South Asia Research Center,*** January 25.
17. UNIDO report on Processed food cluster of Pune, *End of project report, http://www.smeclusters.org/pdf/creports/punepr.pdf*

18. Vase, A.(2004), "*A class for Social Entrepreneur wannabes*", The Stanford Daily, October 12.

QUESTIONS FOR DISCUSSION

1. Discuss the importance of identifying local business opportunities and linking it with the larger issue of women empowerment in India.
2. What role has an investment efficient operations and distribution system played in the success of Lijjat Papad?
3. Why is social entrepreneurship important? What should be essential components of a sustainable business enterprise? Please discuss using insights from Lijjat Papad.

5
Social Entrepreneurship : A Case Study of Divya Thangadurai

Himani Kaul
Shivangi Gupta

ABSTRACT

The venture makes use of handicrafts and relies on efficient supply chain management practices to create an enduring brand called Kai. The authors demonstrate a model of sustainable entrepreneurship also at the same time contributing to sustainable and meaningful entrepreneurship. The growth of the firm in the context of changing socio-economic characteristics. This case critically evaluates the strengths, weaknesses, opportunities and threats and also analyses the financial situation of the firm. The case provides insight into creating successful social entrepreneurship ventures.

INTRODUCTION

Entrepreneurship can be seen as a philosophy of life that focuses on having the confidence and vision to make things happen, to see opportunities to do things differently and to act on those opportunities. (Stokes, 2006). A firm belief in people, an undying passion and a constant zeal to organize efforts towards social contribution are a few characteristics that illustrate the modern day 'Social Entrepreneur'. The word first used in the literature on social change in the 1960's and 1970's has become synonymous with various pragmatic visionaries indulging in worthwhile 'social innovation'. For social entrepreneurs, untapped markets are people or communities in need, who haven't been reached by other initiatives. (Stokes, 2006)

Sandhi Craft Foundation, a venture launched by Divya Thangadurai truly illustrates the definition of a Social Enterprise, a business with primarily social objectives whose surplus are principally reinvested for that purpose in the business or in the community, rather than being driven by the need to maximise profit for shareholders and owners. (Stokes, 2006)

The most significant facet of this style of entrepreneurship is that these people assess their success on the impact they have had on society. Social enterprises create value of a non-financial kind, for example regenerating local neighbourhoods and demonstrating new ways to deliver public services. (Stokes, 2006). Whether the organizations they set up are non-profit or for-profit entities, their innovative ideas are beyond charity to enable efficient solutions to poverty, illiteracy, and health, among others.

INDIAN HANDICRAFTS INDUSTRY: SOCIAL SIGNIFICANCE

At the beginning of the millennium, 260 million people in India did not have incomes to access a consumption basket that defines the poverty line. Of these, 75 per cent were living in rural areas. The agricultural sector is the largest employer of India's poor, with the handcrafted goods sector coming a close second. Low productivity in conjunction with low skills has made employment creation in both these sectors an extremely important priority.

The employment potential of the handcrafted sector is 6 million artisans when we estimate indigenous skills alone. It is likely to be much higher when we include the artisan entrepreneurs who add value to products whilst finalising them for markets.

With economic liberalization, there are opportunities that have arisen in domestic markets. Consumer spending has increased by 11.5% in the last decade and retail spaces have exploded, clocking annual growth rates of 20% every year, thereby opening up the possibility to take handcrafted products from niche markets to mainstream retail markets. The export markets have always held potential to increase craft employment opportunities, with a multiplier of five, according to a recent Government of India report. However, the current share of Indian handicrafts is miniscule, forming only 2% of the global market share. The world market for handicrafts is estimated to be to the order of $235 billion. While China has cornered almost 30 per cent of this, other key players include Taiwan, Korea, Indonesia, Thailand, Turkey and Latin American countries, posing stiff competition to Indian handcrafted products.

BIRTH OF SANDHI

While the market for handicrafts was booming in double digits, the Indian artisans were leading vulnerable lives with unpromising futures. Handicrafts, which were supported through royal or temple patronage earlier, were on a decline, and hand-crafted products were increasingly being viewed by markets as elitist, expensive and impractical. With the Industrial Revolution taking its due course, the machine-made products became more practical as well as cheaper substitutes. This loss of patronage left the artisans with no other route for financing their work. Simultaneously, markets and designs changed, with urban India moving at a different pace from rural India, most artisans were left stranded. For various groups of artisans, who had been involved in creating crafts since generations, this change in scenario was an unforeseen disaster, forcing them to undertake employment in sectors that they were unskilled for or forced migration to urban areas. In both cases, this was the start of a vicious cycle of poverty. This sector has long been the second largest employer of India's poor after agriculture, but still is highly disorganized and fragmented. As a matter of fact, low productivity along with low skills has made employment creation in both these sectors an extremely important priority.

This story begins with a person's passion to utilize her skills, an urge to bring about a difference into people's lives and a keen interest in fashion and crafts. This was complimented by years of corporate experience and together they provided a perfect blend for the establishment of *Sandhi* - Sanskrit for "connection" referring to the work of building bridges to link crafts persons and the marketplace. The story of Sandhi is the story of Divya Thangadurai, its CEO, a young female entrepreneur who dreamt of running an enterprise that empowers people, both who work for it and the ones it works for. At a young age of 28, she took up the challenge to organize a disorganized sector and develop crafts based livelihoods for the numerous artisans, in turn ensuring them economic independence and recognition to their hard labour.

THE SOCIAL ENTREPRENEUR

They are ambitious to achieve. They marshal resources - sometimes from the unlikeliest places - to meet their needs. They are constantly creative. And they are not afraid to make mistakes. Social entrepreneurs are particularly skilled at finding new uses for derelict spaces, second-hand materials, and under-used people; as well as squeezing money out of the commercial and public sectors. The most successful embody a curious mixture of idealism and pragmatism - high mindedness wedded to hard-headedness. (Stokes and Wilson, 2006)

Divya Thangadurai was born on 24th May, 1976, in Trichy, South India. Her father served in the Indian Army and the Indian Government as Civil Services, thus, serving the public sector had been her long cherished dream. Travelling with him, she visited many villages in the interiors of Tamil Nadu and observed the conditions of people below poverty line in India. Her mother was a small-scale entrepreneur herself and aimed at providing employment to women tailors in Chennai (Tamil Nadu). During her travels, she spent a lot of time with the local craftspeople; this inculcated an unknown interest in Divya for crafts which later manifested itself in the form of Sandhi. After completing a bachelor's degree in commerce from Chennai in 1996, she got through one of India's premier Business Schools; The Indian Institute of Management, Bangalore (IIMB) which gave her a head start for a flourishing corporate career. During her 7 years of work with large corporations, there was always a growing ambition to shift her career path at some point to a socially relevant area; and her management bent of mind ensured that her chosen area had to be socially relevant and scalable to have a significant impact.

She left the private sector and first chose to work pro bono in the area of micro finance. Her work in micro finance made her feel that it addressed only a part of the problem by considering just the need for savings and credit. The requirement was a more sustainable infrastructure for income generation and livelihood. She has lived and worked in South East Asia for a brief period, based in Singapore, she travelled frequently to Malaysia and Thailand on work. She also travelled to England to attend the seminar on Social Entrepreneurship hosted by the Skoll Forum at the Said Business School in Oxford. Her project with Craftsbridge, an agency whose establishment was facilitated by the largest private sector bank in India to market Indian handicrafts, helped provide the ideal setting for her to understand the issues ailing the crafts sector and finally led her to choose handicraft as an income generating activity. Divya studied the sector in detail before firming up the plan for Sandhi Craft Foundation.(Please see the appendix for the accolades and achievements for the entrepreneur.)

EVOLUTION OF SANDHI

The Sandhi business plan was developed and the dream of building a sustainable venture that would achieve economies of scale for the hand-crafted sector, by addressing issues of supply chain was pilot tested between September 2005 and February 2006. Divya expressed her thoughts on the experience in a personal interview as: *To me, this is the most pleasant, sweetest journey I had ever undertaken. I felt like I was playing a video game, where I kept moving from one level to the next.*

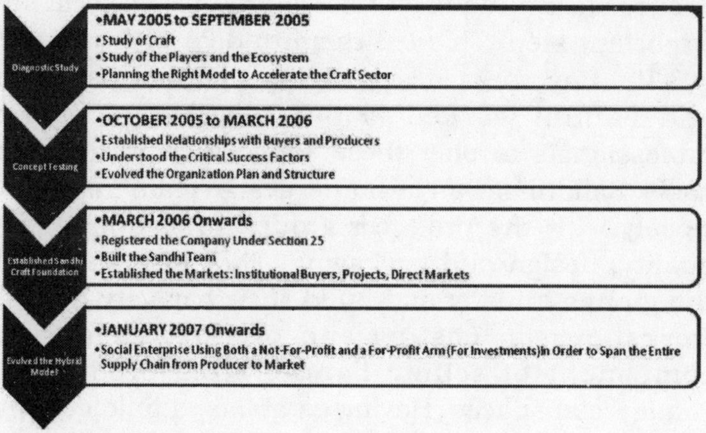

The Philosophy

Sandhi aims to build sustainable livelihood for urban and rural producers engaged in handicraft and handmade products. Sandhi works as a 'network enterprise', bringing together the missing pieces that are necessary to upgrade the crafts sector and the producers involved in this sector by providing:

- *Access to markets by establishing powerful linkages,*
- *Access to capital by partnering with financial institutions to structure financial products keeping in mind the requirements of the sector,*
- *Access to an efficient supply chain along with suitable investments in product development, design and merchandising,*
- *Ongoing support to all players in the sector to build capacity in the long run.*

Access to Markets

Sandhi began with identifying a set of producers and finding their products. Establishing a comfortable relationship between buyers and producers that would ensure a continuous off-take of produce was the next important step. This led them to deal with issues of quality, buyers for design innovation and packaging and Sandhi worked to put together a team of professionals to offer these services on an on-going basis. Sandhi has an in-house design team that works closely with the producer groups to give inputs on quality, design and packaging. They also hand-hold the groups initially and build their capacity through workshops on costing and pricing, an integral component of selling hand-crafted products in commercial spaces. Having established linkages with large retailers, chain stores and wholesalers in India,

Sandhi is proudly looking forward to expand into international markets.

Access to Capital

Providing access to markets and enabling large orders was the beginning of their work. This led the team to realize that another impediment for the groups to grow was their inability to access finance to fulfil orders. Sandhi addresses this gap by working closely with large banks to develop lines of credit for the artisan groups. This includes both short-term and long-term credit through debt and equity investments.

Since generation of economic wealth would enable the individuals and groups to be more self sufficient in the long-run, Sandhi is working with their producer groups to develop innovative methods of profit-sharing by making the artisans shareholders in the projects. With the effort to impact and improve the overall economic status of producers, it is possible for Divya and her team to connect their partners with service providers in the areas of health, education and insurance to extend value beyond economic growth and increasing the quality of people's lives.

Keeping in mind the ethos of Sandhi- not competing with players in the sector, but rather creating an enabling environment for all, they recently signed an agreement with Fab India, in partnership with ICICI Bank, to establish Artisans Microfinance Private Limited, which will provide Rs. 100 crore in five years to the crafts sector. Similar plans to incubate artisans, artisan entrepreneurs and marketing companies for the crafts sector are in the pipeline.

Access to an Efficient Supply Chain

The inability to access larger markets owes a lot to the information asymmetry that exists in the sector.

The Sandhi design team is in touch with larger markets-both domestic and international, to understand changing trends, predict them and transfer this information to their producer groups.

Inefficiencies in the supply chain can lead to delays, increasing costs for the producers and the buyers. Divya and her team's effort is to ensure a smoother supply chain by working with the producers on their forecasting techniques, and identifying other glitches, tackling them as they move along. A recent problem that they have identified is the supply of azo-free dyes to artisans—an issue that the Sandhi team is trying to address currently.

On-going support to all players in the sector

At Sandhi, focus is to create entrepreneurs and enterprises at the grassroot level; opportunities to grow and transform businesses to the next level of business growth; and tools to help entrepreneurs and enterprises sustain their work.

Divya and her team are facilitating the establishment of a retail outlet in Bangalore with one of their partners through financial and management support. Sandhi sees itself bridging gaps in the sector, incubating ideas that might have a high element of market risk by establishing proof of concept and spinning them off to other enterprises thereafter, moving on to cascade enterprises, in its effort to reach out to the poorest of the poor, and enabling economic livelihoods for them.

Integral to the concept of Sandhi's existence as a network enterprise is the willingness to explore risky ventures and innovations for the sector by incubating them within the organisation as 'proof-of-concepts', establishing the credibility of the idea as and then spinning it off to organisations/entrepreneurs. The establishment of proof of concept would also facilitate raising of finances for the ventures, which would otherwise be construed as risky or non-financeable.

Kai: The 'Handi-Crafts' Brand

All Sandhi products are marked with the 'Kai' label, indicating hand-crafted and building livelihoods. The word 'Kai' has meanings in several languages across the world, all of which are relevant in the context of the current label. In Tamil, the word means 'hand' referring to the hand-crafted nature of the products. In Maori, the word refers to food and nourishment. Through the 'Kai' label, Sandhi builds livelihoods, all of which lead to economic upliftment of various families, enabling access to food security for many of them. In Old Welsh, the word means 'rejoicer', signifying the joy that economic empowerment brings to the artisans. In Scottish and Finnish, the word means 'keeper of the keys'. Production of most hand-crafted products involves women. It is no co-incidence then that the word 'Kai' refers to the 'keeper of keys'. Experience has shown us that involving women impacts families in a positive manner, since they tend to translate economic benefits to other members. 'Kai' is a tribute to the million hands that are the 'keeper of the keys'.

Through 'Kai' Sandhi seeks to create an awareness of hand-crafted products across the world and indicate to consumers that the purchase of every 'Kai' certified product helps build livelihoods, allowing for economic empowerment.

The Team

The quality and composition of the team is a critical determinant of organizational performance. (Schjoedt,

2002). Thus, choosing the right kind of people is a critical success factor for the growth and sustainability of a healthy organization. The world outside sees the leader, the entrepreneur behind the organization, but a robust organization requires not only a good leader, but many fertile minds working together. This women dominated Sandhi team comprises of people who have shifted from the "for-profit" sector into developing a socially relevant business. At the heart of their work is economic development through generation of livelihoods in handcrafted products.

As per Divya, choosing the best team for a business is extremely important. She has a firm belief in handpicking the core team so that their diverse backgrounds can be utilized effectively. A common passion to bring about change is also one of the factors that helped Divya choose her Sandhi team. *Most successful entrepreneurs have highly qualified, well-motivated teams that help handle the venture's growth and development. In fact, although the entrepreneur may have the clearest vision of where the firm is (or should be) headed, the personnel are often more qualified to handle the day-to-day implementation challenges* (Hodgetts and Kuratko, 2005). This is obvious looking at the qualifications of the key personnel below:

— CEO, 8 years experience in Private Sector in developing new businesses, MBA – IIMB.

— COO, 8 years experience in Private Sector in managing operations, Chartered Accountant.

— Head of International Business, experience in Banking and Business Dvt., MBA – MDI, Gurgaon.

— Head of Design, 15 yrs. experience in projects with Government.

The Buyer Supplier Network

With fashion cycles changing and consumption growing at a rapid rate, most merchandisers and retailers look for buyers who can deliver high quality products while adhering to stringent timelines. Sandhi understands this need and works closely with buyers to forecast market trends, communicating the same to the suppliers so that products are delivered according to the promised quality and timelines. Members of the Sandhi team interact closely with international trend forecasters to predict trends and ensure that this information is translated to organizations at grass-root level.

Sandhi Craft Foundation aims to build sustainable livelihoods for producers engaged in handicraft and handmade products. Sandhi provides a platform wherein craft producers can connect to markets on a sustained basis, while drawing on Sandhi's knowledge systems to grow their enterprise.

The Sandhi team examines the entire supply chain, beginning with the procurement of raw material to taking the finished product to a mainstream buyer and addresses the gaps that exist along the way. Sandhi is also in dialogue with banks and financial institutions to assist producer groups in getting access to finance and capital to procure high quality raw material, working closely to provide inputs in the areas of raw material sourcing; design inputs, keeping in mind market trends in style and colour, using our trend forecasting techniques; product development; building efficiencies in production processes and order management; quality control; inventory management; business planning; costing of products and long-term capacity building.

Sandhi Budget Utilization And Projections

The budget allocation is depicted in the table below:

Budget Utilization

Description	*Projected*	*Utilized*
Budget Period	Oct 05 to Jan 06	Oct 05 to Nov 06
Budget	14 Lac	22 Lac
Salaries	6	12
Travel, Communication, Admin. & Misc.	8	5.5
Projects	Not projected	4.5

Sandhi Craft Foundation proposes to break even in its 3rd year.

Projected Profit & Loss Statement

	Jan-Dec 2007
Revenues	325 Lacs
Gross Margin (%)	13%
Gross Profit (Rs.)	41.25 Lacs
Salaries	42 Lacs
Other Admin Costs	6 Lacs
Marketing Costs	8 Lacs
Operating Profit/(Loss)	(15 Lacs)

RISK AND SUSTAINABILITY

Divya's objective for Sandhi has been to create a sustainable platform for rural and urban livelihood generation via handicraft. The execution of this idea will be in addressing the entire supply chain from raw material to production to linkages with markets. The "Sandhi way" of working will stand for certain values such as fair wage and fair terms of trade. In addition to this, Sandhi aims to guarantee quality output to the market thereby bridging the gap between producers and their markets. For a novel organization of this kind, the thrust will always be on self-sufficiency for the producer groups and in providing continuous access to markets. For example, Sandhi undertook a project with basket weavers in Badohi, and attempted to create a linkage between the women and the local micro finance institution in order to enable the women to be self-sufficient and capable of producing without depending on intermediaries for capital. Simultaneously, Sandhi also worked to enhance the design of their products and created a market connection for them to ensure a continuous source of work for the women. Refer to the diagram for how Sandhi plans to build a successful and sustainable venture.

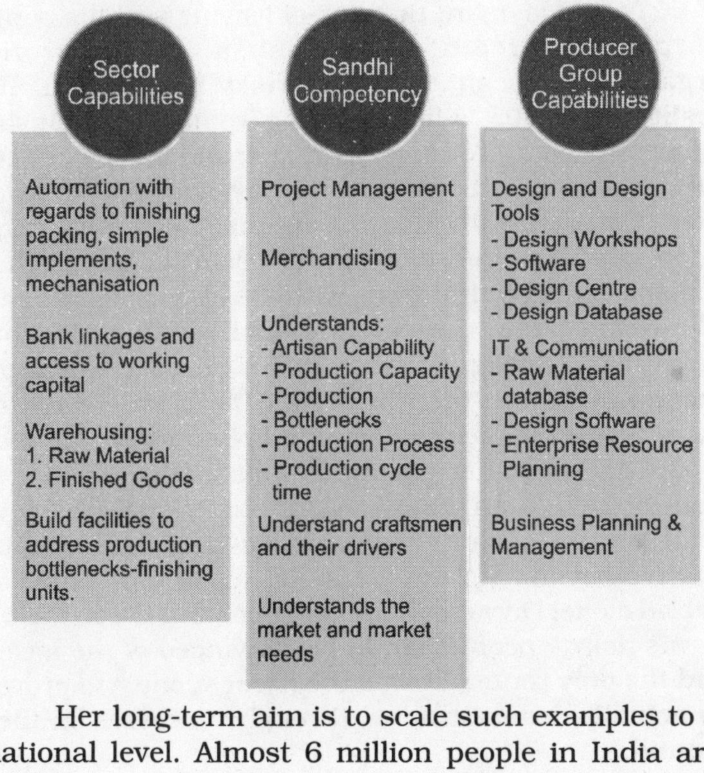

Her long-term aim is to scale such examples to a national level. Almost 6 million people in India are engaged in craft-based activities. While these people remain connected to the larger economy as 'job workers', their ability to negotiate upstream with intermediaries is lacking.

The following are some key issues that have been identified by Divya in the handicraft sector:

- Producers are highly fragmented & unorganized;
- There have been high levels of product rejections due to poor quality;
- Producers do not have access to working capital and financial services;
- Designs are not contemporary and in line with market requirements.

To any layman, the idea of leaving a well paying corporate career to establish a not-for-profit organization is an extremely risky proposition. In reality, mid 2005, a bright young woman abandons a successful and lucrative eight-year old career in the private sector, to begin afresh in a sector she had no prior experience of. Many before her have built very successful for-profit and not-for-profit models in the Indian Handicraft Industry, with the likes of Fab India, The Home Store, Cottons, and Craftsbridge etc. (for profit) and Dastkaari Haat Samiti, Crafts Council of India, AIACA, etc. (not-for-profit). Divya was ready to take up the challenge and attempt to create a new model and fulfil her cherished dream. Her vision for Sandhi is to spin business fundamentals into the unorganized sector, which would be scalable and survive beyond its founders. Attempting to build a hybrid model Divya took the best of both these models. It was risky – people had to be convinced of the idea, and the only route out was the hardest one – to prove by actually demonstrating, through successes on the ground.

Austin, Stevenson and Wei-Skillern's analytical framework provides the lens through which the factors associated with Social Entrepreneurship can be viewed. These five components, discussed in context of Sandhi Craft Foundation are overlapping and interrelated, with social value the central consideration. (Harman, 2007)

OPPORTUNITY FOR THE FIRM

This is the "initiating point" for social entrepreneurship, the vision of the leader and the team. Divya Thangadurai's main driving factor for the establishment of Sandhi was the need to create sustainable livelihoods for the artisans. Creation of a self-sustaining venture by achieving economies of scale in the handicrafts sector, through aggregation in the supply chain would address the issues of alleviating poverty and upholding human dignity.

Human Resources

It is extremely important to understand the industry in which an entrepreneur is planning to enter. Divya and her team carried out a complete market research, competitive analysis and stakeholder review to carry out a successful pilot test. Enabling a good network and a long term commitment to the initiative is a critical success factor.

Capital Resources

As Sandhi is a registered Section 25 company, the profits from the operations are redirected into the company itself. The success of the pilot convinced ICICI to invest in Sandhi and enabled the organization to carry out the business successfully.

Context

Contextual forces are instrumental in creating the

entrepreneurial opportunity. The appalling situation of Indian artisans due to loss of patronage and Industrial Revolution and Divya's long standing interest in crafts prompted the establishment of Sandhi. While on one hand, the Indian economy clocked double digit figures of growth, on the other, an entire sector with huge potential for employment seemed to be declining due to supply chain issues, which if tackled could lead to viable employment opportunities in rural, semi-urban and urban India. Given all of these issues and a solution staring one in the face, it did not take long for Divya to conceptualise 'Sandhi' to tackle the problems at ground level, develop and implement solutions and professionalize the handicraft sector.

Social Value Proposition

The proposition creates value for all its stakeholders. The suppliers gain from Sandhi as it provides a platform wherein craft producers can connect to markets on a sustained basis, while drawing on Sandhi's knowledge systems to grow their enterprise.

With fashion cycles changing and consumption growing at a rapid rate, most merchandisers and retailers look for buyers who can deliver high quality products while adhering to stringent timelines. Sandhi understands this need and works closely with buyers to forecast market trends, communicating the same to the suppliers so that products are delivered according to the promised quality and timelines.

SANDHI SWOT (Strengths Weaknesses Opportunities and Threats) ANALYSIS

STRENGTHS

- Established linkages with producers and markets
- Functional team in place
- Unique business model
- Proven revenue model
- Partnership with other stakeholders like CII, KVIC, Industree, ICICI Bank
- Insights into craft sector and its drivers

WEAKNESSES

- Low margin
- Inefficient partner groups
- Small Team
- Limited ability to operate as a finance service provider for the sector

OPPORTUNITIES

- Untapped demestic markets
- Growing foreign markets
- Unorganized sector
- Ability to leverage partnerships through the network enterprise concept

THREATS

- Lack of funding
- Overdependence on a single funding source
- No entry barrier
- Lack of market acceptance for the network enterprise concept and being viewed as competition by potential partners

CONCLUSION AND LESSONS LEARNT

The Global Entrepreneurship Monitor (GEM) research, 2002 showed that India had the second highest level of entrepreneurial activity among the 37 GEM countries. These findings have generated considerable confidence among the various sectors of the economy, particularly about the on-going economic reforms in the country. However, in GEM 2005 indicated that the level of entrepreneurial activity in Indian women is only 3.6% as compared to a figure of 16.9% for men. Evidently, most entrepreneurial initiatives are need based and not driven by opportunity highlighting the need of the hour is women empowerment both through provision of employment and enterprise creation. Typologically, the former leads to endogenous empowerment, enterprises absorbing women; and the latter gives rise to exogenous empowerment, women creating enterprises. (Mohanty, 2005)

By understanding the bottlenecks and generating revenues from market expansion and minimization of costs by reducing inefficiencies makes clear how Sandhi is different from the private sector players, who are changing the way business is done, but without significantly impacting the livelihood of artisans. With Divya's Sandhi Foundation taking a leap into development of an organization that helps artisans find shelf space in large urban retail stores for their handmade products, it can soon become a significant tool for poverty alleviation. Re-emphasizing that social entrepreneurs are particularly skilled at finding new uses for derelict spaces, second-hand materials, and under-used people; as well as squeezing money out of commercial and public sectors. The most successful embody a curious mixture of idealism and pragmatism – high-mindedness wedded to hard-headedness. (Stokes, 2006)

The most important lesson to draw from entrepreneurial profiles is their attitude towards the venture. Starting a new business is essentially an experiment. Implicit in the experiment are a number of hypotheses or assumptions that can be tested only by experience. The entrepreneur launches the enterprise and works to establish it while simultaneously validating or invalidating the assumptions. Because some will be dead wrong and others partially wrong, an important goal of every business plan must be to continually produce and build on new knowledge. Managers must justify moving to each new stage or milestone in the plan on the basis of information learned in the previous stage. (Block and Macmillan, 1999)

APPENDIX II - ACCOLADES & ACHIEVEMENTS

— Attended the seminar on Social Entrepreneurship hosted by the Skoll Forum at the Said Business School in Oxford.

— Spoke at the Entrepreneurial Summit 2006.

— Sandhi Craft Foundation, in association with AIA has created the League of Artisans (LOA), a platform to build sustainable business enterprises in the craft sector in India.

— Sponsored by the Development Commissioner (Handicrafts), Ministry of Textiles and organized jointly by the Sandhi Craft Foundation as well as the Dastkari Haat Samiti, an exhibition was aimed at instilling a sense of confidence and economic independence in the women of the area by introducing their products in new markets.

— Attended AIACA (launch of a research on Credit to Handloom Sector).

— Attended B2B meet organized by the Ministry of Textiles.

BIBLIOGRAPHY

Basu, A., Casson, M., Wadeson, N. & Yeung, B. (2006) The Oxford Handbook of Entrepreneurship. New York: Oxford University Press.

Calvin, R.J. (2004) *Entrepreneurial Management* Tata. New Delhi: McGraw Hill.

Guirdham, M. (2002) *Interactive Behaviour at Work* (3rd edn) England: Prentice Hall-Financial Times.

Gupta, S.L. & Taneja, S. (2001) Entrepreneur Development- New Venture Creation. New Delhi: Galgotia Publishing Company.

Hindle, K. and Legge, J. (2004) *Entrepreneurship- Context, vision and planning* .New York: Palgrave Macmillan.

Hodgetts, R.M. and Kuratko, D.F. (2005) Entrepreneurship – Theory Process Practice (6th edn.) Singapore: Thomson South Western

Holt, D.H. (1992) *Entrepreneurship- New Venture Creation.* New Delhi: Prentice Hall

Kirby, D.A. (2003) *Entrepreneurship.*London:McGraw Hill

Longenecker, J.G., Moore,C.W. & Petty, J.W. (2000) *Small Business Management-An Entrepreneurial Emphasis.* (11th edn) United States of America: South-Western College Publishing

Mohanty, S.K . (2005) *Fundamentals of Entrepreneurship.* New Delhi: Prentice Hall of India Private Limited

Oates, D. (2006) *A Guide to Entrepreneurship.* Mumbai: Jaico Publishing House

Scarborough, N.M. & Zimmerer,T.W. (2006) *Essentials of Entrepreneurship and Small Business Management.* (4th edn) New Delhi: Pearson Education

Sexton, D.L. & Landstrom, H. (2000) The Blackwell Handbook of Entreprepreneurship. Oxford: Blackwell Publishers

Soundarapandian, M. (1999) *Women Entrepreneurship- Issues and Strategies.* New Delhi: Kanishka Publishers and Distributors

Stokes, D. (2003) Small Business Management (4th edn) London: Thomson Learning

Stokes, D. & Wilson, N. (2006) *Small Business Management & Entrepreneurship.* (5th edn) London: Thomson Learning

Swedberg, R. (2004) *Entrepreneurship- The Social Science View.* New Delhi: Oxford University Press

Wickham, P.A. (2004) Strategic Entrepreneurship. (3rd edn) England: FT Prentice Hall Publishers

Websites

Schjoedt, L. (2002) Entrepreneurial Teams [online]. University of Colorado at Boulder. Available from: *http://www.pesochallenge.org/docs/pes2/entrepreneurial_teams1.pdf* [Accessed 10th April, 2006]

Journal

Block, Z. and Macmillan, I.C. (1999) *Milestones for Successful Venture Planning,* Harvard Business Review on Entrepreneurship, 117-133

Conference Paper

Harman, J., 2007. *Successful Social Entrepreneurship: The Case* *of the Eaglehawk Recycle Shop.*The 2nd International Conference on Services Management,1-2 June 2007 New Delhi. Gurgaon: Institute for International Management and Technology,136-142

QUESTIONS FOR REVIEW

1. What are initial challenges for setting up an entrepreneurial start up firm ? Please discuss in light of the start up experience for Sandhi.
2. What have been the reasons for success for Sandhi? Please discuss specially in the domain of social entrepreneurship efforts.
3. Evaluate the strengths and weaknesses of Sandi as a venture in light of environmental opportunities and threats.

6

SEWA: Creating Women Entrepreneurs

Smitu Malhotra
Madhukar Shukla

ABSTRACT

Self-Employed Women's Association (SEWA) is an all-women "membership organization" which was founded in 1972 in Ahmedabad, India at the initiative of Ela Ramesh Bhatt. The guiding purpose of SEWA is to empower women who work in unorganized/ informal business sectors. From modest beginnings as a small group of poor illiterate women, its membership has grown to around 700,000 throughout India.

SEWA is based on Gandhian principles of self-reliance and full employment, and functions as a democratic institution. Through its innovative practices and initiatives, it has helped its members become fully self-employed and self-reliant. It has been able to do so by mobilizing women and organizing them into unions at the urban and rural levels so that they have better access to social justice, markets and services. There are more than 80 trade/craft-based cooperatives (including SEWA Bank), which help women to promote their products and services by providing them technical, marketing and financial resources.

Often been described as a trade union or a confederation of cooperatives, SEWA is more accurately a movement for social change. Its greatest achievement has been in not only publicizing the issues of self-employed workers, but also in influencing policies to give legal/political visibility to such workers' status and contributions. Moreover, it also provides a scalable and sustainable model for harnessing the entrepreneurial potential in developing societies. This case describes the story of the growth of this unique example of social entrepreneurship, which in turn, transforms illiterate, poor and marginalized women into entrepreneurs and leaders.

The case highlights the following "Lessons Learned" from its success:

* ***Self-sufficiency*** *as a key value underlying SEWA's strategy;*
* ***Nurturance and capability-development*** *among members as a key to growing the business;*
* ***Social network*** *is a means of overcoming "masculine" socio-political hurdles;*
* ***Focus on people and community*** *issues must come before mere performance targets and profits.*

INTRODUCTION

SEWA (Self-Employed Women's Association) is an all-women "membership organization", which was founded in 1972 in Ahmedabad, at the initiative of Ela Ramesh Bhatt. The guiding purpose of SEWA was to empower women who work in unorganized/informal sector. From modest beginnings as a small group of poor illiterate women, its membership has grown to around 700,000 throughout India.

SEWA is based on Gandhian principles of self-reliance and full employment, and functions as a democratic institution. Through its innovative practices and initiatives, it has been helping its members to become fully self-employed and self-reliant. It has been able to do so by mobilizing women, and organizing them into

— Unions at the urban and rural level, so that they have better access to social justice, markets and services;

— More than 80 trade/craft-based cooperatives (including SEWA Bank), which help them to promote their produce and services by providing them technical, marketing and financial resources;

— Providing statute services to its members by partnering with donors and other governmental agencies.

SEWA has often been described as a trade union or a confederation of cooperatives. A more accurate way of defining it would be as a movement for social change. Its greatest achievement has been in not only surfacing the issues of self-employed workers, but also in influencing policies to get the politico-legal visibility to their status and contribution. Moreover, it also provides a scalable and sustainable model for harnessing the entrepreneurial potential in a developing society.

This case describes the story of the growth of this unique example of social entrepreneurship, which in turn, transforms illiterate, poor and marginalized women into entrepreneurs and leaders.

THE BACKGROUND AND INCEPTION

In 1971, a small group of women cart-pullers of Ahmedabad's cloth market came to the office of TLA (Textile Labour Association), looking for help to find housing. Though not TLA's members, they were hopeful, because TLA – India's oldest, and largest trade union at that time – had been successfully organizing and representing workers in their struggle for their rights. TLA was also a unique kind of trade union, founded on Gandhian principles of truth, non-violence and trusteeship in 1920, and which treated workers at par with other members of the society. It was known as "laboratory of human relations" because it focused on development of workers as a total person, and not just as an economic entity.

These women were guided to the women's wing of the organization, which was headed by a woman lawyer, Ela Bhatt. Ela Bhatt – or as she is popularly known, Elabehn - was working for TLA since 1955, which she had joined at the invitation of two of TLA's founders, Anusuya Sarabhai and Shankarlal Banker.

However, she was more than just a qualified lawyer. Her background and upbringing had sensitized her to the plight of the marginalized masses of India. She hailed from a family where Gandhian values were practiced; her maternal grandfather and uncles had taken active part in the freedom struggle, and her mother was active in women's movement. During her college days, she herself was a student leader (where she met her future husband, Ramesh Bhatt). As she recalled later in a speech:

"As the struggle for Independence was won, the atmosphere in the universities and the civic life was full of restless enthusiasm to rebuild the nation. I am a product of that early atmosphere.... Our teachers sent us out to the people of India, particularly to the rural poor. Our parents had their doubts, but they did not very much stop us from our journey to these people. Over a period of time we realised that the right to vote was not enough for the poor and women. They wanted a voice and visibility. As the poor, they wanted more than just day-to-day survival. As women, they wanted opportunities to learn and to act. As workers in India's self employed sector, they wanted to be a part of the labour movement. As Dalits and minorities they wanted to move in from the margins to the mainstream. Yes, they wanted a voice and visibility..."

Elabehn talked to the women cart-pullers, visited the footpaths where they slept, and the market where they worked. There, she also met a group of women who were working as head-loaders, carrying bales of cloth from the wholesaler to the retailer (and getting as less as 30 paisa per trip). As she interacted with these women, she gained a deeper understanding of their deprived working and living conditions, exploitation by merchants and authorities, erratic and low wages, etc. More than that, it also reconfirmed a growing incompleteness that she had been feeling about her work at the TLA's Women's Wing.

The Women's Wing was established in 1954, with the primary purpose of assisting the women belonging to factory workers' household. By 1968, it had also started conducting classes in sewing, knitting, spinning, embroidery, stenography, etc., for daughters and wives of workers. Elabehn, however, was not very comfortable with this largely *"middle-class approach"* towards women's issues. As she recalled, *"All women's programmes were welfare oriented towards making them good mothers and better housewives but their economic role was not recognised. The leadership of the union, which was middle class and high-caste, only addressed their roles as wives and mothers."*

Finding the Niche

What also gradually started dawning on her was the fact that *"there are so many other kinds of economic activities being done outside the formal sector, where there is no specific employer/ employee relationship... if we talk of a labor movement worth its name in my country then it should include these workers who are outside the formal sector. I started calling them self-employed but economists and others call them the informal sector... Most of the production of goods and services is done by the self-employed. In 1972, they were 89% of the workforce, the active working population in the country. Today (2003) that percentage has grown to 96%... but they are outside the purview of the labor legislation. They are outside the purview of rightful access to social security, access to financial services, welfare programs.*

Moreover, these self-employed women constituted a large proportion of this economically active population - as hawkers and vendors, construction and agricultural labours, paper pickers, home-based workers, artisans, salt farmers, cart-pullers, domestic helps, potters, weavers, etc (see Box 1: Profile of The Self-Employed Women). In fact, these mostly rural, illiterate or semi-literate, and socially and economically vulnerable women accounted for 80% of the working women in the country. *"...(what) I realized was that when we talk of women and the women's movement... it is these women who should be playing a leading role in the women's movement."*

Elabehn's initial attempts were to create visibility and awareness about the plight of these self-employed women. She wrote articles about them in the local newspapers. One of her articles about the problems of head-loaders drew a denial from the cloth merchants, testifying to their fair treatment to these women. The Women's Wing turned this denial (and testimony) to their advantage by reprinting the merchants' claims, and circulating it. The merchants were now bound by their own words.

The word spread, and soon a group of used garment women dealers approached the Women's Wing with their problems. These women were paying 10% per day to the money-lenders to get their working capital – besides being harassed by the municipal authorities. In one public meeting in a park, and which was attended by more than 100 women, one of the woman suggested that they should form an association of their own. This was a path-breaking suggestion; there was no historical precedence of this kind of organizing. But it received much support, both from the women, and from TLA itself.

And so, in December 1971, on an appeal from one of the self-employed woman, - and with support from Elabehn, and the president of TLA, Arvind Buch - the ***Self-Employed Women's Association (SEWA)*** *took its birth.*

BOX 1: Profile of The Indian Self-Employed Women

To appreciate the significance of SEWA's contribution and achievements, it is essential to comprehend the nature and size of its constituency, the self-employed workers.

Often classified as part of the "informal" economy, the self-employed constitute the largest, yet surprisingly the most invisible, part of the economically active workforce. According to ILO definition, they comprise (a) *the own-account workers in survival-type activities*, e.g. vendors of vegetables, fruits, meat, fish, etc., and of non-perishable items like locks, clothes, vessels; garbage collectors, rag-and scrap pickers; head-loaders, construction and agricultural workers, rickshaw- and cart-puller, etc. (b) *the paid domestic workers*, e.g., maids, gardeners, chauffeurs, etc. (c) *the home-based workers*, e.g., garment makers, embroiderers, incense stick rollers, *bidi*-rollers, paper bag makers, kite makers, food processors, etc., and

(d) *the self-employed in micro-enterprises*, e.g., road-side mechanics, barbers, cobblers, carpenters, tailors, book-binders, owners of small stalls and kiosks, etc. What they share in common is a lack of secure contracts, worker benefits or social protection.

In India, for instance, the self-employed workers account for 93% of the total workforce. In other developing countries/regions also, informal employment comprises 50%-75% of *non-agricultural* employment, e.g., 78% in Sub-Saharan Africa, 51% in Latin America, 55% in Mexico. Even in developed economies, the temporary/part-time/self-employed – i.e., employment without benefits or protection – account for a large working population, e.g., 30% of total working population in Europe, and 25% in United States.

The contribution of the self-employed workforce to the economic health of a society has largely remained neglected. In India, the "Informal sector" accounts for 60% of Net Domestic Product (i.e., GDP minus depreciation), 68% of income, 60% of savings, 31% of agricultural exports, and 41% of manufactured exports. Even in the urban centers of India, the self-employed account for about 60-67% of the employment.

The Self-Employed Women – The farm workers, vendors, casual construction labour, domestic help, home-based workers – are even far more neglected and unaccounted-for part of the informal economy. This is so, since the self-employed women work from homes and their contribution is mostly not calculated into the national economic data. However, according to the National Sample Survey '05, one-third of the informal sector workforce (about 120mn) comprises of women. Collectively, they accounted for 96% of the female workforce in the country, and contribute to about 20% GDP of India.

THE BEGINNINGS AND STRUGGLE

However, getting SEWA to be registered as a trade union was not that easy. Initially, the labour commissioner's office refused to accept the status of SEWA as a union. It argued that a trade union can only be formed for those who work for an employer. Since its members were self-employed women who had no recognized employer, SEWA did not fall in the legal category of a trade union.

It took much effort to convince the government that a trade union can also exist to unite and develop the workers, regardless of their employment relationship. In an interview in 2003, Elabehn narrated the struggle: "I argued that the purpose of a union is not only to fight, or to be against somebody, you also have to be for something. And that was for changing so many laws and policies. Women may not be able to pinpoint an employer but we have to fight against certain systems. Like the contract system. Like that whole range of middlemen, contractors, and subcontractors, and sub-sub-contractors. That is something that is an exploitative system."

After many weeks of persuasion and convincing, finally the registrar of trade unions reluctantly agreed. In April 1972, SEWA finally got registered as a trade union under the Trade Union Act, 1926, with Arvind Buch as its president, and Ela Bhatt as the general secretary.

At the time of registration, it had a membership of only 320 women, and had a skeleton staff. The first major task, therefore, was to contact and organize the women who were working in different trades and services. SEWA identified 3 main segments of self-employed women as its major stakeholders:

1. Hawkers, vendors and small business women like vegetable, fruit, fish, egg and other vendors of food items, household goods and clothes vendors,

2. Home-based workers like weavers, potters, *bidi* and *agarbatti* workers, papad rollers, ready-made garment workers, women who process agricultural products and artisans, and

3. Manual labourers & service providers like agricultural labourers, construction workers, contract labourers, handcart pullers, head-loaders, domestic workers and laundry workers.

(As SEWA grew, in late 1970s, it also included the rural poor into its fold)

Identifying the working women and their problems was not an easy task. Nirubehn Jadav, one of the earliest organizers of SEWA, recalled: *"First of all we just needed to know what kind of occupations women were doing out there. When we came across new trade groups during our surveys, we kept our eyes open for one or two outspoken women with some fire. We would get these women to go amongst their sister workers and find out what their problems were. They conveyed problems and priorities of their trade groups so that we could call these women together for a meeting."*

ORGANISING THE UNORGANISED

Learning from the successes of such approach, SEWA developed and used a two-step methodology to organize these women.

As the first step its members would conduct quick surveys of different trade groups to get a better understanding of their situation and problems. They would talk to these women, and collect information about their socio-economic status, income, working and living conditions, family, problems, etc. Normally, the investigators for these surveys were also drawn from the same groups, which helped in getting a more realistic picture of the condition of the groups.

While the SEWA members surveyed the different trade groups/communities, the overall picture was far from comforting. 97% of the self-employed women lived in slums, and 93%of them were illiterates. On an average, they had to support a family with four children from a monthly income which ranged from Rs. 50 (for garment makers) to Rs. 355 (for vegetable vendors). What added to their hardships was also the fact that a large proportion among them (varying from 25% to 79%, depending on the nature of their occupation) were always under heavy debt. Since these women needed money for their working capital or for renting the means of production or conveyance, they had to borrow money from the local moneylenders at as high interest rate as 10% per day. SEWA also found, much to its dismay, that in the 1971 census, these women were not even counted as a part of workforce. This invisibility also kept them powerless as producers, traders and workers.

The next step was to contact the women in the trade communities and organize them. Once the findings were ready, the SEWA volunteers would go back to the women and hold discussions with them. Since often the investigators for these surveys were from within the community itself, there was greater acceptance of these efforts. Also, the survey itself helped in identifying the potential leaders from within the community, and in organizing them.

Elabehn understood that the lives of these women will not change unless they *feel* empowered. She was also aware that if the organization depends on charity or is controlled by one person, its member will never feel empowered. A *"truly empowering"* organization, she noted, *"should belong to the women workers themselves. It should be owned by them and democratically controlled by them."*

BOX 2: SEWA Members' 10 Questions

SEWA developed a unique methodology to monitor the success of its work and general direction. It developed 10 questions to evaluate its initiatives, which link its various activities to its twin goals of full employment (q. 1-7) and self-reliance (q. 8-10) for all self-employed women workers.

1. Have our members obtained more employment from our efforts?
2. Has their income increased?
3. Have they obtained food and nutrition?
4. Have their health been safeguarded?
5. Have they obtained child-care?
6. Have they obtained shelter?
7. Have their assets increased? (like their own savings, land, house, workspace, tools of work, licenses, identity cards, cattle and share in co-operatives and all in their own name.)
8. Has the workers' organisation been strengthened?
9. Has workers' leadership increased?
10. Have they become self-reliant both collectively and individually?

GOALS OF SEWA

Correspondingly, SEWA identified **full employment** and **self-reliance** as the two key goals for organizing women into groups (see Box 2: SEWA Members' 10 Questions). In Elabehn's definition, however, full employment represented something more than merely providing income security; it also meant that the women should get the social security that one normally gets with a full-time job in formal sector, e.g., healthcare, insurance, childcare, shelter, etc. The challenge for SEWA was to help the women achieve this goal even in the absence of a social or legal structure which protected or recognized them as "workers".

Similarly, the meaning of self-reliance in SEWA meant both financial self-sufficiency, as well *"taking your own decisions so you are not just beneficiaries or users of the program but you are also manager and owner of the program. You decide and you manage in taking decisions, in managing your own affairs. You are self-sufficient. That is, in very specific terms, what we mean by self-reliance."*

For Elabehn, SEWA is more than just a trade union for organizing women; it is also a tool for personal and social transformation: *"When women organize on the basis of their work, their self-esteem grows and they realize the fact that they are the 'worker' ,the 'producer', an active contributor to the national income and not merely somebody's wife, mother or daughter. While participating in the organization and management of her cooperative or union, her self-confidence and competence grows, a sense of responsibility grows, leadership within her grows."*

Working with the collective strength helped the members of SEWA to struggle for their rights with some success. One of the first struggles for SEWA was for the legal status of women vendors. When SEWA started organizing them, they found that these women were routinely harassed by the police and civic authorities. They were not allowed to sit in the market and were often fined. Initially, Elabehn led delegation to the municipal authorities or the police, to convince them to allow them to sit in the market, or get their fine cancelled.

But then she realized that the problem was with the system itself. In fact, according to the Police Act, women vendors had no legal status (they were considered "encroachers") and, therefore, they were treated like criminals. This was because vending licenses were given only to men by the municipal authorities, and not to the women vendors. She also found that for many years, no licenses were issued by the authorities. SEWA led the fight by printing fliers listing the demand for licenses and for space to sit, led delegations, and held *dharnas* (sit-ins) all over the city.

One of the early successes of SEWA was when the government agreed to accept SEWA's identity cards as equivalent to a license, till it could find a way to give a legal status to the vendors. This was a good opportunity and SEWA used it to start a big membership campaign, and issue identity cards in large number. Since the cards had vendors' photograph and signature, information of type of trade and the place of vending, they also served multiple purposes, such as passes for entering fairs and *melas*, as curfew passes, etc.

In the years that followed, SEWA's activities and membership kept on expanding with more trade groups joining the organization. It fought for legal battle for the sitting space for the vendors; supported home-based workers to demand for higher wages; it carried out campaigns to include garment stitching in the schedule of the Minimum Wage Act; it negotiated with the urban development authorities for housing for the *bidi* makers, and so on. These successes, however, were often also short-lived. If the government changed, or a sympathetic civic official got transferred, many of the achievements of SEWA would get nullified, and it had to start its struggle all over again.

BEYOND TRADE-UNIONISM

In all these struggles, however, SEWA's approach was always based on the Gandhian principle of *Satyagrah* (insistence on truth, or civil disobedience). It tried to solve all issues by leading delegations, staging *dharanas* (sit-ins), or face to face negotiations. To safeguard against harassment by the police, local merchants or civic authorities, SEWA had field workers and volunteers, who would take up the complaints of women workers and directly intervene to get them resolve. It also provided legal aid when required.

A strike or legal action, however, was the last recourse. According to Elabehn, *"My experience and my colleagues' experience has been that by going to the court, in the case of street vendors, yes, we achieved quite a lot, but in the case of home-based workers, piece-rate workers, you win the case but then the workers lose their job. The court may give an order to reinstate them, but the employers, I mean these are small employers who don't forget. They don't want such workers back again. While most of the cases were successful - to raise the wage rate or to reinstate them - the dispute was dealt with by negotiations, with face-to-face talk."*

As SEWA's activities and membership grew, it also realized that just being just-a-union that fought for the rights of the workers was not enough. If it had to organize and empower the poor, self-employed women, it required different strategies. In the context of their fight for day-to-day survival, fighting for their rights, fight against exploitation, getting organized, etc., were not the priority issues. According to Nirubehn Jadev:

"Being a trade union, in the early years, we undertook typical union-type actions like sit-ins and strikes. However, by experience we learned that typical union action alone cannot address the issues of these self-employed workers in India, especially the 80 percent who live in the rural areas of our country. This is because these workers are the most exploited, the poorest of the poor and also the most vulnerable. They cannot hold out during strikes or other such action. If they work today, they eat; if they don't work, they go hungry. It is as simple as that."

In fact, based on the surveys and experience of organizing, Elabehn had concluded that to organize and empower the self-employed women, there were other issues that needed to be addressed, and which did not fall within the ambit of conventional trade union activities. In a pamphlet published by SEWA in 1975, "Profiles of Self-Employed Women", she articulated these goals for the women and for SEWA:

1. To be healthy in order to avoid loss of work days,
2. to be literate enough to avoid being trapped into corrupt practices,
3. to improve their skills by better training in the modern sense, in order to increase their bargaining power, and
4. to learn to save in order to build their own capital or to make use of credit facilities for productive purposes.

This realization led to many social innovations, which changed the nature of SEWA, and evolved it into a very unique and successful experiment in social entrepreneurship. These pioneering activities also helped SEWA to combine the twin goals of struggle and development in its scope of activities.

THE EVOLUTION: SEWA BANK

One of these innovative initiatives, which became the hub of other activities, was the establishment of the Mahila SEWA Sahakari Bank (or the **SEWA Bank**) in 1974.

SEWA's early surveys had shown that the self-employed women remained trapped in cycles of debt and poverty, because they lacked access to credit at fair interest rates. They took money for their working capital from the local moneylenders at interest rates that ranged between as 10% per day to 10% per month. A single day of loss of trade – whether due to illness, weather, social unrest, etc. – would put them in high debt, which would get accumulated. Thus, one of the major challenges for SEWA was to get these women institutional credit at fair interest rates.

Initially, SEWA tried to get these women loans from banks. In the early 70s, the banks had just been nationalized. As a part of poverty eradication program, one of the government's pressure on them was that at least 1% of their loans should go to the poor. Since banks had no previous model of lending to poor, they also welcomed SEWA's help in providing loans to the poor.

SEWA volunteers helped by contacting women in different trade groups, assisting them to fill-up the loan application forms, educating them about how banks worked, and about their responsibility of repayment of loans. They also designed the application forms for the bank, and would accompany the women to banks to help them complete the formalities. This effort was so successful that soon, SEWA's membership swelled to more than 3000.

But soon both the banks, and the women, started

experiencing new kind of problems. The formal bankers had never dealt with this kind of clientele: these women were dirty; they would come in large groups and would also bring along their children to the bank; they would also use the banks' premises to sit down, have their food or smoke *bidi*, and gossip; they would often come before or after the banks' timings for depositing or withdrawing money; they would stand in wrong queues; and would often go to the wrong bank for repayment – and, some time even ask the teller for water to drink!

For SEWA's members too, access to the banks did not entirely solve their problems. The regular bank timings often did not suit them, since that was the time they earned in the market or in the place of their work. They were illiterate, and had to rely on the help of impatient teller clerks to fill-up their receipt. Often they were insulted. Even the size of the loan given to them – Rs.500 to Rs.1500. - was too large for them to handle. They had never seen so much money in their lives, and they would deposit this money to the same moneylenders from whom SEWA was trying to free its members. On the other hand, if they did not deposit this money, it was spent by their husbands or other family members for unproductive purposes.

"Poor, But So Many"

At one of the SEWA meetings called to discuss these problems, one member suggested, *"why can't we have our own bank?"* Many other members picked up this idea enthusiastically. When Elabehn pointed out that they were too poor to start a bank of their own, they pointed out: *"we are poor, but we are so many."*

The SEWA Bank grew out of this apparently wild idea. Women, nevertheless, took responsibility to raise capital required to start the bank, and they went around collecting Rs10/person. Within a period of six months, they were able to raise Rs.4 lacs from 4000 women.

Once again when SEWA went to get the bank registered, it was discouraged. The Registrar of Cooperative Banks was skeptical: how can women who can't even sign their names, operate their account. Moreover, no one in SEWA had any experience in banking sector. SEWA members, however, were certain of one fact: that these women were economically active, and they needed banking service.

One of the challenges was to get 15 promoters of the bank to sign registration document. These were illiterate women – rag-pickers, vendors, garment workers – who did not even know how to write. But at Elabehn's insistence, they sat throughout the night, learning to sign their names, so that they could open the bank. In July 1974, the registration was finally granted to the Mahila SEWA Sahakari Bank.

For the first two years, the Bank acted only as an intermediary for the nationalized bank loans; it did not have enough deposits to extend loans by itself. However, the women now had a bank of their own, where illiteracy was not a barrier, help and counseling was available, and where they were accepted as persons.

Within a year, however, SEWA Bank had to deal with its first crisis. In July 1975, the government pardoned all those who were indebted to money-lenders. Many of SEWA members interpreted this announcement to cover government-sponsored loans as well. The SEWA fieldworkers had to work hard to convince that they were *responsible* to repay their loans, and often came under criticism from their own members for "unnecessarily" pressurizing them to pay.

This experience was also a learning for SEWA. *"This was the first time we came under criticism from our members, and it was painful,"* Elabehn recalled later, *"Even more sobering than the criticism, though, was seeing how deeply our members' economic problems ran. From that point our real work began and we have built a much stronger bank based on that experience."*

Breaking the Cycle of Poverty

The main objective of SEWA Bank, in the words of Jayashree Vyas, its present Managing Director, has remained *"to bring these women out of this whole vicious cycle of poverty,"* and to help them do so, it must also help them in becoming self-sufficient.

SEWA Bank followed a three-stage strategy to achieve this aim. The first step was to get the members out of the clutches of the moneylenders who were charging high interest rates. The bank loaned money to the members to repay back the moneylender at the normal bank interest of 12% per annum. By not paying the high interest to the moneylenders, the women saved a substantial amount.

The second step of "capital formation" was to help women build their savings. SEWA Bank realized that the self-employed women's could only save in small amounts, and encouraged them to deposit as low sum as Rs 5 or 10. In fact, when the bank found that many women find it difficult to visit bank to deposit their daily savings, it pioneered the concept of "doorstep banking" in 1978 – the bank workers would visit the members' localities, collect the money, and update their passbooks. Such savings were crucial to empowering these women, because, as Jayashree Vyas explained: *"...savings is not only one requirement but it is also giving hope because saving is something which you look forward to... when they have a balance in their passbook, that really gives them lots of self-confidence. Really helps them to increase their self-esteem. Also it gives status in the family. When she has money in her hand her status in the family is different, a little different."*

The third step was to provide credit to the members to help them expand their business. For instance, if a vendor had access to larger working capital, her profits would also increase. Similarly, by taking credit to buy an equipment (e.g., a sewing machine), a garment maker could improve her productivity, and therefore, her profits and savings. When their earning, and savings, increased, women could also take loans to improve their living conditions.

Over the years, SEWA Bank has developed a variety of credit schemes – for managing crisis, for women farmers, for housing finance, for developing women's business, etc. - to help its members in capital formation.

Mahila SEWA Trust

SEWA also realized that its members lived – and earned - on a day-to-day basis. If one day they did not work – due to illness, maternity or natural or social calamities – they had no social security to fall back upon. Elabehn felt that women would not feel empowered unless they have the social infrastructure, the skills and appropriate technology to improve their living and working conditions. Often an illness, or delivery of a child, would wipe out their entire savings, and again throw them back into poverty. SEWA tried to address this problem by trying to get them insurance coverage through the institutional sources, but found that the insurance companies were not open to this proposition. For the women workers also, paying a regular insurance premium was not possible.

At Elabehn's suggestion, women decided to form their own trust, and donated one day's wages to start it. From this small amount, and with contribution from TLA, in 1975, the **Mahila SEWA Trust** was established to provide support services to its members. Starting with the Maternal Protection Scheme, soon the Trust was offering a variety of services to its members at modest prices, for e.g.,

— it had started child care centers for vegetable vendors,

— it was providing widowhood assistance to help the members survive immediately after husband's death,

— it provided health care (e.g., eye checkups) to its members,

— it held classes to make them aware of their rights as workers and duties as citizens

— to help the garment makers, it would purchase discarded materials directly from the textile mills, and sell them to members at lower cost (thus eliminating middle-men), etc.

In 1977, when Elabehn received the *Ramon Magsaysay Award*, she donated the Award money, $20,000 to the Trust, which put it on a sound financial footing.

COOPERATIVES: THE BLUEPRINT FOR GROWTH

Another major milestone in the organization's evolution was the formation of the **SEWA cooperatives**.

The transformation of SEWA from just a trade union into a network of cooperatives started in 1977, when it started organizing the *khol* (patchwork quilt)

makers. These women used to work for local merchants and contractors, who would give them the *chindi* (pieces of textile waste, which are stitched together to make *khol*), and then collect finished *khols* to sell them in the market. Each *khol* required about 1-2 hours of work, but in return, women were paid at the meager rate of Rs0.60 per khol as wages.

When SEWA organized 600 *khol* worker into a union, and demanded higher wages for their work, the merchants and middlemen were outraged. Renana Jhabvala, secretary of SEWA, who was one of the key organizers of the *khol* worker's struggle, recounted: *"The local traders were furious. The women had never taken such bold action before. And the retaliation of the traders was swift and ruthless. Many women stopped getting any work, which is of course their lifeline to survival."*

The traders specifically singled out those women who were most vulnerable – the widows and single women – to refuse them work. To support these *khol* makers, the SEWA organizers and the *khol* workers came up with an innovative idea of starting a *khol*-making cooperative. Elabehn was exposed to joint action by trade unions and cooperative during her visit to Israel in 1971, and forming a workers' cooperative seemed a natural step in empowering women workers, and freeing them from the exploitative traders.

The *khol*-cooperative experienced many crisis to get established: the traders tried to break it, undercut prices, hampered with the supply of *chindi*, etc. An even greater challenge it had to overcome was in the shift in mindset of the *khol* workers – from piece-rate workers to worker-owners. But the cooperative survived, and grew up into the first independently registered, self-reliant cooperative of SEWA, Sabina.

Through the success of Sabina, SEWA also discovered the relevance of cooperatives as a powerful organizing and empowering tool. For the first time in their lives, it allowed the women workers to *own* something, and to have the decision-making power over it. It also gave them a steady source of income, lending stability to their lives.

By 1981, SEWA had used this learning to establish cooperatives for many other women trade groups, as well, e.g., for the milk producers, handblock printers, vegetable vendors, handloom weavers, bamboo workers, waste-pickers, etc. It had also established a Rural Wing and an Economic Wing, and its membership had swelled to nearly 6000. Perhaps, more importantly, SEWA had started developing its own unique paradigm for organizing the women workers into autonomous but integrated networked units (see Box 3: Organizing for Empowerment). As one of SEWA's publications notes: *"We did not begin with a pre-determined blueprint for structuring our work. Our vision and ideology have been the guide for constantly evolving our structure and processes in response to the needs of our members."*

BOX 3: Organizing for Empowerment

The SEWA Annual report (2003) describes its approach to organizing the self-employed working women:

"Since her inception as a trade union in 1972, SEWA has grown like a banyan tree. The entire institution is a network of self-help groups, co-operatives, federations, associations, charity trusts and even co-operates! The founders and senior SEWA volunteers have carefully nurtured a culture that strikes a balance between autonomy and integrated effort. All the units of SEWA banyan tree pursue the SEWA mission with sustain ability as a strategy. They are encouraged to

take their decisions freely, but at the same time following the same basic philosophy of SEWA in an integrated manner."

Broadly, the SEWA banyan tree can be seen as consisting of four main "branches": (1) the trade groups & union, (2) the cooperatives, (3) the SEWA bank, and (4) the SEWA Social Security Net.

1. The Trade Groups & Union: SEWA is organized as a cluster of trade-groups (e.g., *bidi* rollers, construction workers, vendors, domestic workers, etc.), which are autonomous in their functioning, and form the SEWA trade union. Women pay Rs. 5 as membership fee, and in 2004, there were 74 such trade groups, with a total membership of more than 7 lakh self-employed women.

The purpose of the trade groups and union is to negotiate with employers/traders, provide social and occupational security through collective action (e.g., protests, rallies, identity cards, etc.), provide legal help to members, lobby with government for protective legislations, and work towards policy changes to benefit the members.

The SEWA union has two-tier level of elected representation: the *Pratinidhi Mandal* (Trade Council) and *Dhandha Samiti* (Trade Committee).

The *Pratinidhi Mandal* (Trade Council) consists of representatives elected by each trade group in a ratio of 1 representative per 100 members. They represent the trade-group in the SEWA's Council of Representatives, which is the foundation of SEWA's governance (in 2004 the Council consisted of around 2000 representatives). The Trade Council meets once a month, and elects a 25-member Executive Committee of the SEWA Union for a term of 3 years. The Executive Committee has additional five members, who are appointed from the SEWA management staff. The Executive Committee, in turn, elects 7 of its members to form the Executive

Committee for a period of 3 years (1 President, 3 Vice-Presidents, 1 General Secretary, and 2 Secretaries). By custom, the President and Vice-Presidents are from the largest trade groups of SEWA. The General Secretary and the Secretaries are responsible for the management and administration of SEWA, and, by constitution, at least one of the Secretaries must be a working class member.

The *Dhandha Samitis* (Trade Committees) are trade-specific, and have no fixed proportion for members, but normally varies between 15 and 25. It is headed by a Member Secretary, and meets once a month to discuss trade-related problems, and possible solutions. The members of *Pratinidhi Mandal* are also members of their respective *Dhandha Samitis*, thus providing a linkage between the trade-groups and the SEWA Council of Representatives.

2. The Cooperatives: Many SEWA members are also organized as member-owners of 86 cooperatives. These cooperatives are a part of the *Gujarat State Women's SEWA Cooperative Federation*, a confederation that was founded in 1992.

Broadly, there are five different kinds of cooperatives in SEWA fold: (1) Workers' cooperatives (e.g., for child care providers, industrial cleaners, domestic workers, etc.), (2) Land-based workers (e.g., for workers in agro-forestry, tree-growers, etc.), (3) Milk Cooperatives, (4) Selling cooperatives (e.g., for vegetable vendors, fish vendors, garment vendors, etc.), and (5) Labour's cooperatives (e.g., for weavers, block printers, embroiderers, etc.). In addition, Video SEWA, one of the services of SEWA, is also organized as a cooperative.

Besides giving control over means of production, and a steady source of income, being organized as a cooperative gives the self-employed women numerous benefits, for e.g.,

* access to raw-material at wholesale prices,

* easy entry to markets,

* increased bargaining power with employers, contractors, middlemen and government,

* access to training and skill-development opportunities, etc.

3. SEWA Bank: From small beginnings (see the case text), SEWA Bank has grown into a large financial institution. In 2004, the bank operated more than 2.5 lakhs accounts, had total deposits of about Rs. 62 crores, and had working capital of approximately Rs.87crores. In the same year, it had advanced loans to more than 53,000 members, and had generated profits worth Rs.88 lakhs.

What makes the bank unique is that the average monthly income of its members is just about Rs.1000, and whose deposits are normally in sums of Rs. 5-100. Though a majority of its loans are unsecured, it enjoys a repayment rate of more than 96%.The bank provides loans to its members on market rates, with a three year repayment period, for *productive purposes*, for e.g.,

* for working capital,

* for purchase of tools of the trade, and

* for capital investment like house, store or work-space.

In addition, SEWA Bank also provides insurance coverage, and social security to its members on nominal premium, conducts workshops for financial counseling for its members, provides mobile banking services, and operates decentralized collection centers. The bank also provides rural banking services to the self-employed women in the villages – who constitute 20% of its account holders - through a network of 3600 self-help groups.

4. SEWA Social Security Net: In addition to the above, SEWA also hosts numerous other service organizations, which provide support to self-employed women through the union, cooperatives or the bank.

Some of these are:

* *SEWA Childcare Centers* take care of the children, during the working hours for the working women. SEWA operates 73 such centers, which also provide healthcare, basic education, meal for the children, and counseling to mothers.

* *SEWA Health*: SEWA Health operates as a cooperative consisting of midwives and health workers-cum-educators, and a turnover of Rs.1crore. It provides not just curative care, but also preventive heathcare, and promotes health awareness to women workers and their family. Its efforts have helped reducing the average healthcare expenses from Rs. 131 to Rs. 74 per household.

* *VimoSEWA* is an integrated insurance program which aims to provide social security to members, covering their life cycle needs and the various risks they face in their lives (death, illness, accident, 'asset loss', etc.). It operates as a cooperative, and offers the services through SEWA Bank. During 2003, it offered insurance to around 1.1 lakh members.

* *Gujarat Mahila Housing SEWA Trust* provides loans to members to build and repair their houses. The Trust understands that the house for the home-based workers is also a production unit, and helps them also with their work-related needs. It also works along with civic authorities to get electricity, water, sanitation, etc., to workers' localities.

* *SEWA's Legal Cell* helps the members by providing legal protection, negotiating with employers, advocating policy changes, educating members about their legal rights and responsibilities.

* *SEWA Academy* provides training in vocational skills and capability building to the members. It also conducts research on issues related to self-employed women workers, and also brings out the two SEWA newsletters, 'Anusooya' and 'Akashganga'.

* *Video SEWA* is a separate unit of the Academy that uses the medium and technology to take up issues of self-employed women to national and international level.

LEAVING THE NEST

In the meanwhile a rift had started growing between SEWA and TLA. Apparently, when TLA had supported the formation of SEWA, it had never anticipated its growth and sphere of influence beyond just remaining "TLA's Women's Wing". The TLA leadership was becoming increasingly uncomfortable with this growing group of assertive women, with their own agenda and views about what a trade-union should be doing.

In many ways, the TLA and SEWA were mutually contradictory in their nature and functioning. TLA was a male-dominated organization, with a predominantly middle- and upper- class leadership, and with a patriarchical top-down decision-making process. SEWA, on the other hand, was an all-women organization (who represented poorest-of-the-poor), and was entirely democratic in its structure and functioning. There was also a conflict of interest between the two, because some of those whom SEWA would confront were often among the allies of the TLA. Also, many of the activities of SEWA (e.g., advancing credit, providing social security, building alternative economic structures, etc.) were not considered to be trade-union activities by the TLA leadership. TLA had often charged Elabehn for neglecting her duties, and going on foreign trips without permission.

These differences became an open conflict in 1981 over the issue of reservations of seats for low-caste students in medical college. When government announced this policy, the high-caste students launched a campaign to abolish reservations, which led to widespread riots in Ahmedabad causing about 40 deaths. Since the TLA had members in both castes, it had decided to remain silent on the issue. Elabehn, on the other hand, took an open public position; SEWA general body passed a resolution supporting the reservations. It also appealed for peace, since the daily wage-earners could not survive curfew for a long time.

Being the only public leader to have taken a forthright stand on the issue, Elabehn's statements were widely quoted in the press. The TLA leadership was disconcerted with these developments, and internal pressures to distance itself from SEWA grew. Within a month or so, Elabehn was charged for "extreme indiscipline" and was expelled from the honorary membership on the TLA, the TLA leaders resigned from the executive positions they held in SEWA, the TLA withdrew its deposits worth Rs. 3 lakhs from SEWA Bank, and SEWA was asked to vacate TLA premises. A few months later, in a meeting of National Labour Organisation, a Gujarat-based confederation of 36 trade-unions, TLA publicly disaffiliated SEWA from its fold, and passed a resolution expelling SEWA from NLO. This was a severe blow to SEWA, since its recognition as a central trade union was through its affiliation with the TLA.

However, the disaffiliation – and the public humiliation and derision – turned out to be a defining milestone in the growth of SEWA. Left to its own resources, SEWA discovered the inner strength it had as an organization. Elabehn called for a meeting of all members. She recalled the sense of solidarity which followed. Elabehn remembers the events: "*...about two thousand women came... and there was fire in their heart* *and eyes. Everyone who had been there (at the NLO meeting) spoke with great courage and indignation about what they had heard and seen. Both leaders and working class women took turns speaking with equal assertiveness. There was such a sense of liberation that there was no man heading the meeting and telling us what to do or think. There was no one we had to be careful not to hurt if we did not pay him enough respect. It was our first meeting without a topee (literally "hat", but meaning, male leader). We passed a resolution that day that men would not be allowed as members or as office bearers of our union. Although insulted at the way we had been thrown out, really, we felt most powerfully, an incredible sense of freedom... We had left the nest."*

Though the breakup with TLA was traumatic, SEWA actually emerged stronger out of that. In a symbolic act to show the connection with its roots, in 1982, SEWA launched a fortnightly newsletter, "Anusuya", named after the co-founder of the TLA, Anusuya Sarabhai, and the person who had invited Elabehn to join TLA. According to Elabehn, *"Like Hindus who have a rebirth... I felt that I should continue the work begun by her in this new context. We chose the name of our paper because Anusuya means, literally, "without rancour". We needed to send out that kind of message at that time."*

INTERNATIONAL AFFILIATIONS

Elabehn also realized that unless there are changes in the policies and legal structure, SEWA's struggle will remain confined to just local protests and negotiations. This required raising SEWA's profile by forming affiliations to international labour bodies, while at the same time continuing the fight for policy changes at national level. Elabehn's own personality, convictions and leadership skills played a critical role in achieving this. As Michela Walsh, who co-founded the Women' World Banking with Elabehn in 1979, once described her: "*The thing about her is that you can never tell where she is uncomfortable. In the slums of Ahmedabad... (to) addressing heads of state and parliament – she wears the same face. And she is the shrewdest political person I know. She never confronts an issue head on, but can walk, for example, through the aisle of the World Bank, drop an idea, you might not even know she said anything, but minds will start to change.*"

With an eye on opportunities, Elabehn represented SEWA and the cause of Indian self-employed women in various international forums. She attended the *World Labour Congress* of the *International Confederation of Free Trade Union* (ICFTU) in Oslo, got SEWA women to attend the *UN Decade on Women's Conference* in Nairobi, collaborated with *ILO* to study the conditions of Home-based workers, she was elected the Chairperson of the *Board of World Women's Banking*, etc. Her work also brought recognition to Elabehn, and to SEWA. In 1984, she was awarded the prestigious Right Livelihood Award by the Swedish parliament (which is considered as the alternate Nobel Peace Prize). The President of India recognized her contributions by conferring the orders of *Padmashri* and *Padmabhushan* on her in 1985 and 1986, respectively. In 1990, the Femme Alliance of France awarded her the Women and Creation Honor.

Her efforts started bearing fruits, when in 1983 SEWA got affiliated to the *International Union of Food and Allied Workers' Associations* (IUF). In subsequent years it also got affiliation from the *International Textile, Garment and Leather Workers' Federation* (ITGLWF) and from the *International Chemical, Energy, Mine and General Workers' Unions* (ICEM). SEWA also became a member of the *International Co-operative Alliance* (ICA), of StreetNet International and of HomeNet, the international alliance of home-based workers' organizations. In 1997, SEWA was instrumental in setting up *Women in Informal Employment Globalizing and Organizing* (WIEGO).

Impacting Policy Changes

At national level, the struggle for policy changes took form of various parallel initiatives, including lobbying, membership drive, surveys to document and highlight the problems of the self-employed, and legal cases, etc. One of the initial successes was SEWA's legal victory in the famous Manek Chowk case.

In 1979, SEWA had organized a large vendor strike in the Manek Chowk of Ahmedabad, in protest to their being evicted by the civic authority. After five days of strike, the civic authorities conceded to SEWA's viewpoint that vending is a legitimate form of livelihood, and the vendors were given back their space. However, by 1981, the government had changed, and the vendors were again getting harassed and evicted. Around the same time, Elabehn received an invitation from Justice Jagadish Bhagwati, inviting her for a seminar on legal aid for poor. Elabehn wrote back a detailed response questioning how can legal-aid or a seminar help if the laws themselves were anti-poor. She also cited many examples, specifically the vendors' plight, where laws worked against the poor.

Justice Bhagwati used the letter to file a public interest litigation on behalf of the legal aid committee which he was heading. The petitioners were Elabehn and three other self-employed women. They invited a

Mumbai-based lawyer, Indira Jaisingh, who had fought a similar case on behalf of footpath dwellers, to fight the case on their behalf. She accepted to fight the case for SEWA free. The case was won in the Supreme Court, which gave the verdict that the vendors have a right to space to sell in the market. This was a landmark verdict in the legal history, since it gave the vendors legal rights.

Another significant milestone in SEWA's progress was when the Government of India accepted their demand to form a Commission for Self-Employed Women. In 1986, SEWA organized a National Workshop on Hawkers and Vendors, and invited the then Prime Minister, Rajiv Gandhi to inaugurate it. To their surprise, not only Rajiv Gandhi accepted the invitation, but also listened to the problems of hawkers and vendors who had come from all over India. He also accepted their demand for the commission, and in January 1987, Elabehn was appointed by the prime minister as a Member of Parliament in Rajya Sabha, and was asked to chair the commission.

SHRAMSHAKTI REPORT

This was the opportunity, Elabehn was looking for. For next one year, this all-women five-member commission and one Government Secretary toured across 18 states, and had almost 800 public hearing of working women. They visited any place where women worked - mines, fields, construction sites, homes, markets, etc. – and talked to them; they also collected inputs from voluntary agencies, activists, government officials, and research organizations, etc.; they set up task-forces to study issues related to self-employed women, their working conditions, health issues, legislative protection (or lack of it), image in media, exploitation, exclusion from access to skills and support, etc.

One year later, this extensive exercise culminated in the commission's report, *Shramshakti*, which was India's first ever document that poignantly, powerfully and in meticulous detail, documented and highlighted the contribution of the self-employed women to the national income, combined with their marginalized status in the society. It listed and classified the various occupations of the self-employed women, and highlighted how the informal sector forms the basis of viability of many formal sector industries, because it absorbs all the risks and fluctuations of the market. It also pointed out how various government policies are biased against the self-employed. In many ways, the findings of *Shramshakti* report confirmed that what SEWA members knew about Gujarat was not unique, it was true for the whole of India.

In 1989, Elabehn got nominated to be the first ever woman member of the Planning Commission. However, by that time, the government had changed/ had other priorities, and the recommendations of *Shramshakti* started getting ignored in terms of their policy implementation. Elabehn, nevertheless, got the report translated in English (and lobbied to get it translated in regional languages), and continued to network with other governmental and non-governmental agencies to get the recommendations implemented. She was perseverant to get the issues enough visibility to warrant legislation and policy change.

In May 1989, SEWA, Ford Foundation and Gandhi Labour Institute organized an international conference on home-based workers in Ahmedabad, with participation from 26 scholars from Asia, Africa and South America. Their deliberations provided sufficient basis for ILO to cover the conditions of home-based workers for the first time in its *Work Digest.* ILO also subsequently set up an expert group to determine the world standards and legislation that should be set up for the home-based workers. Sewa's experiences in this field were also recognized when it was invited to conduct workshops for women's organizations in other countries, e.g., Yemen, South Africa, Turkey, etc.

Meanwhile, SEWA continued to expand its activities and membership. The first artisans' cooperative was formed in 1982. In 1984, it started Video SEWA, a unit to produce videos about and for the self-employed women. In 1986, SEWA formed its first Child Care Cooperative, and Tree Grower Cooperative. This was followed by a cooperative for vegetable and fruit vendors (1989), healthcare (1990), and SEWA Academy (1991), which focused on training and capability building for the self-employed women.

SEWA BHARAT: NATIONAL PRESENCE

By the beginning of 1990s, SEWA's membership had increased to almost 26,000. Though, all its members were still Gujarat-based, it had started networking with self-employed women across the country in 1980s. In 1982, SEWA had formed a 'spearhead team' of a few SEWA organizers to foray into other states, meet other women groups, and explore the possibility of starting SEWA in their states. Elabehn's role in drafting the *Shramshakti* report had also brought her in touch with self-employed women in many other states.

These efforts started bearing fruit in the early 1990s, when SEWA was able to organize self-employed women (e.g., tribal silk spinners in Bihar, the embroiders in Uttar Pradesh, Mithila painters in Madhya Pradesh, etc.) into cooperatives. Like the other SEWA groups, these were formed around different issues, e.g., income generation, to escape exploitation by the middlemen, or fighting against a social evil, etc., but shared SEWA's approach of non-violence, self-reliance and cooperation. These various groups in different parts of India – in Bihar, UP, Madhya Pradesh, Kerala, etc. - formed an affiliation called SEWA Bharat.

SEWA's expansion and reach continued to accelerate during the 1990s (between 1990 and 2000, SEWA's membership grew more than ten-fold, from 26,000 to more than 310,000). It kept on organizing self-employed in different trades into worker-owned cooperatives (e.g., for salt farmers, midwives, traditional handicraft craftsmen, etc.) and bringing them into the SEWA fold. As the number of cooperatives and associations grew, in 1993, SEWA restructured itself into a confederation – SEWA Cooperative Federation. It also launched VimoSEWA in 1992, an initiative to bring insurance and social security to the working women.

Response to Liberalisation

The SEWA vision, along with its evolving decentralized structure, also gave it the capability to adapt to the changes in the business environment. For instance, in the 90s, when the Government of India adapted the path of liberalization and opened its economy to global influences, SEWA's response was pragmatic – it opposed some aspects of the policy, while at the same time, built capabilities to counter the new competitive forces, as well as leveraged on the new opportunities. On one hand, SEWA was critical of the lop-sidedness deregulation process. As Renana Jhabvala pointed out that "*the deregulation has been done mostly for the corporate sector, not for the People's sector. The artisan still faces all types of regulations to obtain raw materials. The vendor still needs licences to sell. Sale of produce for the farmer is still governed by price and movement restrictions."* On the other hand, it also started the SEWA Academy to upgrade the technical & leadership skills among the women workers.

Similarly, it leveraged on the easy access to technology by training its members for computer literacy, computerizing many of its cooperatives, and also using multi-media technology to transfer best practices from one cooperative to another. It also created and upgraded its websites as a tool to promote SEWA and gain access to international markets. According to Elabehn, "*...globalization has given us a very good opportunity to reach the global market. We have our website. Every day we get 10 to 12 queries out of which 8 queries are from abroad. We export. We have an export license... There are opportunities but only because we had an organization which dealt (with them) in a very businesslike way. And we keep to the principle that any product if it sells for 100 rupees then 60 rupees has to go to the actual laborer, the producer, which is very difficult to maintain. But we have been able to maintain that principle."*

In 1999, SEWA created a rural marketing wing, *Gram Mahila Haat* to facilitate sales in larger markets for more than 1000 producers' groups (its turnover in 2003 was around Rs. 3 crores). Likewise, in 2000, SEWA built the SEWA Trade Facilitation Centers (STFCs), which would deliver a wide range of solutions - market support, product development, quality standardization, etc. - to the grassroots organizations. In 2002, STFCs helped the producer export about Rs.

45 lakhs worth of handicraft and fabrics, besides achieving a national sale of about Rs. 75 lakhs.

SEWA TODAY

In 1996, Elabehn retired from the post of SEWA's general secretary, and handed over the reigns to a collective and rotating leadership, which would be elected for a 3-year non-renewable term. In the course of its growth, SEWA had been able to attract many highly qualified women (e.g., Renana Jhabvala, a post-doctoral student from Yale University; Mirai Chatterjee, a Masters in public health from John Hopkins university; Reema Nanavaty, a former IAS officer; Jayashree Vyas, former banker with Central Bank, etc.). While they played – and continue to play - a crucial role in SEWA's activities and management, 80% of SEWA's Executive Committee consists of self-employed women, and takes decisions in a democratic manner.

One of the final vindications for SEWA was when in February 2005, it was recognized as a central trade union (CTU).

Since its breakup with TLA, SEWA had remained unaffiliated with any central union. In 1999, it was also becoming clear that in order to influence the policy making, SEWA needed to become a CTU to be able to participate in Indian Labour Conference, the highest tripartite body which influences the national labour policy. While SEWA met the norm registration requirements in at least five states, it still did not meet the minimum requirements of 500,000 members (it had about 215,000 members).

SEWA launched a major organizing campaign to increase its size and influence. The surge in the membership was phenomenal, and within 3 years, by 2002, SEWA's membership had crossed 5 lakhs.

Nevertheless, the Government of India was still unconvinced to grant it the CTU status, and SEWA had to fight a case in the Delhi High Court in 2005. By now, SEWA's membership was more than 700,000 making it the largest union in the informal sector. Elabehn, however, still emphasizes: *"There are no clear successes or failures— more a series of small victories and compromises. But the important thing is to keep on going on."*

REFERENCES

Bhatt, Ela R. (1997). *Lately Early Year: Sewa's perspectives on Early Years of Independence,* Inaugural Address, The Early Years after Indian Independence: Women's Perspectives, August 9-11, Baroda: organised by Indian Association of Women's Studies, Centre for Women's Development Studies, and Women's Studies Research Centre of M.S. University, INDIA.

Bhatt, Ela R. (2005). Organising for Second Freedom. Harold Wolpe Lecture, South Africa (url: *http://www.nu.ac.za/ccs/default.asp?11,22,5,191*).

Blaxwell, John (2004). SEWA: Empowerment through Mobilization of Poor Women on a large Scale. Scaling Up Poverty Reduction: A Global Learning Process and Conference. Shanghai, May 25-27.

Chatterjee, Mirai (2000). *Interview with Elaben,* Seminar, July, #491 (url: *http://www.india-seminar.com/2000/491/491%20interview.htm*).

Chatterjee, Mirai (1991). *Women taking control: Remaking India's economy,* Multinational Monitor, 12(11) (url: *http://multinationalmonitor.org/hyper/issues/1991/11/chatterjee.html).*

Ela Bhatt-in first person (2004). The-south-asian.com, November, (url: *http://www.the-south-asian.com/Nov2004/Ela_Bhatt.htm*).

Paget-Clarke, Nic (2003). *Interview with Ela Bhatt,* In Motion Magazine, August, (url: *http://www.inmotionmagazine.com/global/ebhatt_int1.html*).

Paget-Clarke, Nic (2003). *Interview with Jayashree Vyas –*

Managing Director of SEWA Bank, In Motion Magazine, August, (url: *http://www.inmotionmagazine.com/global/jv_int1.html*).

Ramon Magsaysay Award (1977). for Community Leadership. Citation: Biography of Ela Ramesh Bhatt (url: *http://www.rmaf.org.ph/Awardees/Biography/BiographyBhattEla.html*).

Rose, Kalima (1992). *Where Women as Leaders*, New Delhi: Vistaar Publications.

SEWA (2000). Building Capacities for Leadership and Self Reliance, X.

SEWA Websites

Banascraft (http://*www.banascraft.org*).

Gujarat Mahila Housing SEWA Trust (http://*www.sewahousing.org*)

Gujarat Shishu Sangh (http://*www.sewass.org*)

Gujarat State Mahila SEWA Cooperative Federation (http://*www.sewa.org/gsmscf*)

Kutchcraft (*www.kutchcraft.org*)

Self Employed Women's Association (*http://www.sewa.org/*)

SEWA Academy (http://*www.sewaacademy.org*)

Sewa Gram Mahila Haat (http://*www.sewamart.com*)

SEWA Insurance (http://*www.sewainsurance.org/*)

SEWA Research (http://*www.sewaresearch.org*)

Shree Mahila Sewa Sahakari Bank Ltd. (http://*www.sewabank.org*)

Shri Mahila SEWA Anasooya Trust (http://*www.anasooya.org*)

Sukhi Mahila Mandal (http://*www.sewa.org/smm*)

Video SEWA (http://*www.videosewa.org*)

Additional Readings:

Bennis, Warren (1998). *Organising Genius: The Secrets of Creative Collaboration*, New York: Perseus Publishing.

Bornstein, David (2005). *How to Change the World*, New Delhi: Penguin India.

Kogut, B. (2000). The Network as Knowledge: Generative Rules and the Emergence of Structure, *Strategic Management Journal*, 21, 405-425.

Kogut, B. and Bowman, E.H. (1995). Modularity and Permeability as Principles of Design, In Edward Bowman and Bruce Kogut (Eds.) *Redesigning the Firm.* New York: Oxford University Press.

Morgan, G and Ramirez, R. (1983). Action learning: A holographic metaphor for guiding social change, *Human Relations*, 37(1), 1 28.

Reich, RB (1977). Entrepreneurship reconsidered: The team as a hero, *Harvard Business Review,* (May-June), 77-83.

QUESTIONS FOR DISCUSSION

1. What was the nature and sources of the obstacles that SEWA had to face during its growth? What generalizations can one draw from these, which would be applicable to social entrepreneurs in general?
2. In terms of SEWA's ideology, people, systems and structure, what were the internal sources of its strength?
3. How was SEWA able to operationalise its key values and goals into its democratic practices? How would you evaluate the nature and sustainability of its democratic nature?
4. As a social entrepreneurship organization, what were the key strategies that SEWA developed and used to grow and overcome barriers?

7

Women Entrepreneurship in Asia: A Singaporean Case Study

Ghee Soon LIM

ABSTRACT

The present case documents the success story of water treatment specialist Hyflux, a young and growing technology company based in Singapore. Founded by female entrepreneur Olivia Lum in June 1989 on a shoestring budget of S$20,000 (US$1 = about S$1.70), Hyflux gradually and painstakingly built its clientele from scratch over a period of more than a decade. On January 17, 2001, Hyflux was listed on Singapore's SESDAQ, the country's stock market for smaller firms. Within three years after the listing, Hyflux chalked up impressive growth results: Revenues quadrupled from the prelisting level of S$20.8 million in 2000 to S$81 million and S$89 million in 2003 and 2004, respectively; profit before tax shot up by more than 200%, from S$8.6 million in 2000 to S$20 million and S$29.5 million in 2003 and 2004, respectively; and profit attributable to shareholders grew from S$6.4 million in 2000 to S$12.3 million and S$26.8 million in 2003 and 2004, respectively. These results were accompanied by the firm's upgrading its listing to the Singapore Exchange main board on April 14, 2003. What factors have contributed to Hyflux's success? What is Hyflux's strategic competency and to what extent is the competency inimitable? How fast and in what ways is the competitive landscape changing? Does Hyflux need a strategic reorientation? These are some of the critical questions that a successful company should consider preemptively before the market or the competitive landscape turns against it.

INTRODUCTION

"It's a historic moment for us after the launch of our IPO," declared Olivia Lum, founder and chief executive of Hyflux, at the opening ceremony of the company's new R&D and manufacturing plant in Changi. It was January 19, 2001, ten days after the company launched its Initial Public Offer (IPO) to prepare itself for listing on Singapore's SESDAQ, a second-tier stock market reserved for smaller firms. "Our marketing thrust abroad will open up fresh opportunities for our employees and suppliers, and be instrumental in putting the Singapore brand name on the global water-treatment map," added the far-sighted chief.[1]

Indeed, the historical moment did not stop at the opening ceremony. In the subsequent three years, the young, tough-minded female technopreneur, who was highly proficient in the technical knowhow of water treatment and highly skilled in nurturing and networking strategic partnerships, successfully brought the company she founded from scratch to new heights. In the two years after the company was listed on SESDAQ in 2001, it successfully clinched, on top of others, several large-scale public and private projects including a S$16 million contract for Bedok Newater Plant, a S$27 million membrane filtration system contract for Chestnut Avenue Waterworks, a S$27.8 million design-and-build contract for a Newater plant in Seletar, the launch of the production and selling of a patented water-from-air machine, and the S$250 million desalination plant (which was Singapore's first).[2]

Table 1 shows that between 2000 and 2004, Hyflux's revenues quadrupled from the prelisting level of S$20.8 million to S$89 million. Profit before tax also shot up by more than 200%, from S$8.6 million in 2000 to S$29.5 million in 2004. Profit attributable to shareholders grew from S$6.4 million in 2000 to S$26.8 million in 2004. Earnings per share stood at 8.5 cents, far above the 4.4 cents in 2000. These results were accompanied by the firm's upgrading its listing to the Singapore Exchange main board on April 14, 2003. By early 2005, Hyflux's market capitalization had ballooned to about S$900 million, 45,000 times as large as its S$20,000 seed capital when it was formed in June 1989. It kept a staff of 600 as of early 2005, compared with just three (including Olivia herself) at the time of formation. Figure 1 shows that Hyflux's share price increased by more than 1,500%, from S$0.21 in January 2001 to as high as close to S$3 in Early 2005 (its January 17, 2001 IPO price was S$0.32).

Table 1 : Key Recent Performance Indicators of Hyflux (S$ million)

	1998	*1999*	*2000*	*2001*	*2002*	*2003*	*2004*
Turnover	6.39	6.93	20.76	27.24	45.27	81.17	88.70
Profit Before Tax And Minority Interest	1.06	.43	8.63	9.45	11.80	19.94	29.50
Profit Attributable To Shareholders	.68	.79	6.37	7.36	12.26	19.51	26.80
Net Tangible Assets Per Share (Cents)	1.17	0.21	6.76	15.50	21.34	27.44	35.70
Earnings Per Share (Cents)	.47	.05	4.40	3.38	5.33	6.27	8.53

Sources: Hyflux website at http://www.hyf;ux.com/ir_b_highlights.html accessed on May 1, 2004; Hyflux Annual Report, various years.

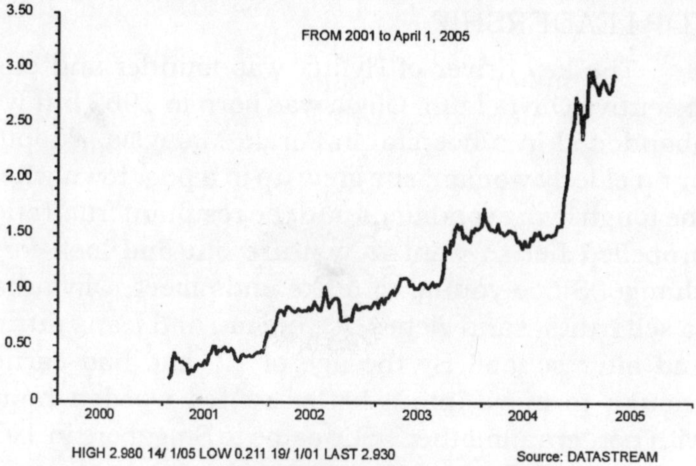

Fig. 1. HYFLUX Stock Price (S$)

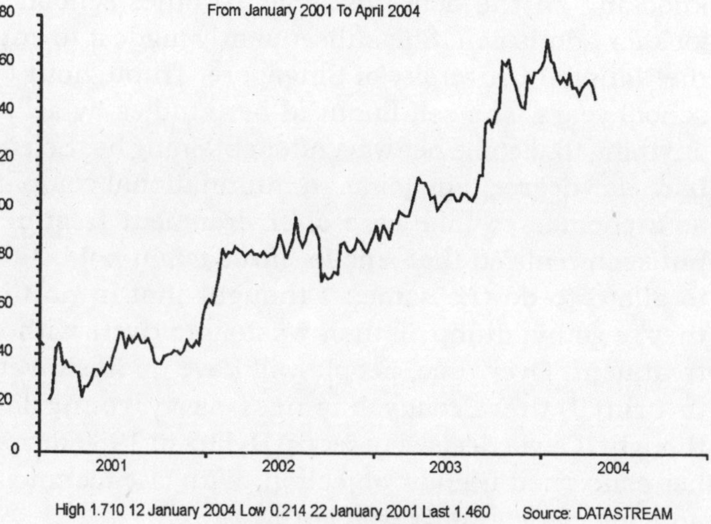

***Source*: DATASTREAM**

Fig. 1(a). Hyflux's Share Price

Hence, despite initial doubts about the company's future at the time of its public listing, Hyflux had successfully proved its worth to its investors. With a holding of 139,912,587 shares in Hyflux as of January 21, 2004, Olivia was currently worth close to S$400 million.[3]

TOP LEADERSHIP

The key driver of Hyflux was founder and chief executive Olivia Lum. Olivia was born in 1962 but was abandoned in a hospital in Perak, Malaysia. Adopted by an elderly woman, she grew up in a poor town where the tough living conditions and the resultant frustration propelled her to want to venture out and look for a change. Since young, to make ends meet, Olivia had to sell fruits, sandwiches, ice cream, and jeans during and after school. By the age of 12, she had earned enough to move into a better rented wooden house with her "grandmother". She came to Singapore in 1977 and entered Tiong Bahru Secondary School—-after knocking on the doors of some 10 other schools to look for admission. She subsequently made it to enter the National University of Singapore. Throughout the school years, she self-financed her studies by selling anything that came her way. After obtaining her Science bachelor degree, she joined a multinational company as a chemist to take care of environment treatment but soon realized that smaller firms might not be able to afford to do the same. "I thought that in no time they're gonna dump all their waste into rivers without treatment. Over time, people will have no fresh water to drink," the already business-savvy young lady thought. Olivia decisively set up Hyflux in 1989 despite her concerned friends' objection. With one technician and one clerk, Hyflux was born.[4]

The initial years of Hyflux were trying. Olivia had to sell her personal assets to finance Hyflux's cash flow and also must brace the uncertainties and dangers to look for business. She traveled to remote areas of Indonesia as well as Maldives, India, and China to talk with factory managers. However, because she grew up in a tough environment, the difficulties of building up her clientele from scratch did not dent her will to want to succeed. Bit by bit, she built up her business through sheer hard work. It was thus not surprising that when Hyflux was listed on the stock exchange, some major investors were convinced by her personal character and decided to invest in the company. For example, Mr Gay Chee Cheong, executive director of investment firm 2G Capital, which held over 21 million Hyflux shares as of January 21, 2004, said of Olivia in November 2002: "At first, I didn't really know what Hyflux did. But I read a Straits Times article about Hyflux's chief executive Olivia Lum and was struck by her strength and capability...(she) really impressed us as being a never-say-die, go-getter...and felt this was one woman we wanted to work with."[5]

Several other invaluable traits on top of her strong character made Olivia good material for entrepreneurship. First, Olivia Lum was highly responsive to feedback from all sources. For example, when someone commented that her Shanghai office was like a "boy scout and girl guide troop," she promptly employed a 65-year-old as general manager. Next, Olivia was shrewd and could grasp the changes around her quickly. For example, commenting on how Singaporean businesspeople were perceived by the Chinese counterparts, she said: "We are no longer being courted. When we first went there, we were treasured because we were a rare commodity. Now, with so many foreigners going to China, a Singaporean could only be just another foreign businessman trying to clinch a deal or run a joint-venture." Third, cost-control was always on the mind of Olivia but being prudent did not mean that she should be risk-averse. "Growing from a small company, we have always been mindful of our costs. At the same time, our area is a growth industry and we are expanding overseas to ride on this growth momentum," she said. Another strength of Olivia was her willingness to share information with investors to capture their heart as there were some 500 other listed companies in Singapore competing for attention and Hyflux was one of the smaller companies. In January 2002, some analyst commented that "another plus for Hyflux is its strong investor relations strategy. Unlike some other IPOs, Hyflux has not shied away from the need to keep stock analysts and the media posted about the company." Finally, Professor Wong Ming Keong of the National University of Singapore, who was Olivia's supervisor for her Honors and Master's thesis, said of her: "She was a quick thinker and efficient worker—and very independent too...I encouraged her to stop her (Master's) course. I said: 'Once your business is successful you can hire professors and PhDs to work for you," which Olivia did in 1999 when she hired a PhD to be her R&D manager.[6]

Olivia's rags-to-riches success story had caught the attention of the Singapore Government as well. In January 2002, Hyflux's profile was raised when Olivia was appointed by Prime Minister Goh Chok Tong as one of two Singapore's representatives to the APEC Business Advisory Council for 2002-2003. On July 2, 2002, Olivia was even sworn in as a Nominated Member of Parliament (along with eight others). Not surprisingly, Olivia also won a number of other awards and recognitions given by non-government entities. For example, in November 2002, Hyflux was given the Most Admired Sesdaq Company Award, given out by SESDAQ. The selection was based on a readers' poll carried out by Smart Investor magazine in August-September 2002. In August 2003, Olivia won the

International Management Action Award, conferred by Spring Singapore and the Chartered Management Institute. In April 2003, Olivia was elected to the council of Singapore Institute of Management. In March 2003, Olivia was chosen as Woman of the Year 2002 by Her World magazine. In August 2003, Business Times crowned Olivia the most creative entrepreneur award based on its readers' poll. Finally, Olivia won the 2003 Entrepreneur of the Year award (manufacturing and products category) given by Ernst & Young. [7]

To Olivia, the expression of entrepreneurship was salesmanship. Olivia liked to sell things—probably because she had to pull herself though the school years—from birthday presents to smoke detectors. "The more I sold, the more I understood people and the human dynamics of pleasing customers, what they really wanted and needed. This dream never died—selling was my link with the business world," she said. Olivia was also active in promoting entrepreneurship and public service. In 2002, for example, she was involved in helping a committee set up by the Ministry of Education to review secondary and junior college education in Singapore. In addition, she also contributed to charitable causes.[8]

STRATEGIC COMPETENCY

Hyflux specialized in supplying water-treatment technology and equipment as well as providing water-treatment consultancy, design, development, manufacturing, commissioning, and maintenance services. Its value-added activities centered on helping clients generate new water sources, recycle and reuse used water, and turn toxic effluent into disposable waste. This line of business fits very well with Singapore's survival as the country was not only water-scarce but also needed ultra-pure water for its electronic, engineering, and biomedical industries. The environmental protection policies of the country required specific industries to treat their waste effluent before releasing it to the open sea. Jurong BirdPark, one of Hyflux's clients, for example, installed a highly eco-friendly and efficient water-recycling system to reuse its sewerage water for washing, cleaning, flushing toilets, and feeding the birds in 2001. The recycling system first filtered out solids, bacteria, and microscopic viruses. It then passed the water through ultra-violet rays and carbon filters. Finally, salts were removed from a reverse-osmosis procedure. The system cut the Park's water bills by about 40%, enabling the Park to recoup its investment in the water-recycling system within three years. In the case of Seletar NEWater plant, Hyflux used its Kristal300 ultra-filtration membranes, reverse osmosis membranes, and ultraviolet technologies to recycle sewerage water. Because of clients' requirements, Hyflux must always be ready to customize its products and services. In the case of a deal with Japanese titanium dioxide plant in Tuas, Singapore, Hyflux must supply high-grade industrial water and deionized water at pre-determined prices. In yet another breakthrough in 2002, Hyflux developed a new membrane system that could filter unwanted elements from organic acids. As for its first project with chip giant United Microelectronics Corp (UMC), clinched in mid-2002, Hyflux's role was to provide waste water treatment services.[9]

Hyflux's water-treatment business also had a socio-political dimension. Because shortage of clean water might result in water-borne diseases, affect food supply, and threaten human survival, countries or regions facing water shortage might experience heightened tensions when they fought over the scarce resource. An Asian Development Bank had reported that 830 million people living in Asia did not have safe drinking water and over two billion lived without adequate sanitation facilities. By exploring new and better ways to generate water that meet the requirements of specific uses, Hyflux thus played a direct or indirect role in reducing such tensions and bettering the life of mankind. In the case of Singapore, its dependence on Malaysia for half of its daily water consumption needs had put it in a difficult position vis-à-vis Malaysia at times. The Singapore Government thus decided to explore new sources of water to reduce the dependence and in 2002, it announced that a new source of reclamation water, called NEWater, would be introduced to help meet Singapore's water needs. Hyflux's water treatment technology had helped make NEWater a reality and when the press produced a series of reports on NEWater, Hyflux enjoyed a great deal of investor attention, resulting in a 10% rise in its share price. "The introduction of NEWater on National Day (August 9) has great significance as it symbolizes the birth of our nation's very own brand of water. Singapore's continuous efforts and focus on the advancement of water technology will serve as an impetus for us to develop into a world-class water-treatment company," Olivia said in August 2002.[10]

Hyflux subscribed to a highly focused philosophy. It defined its mission as: "To create superior value for our stake holders through advanced membrane technology" and its values were: "We embody the entrepreneurial spirit, daring to dream with the aim to excel. We are committed to enhancing the environment and delivering innovative solutions, executed with the utmost professionalism and integrity. We value our partnerships with our collaborations and customers; and every employee and his/her contribution". Hyflux also believed that its main competitive advantage came from having its proprietary technology and hence would spend millions on R&D and upgrading facilities. "When you just buy off the rack, anyone can do the same, so where is your competitive advantage?" Olivia said. "The technology to produce clean water has been around for some time. The challenge going forward is to produce the cheapest water." Indeed, Olivia had attributed Hyflux's success to its staff's knowledge about the company's membranes. NetResearch-Asia analyst Koh Bee Ann concurred and said: "While 'water' demand in general is rising, it will not help companies if they are not positioned in the right sectors or places to benefit from this demand." In other words, water-treatment companies that had their own technology, R&D, and in-house manufacturing capabilities could command higher profit margins.[11]

SINGAPORE'S FIRST DESALINATION PLANT

One of the most talked-about deals in recent Corporate Singapore history was the S$250 million desalination project awarded to Hyflux by the Public Utilities Board (PUB) in January 2003. When the PUB opened the project for public tender (to be closed in June 2002), Hyflux was still a relatively small setup with an annual turnover of S$27.24 million (as of 2001). The S$250 million project was thus way too big for Hyflux to swallow.[12]

Being fully aware of its limitation, chief executive Olivia reckoned that her chance of success would be higher if she teamed up with a larger partner to bid for the project. Her partnership with U.S. energy giant Mirant, however, broke up six months before the tender closed because Mirant decided to pull out of the race to focus its attention on dealing with the repercussions set off by the Enron scandal. Fortunately, Olivia was able to find an alternative partner, French water giant Ondeo (Ondeo was one of the global trade names of Suez Environment—the others included Ondeo Industrial Solutions, SITA and Degrémont), which was looking for a local partner then. Initially, Hyflux sought a 40% ownership in the joint venture but decided to increase it to 70% after it clinched two other local water projects totaling S$55 million. "Along the way, Hyflux kept getting big jobs and, finally, we decided to take a majority stake as it was a strategic project for us. But it was a miracle—when we first started, we were offered only 20% because (our former partner) Mirant thought it was all we could take," said Olivia. In June 2003, Hyflux took over the remaining 30% from Ondeo following trade name owner Suez Environment's restructuring exercise—and owned 100% of it. The project was "guaranteed" by the PUB in terms of a fixed monthly payment for 20 years to cover the fixed costs incurred by Hyflux in setting up and running the plant. For this project, Hyflux would use its membrane technology to filter seawater to remove grease and sand. It would then pass the water to two separate membrane processes to get rid of bacteria, viruses, and other impurities. A series of other processes were carried out to ensure that the quality of the water obtained would meet the standards.[13]

Hyflux won the S$250 million desalination project because its consortium (at the time of the tender) could supply the water at 78 cents per cubic meter (subject to variations arising from fuel prices and inflation) and meet all the technical requirements. The three other competing parties (Keppel Fels Energy, SembCorp

Utilities, and Tuas Power Limited) had put in bids of between S$.96 and S$1.40 a cubic meter. Hyflux could drive the cost of the water down because it would build, own, and operate the plant itself and would use its own reverse-osmosis membrane and avoid using heat to evaporate the water, thus saving on energy costs. The new price compared favorably with the current household tap price of S$1.17 a cubic meter (excluding the 30% conservation charge).[14]

The S$250 million project was almost ten times the total revenues of Hyflux in 2001. It is strategic from Hyflux's point of view because it would add substantial credibility to its capability and help it clinch more mega projects in the future. The plant was expected to supply 10% of Singapore's daily consumption. With the winning of the award, Hyflux suddenly became a "big sister" in the water-treatment industry and could now pit itself against such giants as Suez Environment (of Suez Lyonnaise des Eaux) and Thame Water in an industry that was worth about US$400 billion (as of early 2003).[15]

On December 12, 2003, DBS Bank led a consortium comprising ING Bank, KBC Bank, and Standard Chartered Bank to provide a S$165 million loan to Hyflux to finance the construction of the desalination plant. In fact, the consortium was willing to lend 30% more than what Hyflux was willing to borrow, "a testament to the lending community's faith in Hyflux Group chief executive Olivia Lum and her team". When the plant started operations in 2005/ 2006, it could generate as much as S$1 billion for Hyflux over 20 years.[16]

MARKET AND COMPETITION

In business, you always have competition. Hyflux

was no exception. When Singapore's Public Utilities Board announced in early 2004 that it might consider awarding contracts to private firms to manage its three existing NEWater plants and would open the fourth NEWater plant for open bidding under a build-own-operate arrangement, two competing firms in addition to Hyflux—namely, Dayen and SembCorp Utilities—promptly expressed interests in bidding for the projects. Hyflux's advantage in this quest could be its involvement in two of the existing NEWater plants and the on-going building of Singapore's first large-scale desalination plant. SembCorp Utilities, however, boasted of its track records in supplying chemical plants on Jurong Island with high-grade recycled water and developing similar projects overseas, such as in Fushun, Liaoning (China).[17]

Another indicator of competition was the number of water-treatment companies mushrooming in Singapore. Within the three years after Hyflux was listed, five other water-treatment companies followed suit: Sinomem Technology, Darco Water Technologies, Eco Water, Dayen Environmental, and Asia Environment. In early 2004, Bio-Treat, a China-based water treatment firm and United Envirotech, a Singapore new-kid-on-the-board also joined the fray. Bio-Treat entered the scene in a big way as its February 16, 2004 IPO (Initial Public Offer) price put its market capitalization at S$355.6 million, second only to "big sister" Hyflux's S$484.5 million. The third largest listed water firm as of February 2004 was Sinomem Technoloy with a market capitalization of S$288 million. The other competitors were smaller. For example, United Envirotech had a market capitalization of about S$116 million.[18]

Hyflux used both proprietary Kristal membranes

and third party membranes to treat water. Some of Hyflux's competitors also had their proprietary technology while the rest did not. For example, Bio-Treat had a proprietary technology using micro-organisms to treat water and the technology can be used for portable toilets. Sinomem had a proprietary membrane system—like Hyflux's—that can filter out vitamins and antibiotics from industrial effluent. In contrast, Dayen did not have its own proprietary technology but was able to capitalize on its access to well-know technologies—such as Japanese giant Showa's Unox system (which used highly concentrated oxygen to treat waste water), Kennicott's industrial water systems, and Process Automation's technology in electroplating equipment—and add value in areas like process design, manufacturing, and after sales service. Despite not having its own proprietary technology, Dayen was able to get a share of the pie and had recently started constructing its first build-operate-transfer waste-water treatment project in Shenyang, China.[19]

To compete in the increasingly crowded market, Hyflux paid special attention to building strategic partnerships with key players. For example, set up in November 2003, Hyflux Filtech was a joint venture between Hyflux and a group of Chinese entrepreneurs. Soon after its formation, it announced in early January 2004 that it had clinched contracts worth 40.6 million yuan (S$1 = 4.83 yuan). "Our synergistic alliance will thus give us immediate access to this new market as shown by the deals already secured and will complement our existing marketing presence in the electronics, the pharmaceutical and the biotechnology sectors," Olivia said.[20]

FUTURE OUTLOOK

The immediate future of Hyflux looked bright. As of February 2004, Hyflux had an order book of S$62 million comprising both industrial projects and orders for its consumer products. With the sterling performance of the past few years, Hyflux had become a darling among investors as well. In January 2003, for example, Hyflux made a private placement of 11.8 million shares to Singapore Government's investment arm Temasek Holdings as it was deemed to be "a promising local company with proprietary technology in the high-growth water treatment industry". Commenting on the share placement, Olivia said: "I am happy to welcome SIPL (an investment vehicle of Temasek Holdings) as an investor in the company, especially in the light of our growing business in Singapore and beyond. I believe that this partnership will create value for Hyflux."[21]

Because of the growing gap between water demand and supply in Asia and other parts of the world, an expert had opined that the growth potential for Hyflux in the coming years would be huge. The impressive track records of Hyflux also meant it could now go for more sizable projects in the region. "Backed by these references, it's time for us to go to other markets, particularly Malaysia, Thailand, India and the Middle East," Olivia said.[22]

Indeed, with rapid industrialization across the globe, water treatment is a sunrise industry. This is because water sources have increasingly been polluted while demand for high-grade water grew. One estimate put the global water-treatment market at US$250 billion as far back as early 2000's. In China alone, local authorities' requirements that multinational companies install their own water recycling facilities resulted in a market of US$5 billion a year. Hyflux had thus identified China as one of its key markets in the foreseeable future. In 2003, turnover in China amounted to S$32 million, a 62% rise over 2002 mainly due to growth in the biotechnology and pharmaceutical segments. "China will continue to be a key growth market for the company and our next stage is to tap the booming petrochemicals market there," said Olivia. "China is really going to be the growth engine for us, and we expect orders to keep coming in as the momentum is already there", and "we want to focus on China because it has a twin problem of a chronic water shortage and water pollution". With 44% of its revenues from China as of 2003, it was no wonder that Olivia was highly optimistic that China—where the company had been operating four water treatment plants and was building a fifth one (as of early 2004)—-would be where the action should be in the coming years. Olivia's confidence was further boosted when she learned that experts had estimated that 700 million Chinese people drank dirty water that did not meet minimum state standards and 300 of the 640 major cities faced water shortage, with 100 facing severe shortfall. And with its more than 10 years of presence in China, Hyflux appeared to be well-poised to charge ahead.[23]

Another growth area would be the consumer market, which Hyflux said would contribute 20-30% of its total sales. The company had, for example, recently started to make and sell "Dragonfly" (retailed for just over US$1,000 a unit) under a licensing arrangement, a device that produces drinkable water form thin air (the technological patent belonged to California-based Air 2 Water), as well as Pureflo, a filter attached to water taps to get rid of unwanted contaminants like viruses. Pureflo was priced at S$252 a piece and the company expected to sell 20-30 thousand units a year in Singapore alone. “Nobody knows the chemistry of water better than Hyflux and we have the membrane technology that can be miniaturized for home use. I see great potential in the home consumer market,” Olivia said. The company had plans to bring Dragonfly to Asian countries and the Middle East. However, it must be pointed out that Hyflux was not the only company that produced machines to generate water from thin air. Dewdrops Marketing, for example, also sold a machine made by India-based Killicks, at S$1,200 apiece to offices and households. Another competitor, US-based Liquid Air Inc, was at least one year ahead of Hyflux in markets such as Mexico, US, Central and South Americas, China, Africa, other Asian countries, and the Middle East.[24]

CONCLUSION

Although everything seemed to be rosy for Hyflux, Olivia was not prepared to rest on the laurels. She reckoned that the really big players were those companies with an annual turnover of US$5 billion a year and that Hyflux was no where near that level as yet. “Success is relative. I always see ourselves as the underdog. When we started, we were probably one of the smallest. One by one, we overtook the others to become one of the largest in Singapore. But being the largest in Singapore is relative. If I compare ourselves with the big guys, I don’t think we are a very successful company. There is a lot for us to catch up, a lot to learn.”[25]

Indeed, some analyst had pointed out that the entry barriers in the water-treatment industry were not high and that some players might simply ride on others' proprietary technology to challenge Hyflux's competitive position, even though such players might not enjoy high profit margins. Two good examples were Dayen and Darco, which had been doing a lot of project coordination work in environmental engineering. Others also cautioned that Hyflux "has not had much experience in such plants (referring to the S$250 million desalinization project in Singapore), and it is taking on this contract on its own, which could be financially risky". This reservation was not unfounded as the S$250 million project was several times the annual turnover of Hyflux, even up till this moment. If major problems arose in the execution phase of the plant, then the financial impact on Hyflux might be disastrous.[26]

In essence, Hyflux was currently climbing a very big step up the water-treatment industry ladder. Hyflux could not afford to miss the step. As the chief executive, Olivia appeared to have made up her mind: To ensure that Hyflux could complete the climb successfully and stay high up on the ladder in the years ahead.

SUGGESTED QUESTIONS

1. What personal and environmental factors have contributed to Olivia Lum's success as an entrepreneur? Can her success be emulated in today's environment? Why or why not?
2. What factors have contributed to Hyflux's success in securing the S$250 million contract with the Singapore Government (i.e.,. the Public Utilities Board) to build the country's first desalination plant?
3. Critically evaluate the business portfolio of Hyflux. What are its strengths and weaknesses?
4. Consider the current and potential threats and opportunities in the environment. What would you do differently in the next five years if you were Hyflux's chief executive?

NOTES

1. The Business Times (2001). Hyflux opens $4m R&D center, plant at Changi. January 20. The Business Times (2003). She saw the need for water recycling 10 years ago. August 2.
2. Sharmilpal Kaur (2003). How Hyflux rescued $250m water deal. The Straits Times, January 22.
3. David Boey (2002). Can Hyflux keep up its performance? The Business Times, January 1. Hyflux website at http://www.hyf;ux.com/ir_b_highlights.html accessed on May 1, 2004. The Straits Times (2001). From small-town orphan to big boss. February 11. WWP-Report on Engineering Construction & Operations in the Developing World (2004). Singapore: Construction start-up on planned build-own-operate (BOO) $200,000,000 seawater purifying plant, Hyflux Ltd. February 1.
4. Martin Abbugao (2004). Singapore technopreneur turns waste water into gold. Agence France Presse, February 1. Cheong Suk Wai (2003). You go, girl. The Straits Times, March 16.
5. The Straits Times (2001). From small-town orphan to big boss. February 11. Soh Wen Lin (2002). 2G Capital buys 5% Raffles LaSalle stake for $3m. The Straits Times, November 2. Serena Ng (2001). Picking corporate winners-how two former JIT bosses do it. The Business Times, December 3.
6. Lee Su Shyan (2003). Companies discover fresh growth stories. The Straits Times, December 22. David Boey (2002). Can Hyflux keep up its performance? The Business Times, January 1. The Straits Times (2001). Profs backed her venture with cash. February 11. Tan Tarn How (2004). Want to succeed in China? Be prepared to fail first. The Straits Times, February 29. Bryan Lee and Hugh Chow (2003). China businessmen "getting pickier too". The Straits Times, December 24. The Business Times (2004). Company briefs. January 1.
7. Teh Hooi Ling (2003). Hyflux-led onsortium wins $250m desalination project. The Business Times, January 20. Li Xueying (2003). School of hard knocks made a winner of Ms UPS. The Straits Times, August 24. The Business Times (2003). "Royal Salute" goes to Olivia Lum. August 19. The

Business Times (2003). SGX chief Hsieh to chair SIM council. May 1. The Business Times (2003). Olivia Lum named Woman of the Year. March 4. The Straits Times (2003). Intrapreneurs-New must-haves in any firm, says Tharman. November 1. The Straits Times (2002). Briefly-Corporate reports. January 16. Laurel Teo (2002). Nine NMPs in time for July 8 sitting. The Straits Times, July 3. Simon Wilcox (2002). The 4Cs to helping small enterprises grow. The Straits Times, November 21.

8. The Straits Times (2002). Hey, do you know what kind of entrepreneur you are? April 27. Karamjit Kaur (2002). Wanted-Views on JC, secondary education. The Straits Times, April 7.

9. David Boey (2002). Hyflux wins UMC water treatment deal. The Business Times, June 1. The Business Times (2001). Hyflux opens $4m R&D center, plant at Changi. January 20. Tang Weng Fai (2002). Hyflux in deal to let Temasek vehicle take up 5% stake. The Business Times, December 19. The Business Times (2002). Hyflux bags $28m PUB project. December 27. Leong Chan Teik (2002). Hyflux devises new filter system. The Straits Times, October 22. Siow Li Sen (2002). Hyflux strikes water service deal with ISK. The Business Times, November 5. Margaret Perry (2000). Bird park sets up plant to recycle water. The Straits Times, October 19.

10. The Business Times (2002). NEWater boost for Hyflux. August 9. Sherman Wu (2004). Singapore's Hyflux turns waste water into gold. February 2. Asia Pulse (2004). SIngapore's Hyflux turns waste water into gold. February 3.

11. Kenneth Lim (2003). The challenge is to make cheap water-Hyflux CEO. The Business Times, October 15. The Business Times (2003). Making waves in the stock market. August 30. AFX Asia (2004). Singapore's Hyflux sees 18-26 pct return on desalination project. January 15. http://www.hyflux.com/hyflux_b_vision.html accessed on May 5, 2004.

12. Sharmilpal Kaur (2003). How Hyflux rescued $250m water deal. The Straits Times, January 22.

13. Bryan Lee (2003). Hyflux to recoup plant investment from PUB. The Straits Times, January 21. Sharmilpal Kaur (2004). Newater plant to go private. The Straits Times, January 17. Pang Ai Lin (2003). Interview: Singapore Hyflux/Rev

Desalination Project. Dow Jones Newswires, December 16, 12:19.

14. Sharmilpal Kaur (2003). Singapore awards first seawater plant tender. The Straits Times, January 20. David Boey (2002). Four groups submit bids for desalination. The Business Times, June 1.
15. Angela Tan (2003). Hyflux headed for the big time. The Business Times, January 21.
16. Edna Koh (2003). $165m loan to Hyflux more than 30% oversubscribed. The Straits Times, December 2003. Kenneth Lim (2004). Desalination plant could yield $1b sales for Hyflux. The Business Times, February 12.
17. Reuters News (2004). Hyflux keen to bid to operate S'pore water plant. January 17, 12:55. Kenneth Lim (2004). Privatization of water services gathers pace. The Business Times, January 28. The Straits Times (2004). SembCorp keen to build Newater plant. January 28. Kenneth Lim (2004). Privatization of water services gathers pace. The Business Times, January 28. Kenneth Lim (2004). Big week ahead for Singapore IPO scene. The Business Times, February 9. Lee Su Shyan (2004). China water firm keen to go afloat here. The Straits Times, February 3.
18. Leong Chan Teik (2004). United Envirotech chief to enjoy IPO windfall. The Straits Times, April 19.
19. Pek Tiong Gee (2004). Corporate - Seeking growth through alliances. The Edge Singapore, March 15. Leong Chan Teik (2004). Tapping China's demand for clean water. The Straits Times, January 20. Serena Ng (2004). Dayen too eyes Newater plant contract. The Business Times, January 21. Bryan Lee and Hugh Chow (2003). China businessmen "getting pickier too". The Straits Times, December 24. The Business Times (2004). Company briefs. January 1.
20. Xinhua Financial Network (XFN) News (2004). Singapore's Hyflux unit secures 40.6 mln yuan worth of orders in China. January 2.
21. Azhar Khalid (2004). China sales help lift Hyflux earnings by 59%. The Straits Times, February 27. The Business Times (2002). Hyflux bags $28m PUB project. December 27. Tang Weng Fai (2002). Hyflux in deal to let Temasek vehicle take up 5% stake. The Business Times, December 19. Angela Tan (2003). Hyflux headed for the big time. The Business

Times, January 21. Angela Tan (2003). Temasek's role in Hyflux only as stakeholder. The Business Times, January 21.

22. Asia Pulse (2004). Singapore's Hyflux turns waste water into gold. February 3. Leong Chan Teik (2003). Hyflux rides a 133% profit wave. The Straits Times, August 22.
23. Asia Pulse (2004). Singapore's Hyflux turns waste water into gold. February 3. The Straits Times (2001). Water-treatment firm Hyflux may list on SGX in 3 months. January 2. Azhar Khalid (2004). China sales help lift Hyflux earnings by 59%. The Straits Times, February 27. Serena Ng (2004). Hyflux earnings rise 59% as turnover jumps 79%. The Business Times, February 27. Leong Chan Teik (2004). Tapping China's demand for clean water. The Straits Times, January 20. AFX Asia (2004). Singapore's Hyflux net profit up 59 pct yr-on-yr at 19.51 mln sgd. February 26.
24. Kenneth Lim (2004). Desalination plant could yield $1b sales for Hyflux. The Business Times, February 12. Asia Pulse (2004). Singapore's Hyflux turns waste water into gold. February 3. Genevieve Cua (2003). Hyflux up against US-based rival. The Business Times, January 20. Ginnie Teo (2003). "Why waste air-con water?" The Straits Times, January 18. David Boey (2003). Hyflux in deal to draw water from air. The Business Times, January 17.
25. The Business Times (2003). Grace under pressure. August 2.
26. The Business Times (2003). Making waves in the stock market. August 30.

8

Pioneering Private Education: An Entrepreneurship Challenge in an Economy in Transition —

A Case Study of DOBA, Voted the Best and "Coolest" Private Educational Institution in Slovenia

Carla C.J.M. Millar
Mirjana Mladiè[1]

Mrs. Jasna Dominko-Baloh was sitting at her desk in her office on the first floor of no. 1, Prešernova street in Maribor, Slovenia. She was reviewing the final preparations for the celebration of the 15th anniversary of DOBA Maribor, the private educational institution she owned jointly with her husband and of which she was the managing director. She was checking the plans for a series of events, all carefully organised for different target groups.

ABSTRACT

The case study of DOBA, the largest private education and training provider for youths and adults in **Slovenia,** have focused on entrepreneurship in the education sector of Slovenia.. This case study traces the growth of DOBA and explores the reasons for its growth. It traces the challenges faced by the founding entrepreneur and DOBA's subsequent challenges for future growth. The case study also brings in the industry context and the socio-cultural milieu in which the entrepreneurial venture has flourished.

This case study traces the entrepreneurial journey of Mrs. Jasna Dominko-Baloh, the founder of DOBA. After having worked for ten years in education, she moved on to setting up a private educational institution jointly with her husband. In 15 years, DOBA had educated 75,000 students and contributed towards developing programs for the unemployed. The case study relates the business' growth to the local economic context. The organization team that Dominko-Baloh created was vibrant and had permanent teams that managed functions such as quality control, education and training, marketing, customer satisfaction, IT, projects and business satisfaction. The case discusses initiatives on creating a right work culture, traces the company's competitive dynamics and evaluates the vision of the institution, which has the potential of becoming one of the best schools in Europe. The case study also gives insight on future challenges for DOBA, such as internationalization.

UNEMPLOYED OR SELF-EMPLOYED?

Fifteen years! "Is it really that long ago?" she thought. It seemed like yesterday. She remembered how in 1990, a few days before the 1st of May holiday period, she was informed that she could not return to her previous job at the People's University in Maribor. There she used to organise a variety of courses, mostly skills training for boards of companies, agencies and institutions.

Her employer at the time, The Socialist Alliance of the Working People, was to be officially dissolved within a month. So the news from the People's University was quite a shock to her. She was 35, had little more than 10 years work experience, had never worked in a company or private firm, and was not sure whether she had the entrepreneurial and other qualities it took to start something from scratch. She was an educational psychologist by profession, was married and had a 10 year old daughter. What options did she have? Join the unemployment queue, start applying for jobs, start up her own company? The last one was the most challenging, yet fuelled her ambition. Only a year earlier new legislation had come into force, which allowed individuals to set up their own companies. However, no one yet had established a private educational firm in Slovenia at the time. Would it work? Would she be able to pull it off?

Jasna leaned back in her chair, closed her eyes and let memories flow past. The family had planned to go for a 3-day skiing break. After the bad news of potential unemployment, her first thought was to cancel the holiday - after all they might need all the money they had. But, on second thoughts, going away for a few days might help her clear her mind and decide what to do.

The holiday became a brainstorming session with one question to answer: 'What do I do after the end of May?' Together with her husband she evaluated options and mapped out possibilities. In the end she plunged for setting up a private company for foreign language training: she would exploit her excellent organisational skills and openness to new ideas. The key requirement was top quality staff and teachers, and she knew a lot of excellent linguists she could employ on a part-time basis; also, she would need premises with classrooms. With the help of her husband's financial expertise, she put together her first, very basic, business plan and calculated that in order to break even and carry the cost of herself and an assistant she would need 300 language students a year. At the end of May that year she attended a seminar on how to set up a company – a topic that was totally new to her.

STARTING THE COMPANY

Jasna established DOBA Ltd on the 1st of June 1990 as a private company with herself as the first employee and a director. The name represented the first two letters of her two surnames (DOminko-BAloh): in Slovene it happens to mean an epoch, era, period or season, which she felt was a very suitable image association for the business. They rented premises at 16 Razlagova Street, between the buildings of the University Faculties of Business and Economics and started small. The first products offered were summer holiday courses in foreign languages together with tennis and riding lessons on Pohorje, a mountain range near Maribor. Jasna herself sat in on these courses as an educationalist observer, and found it exciting and quite relaxing – doing something completely new in her life.

During the summer, DOBA went on to become the first training institution to market language courses for pre-school children. The results were utterly surprising: even before the start of September they received over 2,000 registrations (!). It was quite a shock. It also showed that Jasna had discovered a hitherto unexploited market niche. She immediately reorganised DOBA and took on two extra staff. At the same time a computer program was introduced for the registration of course participants; it was completely new and hence tested »live«: data were input during the day and errors and bugs in the computer program were corrected overnight.

Networking and Marketing

Somebody knocked on the door and drew Jasna

out of her thoughts. It was Irena, the principal of the vocational college at DOBA. She brought the lists of the guests of honour for the different events that were to take place. Jasna thanked her and started reviewing them. It was an important part of her PR programme, and she didn't want to leave anything or anybody out. The fact that almost everybody invited did attend the events was proof of the reputation that DOBA had built up and enjoyed not only in the local community but also in Slovenia as a whole. During festive occasions DOBA had been able to welcome not only every minister or state secretary of education, but also the president of the Republic of Slovenia. Also the mayors of Maribor were regular guests at DOBA celebrations.

One of the inheritances of her previous job was that she had been able to create a wide network of contacts from many different areas; it helped her not only to start up her own business, but also to promote it. In the beginning this was a big plus for DOBA; later the results of the programmes themselves and the positive reactions and testimonials of their students created a reputation and further enhanced the image of the institution. DOBA itself was well supported by a solid and carefully planned marketing and promotion programme.

The corporate graphic identity of the institution was the starting point for DOBA's visual communication strategy. The corporate brand DOBA was registered and protected ten years ago, in 1995.

Jasna's reflections turned to the organisation as it had now developed

In 2001 the logo was redesigned and sub-logos were developed for different DOBA programmes. Also, an integrated graphic identity system was designed and launched then.

From 1999 DOBA produced an annual marketing communication plan, which covered a number of activities including the organisation of promotional events, such as the Open Day, the Learning Fair, the Round Tables. Every year DOBA gives at least five interviews to different Slovene media and DOBA organises at least two press conferences per year. Every important event is accompanied by public relations activities. DOBA publishes its own newspaper, DOBA News, twice a year and two years ago, DOBA's students started to publish their own newspaper, with the help of a tutor – one of the Slovene language lecturers.

Sales promotion is also not neglected. Students, lecturers and employees receive birthday cards. When they have successfully completed a course, course participants receive postcards with congratulations, together with information about follow-up or other programmes and information about registration dates and deadlines. Students too receive postcards informing them when they can enrol for further studies. Every course participant or student receives a small present at registration and after he or she finishes a programme or course. And once a year a solemn and formal diploma giving ceremony is organised, accompanied by cultural entertainment.

From 1995 onwards DOBA developed its own market research methodology and the company systematically analyses target groups expectations and needs. For corporate customers a specific research methodology is developed incorporating in-depth personal interviews with CEOs and HR managers to research their needs.

STEPS AND ACHIEVEMENTS THROUGH 15 YEARS

In 15 years DOBA (www.DOBA.si) has become the biggest Slovene private educational and training institution, Jasna thought proudly. Its 30 employees and over 370 part time tutors and teachers, mostly qualified lecturers, have seen more than 8,500 students and course participants go through their hands, in the year 2004/2005 alone. Altogether DOBA has educated 75,000 students and course participants, who have rated the institution 6.1 on a 7-point scale for satisfaction.

Growth in the number of students & course participants

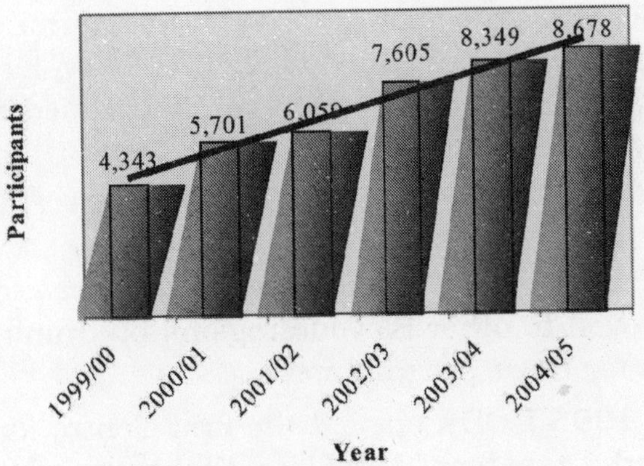

How did DOBA get this far? First, next to their language courses, DOBA invested a lot of time and effort in developing programmes for the unemployed, at that time a large target group in the Podravje region which had suffered much after Slovenia became an independent country in 1991. The infrastructure of the region, the large industrial companies, including all the textile producers, as well as the engineering companies, which had been doing such good business with Arab countries, had fallen apart, as well as the truck producer TAM, operating in the same markets and producing a large number of the military vehicles needed for the Yugoslav army. Many of their suppliers went bankrupt too, all in all leading to an unemployment rate in Podravje of around 25%.

During this period of high unemployment, the Ministry of Education in Slovenia offered financial support for programmes aimed at either retraining the unemployed or teaching them how to start their own business. DOBA decided to develop lifelong learning programmes to train people, discovering and building on their career goals.

1993 saw the start of a secretarial course which DOBA developed itself and which in 1999 evolved into a vocational college that is currently certified by the Ministry of Education. Eleven other colleges in Slovenia have taken over and are now teaching the DOBA programme.

In **1994** DOBA spread its programmes for the unemployed to other Slovene regions by training the trainers for these programmes.

In **1995** DOBA opened the first Centre for Self-Managed-Learning (CSML) in Slovenia, which at present is the largest in the country in terms of the number of participants. Those attending can choose from over a hundred self-tuition learning programmes and in 2003 they have rated the Centre 6.6 out of 7, measuring quality and satisfaction.

From **1996** a new service was started within the Centre, the Knowledge Exchange (KE). This is aligned with the life long learning (LLL) concept and is a facility where people can exchange knowledge and skills like exotic dancing, not-so-common languages like Japanese or Swahili, tattooing, etc., informally and free of charge. The participants rate this service very highly – a 90% satisfaction score.

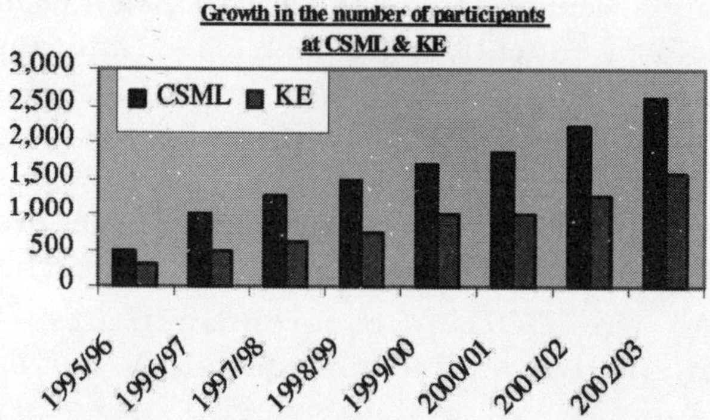

In **1998** DOBA started to offer training programmes and courses in business skills and bookkeeping.

In **1999** DOBA bought and moved to new premises at Prešernova Street, a building that formerly housed the University library.

In **2000** the institution introduced a further programme in business skills at vocational college level and in September 2005 started a vocational college level programme in financial administration. Both programmes are accredited at the Ministry of Education.

In **2001** a Research Institute was founded as a separate unit and registered with the Ministry of Education. The research focuses on current issues in the field of education, through basic and applied research within international, national and local frameworks. It provides a facility for the teaching and administrative staff of DOBA to keep abreast of developments. Currently, DOBA staff includes five The **DOBA premises in Maribor** registered researchers.

At the DOBA Research Institute, both administrative and teaching staff is extremely professional and well informed. They are now constantly asked to serve on national and international professional boards, committees, project councils and associations. Examples are: the Board for Foreign Languages at the Ministry of Education, the Adult Education Board, the International Committee for On-line Course Evaluation, the Project Council for Dynamic Learning and eWork at the Small Business Development Centre (SBDC). Also four members of staff are evaluators for certified foreign language examinations at the State Examination Centre, one is an outside evaluator for degree exams and another is an outside evaluator for EU Leonardo programmes.

2002 saw a consolidation of the company's growth. First, DOBA restructured as a business with two divisions: the DOBA European Business Education Centre, a non-profit institution, and DOBA Knowledge Source Ltd., the business side. In the same year, DOBA acquired an ISO 9001:2000 certificate and introduced an e-learning vocational college for business skills training.

In **2003** the DOBA Business School was founded, with a three-year programme for business studies, an advanced level in comparison to the two levels of secretarial courses taught at the vocational college. Also investments were made in additional classrooms and larger business premises, needed because of the growing number of students and the expected additional growth due to the planned introduction of further new programmes.

The year **2004** was another turning point: a new accredited two-year vocational college programme for public sector engineers was introduced. Also, DOBA obtained certification for their two-year vocational level programme in financial administration as well as an accreditation for the three-year DOBA developed business studies programme, which was already in line with the Bologna requirements. Meeting the Bologna standards is the first level to the international mobility of students and though a step towards the international recognition of the quality of the programmes at particular school. That year DOBA filed an application for the Slovenian Award for Business Excellence, the highest state quality award for business, products or services, based on the European EFQM model, and was the first company in the field of education to do so.

COMPETITIVE ADVANTAGE

All these developments gave DOBA a competitive advantage in a number of areas. Students, course participants and staff work in an inspiring environment, where modern, ergonomically designed and functional equipment including modern ICT devices – computers, internet, overhead projectors and

LCDs are available in every classroom. Designing the premises, DOBA consulted experts on equipment, ergonomics and colours. DOBA uses warm colours, music and fragrances, which provide the pleasant study environment, so important for adults. The premises are also conveniently located in the centre of Maribor.

Other advantages of the institution are the following:

— Nearly all advertised programmes actually take place: thanks to the large number of applicants and the large number of lecturers available, programmes hardly ever have to be cancelled.

— Potential students are able to make well-informed choices and decisions thanks to DOBA's proactive behaviour, giving plenty of information and counselling. According to the DOBA satisfaction analysis this service is highly appreciated.

— Continuous development: as a consequence of their systematic market analysis DOBA is able to develop new programmes timely and in accordance with market needs. And, when students need support, e.g. to enable them to learn more effectively, DOBA immediately responds with new supporting programmes (such as 'Adults learn differently', 'Diploma seminars', and 'Mentoring and Tutoring' programmes).

State of the Art

Currently DOBA's programmes, as a percentage of the number of teaching hours, are structured as follows (the development and international cooperation hours are not teaching hours):

Programme structure by teaching hours

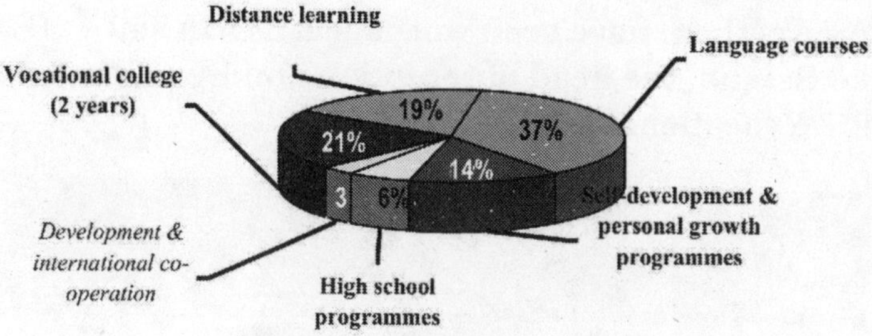

DOBA Organisation Chart
(Since 2002 a Business Group)

Life Long Learning

Many other developments took place: in 1997 DOBA organised the first Week of Life Long Learning with activities aimed at understanding the importance of learning, regardless of age or prior education. This event has been organised every year since. In 1998 DOBA developed a Job Interview Training programme and in 2000 a distance-learning programme was introduced as a predecessor for the e-vocational college for business skills.

Jasna smiled inwardly at the thought of how many people had asked her how one could do so much in so little time. She was not really conscious of what she and her team had achieved till she saw everything written down on paper, in a brochure published for DOBA's fifteenth anniversary celebrations. Oh, yes, nothing could have been done without the right people, the right team.

The Staff

DOBA's administrative staff are visible everywhere: smiling at you from photos in an exhibition in the central hall of the institution, or the ones on the business premises, or in the brochure, and last but not least, when you meet them in real life. They vibrate with energy and enthusiasm to do more and better. Some of them have been working at DOBA since 1990, like Sabina, the head of reception and Irena, the head of the vocational college.

Irena Kristina Sabina Andrea Oton

Nives Nataša Lea Ksenija Dina

In the service business, staff is key to success or failure. Jasna was very much aware of that, so creating benefits, and maintaining loyalty and satisfaction levels of the people working in her company were a very important part of her work. Besides developing her own skills as a leader and manager, she invested energy and assets in developing knowledge, skills and personal growth of her employees: everybody was involved in learning, either inside or outside DOBA, in Slovenia or abroad. Regular visits to foreign vocational training and educational institutions were organised on a yearly basis. Seminars for administrative staff were organised 3 to 4 times per year and often run jointly for staff and lecturers; some of these were developed specially for DOBA. Every employee sent to an outside seminar, fair or on a visit, writes and presents a report for his/her colleagues, including proposals for work improvement. Internal seminars were organised too, called DOBA Thursdays. In 2002, for instance, there were 13 internal seminars aimed at internal knowledge transfer and subsequent reports were made available to everybody through the intranet. Altogether 10% of DOBA's income is invested in personnel / teaching staff education, training and personal growth.

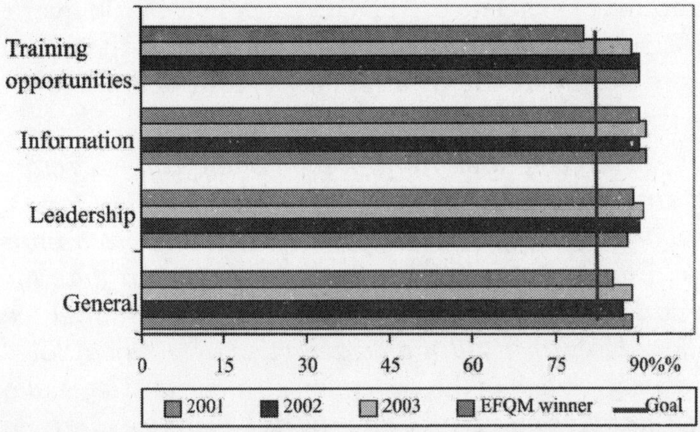

Employee satisfaction 2001 – 2003 in comparison with the EFQM winner

Constantly improving teamwork plays an important role in DOBA. On average, every employee is involved in at least one team, averaging a quarter of his or her time. A number of permanent teams (for IT, marketing, education and training, customer satisfaction, quality and for business efficiency) were established, meeting once a quarter and making their reports available via the intranet. Many of their suggestions were followed up and turned into projects. Every year, at least 5 major improvements are introduced as a result of the work of these teams and the systematic collection of employees' suggestions; and annually more than 15 projects are set up.

Staff satisfaction levels are measured annually, since 2001. Every employee is included in the research, the results of which are available on the intranet within

14 days. The satisfaction levels of lecturers are analysed too, and changes are introduced based on their suggestions.

One staff satisfaction indicator, often used in key business indicators or comparative charts, is the amount of sick leave. At DOBA sick leave is on average 2% per year, which is much lower than that in the state sector in the branch (4.9%) and below the level of the DOBA peer EFQM winner (3%).

The telephone rang. It was one of the secretaries of state from the Ministry of Education inviting Jasna to a working group to evaluate new training programmes for adults. One of the achievements Jasna was most proud of, was the fact that key DOBA personnel were now involved in all major activities at national level – e.g. preparation of the education strategy and legislation, the development of educational practice and new educational and training programmes. Also, DOBA was invited to participate in major projects at local, regional, national or even international level. Since 1999 DOBA has participated in Leonardo and Socrates projects.

COMPETITION

Being part of the international scene helped DOBA to establish contacts with different training and educational institutions all over Europe, which enabled the transfer of good practice on the one side and very solid benchmarking on the other. The fact was that there was not much opportunity to do benchmarking in Slovenia, since DOBA was the first or the best in many fields, always introducing new approaches in adult training and education, well ahead of the state run vocational institutions. Who were DOBA's competitors in Maribor and in Slovenia?

In Maribor, there are two competitors in the field

of language programmes: the People's University (now renamed Andragogic Centre Maribor) and As Asistent (Assistant). A number of other private companies too offer language courses: Lindiè, Lingva and Panteon College. Recently the Berlitz Language School set up a branch in Maribor. However, in comparison to the supply in Ljubljana where more than 50 language schools are operating, competition does not seem too overwhelming. On the other hand, Ljubljana is much larger, and the capital city with embassies and a larger percentage of foreigners and hence possibly has greater demand. Two other vocational colleges in Maribor offer two-year programmes for business skills (the same programme as DOBA), B2 and As Asistent. The latter organises a two-year vocational college level programme for financial administration too, while B2 offers all three two-year programmes that DOBA has in its portfolio.

When comparing itself with other vocational colleges, DOBA usually takes into account competitors from Celje, 45 km from Maribor, (CE), Novo mesto, 90 km from Maribor, (NM), and Ljubljana, 120 km from Maribor (LJ).

Comparison of Selected Vocational Colleges

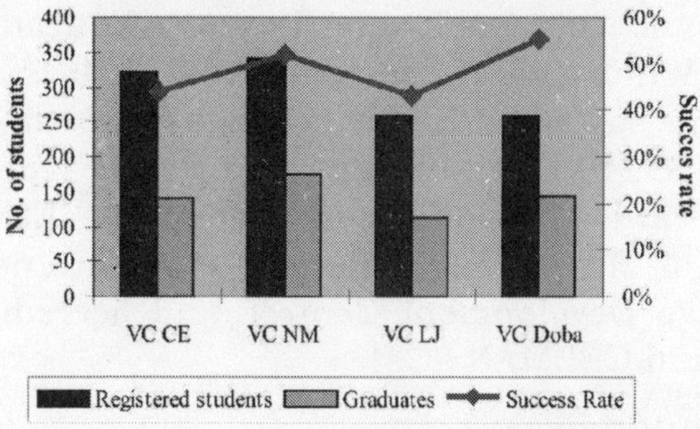

The graph shows a comparison between the

number of registered students and the number of successful graduates. This ratio is considered one of a school's major evaluation criteria for success.

However, the state funded schools and universities should also be taken into account. Some universities too have developed vocational programmes (e.g. the Faculty of Business and Economics at the University of Maribor) albeit at Business school level (e.g. three-year level).

Currently, Slovenia has three universities, in Ljubljana, Maribor and Koper. Possibly that a new one will develop in the next 10 years from the strong vocational colleges centre in Novo mesto, which is an economically strong area with some big and successful global companies like Krka, the pharmaceutical company and Revoz, in the automobile industry.

Professional diplomas are recognised by the state and can be awarded by any organisation that has gained accreditation for the programmes in question. Academic degrees however can be awarded only by the three Slovene universities.

Privatisation of the universities or the establishment of a private university is not expected yet. Nevertheless there are already a few private business schools, focusing on Executive Education and MBAs. While two of the universities, Maribor and Ljubljana, award a Slovene Ministry of Education accredited MBA, the most internationally recognised one is awarded by a private institution, the IEDC-Bled School of Management (formerly the International Executive Development Centre), and accredited by AMBA and CEEMAN (ICA).

Vision and Mission

Systematically comparing DOBA with the best

vocational education institutions in Europe led Jasna to form a challenging *vision*: for DOBA **to become one of the best schools in Europe**, with the *mission*:

— To ensure excellence in the DOBA educational programmes and services,
— To teach course participants to learn,
— To encourage learning in all periods of life,
— To spread and increase the availability of the DOBA training programmes,
— To develop partnerships to satisfy training needs at local, national and international level,
— To respond to the future needs of course participants with new programmes and projects,
— To develop a partnership with course participants through the exchange of qualitative information, through counselling and through progress monitoring.

DOBA has always invested much in communicating its vision and mission to all its stakeholders. And next to communicating these two elements, the firm has communicated its values and strategic goals, regularly and systematically and captured them each year in one slogan-of-the-year. Examples of these slogans are in the table below.

Year	*Slogan*	*Meaning*
1999	At DOBA we all think, we all work	Wherever we work, whoever we are, we contribute to DOBA
2000	We are better every year	DOBA is consolidating and improving
2001	Learning and teaching is our first priority	Intensive introduction of the principles of a learning organisation
2002	Knowledge for development	Acquiring professional knowledge & skills

2003	E-learning for the information society	E-learning is our priority
2004	Quality is our advantage	We summarised our achievements and applied for the Slovenian Award for Business Excellence

DOBA established a procedure for strategy and goal development, which includes consultation with all employees. A "Management team" consisting of 4 or 5 staff-nominated people starts with a concept document and leads the process of feedback, changes and inclusion of additional suggestions before passing the strategy to the Board for finalisation and implementation. This system has guaranteed full staff involvement and subsequent loyalty of the employees and hence is considered to work very well.

"Yes, DOBA has become a well known and recognised brand," Jasna thought contentedly. She remembered another pioneering step in her business career, the application for the Slovenian Business Excellence Award in which she had put together a mosaic of important parts of the DOBA story. One small, but important, piece of information crossed her mind: 98% of students and course participants would highly recommend or recommend the DOBA programmes to other people. "This is really something to be proud of," she thought.

The Lecturers

People matter and the lecturers are crucial for DOBA becoming a recognised, quality driven school. At DOBA a great deal of attention is paid to the selection, education, support and motivation of the lecturers, most of whom work for DOBA on a part time basis. First, they all have to go through the educational qualification procedure, which checks their professional work experience, and their teaching qualifications and references. A lecturer who does not have teaching qualifications or adult education qualifications has to acquire them within five years. DOBA has an agreement with the Faculty of Arts which trains lecturers who do not have such qualifications to help them acquire a certificate of teaching at vocational colleges. The training takes place in Maribor at the DOBA premises, which saves time and money, as otherwise lecturers would have to attend the programme in Ljubljana. Also, the course is adjusted to the profile of vocational teaching, focused on adult education and application to practice. DOBA pays half of the course fee.

Next to this training programme, DOBA organises three or four half-day workshops per year for the lecturers. Annually, in the framework of the staff satisfaction measurement process, lecturers give suggestions for seminars they would like to attend in order to improve their skills. The second part of these workshops is devoted to internal topics, for instance the DOBA strategy and goals, achievements, new programmes and services. This way, part timers are aware of, and involved in, all that's happening at DOBA.

Number of Training Sessions & Workshops for Lecturers

Year	*Number of Training/ Workshop Sessions*	*Number of Educational Hours*	*Number of Lecturers attending*
2001	13	84	187
2002	15	108	192
2003	19	143	205

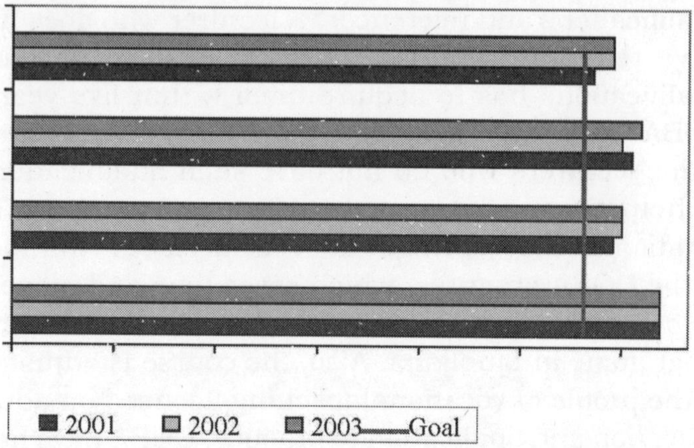

Lecturers' satisfaction levels 2001 – 2003 compared to the goals set

Over the last 5 years DOBA signed contracts with 107 new lecturers and had to end the contracts with 4 of them as they did not reach the DOBA standards. Since 2003 lecturers have to sign an exclusivity agreement with DOBA, through a competitive clause in their contracts barring them from teaching at the same level at competing schools. This was introduced after the University faculties decided not to allow their professors and academic staff to teach at DOBA and similar vocational schools.

Every year, the best lecturers are awarded financial bonuses for their achievements, partly based on the rating given by students and/or course participants. The lecturers meet at The Teachers' Assembly three to four times a year and are included on different boards and committees in the school.

At least twice a year, at the end of the programmes in June and in December, the lecturers are invited to a social event together with the administrative staff and the Board of DOBA. Jasna always personally thanks them each for their dedication and for their work. These meetings are combined with a cultural or leisure entertainment event and are usually well attended. DOBA's intensive HR programme guarantees them an average of 10 unsolicited applications a month either for full time or part time jobs.

Jasna suddenly remembered the last social event, their excursion to Finland this year. The whole management team and the leaders of the professional disciplines, altogether seven people, researched and analysed two of the best vocational institutions in Europe for a full week. "It is always a pleasure to see that you don't have to be ashamed of what and how you are doing in your work," thought Jasna. "On the other hand, one can always learn from others, if only one opens one's eyes and ears."

The most important point they picked up this year was that the school should embed itself in the local economy. DOBA now wants to organise projects through which their students try and help solve practical problems in local companies, free of charge. This year's goal is to find three such companies. A big challenge for all involved! Then there is Europe...

INTERNATIONALISATION CHALLENGE

After Slovenia joined the EU in May 2004 many new challenges appeared. First, there was the Bologna Declaration. Although it is not yet compulsory for DOBA to adjust all its programmes to the Bologna pattern, preparatory activities have already begun. In this year's pre-school meetings lecturers will be briefed on how to structure the new teaching plans for their subjects and the adjusted programmes will be launched in 2006. The new DOBA Business School's programme already meets the Bologna requirements.

Another big challenge is internationalisation. A

first step was taken a couple of years ago, in the form of a test project to transfer distance learning knowledge to Serbia, together with a programme for a vocational college for business skills. Should the first results gain positive evaluation later this year, DOBA will launch the programme itself simultaneously in Serbia and Croatia in 2007.

Only when all the programmes are in accordance with the Bologna standards, will it be possible for DOBA to start cooperating with schools in Europe and e.g. to exchange students. DOBA has already established relations with a vocational college near Vienna and the visit to Finland proved promising in terms of exchanging know-how on distance learning. DOBA wants to expand the co-operation and start to admit foreign students once it has moved to teaching some of the subjects in English.

Jasna looked at the time. It was 5 p.m. already. It was Friday. She decided it was time to stop. A pleasant thought crossed her mind. She checked whether her husband was still working. He was the finance director at DOBA and had to put in long hours recently due to an imminent tax inspection that always required a great deal of documentation. She decided to tempt him away from the office with dinner at that nice Italian restaurant near Pohorje that they loved so much. She knew her daughter, who had been working as an adult education organiser at DOBA for a year now, could not join them. A nice long weekend was awaiting them and she promised herself not to talk about work.

COUNTRY BACKGROUND

Slovenia was established in 1991, following a plebiscite decision by its inhabitants to become independent. In May 2004 it was the only former

Yugoslav republic to join the EU. It has less than 2 million people and is bordered by Italy in the West, Austria in the North, Hungary in the East and Croatia in the South. Slovenia has its own language and culture, 3 universities and its population is relatively well educated.

Slovenian GDP is 75 % of the GDP of the EU-25 group. The unemployment rate in June 2005 was 6.9% and the average monthly salary 720 EUR. In 2003 6 % of GDP was destined for education. In 2004 almost 15,000 people graduated from vocational colleges and higher education institutions. In the same year the percentage of graduates from vocational colleges increased by 46.3 % and represented already 12 % of all graduates.

Further information on Slovenian statistics can be found on the following web sites: *http://www.uvi.si/eng/*, or *http://www.magneti.si/images/zemljevid_slovenija.gif*.

FINANCIAL DATA

The financial statements mirror the company data given above, and show a distinctive growth. Below, please find comparative data over the years 1991 (the first complete financial year of the company), 1995, 2000 and 2004. For the last period the statements for the two organisations that form the DOBA Group: the non-profit DOBA European Business Education Centre (abbreviated to DOBA EPIS in Slovene) and the for-profit DOBA Knowledge Centre, have had to be combined. The figures and the graphs below speak for themselves.

Balance sheet overview 1991 – 2004

in 000 EUR

Position	*1991**		*1995*		*2000*		*2004***	
Immovable property	24	33.0%	49	13,2%	844	62,4%	1.397	56.1%
Equipment	20	27.2%	98	26.6%	150	11.1%	192	7.7%
Liquid assets	29	39.8%	189	51.1%	351	26.0%	774	31.1%
Short-term receivables	2	3,0%	83	22.5%	136	10.0%	481	19.3%
Total assets	**72**	100.0%	**369**	100.0%	**1.352**	100,0%	**2.489**	100.0%
Short-term liabilities towards suppliers	1	1.5%	209	56.5%	105	7.8%	138	5.5%
Short-term loans raised	0	0.0%	14	3.8%	76	5.7%	174	7.0%
Total equity capital	**72**	100.0%	**369**	100.0%	**1.352**	100.0%	**2.489**	100.0%
EUR =	75,7555		105,0788		205,0316		238,8615	

Income statement overview 1991 – 2004

in 000 EUR

	*1991**	*1995*	*2000*	*2004***
Sales income	133	571	922	2.709
Material & service costs	107	445	392	1.461
Labour costs	14	277	451	749
Operating profit	19	-3	150	345
Profit after tax	-	2	127	286
Employee No. (hours base)	1	6	15	22
EUR =	75,7555	105,0788	205,0316	238,8615

* first full operating year (12 months)

** sum of DOBA EPIS and DOBA Knowledge Source

CONCLUSIONS AND LESSONS LEARNED

Surveying this 15-year story of DOBA, one asks oneself: what lessons could be learnt? How will the

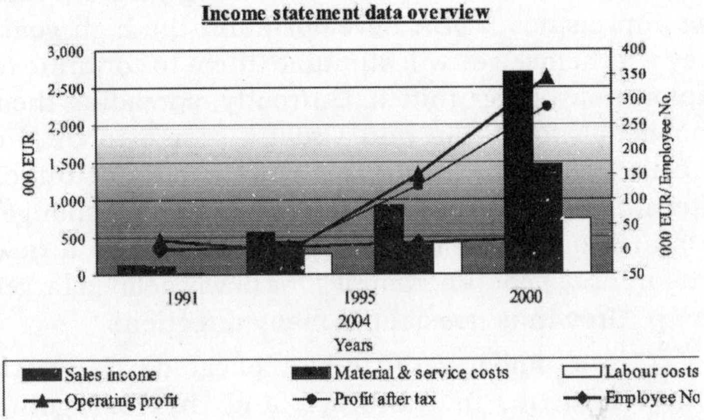

business evolve in the coming years? Can such story be replicated in another situation, culture or country?

DOBA shows what can be achieved when one is under pressure (possible unemployment) provided one has enough entrepreneurial spirit, innovativeness and a firm will. It is difficult to say which trigger had the biggest influence. The fact is that DOBA might not have been there at all if that original threat had not been there, or that very limited time to make such critical decision, to start a new venture. Thereafter however other entrepreneurial skills prevailed: discovering business opportunities and developing methods for systematic scanning thereof, developing managerial and leadership skills, building a brand and reputation through planned marketing tactics, and building the "DOBA team" consisting of internal and external staff and lecturers.

There is no doubt that DOBA is now at a level where dynamic further growth is more difficult to achieve and will involve much larger investments as well as taking much larger risks. Following discussions with Mrs. Dominko-Baloh, we are certain that the institution will not stop here. We strongly believe that the approaches DOBA developed and the high goals they set themselves will stimulate them to continue to exploit new opportunities. Currently, spreading their knowledge to Serbia and Croatia seems to be the challenge; next might be the introduction of international subjects and foreign student exchange. It is also quite possible for DOBA to develop a new two- or three-year programme for a newly defined target group. Growth is possible in many directions.

Can a similar venture be replicated? There are many countries in transition and they are going through the same scenario: transforming and turning to their version of a capitalist system, involving private initiatives, economic transformation and consequently requiring new skills. Together with the economy the schools are transforming including some that become privately owned, with new ideas, new opportunities and new challenges.

QUESTIONS FOR DISCUSSION

1. Discuss the factors which have been responsible for success of DOBA?
2. Critically analyse the competitive scenario for DOBA.
3. Given the financial information , can DOBA internationalise its operations.
4. What are the key strengths and challenges which DOBA needs to address to support future growth?

9

Tejari.com : 'The Middle East Online Marketplace' Under the Leadership of Sheika Lubna Al Qasimi

Linzi J. Kemp

ABSTRACT

Tejari[1], is a premier online business to business (B2B) environment, facilitating procurement in the Middle East. The company's Chief Executive Officer is Sheikha Lubna Al Qasimi (Appendix 1). This case study, considers Tejari's start up and business growth through innovative marketing and technology. It is also a case study describing a personal career, that highlights the capacity of women in the Middle East to be recognized globally as entrepreneurs and leaders.

INTRODUCTION - THE BUSINESS DILEMMA

This case traces the growth of Tejari as it faced the challenges of being a unique business in its region. The country was growing rapidly, new businesses were starting up, others, including the government sector were expanding. The traditional means of communication between buyer and supplier were slow and lacked responsiveness to the changing market conditions. Global trading was increasing and time differences needed to be overcome. Those companies that had an online presence were faced with little compatibility between their systems for purchasing and supplying goods.

THE UNITED ARAB EMIRATES

Tejari is based in the United Arab Emirates, so in this and the following sections a political, economic and technological description of the country is given as a context to the case. That description highlights the swift growth of the country and, following analysis of these sections, students will be able to identify the need for procurement support and thus rationalize the start up of Tejari.

The UAE is a federation of seven emirates[2] or states in the Arabian Peninsula. The national (Emirati) population is 2.4 million, approximately 25% of a total population that also comprises of expatriates and tourists with visas (UAEinteract, 2004). The population has increased on average by five per cent annually over the past 17 years, with an increase of 7.6 per cent in 2003, the highest growth rate in the Arab world. Growth in the national population is attributed to the absence of birth controls and government incentives to produce more children. This growth rate is expected to slow down, due to education of the local populace and the elimination of governmental incentives. The expatriate population has increased due to the expanding UAE economy, although, as Emiratisation is embedded, this growth rate will also slow down. Emiratisation is a policy of reducing reliability on foreign workers. The official language of the UAE is Arabic, for business purposes, English, and other languages are spoken widely.

THE CURRENT BUSINESS CONDITIONS

In order to compete for global business, the UAE is a member of the World Trade Organization (WTO), and, via that membership, is a signatory to a WTO sponsored multilateral trade treaty; the General Agreement on Tariffs and Trade (GATT) (UAE government, 2005). The currency is the Dirham, its value has been fixed to the US dollar since 1980 at the rate of USD 1 = Dh. 3.67 (Gitex, 2005). The UAE has one of the highest per capita incomes in the world, \$18,870, and is ranked 49th in the world on the Human Development Index[3] (HDI). Private consumption of consumer products and services was \$33.8 billion in 2002, an average of \$8,600 per individual in the UAE (Table 1).

Table 1: UAE Income/Expenditure 2002

Income/Consumption	*\$*
Per Capita Income	18,870
Private consumption of consumer products/services	33.8 billion
Average consumption per individual in the UAE	8,600

(based on statistics extracted from UAEinteract.com, 2003).

The Gross Domestic Product (GDP)[4] of the country is rising, though the increase in the population outpaces growth in GDP. GDP is provided mainly by the oil sector, which provides more than two thirds of the UAE's income, but this sector contributes relatively little employment (27,000). The biggest employer is in trade and repair services (392,000 workers), the construction sector was number two in terms of employees (320,000) followed by the manufacturing sector (262,000). The government services employs 224,000 workers, the agriculture and fisheries sector, 163,000 and communication, transport and storage, 131,000. The overall workforce stood at 2.03 million at the end of 2002 and the government is actively encouraging business diversification to continue economic prosperity (Table 2).

Table 2: Employment (2002)

Sector	*Employees*
Trade and Repair Services	392,000
Construction	320,000
Manufacturing	262,000
Government	224,000
Agriculture and Fisheries	163,000
Communication, Transport, Storage	131,000
Oil	27,000
Other	781,000
Total Workforce	2,300,000

(Based on statistics extracted from UAEinteract.com, 2003).

The Emirate of Dubai, where the company Tejari is physically located, is politically stable, is very secure for individuals and property, has a diverse human resource pool and a booming economy. Businesses require a supportive infrastructure to survive and grow and Dubai provides for this in terms of well-connected highways, an international airport and seaport. Dubai Port Authorities (DPA) is ranked number 11 as a world port, it is the leading regional port with a sophisticated e-system that networks the port and customs with the cargo community (Sims, 2000, George, 2004, Qusti, 2004). DPA was also the organization responsible for the electronic automation of the federal government in the UAE, a project in which Sheikha Lubna[5] was closely involved.

Entrepreneurship is encouraged by the Dubai government through free zone areas, set up for the incubation, nurturing and growth of new businesses. Financial benefits to businesses located in the free zones are that the companies can be 100% foreign owned and are tax exempt. There are 3,000 companies in these zones, with an estimated turnover of US$8 billion (Morisonemnon, 2003). Incorporated into the *Jebel Ali Free Zone* (JAFZ) is *Dubai Internet City* (DIC), created as a regional business hub for information technology companies. Besides Tejari's presence in DIC, Dell, Hewlett-Packard, IBM, Microsoft and Oracle have located regional headquarters in the city to stimulate the Middle East's 1% spent on global technology and emerging global markets (Kelaita, 2001).

Within the UAE, there is 29.6% penetration of the Internet, compared to 8.2% usage for Middle Eastern countries as a region, 36.5% for Europe and 68% for North America (Miniwatts International, 2005). There is one state controlled and censored internet and telephony provider (Emirates Telecommunications Corporation or Etisalat). However, for DIC, there is a privately provided internet service, in recognition of the fact that 'the Internet plays a strategic role in any company's ability to survive and compete' (Dubai Internet City, 2005). Laws regarding electronic commerce and security were implemented in the UAE in 2000 to support technology projects such as Tejari and DIC (Suhaili, 2002). The necessity of educating and employing a technologically competent national workforce is recognized by the Chairman of Tejari and the DPA, *"the goal is to have 5 million knowledge workers by 2010"* (Sultan Bin Sulaiman; Smith 2004). Sheikha Lubna (Al Qasimi, 2001), when addressing local faculty, echoed that aim,

"Technology skills are the tools that enable young Arab nationals to become productive members of the economy, creating new jobs and expanding industries that improve the national outlook as whole. A skilled national workforce in turn leads to less dependence on imported labour, and decreases unemployment by creating a sustainable pool of educated workers that can also develop new areas of expertise as the community's needs change. These skilled workers also empower the UAE to compete on a global level as trade opportunities expand".

TEJARI.COM

The Chairman of the DPA conceived the original concept for Tejari as a B2B marketplace for the companies in the free zone area. This idea was expanded on its presentation to the Dubai Crown Prince and UAE Minister of Defence[6], to open up the B2B marketplace beyond the boundaries of these free zones (Suhaili, 2002). The brand name, Tejari, was decided upon because it derives from the Arabic word '*tejarah*' meaning trade, thus creating a regional identity through a name that could be pronounced globally. The company started trading on June 20th 2000 with 15 employees, having taken 60 days to implement from its original conception date.

Shield (2001) questions the decision to launch Tejari as a dot com company, as by 2001 many 'dot coms were under the hammer'. Sheikha Lubna's response is that the dot coms were businesses about technology *"but we weren't"*. In explanation, she has previously described the role of technology in the Middle East's business environment as *"that of an enabler, or a means by which businesses can become more efficient, more customer-focused and supplier-friendly, and ultimately, more profitable"* (Al Qasimi, 2001). Tejari's business focus remained firmly on the core product, the value of procurement, and did not seek to grow rapidly as many of the dot coms did, to their cost. Instead the company sought a more progressive plan based on developing and keeping customers through a relationship of good business practice over the long term. Sheikha Lubna refers to Tejari's business strategy at this time as *"organic world wide"* growth whereby they did not concentrate on the mechanics of business (or in this case the technology) but on the needs of the clients. Sheikha Lubna describes Tejari as *'80% service oriented"* as opposed to being 100% product (technology) driven, the technology in use is to build databases based on services that offer a *"best fit for the clients"*.

The mission statement of Tejari is:

To maximize the business potential of our customers in the Middle East by providing them with innovative online B2B services, enabling them to extend their reach and enhance their competitive standing.

It is a business founded on research into local market trading patterns and needs, *"done here with our own thinking and own culture"* (Al Qasimi; Suhaili, 2002). To Sheikha Lubna that is a *"unique service proposition"* and a core reason for regional success. The benefits offered through Tejari's service proposition are:

* Lowering of procurement costs:
  - Reduction in inventories
  - Reduction in time to market
* Global trade:
  - Via the world wide web (WWW)
  - At all times (24/7)

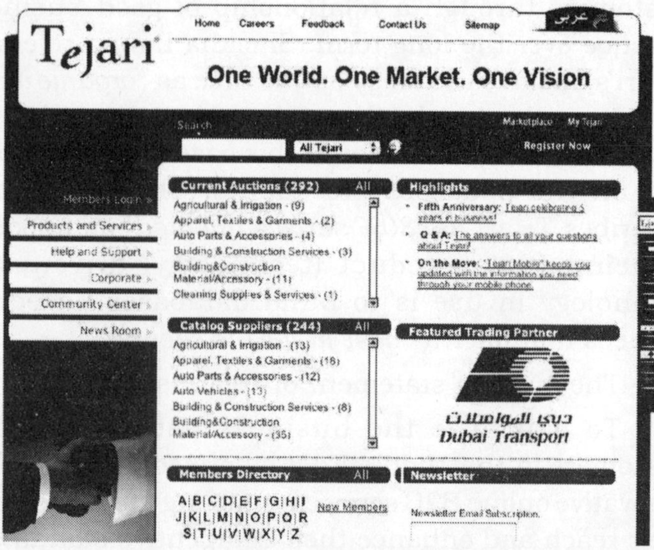

Fig. 1. Tejari.com
(Screenshot from www.tejari.com, November 2005).

Tejari offers a B2B online service for companies wishing to acquire commodities, companies are approved for credit worthiness, registered and their trading information is listed in the marketplace. All trading partners (as they are referred to) can then search for supplies, request and receive quotations, and launch and bid for tenders. The service offered is based on the procurement cycle of purchasing functions, and the duties and responsibilities associated with that process. To enable an efficient procurement cycle, business is conducted via online auctions that bring suppliers and buyers of products together (Figure 1.). The auction scenario is a tool that meets a competitive need to transact business, i.e. to facilitate the buying and selling of supplies on a just in time (JIT) basis (Oakland, 1993). As speed is a factor in the efficiency of businesses today, so supplies can also be purchased immediately through spot purchasing via online catalogs. The online organization is powered by Oracle, which was chosen for its capacity, reliability, up to date technology and scalability as the company grows.

A challenge for Tejari at the outset was to educate users that e-security was efficient and secure, a challenge met through the introduction of national laws protecting e-commerce, and bank to bank financial transactions to avoid potential security problems of credit card abuse. In addition, seminars, workshops and conferences were held locally to educate business users in regard to the security of online transactions.

Since the original concept in 2000, the business expansion strategy has provided: 'Connect' to integrate the systems of clients, 'My Tejari' a website area that can be personalized for the individual trader and 'Catalog' to manage the service and product catalogs of member companies through a data cleansing service. As each client builds his own trading environment (profile) and gains a history of trading, he can focus on the benefits the procurement tool offers. Customers gain data on their procurement costs and, through analysis, can identify efficiencies in their value chain.

By the first quarter of 2003, company statistics showed the number of auctions had increased by 66% in one year, purchase orders had increased from 55 in 2002 to 4,017 in 2003, and Tejari community membership had increased from 482 to 1,528 (Al Qasimi, cited in AME, 2003). In the third year of trading, Tejari had hosted 8,000 auctions, transacted more than $500,000,000 worth of business and Sheikha Lubna's proud claim is that the *"company was also in profit"*. The trading partners in the Tejari environment have to date conducted more than 35,000 online tenders, valued at over $1.8 billion. Currently registered are

3,587 trading partners operating in sectors as diverse as automotives, healthcare, construction, IT, food and beverage, and tourism. It is the governmental sector that has continued to be the most active trader, benefiting from an opening up of the market due to internal market deregulation. For these state operations, deregulation has enabled competitive tendering and the streamlining of business transactions.

In 2005, a consultancy department has been integrated into the environment to advise companies on planning their chain of supply. In line with its service orientation, customer relationship management (CRM) is high on Tejari's goals. Through the bringing together of businesses to collaborate on product research and design (R&D), industry specific solutions will be developed to meet the needs of the trading community. Tejari will be actively targeting the potential new UAE market of real estate, due to an increase in housing construction because of the opening up of the market to non-national purchase, and the increasing housing needs of the growing national and expatriate population. Tejari clients are mainly based in the UAE, although increasing globalization in the region has led to enough trading activity from partners in Jordan and Kuwait to warrant individualized web site environments for these countries. A goal, therefore, is to increase business globally, specifically there is an initiative to seek business in Africa,

"Tejari's revenue model and the growth of our trading community has enabled the marketplace to achieve a leadership position and brand maturity at an accelerated pace. Our challenge now is to develop new services beyond serving as an online trading hub to drive even greater value in the supply chains of our members." (Al Qasimi, 2001; Tejari, 2005).

According to Hillstrom and Hillstrom (2002), and Berns and Hairston (2001), an entrepreneur is an organizer and manager of a new venture, who gathers and allocates the resources needed for that venture's success. This is very much following an economic theory of entrepreneurship, i.e. viewing the contribution of entrepreneurship as the creation of new enterprise (Mitchell et. al, 2002). In the case of Tejari, the main resource lay in technology, a resource that required support from only a few human resources to successfully start-up the business. It is innovation that is the defining characteristic of entrepreneurship, considers Schumpeter (Hillstrom and Hillstrom, 2002; Hadzima, 1994) and entrepreneurs find new ways around problems. The problem was efficient procurement, the innovation was a B2B marketplace for the region and the entrepreneurship was continued as new services were added. Lenko (1995) talks of entrepreneurship in terms of the innovative management of products, this can be considered in relation to Tejari as it markets products through an innovative service that enables itself and other companies to compete in a global market. The provision of jobs nationally and internationally is a feature of a successful entrepreneurial business. A dynamic economy locally was supplemented by Tejari as a business, and the company fed back into the growth of the business in the local area. The business solution was swiftly extended from a single service of the purchasing activity to offer a service encompassing all supply chain activity for businesses. Furthermore, an opportunity was discerned to take the business beyond the public purchasing market within Dubai to private companies in the Middle East and beyond.

Over the years of trading, Tejari has received

numerous business awards including:

* Gulf Marketing Review: Gulf Brand of the Decade Award, 2003 (E-Commerce & IT Category).
* UAE Super Brands Council – Super Brand of 2003.
* World Summit for Information Society, Geneva – Best E-Content Provider in E-business (2003).

Sheikha Lubna ascribes the receipt of awards to the way Tejari disseminated its business quickly to traders, and the subsequent trust, through experience, that customers have put in using the business tools. On the award of UAE Super Brand of 2003, she notes that Tejari *was "the fastest to get* [the award], *usually it takes seven years"*. Sultan bin Sulaiman, (Tejari, 2001), commenting on the same award, said *"no business-to-business online enterprise in the region has a wider reach and more prominent brand recognition than Tejari"*. Sheikha Lubna considers that a company should "*capitalize on receiving awards"*, for example, the award for Best E-Content Provider in E-business (2003), was not only a motivator for Tejari employees, but was a recognition of the capable Information and Communications Technology (ICT) work taking place in the country and the region; as such the award was a *"big deal for people in the Middle East"*.

WOMEN IN THE UAE

Educational and career opportunities for women in the United Arab Emirates are discussed as a context for Sheikha Lubna's career trajectory (Appendix I).

The UAE Constitution states that,

"social justice should apply to all and that, before the law, women are equal to men. They enjoy the same legal status, claim to titles and access to education. They

have the right to practice the profession of their choice" (Al Maktoum, 2001).

According to UNESCO (Statistical Yearbook 1999; World Bank Group 2005), the literacy rate among women in the UAE rose to 88.7 percent in 1995 and by 1997, 72% of tertiary students were female. In the UAE, 6% of internet users are women and, probably due to the exposure to technology whilst studying, the usage of computers in the Emirates is higher for women when compared with other countries in the region (Cisco Learning Institute, 2004). Females comprised about 19.4 percent of the total workforce in 1995 (World Bank Group, 2005), mainly in the civil service, teaching and medicine, and in family businesses,

"women are demonstrating great enthusiasm in taking up jobs to take advantage of their qualifications, social changes, and the support and encouragement of His Highness the President and the UAE leadership" (Representative, Civil Service Council, Gulf News, 2002).

In the health services, women account for 54.3% of the total number of employees, 'one out of every three doctors, pharmacists, technicians and administrators is a woman, as is 81% of the nursing staff (Arabnet, 2002). UAE women employed in the Ministry of Education and the Ministry of Health outnumber national male employees and account for 27 per cent of the civil servants within the 24 government ministries (Gulf News, 2002). The federal government promises a job for every applicant with good benefits and flexible work schedules.

Many UAE national women do not choose to take up employment after education, and legal and societal forces contribute to this scenario. Although law in the UAE states that there is equal pay for males and females, there have been claims that 'at work women remain deprived of equal benefits such as housing and promotion'. (World Bank Group, 2005). According to the UAE constitution, women's roles are positioned within the context of the family,

"the family is the basis of society which shall be responsible for protecting childhood and motherhood. Laws shall be formulated in all fields to observe this protection and care in a way which safeguards the dignity of women, preserves their identity and secures for them the conditions appropriate for a prosperous life and suitable work which is in accordance with their nature and capabilities as mothers and wives and as workers" (ArabNet, 2002).

There may be a personal preference to avoid the inconvenience of a career whilst running a household, the family may raise objections to a wife, sister, or daughter working and a permit has to be issued by the husband/father before a wife/daughter can gain employment. Sheikha Lubna in an interview with Suhaili (2002) talked about the dichotomy of a culture that does not accept women's capability in employment alongside home management. In the context of the need for the national workforce to expand to replace non-nationals, Sheikha Lubna (Suhaili, 2002) calls for males to recognize the possibility of a dual role for females, and that men need to adapt in the light of this,

"here the society starts criticizing by stereotyping, as long as she's doing well in her career that means that definitely she doesn't do well at home, this has to change..... a business with an equal balance between men and women and making half of the society's workforce active will solve a lot of problems like the high dependency on foreign labor. [We need to] *acquire the*

support of men to understand that they have to also be accommodating inside the house".

A career field where Sheikha Lubna notes that women are already established and doing well in the UAE is in engineering, *"honestly I raise my hat to a lot of women in the society who are doing extremely well in the engineering field"* (Suhaili, 2002). She goes on to point out that in medicine, women have careers, but do not gain enough recognition in this profession; *"we have very good doctors, surgeons, and medical professors that didn't get enough accreditation and support."* (Suhaili, 2002). Sheikha Lubna wants to encourage opportunities for national women in nursing careers, although the majority of nurses are expatriates probably because of relatively low pay, long hours and cultural barriers of working in a mixed gender area in a rather intimate setting. In ICT, it is males from India and Pakistan that constitute the major part of the labor force in the UAE (Cisco; World Bank Group, 2005).

In an interview with Sims (2000), Sheikha Lubna saw electronic communication as an employment opportunity for females in her country, *"UAE ladies who may not wish to work outside the home have the opportunity to create their own Internet-based business, or telecommute for an office job through e-mail"*. She talks of other Emirati women besides herself who are now CEOs of technology companies in Dubai and has named women[7] over the years who hold top jobs in Dubai (Sims, 2000); she is pleased to be *"a member of a very prestigious club"*. Sheikha Lubna also encourages women to seek political positions in the Emirates, for e.g. as ambassador or national council member as exampled in her home emirate of Sharjah *"there are about five women in the consultive council and two women in the directing general level in government departments"* (Suhaili, 2002). Thus, she identifies that, within the UAE, women *"already play a strong decision-making role today*" (Sims 2000).

"Arab women are half our community. Sometimes better than men. Perhaps in the past we lagged behind, but today she is growing to better heights in our society and is able to achieve goals within our communities. She will only grow." (His Highness Sheikh Mohammed bin Rashid Al Maktoum, November 11th, 2001) .

THE CEO AND MANAGEMENT TEAM

In this section, we consider the CEO as a leader and entrepreneur, the customer service orientation of the company and the contribution of teamwork. Drucker (1986) is very systematic in his approach to the topic of entrepreneurship considering that it is a tool that can be implemented by an organizational leader to grow a business. In this case we can review the evidence of how that tool was manifested by the leader, using available technology to set up the service and then technological tools to meet customer needs. To continue to be entrepreneurial throughout the life of the organization, Drucker also notes that the company has to be open to and adaptive to change as a positive force.

Sheikha Lubna identifies change management in her career occurring through a trinity of change due to her contribution as an individual business leader in the technology sector, *"I think I am a change agent for life. I am a facilitator, a messenger and a bridge. And in that bridge, I have played it in technology*" (Al Qasimi; George 2001), *"Technology is a catalyst for change"*. To enable clients to adapt to new ways of working, she considers the process begins with introducing change to some users who can act as *"champions"* of change for other traders as they *"buy-in"* to the model. As the business scales up and out, any changes in the platform have to be managed so they are transparent to the end users, *"how we deliver is key"*. For change management to be successful, patience is required as adaptation time will vary according to the perceived needs of individual clients. In her previous roles as a programmer and systems engineer, Sheikha Lubna recognized that businesses involved with technology tended to be

"very self-centered and not close to the end users...in technology companies, the CEOs can be so technology orientated that they never talked about clients. They forget that users use products and that users are number one".

A Tejari trading member, the Department of Health and Medical Services, Dubai, offers credible testimony for such service orientation,

"Tejari is not just a technology platform, it is also a professional consultancy that can advise customers on all of their purchasing processes. We've found Tejari to be a business necessity based on the benefits we've received as a member of the marketplace." (Tejari, 2005).

For public and private businesses to thrive in today's increasingly competitive climate, Sheikha Lubna's personal mantra is that the *"customer is king"* (Al Qasimi, 2001). Her gratification comes from *"making the client happier"* and the practice of Tejari is to encourage clients to speak their needs. Listening to the customer and giving them the services they want underpins Sheikha Lubna's business decision making, in the knowledge that better results are gained through this practice.

In the company's recruitment policy, the philosophy of listening to the customers is followed as employees need to be *"open, courageous and to be able to speak well with clients. It is not about functional knowledge"*. Although Sheikha Lubna has the functional knowledge through her technical acumen, she considers that to improve employee performance *'technical ego'* needs to be constrained. There are many other areas, besides technical competence, that are important to the business and for which an employee may need development to be able to perform effectively. Risk taking is a reoccurring theme in Sheikha Lubna's business belief, which is why courage is a requirement of employees who are expected to take calculated risks. Risk is

"one of the most important aspects of success in business and in life generally. It was again His Highness Sheikh Mohammed bin Rashid al Maktoum who said that not taking risks is, in itself, one of the greatest risks." (Al Qasimi, 2001)

In particular, Sheikha Lubna pays a great deal of attention to feedback in the annual customer survey. If employees are concerned about the possibility of negative feedback in surveys she tells them that such honesty from clients *"will protect employees in the long run as it mitigates risk"*. Risk taking is important as it gives *"the opportunity to innovate, to try new ideas, and to learn from mistakes"* (Al Qasimi, 2001). Most entrepreneurial businesses begin small and extend, as people are willing to work hard and take risks (BBC, 2005; Berns and Hairston, 2001; Shapero and Sokol cited in Hillstrom and Hillstrom, 2002). Tejari is a performance-based company, 60% of earnings are based on performance following the trend of leaders in the field for e.g. Microsoft. Employees are made aware of the expected level of performance as defined in written policies, a *"clear set of deliverables...a clear document from day one"*, and employees with *"stamina will stay"*. Tejari now employs 52 people, but there are at least 120 working with the company as, to reduce the challenge and overhead of recruitment, other human resources have been outsourced[8].

At DPA, Sheikha Lubna managed 100 employees, describing her management style as aiming to "*understand their need* [by] *working closely with them*". At Tejari this style is continued, *"we have operations meetings each week to work closely together"*. When delivery of business is successful, personal *"thank-you"* e-mails are written to individuals. The work hours in Tejari are long - 8 pm until late in the evening, but there are occasions where the work is moved out of the physical building to have *"kick off meetings in Hatta"*[9], here the team leaders present their accomplishments and then, after lunch, everybody moves outside to get together for physical activities. Active teamwork is a key skill that Sheikha Lubna fosters in her leadership, saying that such a skill

> *"cannot be developed in front of a PC or through the Internet, but is nonetheless vital to the long-term growth of the UAE's economy value....the contributions of others, and to appreciate a diversity of ideas and business viewpoints."* (Al Qasimi, 2001)

Nobody works in isolation, but as part of a group striving toward a common goal and, as the group achieves, there is a personal gain and so the individuals do well. An entrepreneur does not succeed alone but needs expert human resources to support them and drive the business forward. In supporting teamwork within Tejari.com, the function of the talented individuals was brought together. The culture of the workplace that Sheikha Lubna fosters is that of the family, *"my success is the success of the team....the team is like a family"*. The physical manifestation of this metaphor[10] is the dining room where employers eat together in an informal setting, as in a *"family kitchen"*. Some senior management do not want to share success with others which Sheikha Lubna says is *"a high risk"* because she consider that if an individual is treated as a member of a family then they will appreciate that the employer cares about their immediate family. In illustration, she mentions an employee whose mother was in an intensive care unit in India, but the employee was reticent about taking any time off to visit her. Sheikha Lubna responded to him by saying that the *"team is in place and we can work with you at a distance"*, but that she would *"never forgive myself"* if he did not return home at this important time. It is unsurprising that Sheikha Lubna uses the metaphor of the family positively as her immediate family has always been very supportive - encouraging her to follow her interests and continue her education (Sims, 2000).

People who work with Sheikha Lubna are from 12 different countries and one of the problems faced is to ensure that people from different cultures work together effectively. The expertise of an international cross cultural manager is brought in at this point. The manager needs to recognize and appreciate employee differences. Sheikha Lubna refers to *"Tejari as a mini-United Nations"* and appreciates the strength such diversity brings to a working environment. She sees technology as a way of bringing the world together,

"the Internet and the ease of global travel, as well as the more than 100 different nationalities living in the UAE, prove to us every day that we do not live and work

in isolation, but as part of a global community." (Al Qasimi, 2001)

Employees are from different religions; the official religion of the UAE is Islam and other faiths are tolerated. Her attitude to that phenomenon is to "*celebrate culture...Christmas, Eid*[11]*, Indian festivals....very sensitive about this as we are all equal*". Her cross cultural appreciation is based on the encounters she has had with diversity and the understanding she has gained from such exposure, "*I learnt through my career to interact with multinationals and, therefore, a diversity of cultures with diverse politics."* (Suhaili, 2002)

Researchers have failed to select or rather to agree completely on a set of personality traits that make up the character of the entrepreneur (Brockhause and Horowitz, 1986; Sexton and Bowman-Upton, 1991; Shaver, 1995; Murphy et al, 2002). But one personality trait is perhaps agreed on more than others (Lanko) and that is commitment. A commitment that comes from the self-motivation to continue despite setbacks that may occur in the life of the organization. Business acumen such as business planning and the knowledge of marketing strategies and technical skills also add into the personality of the successful entrepreneur. Sheikha Lubna has felt the extra pressure on herself as a woman in a senior position dealing with the "*egos*" of male colleagues, "*gender conflict*" is universal, but especially in a society such as this where women in employment is a relatively new concept. On hurdles that she has encountered, Sheikha Lubna states that,

> *"my experience with Dubai Ports Authority was of a male environment. I think I frightened them in many ways as they didn't know how to handle me."*

She deals patiently with colleagues and employees

who do not trust women managers and lets her actions stand as evidence of her expertise, *"you have to deliver before you demand their acceptance. ....You have to have the patience... You have to have the discipline."* (George, 2001). Sheikha Lubna puts her accomplishments down to having *"learnt from failures rather than success,* [and having] *patience and perseverance"*. When failure occurred she learnt from it by speaking with counterparts and deciding where to go from there, she acknowledges that many managers cannot work like that as a *"lot of people have egos"*. However the admission of failure followed by collaboration with others worked for her in resolving many problems and the tactic brought her closer to people as they then sought to support her.

Rewards for the hard work of the entrepreneur include personal satisfaction from the business duties as well as the prestige gained from success (Berns and Hairston, 2001). On her achievement with Tejari, Sheikha Lubna reflects that it was a reward to be appointed to *"set up a company"*, her business acumen having been recognized, as opposed to only being regarded previously as *"a techie"*. Although the appointment gained a great deal of media coverage at the time, Sheikha Lubna considers that the attention was not about her personally, but was an opportunity to *"demonstrate that a woman could succeed at a senior level in a high risk business."*

Influencing the growth of the business was Sheikha Lubna's organizational and managerial ability to further harness together the resources of technology and people. Showing true entrepreneurial spirit, the management team, led by Sheikha Lubna, created a solution to the old and ongoing problem of efficient purchasing.

APPENDIX 1. SHEIKHA LUBNA AL QASIMI, - EDUCATION AND BUSINESS EXPERIENCE.

His Highness Sheikh Zayed bin Sultan Al Nahyan (founder of the UAE) said,

"Nothing could delight me more than to see the woman taking up her distinctive position in society... Nothing should hinder her progress... Like men, women deserve the right to occupy high positions according to their capabilities and qualifications" (Al Maktoum, 2004).

Sheikha Lubna[12] had always been interested in science and maths; as a school-girl her ideas on careers were centered on medicine or architecture. Having studied English in the United Kingdom (UK) for nine months and because of a brother living in California, she became aware of the field of technology. Obtaining a sponsorship from Hewlett Packard, she proceeded to California State University and, by way of the Dean's list for her studies, became one of the first UAE women to gain a degree in technology (1975, Bachelor's degree in Computer Science). Sheikha Lubna considers that her undergraduate studies paved the way for her future business success as the *"foundations were solid*[13]*"* i.e., the curriculum included research, systems operations, engineering and business. She was breaking new ground at the time as a female Emirati student and is proud to have served as a role model for younger women today who are growing up in the UAE. In illustration, she tells the story of a 10 year-old Pakistani girl living in Dubai who recently passed the Microsoft Engineer exams; the youngest ever to do so. On hearing of the student's success, she sent a congratulatory e-mail to recognize the achievement and to offer encouragement for future endeavors. Sheikha Lubna has since earned an Executive MBA (American University of Sharjah[14]), and during her studies was proud that her academic knowledge of business was up to date and was also rather surprised to find she knew as much as she did. That said, it was a busy time, studying and working, and for her, like most students, there were many nights she slept on the couch surrounded by her books!

Sheikha Lubna's career trajectory started in 1981 when she became a programmer for a private company in the UAE. Datamation is a software company that is family owned by Indian expatriates and she was distinguished by not only being the lone woman to work there, but she was also the only Arab. As a private company, the owners expected their employees to finish the job, so she worked outside the contractual hours of 8am to 6pm in order to fulfill her duties. It is perhaps her opinion of systems operations at the undergraduate level, as being *"fun and neat"*, that sustained her through these hours. Her next position was that of branch manager (Dubai General Information Authority) before moving to become Senior Manager at the DPA for seven years. In the latter role, as manager of the Information Systems department, Sheikha Lubna moved from the technical side into more of a business role, but her knowledge of technology kept her in good standing for comprehending the product needs of customers. In her role at the DPA, she also headed the Dubai e-government executive team project to initiate an electronic portal of information for the public sector. The spirit of this initiative went deeper than just producing a source of information, as it was founded in a mission to bring a *"customer service and satisfaction focus to the government sector"* (Al Qasimi, 2001). Based on the leadership that she showed in that project, in 2000 Sheikh Mohammed appointed Sheikha Lubna as Chief Executive Officer for the implementation of Tejari. Sheikha Lubna recognizes an accepting gender environment at Tejari where *"male colleagues are more interested in my ideas and strategic vision for Tejari than bothering about my gender or nationality"* (Sims, 2000). Trust from national male management has helped, *"such people appreciate and value an intellectual, experienced person, with the right educational background, right experience and encourage them to take high positions"* (Al Qasimi; Suhaili, 2002). Admiration in the region towards successful women managers is noted in this story,

" I was once having lunch in a restaurant and then two Saudi businessmen came to me and told me '"we just wanted to say hi and tell you how proud we are of you and your work as an Arab."' (Al Qasimi; Suhaili, 2002)

Currently she lectures at Zayed University[15] and enjoys the role of teaching as it allows her to share knowledge with others. She also shares her knowledge through interviews, international business/ government forums (Microsoft Government Leaders Forum, Arabia, April 25th 2005), as conference speaker on the subject of the Arab world in 2020 (The Arab Strategy Forum, Dec, 2004), as keynote speaker at global events on the topic of "*Emergent Models of Global Leadership,*" (International Leadership Conference, November 2005) and through a webcast (*'Global Conversations with Business Leaders',* 2004) . In the future she anticipates studying for a Doctorate in business or technology or a combination of those subjects at MIT[16]. When questioned how she manages to balance her many roles, Sheikha Lubna's response is a self-deprecatory, *"I don't know"!* Drawing her out on the subject of life balance in an interview with Suhaili (2002), she abhors talk of "*sacrifice*" preferring to advise women that life is about making choices.

Sheikha Lubna perceives that females need to make a positive decision in regards to looking after a home or working to have a career or a blend of both. Having made the decision, then women need to balance their lives to spend time with family and friends, to maintain their health and follow their hobbies in order to achieve a well-rounded life.

Many personal honors have been bestowed upon Sheikha Lubna Al Qasimi during her career:

— Distinguished Government Employee Award (1999).

— Dubai Quality Group: For Support to Leadership, Quality, and Change year (2000).

— ITP: The Best Personal Achievement Award year (2000).

— Datamatix: IT Woman of the year (2001).

— Commonwealth of Kentucky: Honorary title: "Kentucky Colonel" (2003).

— Entrepreneurship award for contribution to e-business in the Middle East - House of Lords, UK (2004).

She is admired in the community as a

"preeminent UAE woman and role model....a recognized expert in the field of information technology....who did not just talk about e-business and e-commerce but she has actually put it into practice" (Boardman, College Director, 2001).

In 2004, Sheikha Lubna became the Minister of Economy and Planning[17], the first woman in the UAE to assume a cabinet position (George, 2005), '..there are other women ministers in Gulf countries, in Bahrain, Oman and Qatar, but Sheikha Lubna's role is the most senior to date..' (Wheeler, 2004).

Sheikha Lubna has however faced challenges to her role from outside the region, as she believes there are many deep felt assumptions held about Muslim women. She (like many others of her religion) wears an abaya[18] in public, her hair is covered although her face is unveiled but she considers there is a stigma ascribed by non-Muslims to this mode of dress. The stigma derives from a principle that such clothing somehow "*blocks energy to the brain*" and that there remains a strongly held belief that because some Muslim women "*choose to be this way*" that they have "*no brain*",

"*especially after the September 11 events, the projection of the Arab and Muslim society is projected in a very negative way. One of the effective ways we can change this image in the West is by putting women in high positions, because usually in the western culture they judge the quality of any society by looking at how developed the women are.*" (Al Qasimi; Suhaili, 2002)

As Sheikh Mohammed had the foresight to appoint a woman to such a position, she reflects that at the end of the day it was a matter of personal integrity to succeed. To illustrate the acceptance of success of women in UAE businesses, Sheikha Lubna quotes Sheikh Mohammed as reporting to male colleagues that he might "*replace some of you with them!*"

In 2000, Sheikha Lubna was asked by Sims in an interview, "*Where do you see yourself career wise in the next 5 years?*" Her response in 2000 was this,

"*I think running Tejari will present me with enough challenges and triumphs to keep me interested for at least the next five years. I'm equally dedicated to my personal mandate of sharing my experiences with other UAE women. The next five-year period is a long road with so many things left to do. It takes courage to believe in your life's conviction - check back with me in 2005 and we'll see where I am".*

In this case study we have read about the challenges and triumphs that have kept the company and leader interested. Working within a plan that she had set to make herself dispensable, life is now changing for Sheikha Lubna Al Qasimi, having been appointed as a member of the Tejari board, she hands over the reins of CEO and Managing Director to a colleague. Her role as a prominent member of the UAE Council of Ministers continues.

REFERENCES

Al Maktoum, H.H. Sheikh Mohammed bin Rashid. (November 11th, 2001). History of Women, *http://www.sheikhmohammed.co.ae/english/history/history_women.asp*

Al Qasimi, L. (2001). HCT Annual conference, Shaping the Future, *"Technology and Business Skills Development for the UAE's Future"*, Videotape.

Al Qasimi, Sheikha Lubna (August 16th 2005). Interview with Linzi J Kemp.

Alvesson, M. (1993). *The Play of Metaphors* in J Hassard and M Parker, (eds). Postmodernism and Organizations, London: Sage.

AME info. (2001). Sheikha Lubna Al Qasimi, http://www.ameinfo.com/20201.html

American University of Sharjah. (August 2005). Information, http://www.american.edu/sharjah/partnership.html

ArabNet (2002). *http://www.arab.net/uae/ue_womenconstitution.htm*

Austin, N. and Peters, T. (1995). A Passion for Excellence: The leadership difference, London: Collins.

BBC (2005). Are you an Entrepreneur? The Money Programme, Open2.net.

Bennis, W. (Nov 5th 2000). *Leadership and Management: New Roles and Challenges...A farewell to (the Old) Leadership,* Paper presented at the Sixth Annual Leadership and Management in the Information Age Conference, Emirates Centre for Strategic Studies and Research, Abu Dhabi, 5-7 Nov 2000.

Berns, R.. G., and J. E. Hairston. (2001). "Entrepreneurship." *Encyclopedia of Business and Finance*. Ed. Burton S. Kaliski. Vol. 1. New York: Macmillan Reference USA, pps. 303-308. 2 vols. *Gale Virtual Reference Library*. Thomson Gale. Retrieved from EMPIRE.

STATE COLLEGE SUNY. 08 November 3, 2005 2005 <http://find.galegroup.com.library.esc.edu/gvrl/infomark.do?&type= retrieve&tabID= T001&prodId= GVRL&docId= CX3402700171&eisbn=0-02-865897-3&source= gale&userGroupName=esc&version=1.0>.

Bloom, B. S. (1984). *Taxonomy of educational objectives*, Boston, MA: Allyn and Bacon.

Boariu, M. (2002). The Veil as Metaphor of French Colonized Algeria. *http://hiphi.ubbcluj.ro/JSRI/html%20version/index/no_3/maria_boariu-articol.html*

Boardman, D. (2001). HCT Annual conference, Shaping the Future, *Inroductory Speech*, Videotape.

Cisco Learning Institute. (2004). Gender, *http://gender.ciscolearning.org/Strategies/Strategies_by_Region/Middle_East/United_Arab _Emirates/Index.html.*

Drucker, Peter F. (1986). *Innovation and Entrepreneurship: Practice and Principles*, Harper and Row.

Dubai Internet City. (2005) *http://www.dubaiinternetcity.com/*

George, V. (2004). Shaikha Lubna Al Qasimi, *"I have earned my desk". http://www.womenone.org/faceslubna04.html*

Gitex, (2005). The UAE Currency, http://www.gitex.com/visitos/currency.html

Grant, D. and Oswick, C. (1996). Getting the Measure of Metaphors in D. Grant and C. Oswick, eds, *Metaphor and Organizations*. London: Sage.

Gulf News. (December 16th 2002). National women surpass male compatriots in government jobs. *http://www.gulf-news.com/Articles/news.asp?ArticleID=71228*

Hadzima, J. (1994). Pinpointing That Critical Entrepreneurial Spark, *Boston Business Journal*.

Hillstrom, K. and Hillstrom, L, C., (Eds). (2002). "Entrepreneurship." *Encyclopedia of Small Business*. Vol. 1. 2nd ed. Detroit: Gale, 2002. 445-449. 2 vols. *Gale*

Virtual Reference Library . Thomson Gale. Retrieved 08 November 2005 from <http://find.galegroup.com.library.esc.edu/gvrl/infomark.do? &type=retrieve &tabID=T001 &prodId=GVRL &docId=CX3404300235 &eisbn=0-7876-7725-6 &source=gale &userGroupName=esc &version=1.0>.

Hindery, R. (April 1 2005). Seven Who Tap Power to Provoke Change, http://www.womensenews.org/article.cfm/dyn/aid/2132.

Kemp, L .J. (2002). Organisational Team, Modern and Postmodern Perspectives in Primary Health Care, PhD Thesis, London, UK: British Library.

Kelaita, K. (June 4th 2000). Dubai Investing in Information Trade, *Time Magazine*, Vol. 157 No. 22. *http://www.time.com/time/interactive/business/dubai_np.html*

Kotler, P. and Armstrong, G. (2006). Principles of Marketing, 11th ed., New Jersey: Pearson.

Lakoff, G. and Johnson, M. (1980). Metaphors We Live By, Chicago: University of Chicago Press.

Miniwatts International (2005). Internet World Statistics. *http://www.internetworldstats.com/stats5.htm*

Mitch., L. (July-August 1995). "Entrepreneurship: The New Tradition." *CMA—The Management Accounting Magazine.*

Mitchell, R. K., Busenitz, L. Lant, T., McDougall, P. P., Morse, E. A, Smith, J. B. (Winter 2002). Toward a theory of Entrepreneurial Cognition: Rethinking the People Side of Entrepreneurship, Entrepreneurship Theory and Practice, Baylor University, pp. 93-104

Morisonemnon Chartered Accountants (2003). Doing Business in UAE and UAE Free Trade Zones, *http://www.doingbusinessinuae.com/*

Morgan, G. (1986). Images of Organization, London: Sage.

Morgan, G. (1991). Paradigms, metaphors, and puzzle solving in organization theory in J Henry, (Ed.), Creative Management, London: Sage

Oakland, J. S. (1993). *Total Quality Management, the route to improving performance*, New Jersey: Nichols Publishing.

Onsman, H. (November 16th 1998). 'The power of the image: how metaphor can transform management', *Business Review Weekly*, (online). *http://www.brw.com.au/content/161198/BRW54.html*

Qusti, R. (2004). Breaking the Boundaries: UAE Appoints First Female Minister, Arab News *http://www.arabnews.com/?page=6&section=0&artide=53904&d=3&m=11&y=2004*

Schein, E .H. (1992). Organizational Culture and Leadership, (2nd ed.), San Francisco: Jossey Bass Publications

Shields, M. (2001). Dot Coms under the Hammer, *BBC News, http://news.bbc.co.uk/1/hi/business/1229279.stm*

Sims, J. (2000). Sheikha Lubna Al Qasimi - the B2B Woman, Go Dubai *http://www.godubai.com/citylife/ls1.asp?article_id=2000/ABW%235*

Smith, L. (July 2004). The Road to Tech Mecca, *Wired Magazine*, Issue 12.07. http://www.wired.com

Suhaili, Y. A. (2002). Interview with Sheikha Lubna Al Qasimi, http://www.eqarat.com/j2ee/examples/english/newsletter/sheikha_lubna_interview.htm

Tannen, D. (1998). *The Argument Culture*, London: Virago.

Tejari. (June 20th 2005). Region's First Online Marketplace Celebrates Fifth Anniversary, *Highlights New Consulting Practice*, Press Release. *http://www.tejari.com/English/NewsRoom/PressReleases/35.html.*

UAE Interact. (Feb 7th 2004). UAE population growth highest in Arab world, *http://www.uaeinteract.com/news/default.asp?cntDisplay=10&ID=134.*

UAE Interact. (April 25th 2005). Lubna Al Qasimi opens 2nd government leaders forum, *http://www.uaeinteract.com/news/default.asp?ID=64.*

United Arab Emirates. (2005). Government, Business, http://www.uae.gov.ae/Government/business.html

United Nations Development Program. (2003). What is the Human Development Index?, http://www.undp.org/hdr2003/faq.html#21.

Wheeler, J. (Nov 2nd 2004). UAE to get first woman minister, *http://news.bbc.co.uk/1/hi/world/middle_east/3974447.stm*

Wikipedia. (2005). Definitions. *http://en.wikipedia.org/wiki/Gross_domestic_product*

World Bank. (2005). *http://web.worldbank.org*

Zeithaml, V.A., Bitner, M.J., Gremler, D.D., (2006). *Services Marketing, Integrating Customer Focus Across the Firm,* Boston: McGraw-Hill Irwin.

Further Sources

American Marketing Association. http://www.marketingpower.com

Arab Strategy Forum. *http://www.dubaistrategy.com/lubna.htm*

Encyclopedia of the Orient. http://i-cias.com/e.o/uae.htm

International Leadership Association. http://www.ila-net.org/conferences/

Microsoft. *http://www.microsoft.com/middleeast*

Sheikh Mohammed. *http://www.sheikhmohammed.co.ae/english/history/history_women.asp*

United Arab Emirates. *http://www.uae.org.ae*

WF360. *http://www.wf360.com/*

Questions for Discussion

1. Analyze the integration of technology and marketing within the Tejari business. How has Tejari combined innovations in technology and marketing effectively?
2. Generalize how marketing contributes to the growth of a business. Where do you see marketing in action in this case study?
3. Predict the future trends for internet usage in the region. What trends for internet usage can be identified in the case?
4. Describe the skills, knowledge and abilities of a leader. In what ways has Sheikha Lubna's career trajectory contributed to her skills, knowledge and abilities as an entrepreneurial leader?

Notes

1. Tejari is named thus in this case study, however, following the trend of other e-commerce businesses it is referred to as 'Tejari dot com' (e.g. Amazon.com)
2. The Emirates are: Abu Dhabi, Dubai, Sharjah, Ajman, Umm Al-Qaiwain, Ras Al-Khaimah, Fujairah.
3. HDI measures a country's average achievements: longevity, knowledge, and a decent standard of living (UNDP, 2003).
4. GDP measures the amount of the economic production of a particular territory in financial capital terms during a specific time period (Wikipedia, 2005).
5. Sheikha Lubna is referred to as such by many in the region.

British English spelling has been used here but her title is also spelt elsewhere as '*Shaikha*'.

6. His Highness Sheikh Mohammed bin Rashid Al Maktoum, referred to later in the case study as Sheikh Mohammed.
7. Mona Al Marri -Dubai Press Club, Maroua Naim - Emirates Internet and Multimedia, and Anita Mehra - Department of Civil Aviation.
8. Outsourcing - a company contracts outside its own employee pool to gain a service or product.
9. Hatta, a village outside Dubai with a quiet, calm, stress free environment.
10. Metaphors are powerful devices that we use in everyday language to express ideas, information being relayed about phenomena in a vivid manner (Kemp, 2002 citing Onsman 1998, Tannen 1998)
11. Eid is the Arabic word meaning any Muslim festival.
12. Niece of H.H. Dr. Sheikh Sultan bin Mohammed Al Qasimi (Ruler of Sharjah, UAE).
13. Where Sheikha Lubna is quoted without a date, the quotation is taken from an interview with the author (Kemp, August 16th 2005).
14. American University of Sharjah, a university on the American model in partnership with the American University in Washington, D.C.
15. A University for national women.
16. Massachusetts Institute of Technology, a leader in science and technology education.
17. Ministerial positions are appointed. The government of Dubai is not democratically elected.
18. A black garment, that covers hair and body.

10

Sustainable Entrepreneurship-The Case of the Body Shop

Vinnie Jauhari

ABSTRACT

The case on **The Body Shop International (a UK based entrepreneurial initiative)** discusses the entrepreneurial initiatives of Anita Roddick. Every entrepreneur needs to answer a fundamental question – Will he create a wave or will he ride an existing wave?. The case of, "The Body Shop" is about creating a new wave where there was none. **The Body Shop International** is a high quality skin and body care retailer operating in 52 markets with 2045 stores, spanning 25 languages and 12 time zones. It has retail sales amounting to 708.7 million pounds in 2004/2005. The Body Shop business consists of a combination of company owned and franchised markets developed with direct selling organization - The Body Shop at Home and online retail in the US. The Body Shop directly employs 6788 people with approximately 14,000 additional employees working for the franchised network "as consultants in The Body Shop at Home and online retail in the US." Annually, it deals with 69 million customer transactions offering more than 900 products and 200 accessories. The supplies are screened under The Ethical Trade programme. The sole manufacturing operations are at a 100 strong factory in Glassgow. In 1999, The Body Shop was voted as the second most trusted brand in The UK by the Consumers Associations. According to 1997

Interbrand survey criteria, the company was named as 28th top brand in the world, second in the retail sector. In a 1998 report, a survey of international chief executives in The Financial Times ranked The Body Shop the 27th most respected company in the world.

This case study traces the route of growth adopted by the enterprise, the journey from a standalone unit to a firm having 2045 stores in which 25 languages are spoken.

INTRODUCTION

Entrepreneurial initiatives have interesting lessons for future entrepreneurs. As Bhide (1998) remarks, every entrepreneur needs to answer a fundamental question – Will he create a wave or will he ride an existing wave? A review of entrepreneurial successes and failures offer many interesting lessons for future entrepreneurship. Riding a rising wave may be a temporary wave. If the entrepreneurial venture lacks a truly necessary product or a service offering, it will die over a period of time. The case of "The Body Shop" is about creating a new wave where there was none. Often different motivations are attributed when exploring the reasons for the birth of an enterprise. Roddick's Body Shop endeavour seems to defy a conventional logic. It was characterized by extraordinary enthusiasm. This coupled with following an unconventional approach to business resulted in an unusual way of doing business.

This is as story about creating a brand in an unconventional manner. It is not about printing advertisements and TV commercials done the conventional way but about doing business differently-getting connected to people.

THE BACKGROUND

The Body Shop International is a high quality skin and body care retailer operating in 52 markets with 2045 stores, spanning 25 languages and 12 time zones. The Body Shop has retail sales amounting to 708.7 million pounds in 2004/2005. The Body Shop business consists of a combination of company owned and franchised markets and developing multi-channel service with direct selling organization - The Body Shop at Home and online retail in the US. The Body Shop directly employs 6788 people with approximately 14,000 additional employees working for the franchised network "as consultants in The Body Shop at Home and online retail in the US." Annually, it deals with 69 million customer transactions offering more than 900 products and 200 accessories. The supplies are screened under The Ethical Trade programme. The sole manufacturing operations are at a 100 strong factory in Glassgow. In 1999, The Body Shop was voted as the second most trusted brand in The UK by the Consumers Associations. According to 1997 Interbrand survey criteria, the company was named as 28th top brand in the world, second in the retail sector. In a 1998 report, a survey of international chief executives in The Financial Times ranked The Body Shop the 27th most respected company in the world.

The Body Shop was about the business of beauty. Here is the founder Anita Roddick's views on the beauty business:

"*I hate the beauty business. It is a monster industry selling unattainable dreams. It lies. It cheats. It exploits women. Its major product lines are packaging and garbage.*" Roddick & Miller (1991).

Elizabeth Arden once said that the cosmetics

business was the nastiest in the world. Anita Roddick related beauty with vivaciousness, energy, commitment, self esteem rather than the ideal arrangement of limbs and features as celebrated in fashion magazines and beauty pageants. She related beauty with health and well being. In her ideology, it is immoral to trade on fear, to make women dissatisfied with their bodies, to deceive a customer by making miracle claims for a product and to use a photograph of a sixteen year old to sell a cream to a forty year old. In this kind of a mindset which prevailed in the industry, an entrepreneurial idea was born. The existing beauty market had operators who were willing to sell false hopes and sell through creating a hype. In this kind of a market scenario, Anita Roddick redefined the business of beauty. She initiated a product line and made packaging irrelevant, testing on animals repulsive and spent millions on market research asking what the customers wanted and getting it for them. In an industry which thrived on advertising, here was a business which never spent money on advertising and worked for protection of the environment and involvement with community.

Anita Roddick was born Anita Perella in Littlehampton in Sussex on October 23, 1942. She was the third of four children to Glida and Donny Perella who were the owners of the Clifton Café. It was in their parents business where these children would learn their strong work ethic. She attended Maude Allen Secondary in Littlehampton and started her tertiary education to become a teacher. She went to Israel in 1962 when she got an opportunity to work and set up on a "hippie trail" visiting places like Tahiti, New Hebrides, New Caledonia, Reunion, Madagascar, Mauritius, Australia and South Africa. She got introduced to Gordon Roddick and the bond was instant and they got married in 1971 and ran their own restaurant. Her husband had set off on a trek to America when she opened a cosmetic shop in Brighton by the name of Body Shop. The shop was painted green to cover damp spots. She started with 15 products that she had made herself and which were based on the cleaning rituals of women that she had experienced on her travels. By the time her husband returned, from his 10 month trek, she had already opened a second store – she had made a deal with Ian McGlinn for a 4000 pound loan for half the business. Family and friends ran the first few shops. However, the demand for her shops and products were great, so they set up a franchise system for The Body Shop even though franchising was a relatively new concept in the UK at the time. The firm went public in 1984.

It evolved from one small shop in Brighton on the south coast of England with only 25 hand mixed products on sale to worldwide network of shops (The Body Shop, 2005). Franchising allowed for rapid growth and international expansion as hundreds of entrepreneurs worldwide bought into Anita's vision.

The evolution of the firm can be broken into the following distinct categories:

THE SEVENTIES: THE STORY BEGINS

The Body Shop operations began on 26th March 1976. The operation used natural ingredients in manufacturing creams and other cosmetics. It used natural ingredients such as – aloe vera, jojoba oil, rhassoul mud, cocoa butter and many more. In two years time (1978) the company started its franchised outlet in Brussels.

The Eighties

The operations took off with the business expanding. New Shops opened at a rate of 2 per month. 1985 was its first year as a public company. The Body Shop sponsored posters for greenpeace. In the mid-eighties, the firm also started campaigning for environmental concerns. In 1986, it created an Environmental Projects Department of its own. Save the Whale, with Greenpeace in 1986 which was the first major campaign for The Body Shop. In 1986, the first community trade product for The Body shop was a footsie roller, produced by a supplier in Southern India. This trade in footsie rollers has evolved into the current trade with Teddy Exports in India. In 1989, "Stop the Burning Campaign" called for the Brazilian Government to bring a halt to the mass burning of the tropical rainforests. One million customers signed the petition that Anita presented to the Brazilian embassy.

The Nineties

In 1990, a year after launching in the USA, there were 2500 applications for the franchise. The demand for the Body Shop product was vast driving a geographical expansion that saw the business trading in 39 countries. In 1994, the The Body Shop at Home was launched in the UK in 1994, Canada in 1995 and Australia in 1997. The Body Shop at Home was launched in 2001 in Ireland and then USA later in the year. In the US getting start up money is easy according to Roddick (Roddick, 1992). "You could get money for starting a dog's funeral service if you wanted to. In Britain it is more difficult. We have too much respect for 'business' as perceived by 'businessmen."

From early to mid 1990's, the Body Shop's forward momentum began to lag. The company's rapid expansion into the United States coupled with a franchise revolt as profits were squeezed by a half dozen me-too competitors and by similar nature based formulas from more conventional marketers created worries for informed shareholders (Davis, 2002). In 1998, after profits started collapsing, Anita Roddick handed over the business to Frenchman Patrick Gournay, a former director of food giant Danone, who subsequently resisted several takeover approaches. In 2002, Amercan born, Saunders who headed The Body Shop's American operation, took the helm in 2002, and the chain "turned the corner". He joined and launched a 100 million investment programme and The Body Shop's share price surged valuing the group at more than 464 million. He started investments in new systems and cutting staff numbers and stores. Saunders strategy has been to reinvent the chain to appeal to more affluent customers. Saunders most successful initiative has been the launch of Body Shop at Home. Consultants organize cosmetics parties in customers' homes and the concept now accounts for seven percent of Body Shop's sales. It is expected to hit 35 percent of operating profit within three years (Lyons, 2005). In 2002, the Roddicks resigned as Co-Chairs and continued to remain as non-executive directors and Anita Roddick would be a consultant for two years on product, marketing and values (Hobday, 2002).

In 1995, Anita Roddick established "The New Academy of Business". The innovative management degree addressing social, environmental and ethical issues run at The University of Bath. Today in UK, there are over 3000 consultants who have introduced 940,484 customers to The Body Shop.

Business Context for Body Care Products

The women's body care market has evolved to meet the changing consumer demands. Today's body care products must meet expectations such as anti-cellulite, anti-ageing, slimming, aromachology, intense moisturizing and sun protection factor. The Mintel Report, 2005 categorises premium brands as Clarins, Lancome, Clinique, Estee Lauder, Elizabeth Arden, Chanel, Helena Rubinstein and Shiseido as well as Molton Brown and Sisley. Mass market brands include L'Oreal and Garnier, Johnson and Johnson, Nivea, Oil of Olay, Simple and any own brand name.

Mintel Report forecasts that the women's bodycare market will show a healthy growth of 37% at current prices between 2005 and 2009 to attain a market value of £322. This is equivalent to an increase of 28% in real terms when the effects of inflation in the chemist goods are considered. The factors influencing the growth of women's bodycare products are – growing affluence in the population, increase in the number of working women and the growing number of old women

Toiletries and Cosmetics Retailing – UK, May 2000

Consumers spending on toiletries and cosmetics have increased each year with a trend to premium products and more frequent usage counterbalancing price promotional activity. The market size for toiletries, cosmetics and skin care is expected to be £4.64 billion in 2000. The high level of product development, innovation and marketing activity has stimulated growth in cosmetic sales. Boots is the most commonly used sources of toiletries and cosmetics being used as a main source of purchase by 23% of toiletries purchasers and by 38% of cosmetics/skincare purchasers. Some 17% of toiletries purchasers and

10% of cosmetics purchasers claim to use Tesco as their main source of purchase. Asda and Sainsbury's are also popular sources of toiletries purchase. The majority of consumer research respondents prefer self service when shopping for toiletries and cosmetics. Some 44% say that they buy toiletries along with the weekly shop, but only 24% buy cosmetics and 18% buy skincare products in the same way. Toiletries appear to be more price sensitive than either cosmetics or skin care. Loyalty cards can be used to good effect. Some 9% of respondents said that loyalty card promotions had persuaded them to buy products they might not have otherwise have bought. The customers are willing to buy retailer brand products as gifts and are particularly interested in buying gift products from Boots. The Body Shop and Marks and Spencer's trade research respondents feel that gift market is under exploited by retailers.

The specialist beauty retailer market is struggling. The Body Shop has suffered a period of falling sales and profits and is viewed in need for a new image. Its direct selling activities are increasing and the company is trialling new store formats and new pack designs. Virgin Vie has failed to live up to initial expectations and has changed its name to Virgin cosmetics appearing to focus on direct selling rather than retail activities. Bath and Body Works, Origins and Sephora are still in initial stages of UK development.

Traditionally popular with middle class teenage girls, Mintel's consumer research indicates that The Body Shop has extended its popularity to the 25-34 age group.

The Body Shop International Financial Performance 1994-99

UK				*International*		
Year	*Sales £m*	*Operating profit £m*	*Operating margin %*	*Sales £m*	*Operating profit £m*	*Operating margin %*
1994	91.1	11.4	12.5	104.3	18.7	17.9
1995	96.5	12.9	13.4	123.2	21.6	17.5
1996	104.8	12.9	12.3	151.7	20.8	13.7
1997	106.1	13.6	12.8	164.7	18.3	11.1
1998	116.2	11.2	9.6	176.9	26.9	15.2
1999	121.7	4.9	4.0	182.0	15.2	8.4
%change 1994-99	+33.6	-57	-8.5	74.5-18.7		-9.5

The company recognized its problems and installed a new operational and management structure, designed to focus on its retail activities and product development. Manufacturing was to be outsourced to third parties. Body Shop Direct is a direct selling operation which recruited more than 1800 consultants. In autumn 1999, the company announced the acquisition of 41 of its franchised stores. Some 134 Body Shop UK stores, representing 59% of total UK retail sales are now company owned.

The Body Shop Five Year Summary*

	2005£m	*2004*	*2003*	*2002*	*2001*
Sales	708.7	672.5	675.3	659.9	657.3
Turnover	419	381.1	378.2	379.6	374.1
Operating Profit	36.2	30.3	24.3	15.2	18.2
No. of Stores	2,045	2,007	1,968	1,954	1,830

****Source**: The Body Shop International PLC Annual Report and Accounts 2005

2005 is a landmark year for the Body Shop International as there are plans on focusing on expansion of the brand across the world with a £100 million investment plan. These expansion plans have been supported by a repositioning of the brand to the massive consumer sector (between mass & prestige in the cosmetics market). This has required a new brand identity, product innovation, a new shop design the development of a multi-channel services and compelling values campaigns to ensure that customers' needs are met. The new branding incorporates. "Passion Panels" which tell customers the stories behind ingredients and the products. The campaign to 'Stop Violence in the Home' is now making a real difference in 26 markets. Significant funds have been collected globally to support Tsunami disaster victims and promote HIV/AIDS awareness and research.

ENVIRONMENTAL PRACTICES AT THE BODY SHOP

Anita Roddick has been a very strong propagator of environmental practices. The Body Shop invested a 15% stake in a wind farm in Wales in 1994 to help offset electricity used in UK operations. In 2001, The Body Shop UK region and service centre head offices switched to Ecotricity providing them with energy from renewable sources. In addition, 127 of The Body Shop UK stores have now converted to green electricity with the rest of the stores to follow suit. In 1996, The Body Shop had initiated Against Animal Testing campaign which led to the largest ever petition with four million signatures being delivered to the European commission in 1996. The campaign led to a UK wide ban on animal testing on cosmetic products and ingredients in November 1998.

In 1997, The Body Shop was the first international cosmetics company to sign up to the Humane

Cosmetics Standard supported by leading animal protection groups. The Body Shop Value Reports in 1995 and 1997 were recognized by United Nations Environmental Program and Sustainability as trail blazing and ranked highest in their review of International Corporate Environmental Reports.

Though The Body Shop retains the naturally inspired products using traditional recipes, it has created a Community Trade Programme that creates sustainable trading relationships with disadvantaged communities around the world. The goal is to help build livelihoods and to explore trade based approaches to supporting sustainable development by sourcing ingredients and accessories from socially marginalised producer communities. The Body Shop trades with over 35 suppliers from some 25 countries.

The Mission Statement of the Body Shop is as follows:

1. "To dedicate our business to the pursuit of social and environmental change.
2. To creatively balance the financial and human needs of our stakeholders: employees, customers, franchisees, suppliers and shareholders.
3. To courageously ensure that our business is ecologically sustainable: meeting the needs of the present without compromising the future.
4. To meaningfully contribute to local, national and international communities in which we trade, by adopting a code of conduct which ensures care, honesty, fairness and respect.
5. To passionately campaign for the protection of environment, human and civil rights and against animal testing within the cosmetics and toiletries industry.

6. To tirelessly work to narrow the gap between principles and practice whilst making fun, passion and care part of our daily lives."

As a retailer with strong social and environmental beliefs, an umbrella statement, "Made With Passion" encapsulates the very DNA of The Body Shop. The strap line has been created to sum up five core values of the organization (Bawaba, 2005):

1. Against Animal Testing

"We consider testing products or ingredients on animals to be morally and scientifically indefensible."

2. Support Community Trade

"We support small producer communities around the world who supply us with accessories and natural ingredients."

3. Activate Self Esteem

"We know that you are unique and we will always treat you like an individual. We like you just the way you are.

4. Defend human rights

"We believe that it is the responsibility of every individual to actively support those who have human rights denied to them."

5. Protect our planet

"We believe that a business has the responsibility to protect the environment in which it operates locally and globally."

***Source*: The Body Shop International plc.**

The Body Shop does not sell any products which consume a disproportionate amount of energy during their manufacturer or disposal, cause unnecessary waste, use ingredients derived from threatened species or threatened environments or adversely affect other countries, particularly in the third world. The Environmental Projects Department which monitors the company's practices and products to ensure they are environmentally sound and up to date, organizes campaigns, co-ordinates global projects, gives guidance and supports local activities and liaises with pressure groups. The Body Shop uses its shops as arenas of education to proselytize among staff, customers and passers by on issues as diverse as the destruction the rainforests and the spread of AIDS. Every shop has its own local community project run by volunteers from the staff.

GOVERNANCE AND MANAGEMENT OF THE FIRM

The Body Shop Board of Directors is responsible for corporate governance in compliance with London Stock Exchange regulations and UK company Law, as well as representing the interests of shareholders and monitoring compliance with formal company policies, including ethical policy. The Board meets formally six times a year and is responsible among other things for strategy, allocation of financial resources, annual and interim results, acquisitions and disposals and risk management. For each formal meeting, the board reviews how the Company has performed against its Values.

THE PHILOSOPHY

Roddick believes "Sustainable profit does not come from an obsession with profit. Neither does change come from an explicit effort to make change, and it absolutely never comes about at the urging of outside consultants or as a result of bloodless strategic planning." Roddick is a strong propagator of work ethics and an incredible power of love as a life force. As an entrepreneur she strongly believes that one neither needs skills nor money to be successful. What one needs is optimism, humanism, enthusiasm, intuition, curiousity, love, humour, magic, fun and most of all euphoria. The fundamental philosophy of the venture is to have a product which channelises resources at the grassroot levels. It allows them to use success to act as a force for social change, to continue the education and consciousness raising of their staff to help the Third World protect the environment. She also feels that the business is to keep the company alive and breathlessly excited, to protect the workforce, to be a force for good. In her words,

"I see business as a Renaissance concept where the human spirit comes into play. It does not have to be drudgery. It does not have to be the Science of Making Money. It can be something that people genuinely feel good about".

So how does one ennoble the spirit by selling as inconsequential as a cosmetic cream? Anita Roddick answers this as creating a sense of holism, spiritual development, feeling connected to the workplace, environment and relating with one another.

"When one satisfies one's own basic material needs in a way that you are serving the needs of others honourably and humanely, one feels great even about selling a moisturizer."

Roddick believes that leaders of the company have a responsibility to make their company profitable, but not at the expense of human right abuses, the environment or preventing employees from having a sense of pride in what they do. Two of her biggest concerns are the issues of child slavery and sweatshop labor (Coomber, 2005).

PR AND THE BODY SHOP'S SUCCESS

"We built a major brand solely on PR", she replies. To do what we did without PR would have been impossible. We were interesting. We had stories" (Hill, 2005). An employee of a branding agency who was a trusted person at Body Shop says, "She was a voracious consumer of other people's ideas. We would often find ourselves being swamped with new people. If someone else came up with a brighter idea she would move on to them. She is tireless in developing programmes around the world that link The Body Shop to social issues and community issues and community initiatives (Rogers, 2005). Roddick has used her stores and products to help communicate human rights and environmental issues (2004). Globalisation makes corporations move offices and plants across the globe seeking lower wages, looser environmental regulations and the most docile and desperate workers. Businesses can go global but businesses need to listen to responsibilities which come with it."

A PR initiative involving millions of people is no ordinary effort. It comes with keeping in mind a larger picture. It comes with a passion about thinking about things differently. It comes with doing the things "the right way." Campaigns in which people sign up for a common cause generates an unprecedented loyalty. Subsequent to this, the question is not about buying a product but supporting social causes. The Body Shop campaigned on environmental and social issues. They helped in procuring more than 1million signatures to protest against the burning of rain forests. They used The Body Shop outlets as campaign platforms. The Body Shop joined hands with Greepeace in 1985. They paid for hundreds of posters showing the Greenpeace slogan that said, "You can join Greenpeace at the Body Shop." (Needle & Lecker, 1997). The socially conscious effort continues today with involvement in Save The Whale campaign, 'Friends of the Earth' and 'Amnesty International'.

The Body Shop also initiated 'Values Reporting'. It focuses on the challenges confronted by The Body Shop. They have taken a stakeholder approach which provides them with valuable ideas for improvements. The Report is not a comprehensive mapping on overview of the Values activities but an account of the key risks and opportunities facing the Body Shop over the coming years. The stakeholders have been invited to comment on the role of the Body Shop on business in general and on some of the global community's greatest challenges, such as HIV/AIDS, tropical deforestation, domestic violence, animal testing and economic development of the poorest communities.

In 2003, The Body Shop joined the Business Leaders' Initiative for Human Rights to promote the idea to other companies that defending human rights is and should be the norm and an integral part of doing business. As part of their work within this business network, a commitment on road testing a set of draft, 'Norms on Human Rights' – a list of commonsense initiatives that translate the UN Declaration of Human Rights into a form suitable for use by companies. The Body Shop has been a long standing supporter of the Forest Stewardship Council (FSC) certification scheme, which aims to ensure environmentally appropriate, socially beneficial and economically viable forestry products. In 1996, The Body Shop committed to purchasing all timber by 2010 that is certified as sustainable for use in all their retail products and shop fits. The Body Shop joined the UK based World Wildlife Fund 95 Plus Group, now the WWF Forest & Trade Network, to help them achieve the target. The company is actively encouraging and supporting suppliers to achieve FSC certification. In many countries, this is a complex, time intensive process. It is a particularly challenging for those Community Trade suppliers who are located in some of the most remote areas of the world. For example, in Siberia they worked with their Community Trade partner Altai to achieve the regions' first certified birch forest.

In a response to Management Today (2000) on what kept her ready to face the challenges time and again without going stale, Anita Roddick responded, "There is only one way for me to keep moving, stay passionate and avoid going stale. I take it personally. It being the imbalances, injustices or irrationalities that I come across every day in my job. It is why the Body Shop has spent two and a half years creating the world's biggest human rights award. It is when I joined the protests against the WTO in Seattle last year. It is why I have just been in Eastern Europe helping children on the Edge, the initiative we fund there to mark 10 years of work in Romanian orphanages." As Roddick (1991) puts it,

"The Body Shop existed for one reason only-

— To allow us to use our success as a force for social change.
— To continue the education and consciousness of our staff.
— To assist development in the Third World.
— Help protect the environment".

LESSONS LEARNED

As Roddick & Miller (1991) reflect about their organization, "To run the business, skill and money is not the answer. What you need is optimism, humanism, enthusiasm, intuition, curiosity, love, humour, magic, fun and - secret ingredient - euphoria'. None of this appears in a curriculum of a business school." The status quo stand is, 'the business of business is to make profit." The idea is to keep the company alive and breathlessly excited, to protect the work force, to be a force for good. To sum in Roddicks' (1991) words.

"I see business as a Renaissance concept where the human spirit comes into play. It does not have to be drudgery. It can be something that people genuinely feel good about".

Her ideas about people management are different. It is about making people feel connected to the workplace, it is about environment and relationships with one another, it is about making Monday-Friday a sense of being alive. It is about creating opportunities for people to do as a good job. In her words, it is about communication with passion,

"I want a society and a job that values me more than GNP,

I want work that engages the heart as well as the mind and the body I want a government that fosters friendship and nourishes the earth.

I want something in my life not just to invest in but to believe in.

Year 2000 and beyond

France-based L'Oreal paid £652 million in 2006 for the environmentally aware Body Shop in a deal that initially raised some eyebrows because of the apparent tension between the two businesses.

Post acquisition by L'Oreal , by May 2007, The Body Shop reported that pre-tax profits for the full year were up 1.38 per cent to £29.2 million, from £28.8 million last time around. Operating profits rose 6 per cent to £41.5 million. (Times Online May 2007)

The financial situation at the L'Oreal is described in Inset 1 below (L'Oreal Corporate, 2007):

Inset 1: Loreal Acquisition of ***The Body Shop***.

The acquisition of *The Body Shop*, consolidated from July 1st 2006 onwards.

Like-for-like (i.e. based on a comparable structure and identical exchange rates), the growth in the group's total sales amounted to + 5.8% at December 31st, 2006 (+ 5.7% excluding *The Body Shop*).

In the 4th quarter, the growth rate was + 6.5%.

Commenting on the figures, Mr Jean-Paul Agon, Chief Executive Officer of L'Oréal, said:

"The strong growth of our sales at the end of the year enabled us to achieve the announced growth target for 2006.

This growth was achieved thanks to the renewed dynamism in Western Europe and the remarkable performance in the new markets, particularly in Brazil, Russia, India, Mexico and China. The Body Shop delivered a good second half performance, strengthening the group's growth.

Overall, the organic growth of our brands and the significant contribution made by the acquisitions led to a strong increase in the group's sales of + 8.7%. These good figures mean that we can confirm our profit targets".

Sales by operational division and geographic zone:

At December 31st, 2006

	At 31/12/06€ million	*Growth Life-for-like At 31/12/06(*)*	*Growth Reported At 31/12/06 (*)*
By operational division			
Professional Products	2,126	+3.8%	+3.2%
Consumer Products	7,903	+5.8%	+5.4%
Luxury Products	3,773	+5.1%	+5.3%
Active Cosmetics	1,128	+12.2%	+14.4%

Cosmetics total	15,011	+5.6%	+5.6%
By geographic zone			
Western Europe	6,992	+3.5%	+3.7%
North America	3,954	+2.7%	+2.2%
Rest of the world, of which:	4,065	+12.7%	+12.8%
- Asia	1,476	+7.9%	+7.4%
- Latin America	1,021	+16.1%	+18.6%
- Eastern Europe	850	+22.0%	+24.8%
- Other countries	718	+8.5%	+4.5%
Cosmetics total	15,011	+5.6%	+5.6%
The Body Shop	435	+9.7%	
Dermatology(1)	344	+8.6%	+8.1%
Group total	15,790	+5.8%	+8.7%

(Provisional, unaudited figures).

(1) Group share, i.e., 50%

	At 4th quarter 06€ million	*Growth Life-for-like 4th quarter 06 (*)*	*Growth Reported 4th quarter 06 (*)*
By operational division			
Professional Products	528	+4.8%	+0.8%
Consumer Products	1,923	+6.5%	+2.4%
Luxury Products	1,080	+5.4%	+2.5%
Active Cosmetics	233	+11.3%	+9.5%
Cosmetics total	3,781	+6.1%	+2.5%
By geographic zone			
Western Europe	1,702	+3.1%	+3.1%
North America	990	+3.6%	-4.3%
Rest of the world, of which:	1,089	+14.0%	+8.6%
- Asia	385	+9.4%	+3.6%
- Latin America	277	+14.7%	+8.3%
- Eastern Europe	247	+23.9%	+25.0%
- Other countries	180	+11.0%	+1.5%
Cosmetics total	3,781	+6.1%	+2.5%
The Body Shop	263	+10.3%	
Dermatology(1)	105	+9.2%	+4.5%
Group total	4,148	+6.5%	+9.5%

(Provisional, unaudited figures).

(1) Group share, i.e., 50%

Anita Roddick expired on 10th of September 2007 at the age of 64(Times Online, 2007). She was suffering from Hapatitis C and had died of a haemmorage. When the company was bought by L'Oreal in 2006, the Roddicks netted roughly £130 million. Rich tributes were paid to Anita Roddick after her death. Tony Juniper, the Friends of the Earth director, said she was "a leading light of the modern green movement, and one of the first people to combine a profitable business with environmental responsibility".

John Sauven, executive director of Greenpeace, said she was a "pioneer", adding: "She was so ahead of her time when it came to issues of how business could be done in different ways, not just profit-motivated but taking into account environmental issues. When you look at it today, and how every company claims to be green, she was living this decades ago."

John Bird told BBC Radio 4's The World Tonight: "Anita was the mother of the Big Issue. There is absolutely no way the Big Issue would have happened if Anita and her husband Gordon hadn't started a business that created a social engine that drove people like us to get creative."

The executive director of a charity she founded said she inspired entrepreneurs with a conscience to "get their hands dirty". Brendan Cox, of Crisis Action, added: "Anita challenged social entrepreneurs to raise their game. 'Enough of bring-and-buy sales, let's change the global economy.' She showed that tinkering at the edges wasn't where we should stop, we should get involved, get our hands dirty and change the world trying."

In her own words

"I was a natural outsider, and I was drawn to other outsiders and rebels."

— on her childhood as the daughter of an Italian immigrant couple in an English seaside town,

"Nobody talks of entrepreneurship as survival, but that's exactly what it is and what nurtures creative thinking."

— on founding The Body Shop

"Campaigning and good business is also about putting forward solutions, not just opposing destructive practices or human rights abuses."

— on activism and business ethics

"I don't want to die rich. Money does not mean anything to me."

— on philanthropy

"Having hep C means I live with a sharp sense of my own mortality, which in many ways makes life more vivid and immediate. It makes me even more determined to just get on with things."

— on the disease that she carried for more than three decades

"The most exciting part of my life is now – I believe the older you get, the more radical you become."

— on remaining active in her sixties

Source: Times database.

REFERENCES

Al Bawaba (2005). *The Body Shop, Al Bawaba,* October 4, pp. 1.

Coomber, S. (2005). Radical Roddick, *Business Strategy Review,* 16(2), 80.

Davis, D. (2002) Unforgettable, *Global Cosmetic Industry,* New York, September, 170(9), 67

Hobday, N. (2002) The Body Shop Loses its Head, *The Daily Deal,* New York, February 12, pp. N.A.

Hill, A. (2005). "I'm an Activist. I'm too old to bullshit." *PR Week* (London ed.) London, Jun 17, 2005. pp..24, 2 pages.

Lyons, T. (2005). Body Shop is Back – and Fitter than Ever, *Knight Ridder Tribune Business News*, Washington, October 16.

Management Today (2000). From the Top, *Management Today*, October, pp. 61, 7 pages.

Lecker, M.J. & Needle, T.K. (1997) Psychoethics: A Discipline Applying Psychology to Ethics, *Review of Business*, Vol. 18, No. 3.

L'Oreal Corporate (2007) L'Oreal Press Release Retrieved from http://www.loreal.com/_en

Roddick, A. and Miller, R. (1991) *Body and Soul*, London: Vermilion.

Rogers, D. (2005). Roddick still has the flair to walk the walk, *PR Week* (London ed.) London: Jun17, pp.23, 1 page.

Times Online (2007) Anita Roddick the Green Queen who Inspired Millions, Died, Times Online, September 11, 2007. Retrieved from http://www.timesonline.co.uk/tol/news/uk/article2426935.ece

Times Online (May 2007) Profits inch higher at Body Shop, Retrieved from http://business.timesonline.co.uk/tol/business/industry_sectors/retailing/article713542.ece

Koon, C.P. (2004). Businesses have the Power, influence to do Good, *Business Times*, Kuala Lumpur, November 23.

QUESTIONS FOR DISCUSSION

1. Body Shop as a business venture gives insight on how expansion can be linked with community welfare. Draw suitable examples from the case study to highlight the achievements of Body Shop.
2. Body Shop became an extremely publicized venture. What were the driving factors which led to Body Shop emerging as a global brand.
3. What are the lessons which can be drawn from the life of Anita Roddick which could inspire new entrepreneurs to think and act differently rather than blind pursuit of wealth?

11

Barbara Corcoran's Successful Career in Real Estate: A Story of Resourcefulness, Marketing Prowess and Creativity

Janet Rovenpor

ABSTRACT

The case study on **Barbara Corcoran**, **Janet Rovenpor** gives insight into and traces the growth of her successful real estate business in New York City. Climbing to the top of the residential real estate market in New York City is no easy feat. Rents and sale prices for apartments in the borough of Manhattan have been the highest in the United States for decades. While the real-estate business has had some difficult years, especially after the stock market crash in 1987 and then again in 2001 after the terrorist attacks on the World Trade Center, demand continues to outpace supply. As the monthly inventory of available apartments declined, the average sales price for an apartment rose to over $1 million for the first time in 2004. Strict land-use regulations and high construction costs curtail the pace of new development. Real estate firms are resorting to aggressive tactics; owners lure away each other's most productive brokers; sales agents follow strangers into open houses in an attempt to earn a share of the commission; brokers post the exclusive listings of other agencies on their web-sites without the agencies' consent

The Corcoran Group has survived and prospered within this competitive residential real-estate market. As founder of the firm, Corcoran has been its source of inspiration and the creator of its prestigious public image. Corcoran established her first realty in 1973 with $1,000 from a partner, then ultimately took her share of the assets of the business and opened her own agency. Over a period of 30 years, the firm grew steadily under her stewardship from renting cooperative apartments, to selling condominiums, townhouses and lofts. Corcoran's advice on up-and-coming neighborhoods was widely sought. In 2001, she sold her firm for approximately $70 million, though she retains the position of chairwoman. At the time of the sale, the Corcoran Group operated 11 offices city-wide, employed 500 brokers and maintained a support staff of 200 and collected gross commissions of $85 million on home sales of $2.2 billion.

This case study traces the growth of the Corcoran Group over time and discusses Corcoran's personal characteristics and background. The growth of the venture is enmeshed with the literature on women entrepreneurs. Raised in Edgewater, New Jersey as one of a 10 children family, Corcoran's early years taught her how to get along with people, to stand out in a crowd, and to get what she wanted. She successfully overcame personal hardships and entered a challenging profession dominated during the 1970's by men.

With limited resources, Corcoran created brand name recognition for her firm and introduced several technological innovations that changed the nature of the real estate business. She shared information on real estate statistics by starting "The Corcoran Report", used her media contacts to enhance her firm's reputation and client base, and adopted new technologies that increased her firm's efficiency. Despite initial resistance from her employees, she created a paperless office in 1984, established email communication as the way to update real estate listings, and allowed brokers to work at home with IBM compatible computers. She produced videotapes of her properties and put them on the Internet five years before most competitors had websites. Today her namesake firm has grow domestically and internationally.

"Leaders come in two flavors, expanders and containers. The best leadership team has a mix of both. Expanders, like me, are naturally inclined to make more and more of something. Containers, like Esther, are naturally inclined to keep everything in order. One without the other always runs into trouble, because after a great idea is birthed, it needs to be nursed."

(Barbara Corcoran, 2003, p. 65)

INTRODUCTION

Climbing to the top of the residential real estate market in New York City was no easy feat. Rents and sale prices for apartments in the borough of Manhattan had been the highest in the nation for decades. While the real-estate business encountered some difficult years, especially after the stock market crash in 1987 and then again after the terrorist attacks on the World Trade Center in 2001, demand continued to outpace supply. As the monthly inventory of available apartments declined, the average sales price for an apartment rose to over $1 million for the first time in 2004 (Rich, 2005c). The upward trend for rental units was a bit more moderate. As vacancy rates dropped, average Manhattan rents increased in 2004 to $2,397 a month from $2,334 a month in 2003 (Rich, 2005c). Strict land-use regulations and high construction costs curtailed the pace of new development (see Exhibit 1 for a history of the New York City residential real estate market).

At the same time, a growing number of individuals entered the real estate profession. The total number of licensed brokers and sales agents in Manhattan reached 26,200 in 2004; an increase of 42% from 2000 (Rich, 2005a). They were attracted by the opportunity to earn commissions of 5-6% on soaring sales prices. Yet, the number of units available for sale was limited. So, there were more brokers trying to sell fewer units that were harder and harder for the average New Yorker to afford. Real estate firms resorted to aggressive tactics: owners lured away each other's most productive brokers; sales agents followed strangers into open houses in an attempt to earn a share of the commission; brokers posted the exclusive listings of other agencies on their web-sites without their consent (Rich, 2005b).

It is within this competitive residential real-estate market that The Corcoran Group survived and prospered. Barbara Corcoran, the founder of the firm, was its source of inspiration and the creator of its prestigious public image. Corcoran established her first realty in 1973 with $1,000 from a boyfriend/business partner. When the romantic relationship ended, Corcoran took her share of the assets of the business and opened her own agency. Over a period of more than 25 years, the firm grew steadily under her stewardship. From renting apartments, she moved on to selling cooperative apartments, condominiums, townhouses and lofts.

Corcoran became a real estate expert whose advice on up-and-coming neighborhoods was widely sought. In 2001, Corcoran sold her firm for approximately $70 million (Sorkin & Blair, 2001). She retained the position of chairwoman. At the time of the sale, The Corcoran Group operated 11 offices city-wide, employed 800 brokers and maintained a support staff of 200. The firm collected gross commissions of $85 million on home sales of $2.2 billion in 2000 ("NRT Agrees," 2001). Among the firm's celebrity clients were: Pamela Anderson, Robin Williams, Robert De Niro, Harrison Ford, Keith Richards, and Britney Spears (Warren, 2004).

This case study traces the growth of The Corcoran Group over time. Barbara Corcoran's personal characteristics, background and career trajectory are described in order to document the ways in which some women, with limited resources, can become entrepreneurs. Corcoran was raised in Edgewater, New Jersey and came from a family of 10 children. With so many siblings competing for the attention of their parents, she learned how to get along with people, how to stand out in a crowd and how to get what she wanted. After working at a number of different jobs at a young age, including waitress and nurse's aide, Corcoran entered the challenging real estate profession with limited experience and minimal startup funds. At the time, the ownership and management of Manhattan real estate firms were mostly in the hands of men.

BARBARA CORCORAN'S EARLY LIFE AND CAREER

Barbara Ann Corcoran was born on March 10, 1949 to Florence, a hard-working, stay-at-home mother and Edwin, a fun-loving, printing press manager who held a second job as a night watchman. She was the second of ten children in a family with an Irish heritage. Barbara grew up in a working class neighborhood in Edgewater, NJ. Her family occupied the first floor of a three family house on Undercliff Avenue. Barbara lived in a middle room with her sisters. Her brothers occupied a back room while her parents slept on a convertible sofa bed in the living room (Corcoran, 2003).

Barbara went to the Holy Rosary School where she experienced difficulty with arithmetic and reading. At age 7, she was put into a remedial classroom. She became upset when a teacher called her "stupid" (Corcoran, 2003, p. 25). The disapproving looks and old-school discipline she received from her teachers in Catholic school were counterbalanced by the love and support she got from home. Barbara's mother praised her for her great personality and wonderful imagination and her grandmother predicted that she would be wealthy one day. Throughout much of her schooling, Corcoran earned what she called "charity" D's (Kalb, 1999). Corcoran would learn later in life that she had dyslexia.

Unlike many young people in her town, Barbara did not want to get married immediately after high school (Corcoran, 2001). She went to St. Thomas Aquinas College in Sparkill, New York. She graduated in 1971 with a bachelor's degree in English. One of her positive experiences occurred in a creative writing course in college when a professor praised an imaginative essay she wrote about a raindrop (Corcoran, 2001). In her last year in college, Corcoran worked as a waitress at a diner in Fort Lee, NJ. She started dating a customer, Ray Simone, who was several years her senior. He was divorced and the father of three children. At his suggestion, she moved out of her family residence and got a room at the Barbizon Hotel for Women in Manhattan. Simone footed the bill and gave her some money to buy a new outfit. After finding a job, Corcoran moved out of the hotel. She rented an apartment with two other women on East 86th Street (Corcoran, 2003).

Corcoran worked as a receptionist for the Giffuni

Brothers. Andrew and his brother, Joseph, were real estate developers who at the time owned apartment buildings in Manhattan and Brooklyn. In order to supplement her income, Barbara worked on the weekends renting apartments for one of the Giffuni brothers' sons. She found that she could make more money in one weekend than she did all week (Sorter, 2003). There were two additional benefits. Barbara enjoyed talking to people and people liked her for her honest manner. She derived a sense of satisfaction from having the keys to open and lock doors around town. She felt in control. This paralleled her enjoyment of the waitressing job. At the diner, she controlled her own territory (tables and countertop) and could charm customers with her outgoing personality (Sorter, 2003).

After several months, Barbara decided that she would like to run her own realty. She estimated that the startup costs were minimal. All that was really needed was a telephone and access to the advertisements in the Sunday edition of the *New York Times* (Corcoran, 2003). She asked Simone, who was a real estate developer, for $1,000. He gave her the funds but went in as a partner with 51%, compared to her 49%, ownership of the business. The company, "Corcoran-Simone;" operated its rental service out of Barbara's apartment starting in 1973.

Corcoran's first commission came from renting one of her former employer's apartments. She found a way to differentiate a one bedroom apartment from all the others that were advertised in the newspaper. She convinced Joseph Giffuni to put up a wall to separate the living room from the bedroom. She was able to rent it for $20 more a month by featuring it as a "one bedroom plus den." Corcoran spent most of her one-month's commission of $340 on a fancy coat that she bought at the upscale store, Bergdorf Goodman. She felt she needed to look the part. If she looked good, she would feel more confident and people would assume that she was successful. Once she created the image of success, she would feel pressured to work hard to live up to the image she had projected (Corcoran, 2003). Corcoran was so successful, with clients coming in and out of her apartment, that her landlord thought she was a prostitute and sent her an eviction notice. Barbara convinced him to let her try to rent out some of his vacant apartments. He agreed and she ended up getting even more business.

In 1976, Corcoran made her first sale. It came about by chance. Her client, an engineer working for Union Carbide, was being transferred from St. Louis to NY. The engineer told her he was interested in buying not renting. Up until that time, Corcoran had been solely a rental agent. She decided to show the client different neighborhoods in Manhattan in order to buy time and prevent him from going to someone else. That night, she responded to newspaper ads and set up appointments for the next day. She sold the engineer a two bedroom cooperative apartment for $54,500 on East 84th Street. She earned a commission of $3,800 which was much more than the fee she had been receiving for renting apartments (Personal Communication, September 28, 2005). Needless to say, that gave her an incentive to continue selling.

Not everything proceeded smoothly. Corcoran suffered a major setback in her personal life when Simone told her that he was going to marry her secretary. It took Corcoran almost two years to get the nerve to tell Simone that she wanted to divide the assets of the business and go out on her own. Since Simone was the majority shareholder, Corcoran allowed him to take the first pick of the company's assets. Simone kept the company office, main telephone number, and top-producing salesperson. Corcoran got what she secretly wanted the most. She needed Esther Kaplan, a dedicated and well-organized sales agent, to help her run the business. She also took with her seven out of the fourteen salespeople. Towards the end of the 1970's, Barbara opened "The Corcoran Group" in an office a few flights above her former location.

On the one hand, Corcoran benefited from excellent timing. Co-op sales in Manhattan had just started to rise again after having fallen from their all-time peak in 1969 (Sterne, 1976). New Yorkers had regained their confidence in the fiscal health of the city and were attracted to its good private schools, convenience to work and shopping, and rich social and cultural life (Sterne, 1976). On the other hand, the residential real estate market was not very friendly to women. In 1975, fewer than 4 out of 10 full-time sales agents were women; they earned 60% of what men did (Kennedy, 1992). By 1987, 2/3rds of sales agents were women. The National Realtor's Association reported that 28% of its members in the Women's Council had ownership interests in real estate firms in 1990 (data for prior years were never compiled; Kennedy, 1992). In a 2005 survey, the Women's Council of Realtors found that only 22% of its respondents had any ownership interest in their companies even though women made up 52% of real estate brokers (Evans, 2005).

The attitude of some male professionals to women was appalling. Al Klipel, president of Havendale Realty in Long Island, was quoted as saying in a national newspaper that he did not want women in the home resale area of his agency: "Men and women just don't mix in business . . . A woman should be home taking care of her house and children" (Rejnis, 1970, p. 150). Women in sales were viewed with suspicion because the residential market had once consisted of women with social connections who had fallen on difficult financial times and were merely "dabbling" in sales. The assumption was that women were not knowledgeable about tax laws, cooperative regulations and zoning ordinances (Rejnis, 1970). Women faced even greater gender bias in office leasing (Rejnis, 1970), commercial sales (Goodman, 1981) and realty management and construction (Fried, 1977).

The predominance of men in real estate made Barbara Corcoran feel like an outsider. She felt it every time she was in a large room at an industry conference. She realized that she did not have the same background as the "silver spoon boys" of real estate who were well-connected, went to all the right schools and came from wealthy families. Yet, Corcoran did not let the financial and cultural gap bother her. She was too busy trying to develop her business so that she could pay her bills (Personal Communication, September 28, 2005).

BARBARA'S FRESH START AS HEAD OF THE CORCORAN GROUP

Barbara Corcoran reported that she was apprehensive right before the opening of her own realty (Corcoran, 2003). Even though Ray Simone had never played an active role in running Corcoran-Simone, he had been her companion and someone who had given her a start in the business. He constantly told her that she was "great" at everything she did — positive feedback that she had gotten only from her mother. Now, she was on her own. Corcoran decided to prepare carefully. She developed a plan for how she would greet her employees and organize the work setting. She drew from her prior experience about what worked and what did not in managing a real estate agency. Barbara announced to her employees that they would be eating breakfast together every Monday morning between 9:30 am and 10:15 am. The breakfasts enticed salespeople to arrive at the office on time for the start of the work week. They served as forums within which to communicate information, praise salespeople in front of their peers, and promote new properties.

Barbara remembered how her mother had an efficient method for everything needed to run a well-organized household with 10 children (Corcoran, 2003). Socks were found in the sock drawer; laundry was sorted into white and colored piles as well as into heavy and light fabrics; polished shoes were dried on radiators the night before a school day. She used these memories to help her organize her office. Corcoran created a color-coded filing system so that listing information for studio apartments would be recorded on white cards, one-bedrooms on yellow cards, two bedrooms on blue cards, and three bedrooms and larger on pink cards. This made it easier for salespeople working with a client to retrieve information quickly based on a client's needs. It also reduced the number of mistakes in filing. It is possible that Corcoran's insights also stemmed from her experiences with dyslexia. For people with learning differences, multi-sensory stimuli — words, colors, images, and smells — aid the learning and retention process. Dyslexics often find that pastel colored forms are easier to read than white colored forms (Msonthi, 2000). Such strategies can be of assistance to employees everywhere.

Commission request forms were green. On the back, Corcoran developed a list of questions.

Salespeople were instructed to indicate where they got their client; whether or not the client answered an ad, went to an open house or were referred by a friend or business associate; and how long the property had been on the market before it sold. Commissions would not be paid without checking the appropriate boxes on the forms. The information recorded by salespeople helped Corcoran predict emerging trends. In the late 1970's, for example, she discovered that property values on Manhattan's West Side were catching up to those on the East Side. Buyers in their 30's, whose affluent parents lived on the East Side, were at the forefront of the buying spree. Despite skepticism from others, Corcoran opened a large office on the West Side (Corcoran, 2003).

Corcoran believed that it was important to expand a business before being ready so that managers would feel pressure to work harder to justify the expense and the increased size. As Corcoran said, "Common wisdom dictates that businesses often fail because they grow too fast and outstrip their cash flow. I have found that businesses get bigger faster when forced to run like hell to pump up their cash flow. Just as it's never really the right time to have a baby, it's never the right time to open your next office. For me, *now* always proved to be the best time" (Corcoran, 2003, p. 82). Even though it took time for early investments in new neighborhoods to generate revenues, they gave Corcoran a significant head start on her competitors.

The Corcoran Group grew to 60 employees and performed well during the early and mid 1980's. This period of time is noted for Barbara's marketing efforts. In 1981, Barbara wrote *The Corcoran Report*. Real estate firms, especially in New York City, rarely shared information with one another or with the public.

Corcoran saw how she could satisfy the hunger for basic real estate statistics. She summarized the data that were already conveniently compiled and stored in her color coded filing system and sent her report to the *New York Times.* The report announced that the average selling price of a 4 1/2 room two bedroom, luxury apartment in Manhattan in the first six months of 1981 was $255,000 (Horsley, 1981). Apparently, the calculations were based on only 11 apartments. Yet, it was a great publicity stunt. "People started ringing me for comments, and all of a sudden everybody in the business knew who I was," said Corcoran (quoted in Sherman, 2004b, p. 1). The report was one of the first of its kind; every major brokerage subsequently issued its own assessment of the market.

The real estate industry suffered a major downturn when the stock market crashed in 1987. Wall Street executives, who had bought property and who had contributed to the rise in housing prices in the previous years, were laid off. Large corporations, including JC Penney, Mobile Oil and Exxon moved their headquarters out of New York City (Richter, 1990). Vacancy rates rose and property values declined. Tenants could not pay their rents; owners defaulted on their mortgages. No longer could single properties could be sold or "flipped" three or four times in a few months (Grant, 1990). Large real estate developers experienced cash flow problems. Martin J. Raynes, for example, scrambled to renegotiate his bank loans on buildings he was in the process of converting to cooperatives and condominiums (Lenzner, 1990). Donald Trump, a long-time symbol of real estate success, faced the prospects of bankruptcy and was forced to sell the Plaza Hotel and the Trump shuttle (which he had recently purchased from Eastern Airlines).

In 1990, four large residential brokerages closed (Dullea, 1990). Many others were forced to cut back on staff and expenses. Small boutique firms had to find creative ways to stay in business. The Stern Organization, for example, packaged unsold shares in cooperative apartment buildings and sold them at discounted prices to foreign investors (Grant, 1990). Eastern Consolidated decided to focus on information gathering; it hired top performing brokers from bankrupt firms and took advantage of their networks of contacts (Grant, 1990).

The Corcoran Group, too, was faced with debt and almost closed. Corcoran had just opened a new and renovated Madison Avenue office with 5,500 square feet. She had used most of a $350,000 loan from Citibank to pay for it (Barron, 1993). Sales declined steeply. Corcoran had trouble paying the company's bills. She resorted to extreme measures to survive. She took a job as a sales manager for the Albanese brothers who had built a new condominium complex across from the United Nations. Corcoran also continued to teach real estate courses at New York University. Refusing financial assistance from some of her close employees, Corcoran sold her apartment in Manhattan and moved into a rental. She mortgaged her weekend home in Pawling, New York for $450,000. She used her extra income to keep the business afloat. Her spunk as well as her sacrifices were noted by her employees who worked harder as well. "If you expect people to deliver 150% in bad times, it looks better if you're doing 150% yourself," noted Corcoran (quoted in Schleier, 2003).

The firm's turnaround came in April 1991 when Corcoran developed a plan to sell 88 apartments owned by Bernie Mendik and his investment partner, the Equitable Life Assurance Society. The apartments had been on the market for three years, were not very attractive and came with high maintenance fees. She proposed a one-day sale in which all apartments of similar sizes would be sold for the same price regardless of their condition or location. All studio apartments, for example, on high or low floors, with or without kitchens, would be priced at $49,500. There would be no monthly maintenance fees for two years. The apartments would be sold on a "take it or leave it" basis with those customers showing up first getting their first choice of apartments (Corcoran, 2003). Since she did not have funds to spend on marketing, Barbara asked her salespeople to tell only their closest friends and suggested that interested buyers had better come early (Barron, 1993). The one-day fixed-price auction was a success. There was a large turnout. The sales event generated $1 million in commission for The Corcoran Group.

Traditional auctions, popular during soft housing markets, sold properties to the highest bidders. What was unusual about Corcoran's approach was the fixed-price, one-day sale and the use of word-of-mouth advertising to generate interest in the sale. Corcoran realized that these types of "sweepstake" sales created excitement (Kennedy, 1991). As she wrote, "Competition always communicates the message that there's a good deal to be had . . . buyers could plainly see the number of customers ahead of them and behind them in line. Even the customers who weren't sure they wanted an apartment decided they wanted one as the litter thinned" (Corcoran, 2003, p. 164). Corcoran held these auctions more than once.

The cooperative and condominium market soon rebounded. Corcoran estimated that her firm entered the real estate slump ranked 17 or 18 in the industry and emerged as number 4 (Pinckey, 2004). By 1993, Corcoran's net worth surpassed $1 million (Barron, 1993). In 1997, *Crain's New York Business* ranked The Corcoran Group as being the second largest residential real estate brokerage in New York City. Its property sales reached $925 million and it employed 280 agents (Cullen & Lopez, 1999). It maintained its number 2 rank for the following three years. In 2001, property sales were 2.4 billion and 670 agents worked for The Corcoran Group (Rodrigues, Southwood & Mason, 2002). This placed the firm in 3rd place (see Exhibit 2). Nationwide, The Corcoran Group's sales rank put it in 38th place in 2001 (Bresnahan, 2002).

BARBARA CORCORAN'S BOLD MARKETING STRATEGIES

Corcoran's basic marketing strategy was to put herself and her firm in the limelight. She did everything she could to draw attention to her business. She believed that her greatest asset was as a marketer and not as a real estate broker (Kalb, 1999). She realized the importance of having the right look and creating name recognition early in life. As a child, Barbara got into trouble for engraving her name in a newly cemented retaining wall belonging to one of her neighbors. Her home in Edgewater, New Jersey, was always easy to find because it was located right under the big "L" of the Palisades Amusement Park sign. When she couldn't compete with a well-rounded waitress at the Fort Lee Diner, she put ribbons on her pigtails to stand out (Corcoran, 2003).

Corcoran used similar tactics in business. She put her own image on large billboards with the catchy slogan, "Where do you want to live?" She advertised her firm's sales agents as the "Power Brokers" even when the agency was still small (Pinckney, 2004). She had the photographs of her agents air-bushed so they would look younger on their business cards (Warren, 2004). She did things with style. She paid for television advertisements to launch her web site, www.corcoran.com, with the 1951 popular song by Rosemary Clooney called, "Come On-A My House," playing in the background.

Corcoran was not the only person in the industry to recognize the importance of a slogan, a gimmick or a trademark. Clark Halstead, founder of the Halstead Property Company, also personalized himself and his company. He imported an English taxi cab and painted the firm's circular logo on its side; he spoke about the real estate market on his own radio talk show; he formulated a plan to drop thousands of ping pong balls (with the firm's logo) on concert goers in Central Park (Rozhon, 2001).

Corcoran differentiated between advertising and publicity (Corcoran, 2003). Advertising was expensive; the firm's budget was $11 million annually (Philippidis, 2003). Advertising required a firm to convince others that it was reputable and offered a valuable service. People either believed the message or did not. Publicity, which was free, required getting the attention of the media. Reporters were eager for good stories and it was important for Corcoran to become one of their reliable sources. When a major newspaper portrayed a positive image of a company, everyone believed it. She used three techniques to publicize her firm (Corcoran, 2003):

* She linked her company to news, hearsay and rumors that were already in circulation. When Corcoran heard that Madonna was house hunting for an apartment in New York City, she drew up

a checklist of what the singer might be looking for (e.g., security, space, and a view). She sent copies to the media. Soon, she was asked to comment on CNN. People began to assume that Madonna was one of Corcoran's clients. As a result, the firm did attract a number of celebrity clients. Corcoran used the same tactic when she heard that the Clintons were looking for a house in Westchester County, New York (Kalb, 1999).

* Since it was a breach of confidentiality for agents to talk about their own famous clients, Corcoran discussed the sales of her competitors and often got credit for them. A competitor once sold a Park Avenue triplex for a record $37 million. Corcoran called it a "steal of a deal" and was interviewed on CBS news (Kwon, 2003). The anchor introduced her as the agent that made the sale. Even though Corcoran corrected him, people still thought of her as the agent.

* She tried to think of ways to stand out and be interesting. Corcoran hired a professional dog trainer to groom and shape the behavior of dogs of clients so that cooperative boards would be more accepting of them. She used a ritual performed by American Indians to remove evils spirits from an apartment whose owners had been involved in a violent marriage. The press loved such off-beat stories.

Another way that Corcoran satisfied the media's and the public's need for information was to continue to issue *The Corcoran Report* twice a year. She published it even when the real estate news was negative, withstanding pressure from her competitors. They had wanted her to skip the report during the real estate slump of the late 1980's (Dullea, 1990). In 2004,

The Corcoran Group dedicated a 6 figure budget to *The Corcoran Report* and employed three staff members (including a copywriter) for each document. An outside creative agency designed the layout. Each print run totaled almost 300,000 copies (Sherman, 2004b).

Corcoran also sent the media other catchy and irresistible items. Her brokers identified 10 buildings in Manhattan that were receptive to trick-or-treaters on Halloween. Residents of these "kid-friendly" buildings put up decorations, held parties and placed welcome stickers on their doors (Malanga, 1997). More recently, the firm compiled a list of regions in the country that were attractive to seniors ("Astoria Ranks," 2005). Astoria, Queens was the best place for people who wanted some peace and quiet (the average home cost $156,000) and Sparks, Nevada was the best place for physically active adventure seekers (the average home cost $250,000). On the ABC morning show, "The View," Barbara Corcoran identified the "sexiest suburbs" in the US, with La Jolla, California on the top of the list. The criteria used were: a suburb's proximity to a major city; aesthetic appeal; average age of residents; nightlife; and number of shops, plastic surgeons and gyms (Huppke, 2005). Thus, Corcoran established herself as an authority on life-styles and trends.

As these examples show, Corcoran had a deep understanding of people and sometimes intuitively used psychology to get what she wanted. People loved to hear about celebrities. Whenever she could she tried to give the public a peek into their private lives. By linking her company with famous people, she could bring in more business. Corcoran even hired a psychotherapist, who was an expert in the family dynamics of wealthy individuals, to teach her brokers how to sell to celebrities and how to present them to cooperative boards ("How to Be," 2001). They learned that some celebrities were "introverts" who needed time and space to think about what they had seen. Celebrities should be coached to dress simply and not wear a lot of jewellery or make-up when meeting board members. Corcoran became a celebrity herself and her firm attracted other brokers, such as Dennis Mangone, who wanted to create "a brand within a brand" (Sherman, 2004a).

Corcoran promoted her business knowing that people tended to want the same things that other people wanted. During difficult economic times, buyers rushed to her one-day auctions and purchased slow-moving apartments. One of her agents once asked her for a Bentley and a chauffeur to show condominiums to an important client. Corcoran agreed but made sure that the agent was interrupted by calls on her cellular phone. The client was led to think that the agent was more in demand than she actually was. This probably left a favorable impression on the client. If the agent was working with lots of important clients, she must be good, so he should stay with her until he finds a suitable condominium for himself.

People also responded to lists. Buyers routinely check *Consumers Report* ratings for appliances; magazines publish a range of guides such as the *Fortune 500* list of major US corporations or the 100 Best Companies for Working Mothers. Lists help people to organize information and to simplify the many choices they have to make in their lives. With Corcoran's lists, seniors could locate an appropriate place to live; young people could move to trendy cities. People's memories are unreliable. Research has found that some individuals regard news stories as true even though they were retracted by the media because of an error (Begley, 2005). People were willing to assume that Corcoran was the agent for some of the largest real estate transactions in Manhattan even when she denied it.

Barbara Corcoran's emphasis on branding and marketing was taken to new heights by other residential real estate firms in 2004 and 2005. Brokers used names of celebrities to sell homes in several ways. A broker at Keller Williams Realty in California advertised a "fabulous beachfront hacienda," that had previously belonged to Dudley Moore for $4.35 million. He admitted that he had hoped to sell the home for a premium to a fan of the actor (Kaufman, 2004).

Developers, often at the suggestion of their sales agents, offered discounts on luxury condominiums or first choice on a unit in a building still under construction, to famous people in exchange for use of their names to promote sales. A celebrity publicist might be asked to "leak" news of the purchase to the media or the famous person might appear on a billboard (Schoeneman, 2005). In an industry preview party for the Cipriani Club Residence (55 Water Street), marketing agents handed out promotional brochures with photographs of model Naomi Campbell, actor Mickey Rourke, and the daughter of an Italian knitwear family, Margherita Missoni. All three received discounts on apartments in exchange for permission to use their photographs in marketing materials. Actor Jeremy Piven got his first choice on an apartment in the Sundari Lofts & Tower in Manhattan. He promised to attend the ribbon-cutting ceremony when the building was completed. Such celebrities might attract additional buyers, cause prices in the building to rise, and sell the unit before even moving in.

Developers of several new buildings began to market their apartments as luxury brands. They featured habitats designed by well-known architects and interior decorators. They included the usual amenities — Miele appliances and Italian marble floors — and more. Downtown by Philippe Starck (where a studio was priced at $410,000 and a three bedroom duplex was priced at $3.5 million) offered a yoga-ballet studio and a bowling lane as a bonus for residents. Tenants at the Orion Condominium (where a one bedroom was $465,000 and a 2 bedroom penthouse was $1.9 million) could eat breakfast every morning on the 29th floor lounge. As Pamela Liebman, CEO of The Corcoran Group, remarked, "It used to be location, location, location. Now it's location *and* lifestyle" (cited in Robledo, 2005).

BARBARA CORCORAN'S USE OF INFORMATION TECHNOLOGY

The residential real estate industry was notoriously slow in embracing new technologies. The Internet, which had the potential of linking buyers and sellers of properties directly, was seen as a great threat to the lucrative commission structure in the business (Barron, 1999). In 1999, it was estimated that US home sales generated approximately $30 billion a year for sales agents (Barron, 1999). In 2004, the amount more than doubled — to $61.1 billion (Rich, 2005a). Agents typically charged 5-7% commission fees on sales of homes. Web-based sales would lower or even eliminate these commissions. Nonetheless, Barbara Corcoran was an early adopter of new technologies to both improve office efficiency and to sell properties on the World Wide Web.

In 1984, Corcoran took the lead in encouraging

her offices to go paperless. She decided that 2,000 hand-written cooperative and condominium listings filed in binders would be destroyed. She held a book burning party in her home. Approximately 1/3rd of her brokers refused to discard their listings books (Corcoran, 1994). They held on to them as if they were "life preservers in a sinking ship" (Personal Communication, September 28, 2005). The brokers never thought that computers would work. So, for almost a year, Corcoran ran two parallel systems. She installed a DOS-based computer system with data entry capabilities and maintained the hard copy filing system in which new listings replaced old listings in loose-leaf binders.

By 1994, computerized databases held more than 8,500 listings that were updated daily. Previously, it took 4 people to make 225 new entries. Now, one person was able to enter 900 new entries. Brokers also filled out the dozens of forms needed for each property from their terminals (Corcoran, 1994). Next, floor plans were computerized so that they could be faxed via the computer directly to buyers. Before personal computers, brokers would individually log changes to their listings in the office. With e-mail, these messages could be quickly sent to all the brokers in the office.

The next step was to allow brokers, especially those who cared for children or those who wanted to work part-time, to telecommute. Corcoran could expand her sales force without significantly increasing her overhead costs. It was a "poor man's way of expanding the market share," noted Corcoran (Personal Communication, September 28, 2005). By 1996, 1/4th of Corcoran's 220 brokers worked outside of the office (DeNitto, 1996). They used IBM-compatible personal computers and were connected to the office's mainframe via modems. Two underperforming brokers, whom Corcoran had wanted to fire, asked to work from home. As a result, their sales quadrupled; they became two of the firm's top performers because they worked best outside the office's competitive environment. The strategy was cost-effective. Corcoran paid for the computers and the telephones but she did not have to rent new office space or furnish it. Owners reported that it cost between $25,000 to $45,000 (including rent) for each agent to work in the office (DeNitto, 1996).

In May 1993, Corcoran opened a residential real estate gallery on Broadway and 81st Street (near the gourmet shop, Zabar's). The entrance to the store featured a sign on a dark green canopy which read: "Come in and Browse!" It was a revolutionary concept — a "store, a library and a gallery all in one" — noted Corcoran (quoted in White, 1993, p. 31). Apartment hunters could look through the real estate offerings in the same manner that they might look for a pair of shoes in a department store. The difference was that the gallery was "high-tech." Video monitors displayed apartments, lofts and townhouses that were being offered by The Corcoran Group exclusively. Signs, like "Find Your Two-Bedroom Here," helped visitors to zero in on what they wanted. They could use computers to access information on more than 6,000 property listings in Manhattan. They could also take home floor plans. Staff members were available to answer questions and help with searches. Some people used the computers just to get an indication of what their own homes were worth.

The gallery's décor was changed periodically just like the window dressings in a retail store. In August, for example, the window featured a summer theme and displayed the outdoor spaces of penthouses (White,

1993). The setup cost $135,000 and had an annual operating budget of $180,000 (White, 1993). Within the first six months after its debut, the gallery had been visited by over 2,000 people; it generated 12 sales, 150 listings, and 10 exclusives (Temliak, 1993). In December 1993, Corcoran opened a second gallery on Hudson Street in Tribeca. "People use the store to get familiar with a neighborhood, obtain an overview of product availability and winnow down the selection of apartments to look at. It takes some of the time-consuming leg-work out of home hunting," said Corcoran (quoted in Temliak, 1993).

In 1994, Corcoran launched Corcoran.com. She established the web-site before any other large real estate agency in New York City. Interestingly, her motive was not profit-oriented. She did it to "save face" (Personal Communication, September 28, 2005). She had just spent a substantial sum of money videotaping properties which her brokers refused to distribute to their clients. By putting the videos on the web, she could claim that her project had a successful outcome. Her move onto the web was fortunate. Statistics by the National Association of Realtors showed that the percentage of home buyers who used the Internet to look for houses rose from 2% in 1995 to 75% in 2004 (Koprowski, 2003; O'Donnell & Kirchhoff, 2005).

The Corcoran web-site was soon reconfigured to include floor plans, photographs of apartments, email links to brokers, 3D virtual tours, and a database enabling prospective buyers and renters to search for properties with specific amenities, in different neighborhoods and within certain price ranges (Blair, 2000). In 1999, a chat line was added. Web users could ask a broker questions between the hours of 9 am and 5 pm. As part of their training, brokers were required to learn how to explain what a co-operative apartment was in 20 words or less ("Real Estate," 1999). In 2002, 2003 and 2004, Corcoran.com received the "Best Real Estate Web Site" award given by the Web Marketing Association (Bresnahan, 2004). It attracted 1.2 visitors a month.

The web site was successful because Corcoran staff listened to end users and responded to their feedback. Employees introduced a feature that enabled clients to search for agents by face. A client might have met a broker at a party but had forgotten his name or lost her business card. Clients could choose an agent online who spoke the same language or shared the same interests. A Corcoran vice president once make a valuable contact with a client in the UK because she rode a vintage bicycle (Whitaker, 1998). The site could be translated into different languages and used by clients around the world. Clients could register their "dream home" with information on the right location and right price. They would be notified by e-mail as soon as a property matching their description became available (Bresnahan, 2004). The site's greatest value seemed to be the convenience it afforded young, technology-savvy buyers. Buyers used to work with an agent for several months and physically visit 20 or 30 different properties before choosing one. Buyers who used the Internet came to a broker with lots of prior knowledge and might see between 4 to 8 properties during a month's time before making a decision (Russer, 1998; Levine, 2004).

"Winning over the sales associate is the piece of the tech puzzle that's been the most undervalued," warned Corcoran (quoted in Freedman, 2000, p. 42). How, then, did she handle initial resistance from employees? Brokers refused to discard their listing books. Sales people never returned e-mail messages from clients. Brokers eventually realized how cumbersome the old filing system was. Every day they would receive new listings recorded on 7 to 8 sheets of paper. They would take them home, cut the listings into slips of paper and paste them into their binders. They would then try to remove the old listings that were pasted on the loose-leaf paper. It slowly became apparent that they could let the computer do the work for them. Corcoran personally wrote e-mail messages with apologies to clients who had never heard from the sales people. She patiently waited for about three years before her sales people became comfortable with e-mail (Personal Communication, September 28, 2005).

Extensive training and the adoption of user-friendly systems played a key role in the successful implementation of new technologies. Training was made "easy" and "convenient" (Freedman, 2000). In 1998, for example, the company offered 15 training classes a week for 150 people; the content covered included computers, email and the Internet. The information systems department ran a "help desk" for people with questions about the company's software and the Internet. The department's director made sure that those employees who used the help desk frequently were persuaded to enroll in classes (Russer, 1998).

Most importantly, the Internet was given a "human face" (Freedman, 2000). On the firm's intranet, brokers could view photographs of their colleagues who had made web-based sales and read histories of the clients who bought properties using the World Wide Web. The message was that real people were making real deals. Six buyers were invited to a sales meeting at the St. Regis hotel. Over breakfast, they explained passionately how the Internet had helped them search for real estate. Several of the buyers were fairly prominent individuals in the news and television industry. They had busy schedules which prevented them from relying on the *New York Times* for leads regarding suitable apartments. It was more convenient for them to surf the web; they found what they liked on the Corcoran site. They could e-mail the listing agent to express their interest in a property in the middle of the night. "For the associates, the buyers were living proof that the Internet is not about computers but about people," remarked Corcoran (quoted in Freedman, 2000, p. 42).

The technologies used by real estate brokers and their firms became increasingly sophisticated. By 2005, listing agents could go to their seller's home with digital cameras and create high quality, color brochures within a day. The photographs were quickly posted on the agency's web site. Using wireless access to the Internet (via laptop computers, Blackberry devices or personal digital assistants), agents could find the price, number of bedrooms and square footage of a home whose for sale sign a client had just seen while driving around in a car. Offices began to use a centralized scheduling desk. A prospective buyer might call an agency and find that his or her agent is out showing properties. A staff member could send an electronic message to the agent's Blackberry and propose a time and place for the agent and the client to meet. The agent had the option of accepting or rejecting the details of the appointment (Rafter, 2004). By 2010, experts at a real estate conference in California predicted that a typical home would go from listing to signed sales agreement in just one hour (Collins, 2005)!

BARBARA CORCORAN CREATES A UNIQUE ORGANIZATIONAL CULTURE

Corcoran's philosophy, although never articulated in any one place, consisted of: (a) projecting a love for New York City and its residents; (b) maintaining an open and supportive environment for her staff and brokers; and (c) creating a relaxed and fun place to work. Corcoran showed that she really cared about the city in which she built her business. The border on the glass-enclosed reception area of her main office once featured quotes about New York. One from 1910, by O. Henry, the American short-story writer, read: "It couldn't have happened anywhere but in little old New York" (Ricci, 2004).

After the sale of her company to NRT Incorporated in 2001, Corcoran had planned a lavish party for September 25 at Rockefeller Center's ice skating rink. She cancelled those plans after the terrorist attacks on the World Trade Center. Instead, she spent $100,000 to take 700 brokers out to dinner in 40 different downtown restaurants. She wanted to show her continued support and commitment to such badly affected neighborhoods as Tribeca and Soho (Schoeneman, 2001). Many of Corcoran's employees became regular patrons of these restaurants. The Corcoran Group closed its doors to business on the first anniversary of 9/11. Four years later, a senior vice president, Barrie Mandel, opted not to hold open houses on September 11 — even though the date fell on a Sunday (the busiest day of the week for residential real estate). "Commerce and business as usual and profit motives don't belong on that day," said Mandel (quoted in Kantor, 2005, p. G1).

Corcoran created a friendly, supportive and family-like atmosphere in her firm. It was important that her sales people learn to "love each other" (Personal Communication, September 28, 2005). Employees hiked and played softball, bridge, and golf together. Corcoran believed that her job was to be a "grandparent," not a "nervous parent" to her employees (Fitzgerald, 2003). A good manager should not try to control the behavior of employees. He or she should praise them, nurture them and even spoil them. A former employee remarked, "Barbara always made you feel you were very important to her, and because of that you wanted to do well for her. She really wanted to hear what you had to say, and she actually incorporated it into the business" (quoted in Witchel, 2003, p. 9).

Corcoran hated secrets and expected her employees to be open and honest with one another. Sales people were naturally competitive; they chased after the same properties and the same customers. She had to make them feel like friends and share information. Corcoran was quick to fire a salesperson — even a most productive one — because she did not abide by the firm's "share and share alike" listing policy. The policy required that all sales people post new property listings in the office files within one hour of getting the listing. Corcoran publicly confronted the sales woman and found piles of papers in her desk drawer with information about apartments that she had hidden from the others (Corcoran, 2003). The incident became known as the "Tale of the Pocket Listing Lady." Every new salesperson joining the firm heard about it for years to come (Corcoran, 2003).

The Corcoran Group was also a fun place to work. Corcoran once hired five rickshaws for $40 an hour to take some of her salespeople and their families to see the Christmas tree at Rockefeller Center (Barron, 2000).

She paid a street vendor to attend a meeting and hand out cotton candy (Kalb, 1999). She held a party for 75 executives at Mohonk Mountain in the Catskills. The 136 year old dress code in the dining room was "no jeans or sneakers, men to wear coats." For this party, employees were required to wear pajamas and slippers ("We Hear," 2005). Fun had a purpose. It helped Corcoran develop effective people skills; she learned that barriers broke down when people played together (Gleeson, 2003).

The office décor and company amenities reflected the values of openness, support and fun. As CEO Pamela Liebman noted, "You can see the whole philosophy the way these open offices were designed with lots of glass. That's the kind of environment we have. The most important thing here is that our brokers are feeling good and set up so they can maximize their earning potential, which is why we have free sodas, a massage therapist who comes in twice a week, and yoga classes. We're a very forward-thinking company. My motto is: We have the power and the strength of the big, but the heart of the small" (quoted in Ricci, 2004). When The Corcoran Group was sold to a subsidiary of the Cendant Corporation in 2001, the buyers promised to keep the firm's culture intact. NRT's president, Bob Becker, commented, "I know that she [Barbara Corcoran] does a lot of things that are unusual with the food and the messages and whatever it is. It works. It's a different and more fun way of going about it, but the results that she has produced are phenomenal... We're looking to learn from her" (quoted in McGeveran & Netburn, 2001, p. 13).

BARBARA'S MENTORS, ROLE MODELS AND SUPPORT NETWORK

Barbara's primary role model was clearly her mother (Bloomgarden, 1996). She referred to her mother's brilliant organizing skills and nurturing child-rearing practices in her memoir. She applied many of her mother's techniques to running her business. Florence, for example, identified the "special gift" that each of her children possessed, praised them for it and encouraged them to believe in themselves. Barbara was the creative one, so her job was to sing, dance and entertain her younger siblings. Eddie, the oldest brother, was a "born leader" who everyone else looked up to. Ellen was Florence's helper and would some day make a "great mother" (Corcoran, 2003). Almost every one of Barbara's siblings became either professional health care providers, independent contractors or business owners (Personal Communication, September 28, 2005).

When interviewing new hires, Corcoran found out what they did best and created a position to match their talents or skills. She believed managers should "make jobs for people" and not "squeeze people into jobs" (Corcoran, 2003, p. 66). Corcoran hired a young woman working in a florist shop to meet and greet visitors because she had a great smile. She transferred a salesperson who did not want to sell anymore to a training position in which he taught other salespeople how to promote themselves and attract more business. Corcoran expected her agents to be productive. They were required to have at least one signed contract within the first three months on the job (Schleier, 2003). She would routinely fire the bottom 25% of the sales force (Corcoran, 2003). Those who performed well were rewarded with public praise, notes, e-mails, flowers, trophy ribbons and small gifts. Corcoran, in effect, became a mentor to others.

Corcoran attributed her sense of humor to her father, Edwin. He taught her how to have fun. He "believed that play came first, which drove my mother nuts," said Corcoran (quoted in Hicklin, 2003). Edwin would allow them to use a ladder as a sled in the snow and race dangerously down a hill near their home in New Jersey (Corcoran, 2003) or to jump into a lake during a hail storm while their mother begged them to get out (Hicklin, 2003). He signed their report cards with names like "Rock Hudson" or "Eliot Ness" instead of his own (Corcoran, 2003). Corcoran used humor in business. When she first met Donald Trump she joked, "My husband is the poorer version of you" (Dean, 2004). He remembered her and later gave her the opportunity to sell eight blocks of property for him, earning a commission of $2 million.

Barbara Corcoran's second husband was Bill Higgins, a former FBI agent and navy captain. He played an instrumental role in several of Corcoran's innovations. The couple met at a real estate conference in Suffern, NY. Corcoran found herself sitting next to Higgins. She complained about a competitor who had just been quoted in a *New York Times* article. Corcoran wanted some media attention too. Higgins put Corcoran in touch with a public relations company he had used. When the public relations company's fee was too steep, the agent gave Barbara some free advice: "The best way to make your company known is to put out some sort of survey or report on the marketplace. Something with a lot of numbers — the media loves numbers. May be compare this year's prices to last year's" (Corcoran, 2003, p. 71). That was how Corcoran got the idea for *The Corcoran Report*.

Higgins also helped Corcoran realize the potential

of the Internet. In 1993, Corcoran had conceived of a new way for people to shop for homes. She used $71,000 to create professional videotapes of the firm's listings. The videos featured floor plans, the interiors of apartments, the lobbies of the buildings, and the photos and telephone numbers of the listings agents (Corcoran, 2003). Clients could take the videos home for a $20 refundable deposit. The project was a failure. Salespeople did not want to distribute the videos to their clients because they also displayed the face and contact information of a colleague. Clients preferred working in person with an agent. Around this time, Corcoran's husband described a recent trip with the US navy in which he participated in military exercises in real-time over the Internet. He explained how the Internet would help people from around the world exchange information. Corcoran quickly decided to register a domain name. She uploaded the videos onto the Internet five years before her competitors even had a web-site (Pinckney, 2004).

Corcoran also picked up tips about how to be successful at the many jobs she held before starting The Corcoran Group. When she was 17, for example, she worked at a five and dime store in Fort Lee, New Jersey. When she left to work as a sales clerk across the street at another business, her former employer warned her about the difficulties outsiders encountered when they worked for family-owned businesses. Although she was the best salesperson at the new job, she never got promoted because the owner advanced his nieces and nephews instead. She remembered that lesson — when she started working in real estate at the Giffuni Brothers, she made sure she stayed there for only nine months ("The Best," 2003).

A LINK BETWEEN LEARNING DIFFERENCES AND ENTREPRENEURSHIP

Jerry Porras, a Stanford University professor and author of the best selling book, *Built to Last: Successful Habits of Visionary Companies*, once remarked, ". . . it's clear that many CEOs who have struggled with learning differences have been among the most gifted entrepreneurs" (quoted in Thompson, 2004, p. 52). These learning differences include dyslexia and attention deficit disorder (ADD). Dyslexia is a language-based disorder that affects reading. ADD is a disorder that results in hyperactivity, inattention, and difficulty completing tasks.

In the case of dyslexia, Julie Logan, a researcher at Simfonec, a research center at Case Business School in London, found that 20% of entrepreneurs (business owners employing at least one person) were dyslexic whereas 4% of employed managers (those supervising at least one person) were dyslexic ("Entrepreneurs," 2004). Logan discovered that the entrepreneurs in her study had often failed in school but succeeded in business because of their creativity and tenacity ("Dyslexia," 2004). In her book, *Overcoming Dyslexia*, Dr. Sally Shaywitz, a co-director of the Yale Center for the Study of Learning and Attention, pointed out that dyslexia had nothing to do with low intelligence or laziness. Dyslexic individuals were very bright and succeeded in all fields (including medicine, law, auditing, finance, insurance, politics, music, art, and consulting). The problem was that members in society assumed that spelling was associated with creative writing; slow reading was incompatible with sharp thinking; and scores on standardized tests were the best predictors of subsequent performance (Shaywitz, 2003).

During her career, Barbara Corcoran acknowledged publicly that she had dyslexia. In an interview with Neil Cavuto on Fox News in 2004, she admitted that growing up with undiagnosed dyslexia was difficult: "So, I just became a very quiet student, more than anything else. So fearful that someone would find out how stupid I was. You know, there is so much peer pressure in school and you are judged so much by grades and how well you perform next to the next kid. And so for me it was a terribly painful experience, actually for me it was a jail sentence, I couldn't wait until the day I got out of school" ("Neil's Heroes," 2004). In adulthood, Corcoran was able to turn her dyslexia into an asset. It enabled her to read people, size up situations and invent new ideas (Corcoran, 2003). Corcoran's learning difference shaped some of her business ideas and community service activities. She donated the proceeds from her book to the Windward School which educates children with language-based learning disabilities. She contemplated opening a school for dyslexic children.

Barbara Corcoran was not alone. Many other business leaders, including John Chambers (Cisco Systems), Richard Branson (Virgin Group), Craig McCaw (McCaw Cellular Communications), Charles Schwab (Charles Schwab & Company), David Neeleman (JetBlue Airways), Alan Meckler (JupiterMedia), and Paul Orfalea (Kinko's), began to discuss their own learning differences. Some like David Neelman suffered from attention deficit disorder while others like John Chambers suffered from dyslexia. Orfalea had both dyslexia and ADD. Many of these business people learned about their learning differences only when their own children were diagnosed with similar conditions. They were supported by a special person, a parent or teacher, who saw their talent and nurtured it. It was also helpful if they were able to excel at some activity (e.g., sports) early on. These executives decided to speak out publicly about their difficulties in order to better educate people.

Self-reports of CEOs about the challenges they faced suggest that they shared some of the following personal characteristics (Thompson, 2004):

— They recognized their strengths and weaknesses and hired qualified individuals who possessed excellent skills in their weak areas. Barbara Corcoran hired Esther Kaplan to help her manage The Corcoran Group. She later offered her a partnership. When Kaplan retired, she eventually replaced her with Pamela Liebman. Corcoran once admitted that she never read financial statements — she could not (and did not want to) understand them (Hicklin, 2003). Liebman, on the other hand, had taken accounting classes as the University of Massachusetts and was responsible for negotiating the eventual sale of The Corcoran Group to the Cendant Corporation's NRT subsidiary.

— They realized that a great team is needed to build a great company. Corcoran learned the importance of teamwork during the real estate slump of the late 1980's. Her employees formed a team and helped each other list apartments and negotiate deals; they took pay cuts, agreed to reductions in advertising, taught workshops and helped each other complete sales. As she wrote, "Nothing is more powerful than a team working together. Teams can accomplish anything, but to create an exceptional team, the members must totally believe that no one of us is as smart as all of us" (Corcoran, 2003, p.151).

— They prepared a lot in advance and developed good communication skills for issues they believed in with a passion. Corcoran once spent 40 minutes in the broom closet of a restaurant to practice a speech at a company awards ceremony (Finnerty, 2000). She became quite comfortable talking about her company as keynote speaker at the Key Financial Forum for Women, providing career advice to teenagers around the country and discussing politics on Fox News. She estimated that she had given 500 speeches all over the world (McDonnell, 2005).

— They could see multiple dimensions of a problem and made issues clearer and simpler. Corcoran did not appreciate fancy business terms such as "mission statement" or "business plan." She led her firm by the simple belief that all business managers, not just heads of real estate agencies, needed to understand people and how to aggressively market their company's products and services.

BARBARA CORCORAN'S SEARCH FOR A NEW CAREER

In 2001, Corcoran sold her firm to NRT, Incorporated, a subsidiary of the Cendant Corporation. She stayed on as chairwoman for the following 4 years. Usually, newly acquired brokerages were merged into one of three Cendant groups: Coldwell Banker, Century 21 or ERA. The Corcoran Group, because of its valued reputation, remained an independent brand. Corcoran's motivation for selling was two-fold: she wanted to spend more time with her husband and son; she felt that her company's future growth, especially into national and international markets, required the resources of a large corporation. With sales of $149 billion in 2002, NRT had 900 offices, 52,000 sales associates and operated in 30 of the largest metropolitan areas in the US. Under NRT's ownership, The Corcoran Group acquired brokerages in Long Island, New York and in Palm Beach, Florida. It also bought Citi Habitats Incorporated, the largest residential rental brokerage firm in New York City (See Exhibit 3 for more information about The Corcoran Group).

Corcoran went through a difficult transitional period. She said, "I heard the silence of having sold the business and felt the tremendous challenge of reinventing myself. It was shocking to me what a vacuum it was" (quoted in Galant, 2005). She thought about starting a public relations firm, creating a talent pool for women job sharers, and opening a school for dyslexic students (Morgenstern, 2005). She finally realized that she was a good motivational speaker and television personality. On August 19, 2005, Corcoran announced that she was resigning as chairwoman of The Corcoran Group. She planned to devote all of her energies to real estate-related content for network television (Yulico, 2005). The new company, not surprisingly, was named, "Barbara Corcoran Productions." On November 15, 2005, when Barbara Corcoran's resignation from The Corcoran Group took effect, a new chapter in her career began.

REFERENCES

Astoria ranks no. 1 place to retire. (2005). *The Daily Astorian*, Retrieved 9/8/05, from the World Wide Web: http://www.dailyastorian.info, August 10.

Barbara Corcoran (1999). Profile of an Entrepreneur in Residence, Lubin School of Business, Pace University, Retrieved 6/10/

05, from the World Wide Web: http://appserv.pace.edu/execute/ page.cfm?doc_id=2031, (Fall).

Barron, J. (1993). The new millionaires: Making it in tough times. *New York Times*, p. F1, Retrieved 6/12/05, from ProQuest Historical database, August.

Barron, J. (2000). Public lives. *New York Times*, p. B2, Retrieved 6/10/05, from ABI/INFORM (ProQuest) database, December 8.

Barron, K. (1999). Realtor 1, Web 0, *Forbes 163* (3), p. 64. Retrieved 6/10/05, from ABI/INFORM (ProQuest) database, February 8.

Begley, S. (2005). People believe a 'fact' that fits their views even if it's clearly false, *Wall Street Journal*, p. B1, Retrieved 2/8/05, from ABI/INFORM (ProQuest) database, February 4.

Blair, J. (2000). Apartment hunt goes virtual; Buying a place unseen, other than online, *The New York Times*, p. B1, Retrieved 6/10/05, from LexisNexis Academic database.

Bloomgarden, K. (1996). 75 most influential women; all in the family, *Crain's New York Business*, Retrieved 7/13/05, from the World Wide Web: http://newyorkbusiness.com, March 25.

Bresnahan, B. (2002). 2001 Power Broker 350. RISMEDIA-NRRE. Retrieved 11/16/05, from the World Wide Web: *http://www.ismedia.com/index.php/article/articleprint/643/-1/162*, , May 29.

Bresnahan, B. (2004). NRT's The Corcoran Group sets the standard for online marketing, *Real Estate News*, Retrieved 6/16/05, from the World Wide Web: http://www.nycexclusives.com/ aboutus/ index.aspx?page=ManagerArticle&userid=PL&pub_id=1975.

Collins, J. (2005). Real-estate industry officials predict a move toward quicker transactions, *Knight Ridder Tribune Business News*, p. 1. Retrieved 9/23/05, from ABI/INFORM (ProQuest) database, September 21.

Corcoran B. (2001). An insult was my motivation, *New York Times*, p. C8. Retrieved 5/7/05, from ABI/INFORM (ProQuest) database, August 8.

Corcoran, B. (1994, October 19). Corcoran Group enters new age of brokerage, *Real Estate Weekly 41* (11), p. B2.

Corcoran, B. (2003). *If You Don't Have Big Breasts, Put Ribbons on Your Pigtails,* NY: Penguin Group.

Cullen, J. F. & Lopez, D. (1999). NYC's largest residential real estate brokerages, *Crain's New York Business, 1999 Book of Lists, 14* (52), p. 80, Retrieved 7/13/05, from EBSCO host database.

Dean, S. (2004). The last laugh. *Reader's Digest.* Retrieved 6/16/05, from the World Wide Web: http://www.barbaracorcoran.com/ images/BarbaraCorcoran_PressKit.pdf+%22the+last+laugh%22+reader%27s+digest+barbara+corcoran&hl=en, September.

DeNitto, E. (1996). Residential report; Brokers do home work; real estate firms plug in incentives for work at home to boost productivity, *Crain's New York Business,* Retrieved 7/13/05, from the World Wide Web: http://www.newyorkbusiness.com.

Dullea, G. (1990). When finding the gold can take a little brass, *New York Times,* p. B5, Retrieved 6/12/05, from ProQuest Historical database, July 20.

Dyslexia no bar to success for some British entrepreneurs. (2004). *Knight Ridder Tribune Business News,* p. 1, Retrieved 6/12/05, from ABI/INFORM (ProQuest) database, November 18.

Entrepreneurs five times more likely to suffer from dyslexia. (2004). Cass Business School, City of London, Retrieved 7/13/05, from the World Wide Web: http://www.cass.city. ac.uk/media/stories/story_8_45816 _44300.html, November 22.

Evans, M. (2005). Real estate's all-stars, *Realtor Magazine Online,* Retrieved 11/16/05, from the World Wide Web: http://www.realtor.org/ rmomag.nsf/pages/feature1july05?OpenDocument, July 1.

Finnerty, A. (2000). What do you do all day?: The big-city realtor/Barbara Corcoran, *New York Times Magazine,* p. 52, March 5.

Fitzgerald, J. (2003). Hiring the right person, *Chicago Tribune,* p. 2, Retrieved 5/7/05, from ABI/INFORM (Proquest) database, March 26.

Freedman, R. (2000). Taking the e-savvy approach, *Realtor Magazine Online,* Retrieved 6/13/05, from the World Wide Web: http://www.realtor.org/rmomag.nsf/pages/bestpracticefeb00, February 1.

Fried, J. P. (1977). The fight to shatter realty management's male mystique, *New York Times*, p. 42, Retrieved 6/12/05, from ProQuest Historical database, January 10.

Galant., R. (2005). A real estate tycoon finds her own space, *Newsday.com*, Retrieved 5/11/05, from the World Wide Web: http://pqasb.pqarchiver.com/newsday/834816251.html?did= 834816251&FMT= ABS&FMTS= FT&date=May+9%2C+2005 &author= RICHARD+GALANT &pub=Newsday&desc= MONEY+ %26+ POWER%2C +A+real+estate+tycoon+finds+her+own+space, May 9.

Gleeson, J. (2003). Learn from failures, exec says, *The Journal News*, Retrieved 9/22/05, from the World Wide Web: http://www.corcoran.com/aboutus/article_bccom.asp?pub_id=963, May 20.

Goodman, G. W. (1981). Slowly, women progress in commercial brokerage, *New York Times*, p. R1, Retrieved 6/12/05, from ProQuest Historical database.

Grant, P. (1990). Small firms disappear amid drought of deals, *Crain's New York Business, 6* (23), p. 19, Retrieved 7/23/05, from ABI/INFORM (ProQuest) database, June 4.

Hicklin, A. (2003). Barbara Corcoran profiled, *The Sunday Herald*, Retrieved 6/16/05, from the World Wide Web: http://www.corcoran.com/aboutus/article_bccom.asp?pub_id=781, January 1.

Horsley, C. B. (1981). Study shows coop prices nearly quintupled, *New York Times*, p. 324, Retrieved 6/12/05, from ProQuest Historical database, August 30.

How to be a broker to the stars. (2001). The *New Yorker 77* (17), p. 25, Retrieved 9/8/05, from ABI/INFORM (ProQuest) database, July 2.

Huppke, R. W. (2005). Oak Park, do you think you're sexy?; Well, one author does, putting you up there with La Jolla, Calif., and Coral Gables, Fla. *Chicago Tribune*, p. 2, Retrieved 9/12/05, from ABI/INFORM (ProQuest) database, July 24.

Kalb, P. E. (1999). Barb wired, *New York Magazine*, Retrieved 4/16/05, from the World Wide Web: http://newyorkmetro.com/nymetro/ realestate/features/1669, December 13.

Kantor, J. (2005). 9/11: Light a candle or party on? *New York Times*, p. G1, Retrieved 9/26/05, from ABI/INFORM (ProQuest) database, August 18.

Kaufman, J. (2004). Using the glow of celebrity to sell, *New York Times,* p. 11, Retrieved 9/26/05, from ABI/INFORM (ProQuest) database, November 14.

Kennedy, S. G. (1991). Prices halved, 13 co-ops sell in hour in Manhattan, *New York Times*, p. B6, Retrieved 6/12/05, from ProQuest Historical database, June 28.

Kennedy, S. G. (1992). A growing leadership role for women, *New York Times*, p. R1, Retrieved 6/12/05, from ProQuest Historical database, January 5.

Koprowski, G. J. (2003). Who owns listings?; Realtor battle pits old line vs. online, *The Washington Post*, p. F1, Retrieved 6/15/05, from ABI/INFORM (ProQuest) database, March 22.

Kwon, B. (2003). Use what you've got. *Fortune Small Business*, Retrieved 5/11/05, from the World Wide Web: http://www.fortune.com/fortune/smallbusiness/smallbiznotes/0,15704,423332,00.html, February 14.

Lenzer, R. (1990). Bad old times in the big apple from cabbie to broker, everyone's feeling pinch of latest slump, *Boston Globe*, p. 43, Retrieved 7/23/05, from ABI/INFORM (ProQuest) database, June 27.

Levine, J. (2004). Shopping online; Know the facts before you visit the dealer, *PC Magazine 23* (16), p. M16, Retrieved 6/15/05, from ABI/INFORM (ProQuest) database, September 21.

Malanga, S. (1997). NYC market really spooky, *Crain's New York Business 13* (43), p. 6, Retrieved 9/12/05, from ABI/INFORM (ProQuest) database, October 27.

McGeveran, T. and Netburn, D. (2001). Corcoran's dream: One tremendous, profitable family, *The New York Observer,* p. 13, Retrieved 6/16/05, from NOVEL database, October 8.

Morgenstern, J. (2005). Barbara Corcoran's second act, *O: The Oprah Magazine 6* (3), p. 163. Retrieved 6/10/05, from ABI/INFORM (ProQuest) database, March.

Msonthi, M. (2000). Office hours: Ways with words: Yes, it is possible to be dyslexic and a good secretary, *The Guardian*, p. 5, Retrieved 6/12/05, from ABI/INFORM (ProQuest) database, November 6.

Neil's heroes: Barbara Corcoran (2004). Transcripts of an interview from "Your World with Neil Cavuto," *Fox News Network*, Retrieved 9/12/2005, from the World Wide Web: http://

www.foxnews.com/story/0,2933,122247,00.html, June 8.

NRT agrees to buy New York City Realtor Corcoran Group (2001). *Wall Street Journal*, p. C12, Retrieved 5/11/05, from ABI/INFORM (ProQuest) database, September 25.

O'Donnell, J. & Kirchhoff, S. (2005). Discounters setting sights on traditional real estate market; Internet also changing home search, sale technique, *USA Today*, p. B1, Retrieved 6/15/05, from ABI/INFORM (ProQuest) database, June 6.

Philippidis, A. (2003). Media mastery pays off for broker Corcoran, *Westchester County Business Journal 42* (22), p. 17, Retrieved 5/10/05, from the World Wide Web: http://www.amazon.com, June 2.

Pinckney, B. (2004). Women share great (and not so great) ideas, *Business Review 31* (12), p. 3, Retrieved 5/7/05, from ABI/INFORM (ProQuest) database, June 25.

Rafter, D. (2004). Plugged into the market, *The Washington Post*, p. F1, Retrieved 9/23/05, from ABI/INFORM (ProQuest) database, September 11.

Real estate chat line opens. (1999). *Real Estate Weekly*, Retrieved 7/13/05, from the World Wide Web: http://www.looksmart.com, November17.

Rejnis, R. (1970). Women in realty making headway in home sales, *New York Times*, p. 150, Retrieved 6/12/05, from ProQuest Historical database, July 5.

Ricci, J. (2004). Manhattan's hottest property, *UMassMagOnline*, Retrieved 6/18/05, from the World Wide Web: http://umassmag.com/Spring_2004/Manhattan_s_Hottest_Property_657.html, September.

Rich, M. (2005a). Middleman now rich man in real estate boom, *New York Times*, p. A1, Retrieved 7/22/05, from ABI/INFORM (ProQuest) database, May 31.

Rich, M. (2005b). Realty agents add elastic to their ethics, *New York Times*, p. F1, Retrieved 5/11/05, from ABI/INFORM (ProQuest) database, May 5.

Rich, M. (2005c). Average Manhattan apartment remains over $1 million, *New York Times*, p. B3, Retrieved 5/13/05, from ABI/INFORM (ProQuest) database, January 3.

Richter, P. (1990). From high rise, Manhattan takes a steep downturn, *Houston Chronicle*, p. 6, Retrieved 7/23/05, from ABI/INFORM (ProQuest) database, July 1.

Robledo, S. (2005). The height of fashion, *New York Magazine,* pp. 42-44, November 7.

Rodrigues, J. H., Southwood, D. and Masson, S. (2002). NYC's largest residential real estate brokerages, *Crain's New York Business, 18* (52), p. 84, Retrieved 7/13/05, from EBSCOhost database, December 30.

Rozhon, T. (2001). Midsize Brown Harris is buying Halstead, a big real estate firm, *New York Times,* p. 8, Retrieved 11/16/05, from ABI/INFORM (ProQuest) database, January 25.

Russer, M. J. (1998). The Corcoran Group: An early Internet adopter pushes ahead, *International Real Estate Digest,* Retrieved 9/14/05, from the World Wide Web: http://ired.com/news/industry/ 990127.html.

Schleier, C. (2003). Her can-do spirit lifts sales, *Investors Daily,* Retrieved 6/16/05, from the World Wide Web: http://www.corcoran.com/aboutus/article_bccom.asp?pub_id=861, March 24.

Schoeneman, D. (2001). Corcoran's dinner for 700. *The New York Post,* Retrieved 6/16/05, from the World Wide Web: http://www.corcoran.com/aboutus/article_bccom.asp?pub_id=295, October 24.

Schoeneman, D. (2005). The home front: Housing aid for the A-list, *Wall Street Journal,* p. W1, November 4.

Shaywitz, S. (2003). *Overcoming Dyslexia,* NY: Random House.

Sherman, G. (2004a). Meet the celebrity broker, latest boldface aspirants, *The New York Observer,* p. 15, Retrieved 9/14/05, from the World Wide Web: http://www.observer.com, November 22.

Sherman, G. (2004b). Is the $1 million apartment sale an urban legend? *The New York Observer,* p. 1, Retrieved 6/17/05, from the NOVEL database, September 13.

Sherman, G. (2004c). Monster brokers Elliman, Corcoran brawl for luxury, *The New York Observer,* p. 1, Retrieved 6/17/05, from the NOVEL database, January 5.

Sorkin, A. R. and Blair, J. (2001). Corcoran sells realty firm she founded, *New York Times,* p. A20, Retrieved 5/7/05, from ABI/INFORM (Proquest) database, September 25.

Sorter, A. (2003). People to pay attention to — Barbara Corcoran, *ADDitude,* Retrieved 6/16/05, from the World Wide Web:

http://www.corcoran.com/aboutus/article_bccom.asp?pub_id=912, June 1.

Sterne, M. (1976). Co-op sales rise is hailed as healthy economic sign, *New York Times*, p. 31, Retrieved 6/12/05, from ProQuest Historical database, November 29.

Temliak, B. (1993). Real estate marketplace, *New York Law Journal,* Retrieved 6/18/05, from LexisNexis Academic database, December 22.

The best career advice I ever got. (2003). *Smart Money,* Retrieved 9/22/05, from the World Wide Web: http://www.corcoran.com/aboutus/article_bccom.asp?pub_id=948, June 1.

Thompson, M. C. (2004). Creative learning, *Chief Executive*, p. 52, Retrieved 6/12/05, from ABI/INFORM (Proquest) database, April.

Warren, M. (2004). Meet the world's richest estate agent, Retrieved 5/11/05, from the World Wide Web: http://telegraph.co.uk/global/main.jhtml?xml=/ global/2004/06/04/prich02.xml, June 4.

We hear . . . (2005). *New York Post,* p. 6, Retrieved 6/16/05, from NOVEL database, March 16.

Whitaker, B. (1998). House hunting with cursor and click, *New York Times*, p. G1, Retrieved 5/27/05, from LexisNexis database, September 24.

White, J. (1993). When the going gets tough, the tough get creative, *Journal of Property Management, 58* (6), p. 31, Retrieved 7/23/05, from ABI/INFORM (ProQuest) database, November/December.

Witchel, A. (2003). How a d (for dyslexia) pupil rose to realty's a-list, *New York Times,* section 9, p.1, Retrieved 5/7/05, from ABI/INFORM (ProQuest) database, February 2.

Yulico, N. (2005). Corcoran ready for her close-up, *TheStreet.com Technology Report,* Retrieved 9/8/05, from the World Wide Web: http://www.thestreet.com/_yahoo/markets/realestate/10239167.html?cm_ven=YAHOO& cm_cat=FREE& cm_ite=NA, August 22.

EXHIBIT 1: THE NEW YORK CITY RESIDENTIAL REAL ESTATE MARKET: A DECADE BY DECADE SUMMARY OF KEY ISSUES

Early History:

The first great New York City (NYC) real estate deal occurred in 1626. Peter Minuit, director of the Dutch West India Company, purchased what is now known as the island of Manhattan from the local Indians in exchange for trinkets and other goods worth 60 Dutch guilders (approximately $28 at current exchange rates). Ever since those early days, real estate has been the talk of the town. As Pamela Liebman, The Corcoran Group's CEO, once observed, "Go to a dinner party in New York and the most popular topics are sex and real estate, and not necessarily in that order, depending on the party." Below is a summary of the NYC economy and real estate developments from the 1970's to the 2000's.

1970's:

Between 1969 and 1977, NYC lost 600,000 jobs. Its population fell by almost 1 million as residents moved to the suburbs and to other parts of the country. The city's expenditures were three times higher than its revenues, creating a fiscal crisis. Its short-term debt grew from near zero in 1970 to $6 billion in 1975. Starting in 1977, the local economy began to recover. Employment increased in the insurance, construction, finance and real estate sectors. The city began a massive program to rebuild deteriorating bridges, parks, sewers and highways. Its financial problems were alleviated in 1978 when the federal government provided a financial aid package totaling $4.5 billion.

In 1973 and 1974, the City Commission on Human Rights accused several real estate firms of "racial steering" (sending white home buyers to all-white neighborhoods and blacks to mixed or all black areas) and "blockbusting" (exploiting racial and ethnic fears in order to induce the panic sale of homes at low prices). Maximum fines for racial discrimination amounted to $500; an offender's license could be suspended or revoked. In 1974, the Justice Department settled a price-fixing case against the Real Estate Board of New York and NYC's tenant-owned Apartment Association. Without admitting guilt, the two groups agreed to state in all their forms that the commission between a real estate broker and client is negotiable.

In 1979, the prices of cooperative apartments and condominiums reached new highs. Based on a survey of 200 luxury buildings in Manhattan, the average selling price per room was $26,417 in 1979 compared to $16,426 in 1978. The total sales volume for the year ending June 30, 1979 was $146.8 million compared to only $53 million for the year ending June 30, 1975.

More and more real estate firms, especially those involved in the service sector (leasing, sales, management and insurance), became interested in expanding nationally by establishing branch offices or forming alliances with other companies. They wanted access to a larger number of customers and real estate experts who understood recent changes, such as the new accounting practices. This meant that owners and their agents would need to learn about regional differences (e.g., companies on the West Coast started and failed more frequently than those on the East Coast resulting in greater tenant turnover and shorter leases).

1980's

In 1980, NYC's budget was balanced for the first time in years. This was attributed to a stronger local economy, rigid control over expenditures and new taxes. The city had regained 100,000 out of the 600,000 jobs it had lost in the previous decade. Ed Koch was the mayor and was credited with fostering a favorable business climate. Nonetheless, census data commissioned by NYC found that more than half of all tenants in Manhattan were paying close to 30% of their gross income on rent. Central Manhattan was becoming a neighborhood that only affluent individuals, unattached professionals or childless couples with two incomes could afford.

By 1985, there were 16,852 licenses real-estate brokers and agents in Manhattan (up from 13,138 in 1981). In 1986, the market enjoyed strong growth. Brokers would read obituary notices in newspapers to find sources of vacant apartments and prospective tenants might be willing to pay money under the table to a superintendent in order to secure a rental apartment. Agents might also try to learn which couples were getting a divorce. Construction projects would bring 15,000 new condominiums to the market, causing some to predict a surplus of luxury units.

On October 19, 1987, the Dow Jones industrial average fell 508 points. The day became known as "Black Monday." Koch ordered a 90 day freeze on hiring for government jobs, suspended a 5% pay increase for management-level employees and asked officials to reduce the city's budget by $500 million. Commercial banks and investment banking houses laid off 40,000 employees. Major employers — JC Penney, Mobil Oil and Exxon - moved their headquarters out of Manhattan. The buying power of Wall Street professionals eroded and resulted in some lean years for real estate. Sellers used different types of incentives — 6 months free maintenance, airplane tickets to

Hawaii, free Jacuzzi whirlpool tubs, cheap financing and low down payments — to attract buyers.

1990's

Between 1990 and 1993, apartment prices continued to decline. The real estate slowdown had a ripple effect on other types of related businesses. Sales of carpeting to commercial and residential customers by a large dealership fell 20%. Business was down 30% for local moving companies. Interior decorators lowered their fees. Drapery and furniture businesses closed. Volume was up, however, at law firms because lawyers were busy restructuring real estate loans.

By 1994, the economy in NYC stabilized. The real estate market encountered a "boomlet." Apartment rents and sales prices started to rise in the West Side of Manhattan and in the downtown Wall Street area. The improvement gradually spread to the rest of Manhattan and then to the outer boroughs. In 1996, residential real estate firm sought new sources of revenue. Brokers joined forces with architects, construction firms, mortgage brokers and lawyers. Century 21 (a national residential real estate franchise based in Parsippany, NJ), for example, entered an agreement with Amre Incorporated (a large home improvement company based in Dallas) to offer home buyers discounts on vinyl siding, cabinet re-facing, decks and roofing materials.

In 1997, buying an apartment once again became a "singular New York ordeal." Supply was short because few new buildings had been constructed and the rate of converting rental apartments to cooperatives had slowed. Rents and sale prices soared. Bidding wars broke out and apartments were sold for more than the asking price. Cooperative boards became selective regarding which buyers they would approve and brokers scrutinized the financial qualifications of buyers more carefully. The economy in NYC remained healthy through 1999.

2000's

The new millennium did not begin well for NYC or the rest of the country. An economic slowdown took hold of the city. In April 2001, stocks on the Nasdaq fell and dot.com firms failed. In September 2001, the World Trade Center was attacked and demolished by terrorists flying in two hijacked US airplanes. Approximately 3,000 people were killed. Corporations moved out of the city, tourists deferred their visits, and new construction was suspended. 60,000 jobs were lost. Some feared that the financial district in downtown Manhattan would never recover.

The downtown residential real estate market soon improved due to the promise of help from the government. Federal grants — totaling $280 million — were made available. Individuals who made a two year commitment to live in the immediate impact area of Ground Zero could get $12,000; families could get $14,500. In other parts of the city, the lower end of the market — studios and one bedroom coops — recovered first. Interest rates were low; individuals took money out of the stock market and put it into real estate; bargain hunters realized it was cheaper to buy than rent.

Tourists returned to Manhattan in 2004 but they stayed for shorter periods and spent less money. Jobs were created in the education and finance sectors. Income tax and sales tax receipts rose to the point that the mayor considered the building of new stadiums and larger civic centers. In a symbolic move, the cornerstone for the new Freedom Tower at Ground Zero was laid on July 4, 2004. The average sales price of an apartment exceeded $1 million and average rents for an apartment rose to $2,397 a month in 2004. An annual survey by the Census Bureau revealed that 44% of New Yorkers spent 35% or more of their household income on mortgages while 42% of New Yorkers spent 35% or more of their income on rent.

A number of new sales tactics became popular. A limited number of large apartments (units with four or more bedrooms) was available. A broker with a listing in a particular building might approach the seller's neighbors to see if they, too, were interested in selling. Separate apartments could be combined into one large unit (and sold at a premium) as long as they were adjacent, across the hall, or upstairs/downstairs from one another. In 2004, 4.1% of all apartment sales were combinations (up from 2.9% in 2003 and 1.7% in 2000). Advertisements for luxury buildings in which celebrities lived were common. Apartment owners were bombarded with fliers and postcards asking them if they wanted "to get rich and retire to Florida" and announcing that "there was no better time to sell than now."

The residential real estate market in Manhattan was competitive because firms were not required to share their listings through a Multiple Listing Service. Starting in 2003, however, the Real Estate Board of New York required its 120 member brokerage firms to share all their listings within 72 hours of obtaining them. It was easy to violate the rule. A broker might decide not to inform his seller that a buyer from another firm was interested in his property. Or, the broker would wait a week before letting another agent show the property to a prospective buyer. The broker might try to hold out until she herself could find a buyer and, as a result, keep more of the commission.

Mortgage rates rose and the cost of gasoline approached $3 a gallon in 2005. Home heating prices were expected to soar. The average sales price of coops and condominiums began to decline in the third quarter of the year. Some observers predicted that the housing bubble was about to burst.

REFERENCES

Dunn, J. (2005). He's the most successful young real-estate brokers in New York, *New York Magazine*, p. 38, Retrieved 11/18/05, from ABI/INFORM (ProQuest) database, April 4.

Fried, J. (1976). Allegations heard on bias in rentals by realty brokers, *New York Times*, p. 29, Retrieved 11/18/05, from ProQuest Historical database, October 7.

Garbarine, R. (1996). Real estate; A residential real estate chain is getting into the home repair business as the industry diversifies, *New York Times*, p. D15, Retrieved 11/12/05, from ABI/INFORM (ProQuest) database, January 12.

Goldman, J. (1986). Same tall ships, a 'new' New York City has made big strides in 10 years since bicentennial, *Los Angeles Times*, p. 4, Retrieved 11/18/05, from ABI/INFORM (ProQuest) database, June 30.

Grant, P. (1990) Real estate's ripples batter service firms, *Crain's New York Business 6* (16), p. 1, Retrieved 11/11/05, from ABI/INFORM (ProQuest) database, April 16.

Haberman, C. (1981). Who cured fiscal crisis in the city? *New York Times*, p. 25, Retrieved 11/18/05, from ProQuest Historical database, March 7.

Herman, E. (2002). New York's downtown real estate has rebounded in year since Sept. 11 attacks, *Knight Ridder Tribune Business News*, p. 1, Retrieved 11/9/05, from ABI/INFORM (ProQuest) database, September 12.

Herman, R. (1980). Costs force life of compromise for apartment dwellers in city, *New York Times*, p. A1, Retrieved 11/18/05, from ProQuest Historical database, January 22.

Horsley, C. (1979). Apartment prices reach new highs in luxury market, *New York Times*, p. R1, Retrieved 11/18/05, from

ProQuest Historical database, September 23.

Marino, V. (2005). Good neighbors make good profits, *New York Times,* p. 11, Retrieved 11/13/05, from ABI/INFORM (ProQuest) database, February 27.

Polgreen, L. (2004) Regional income steady; city housing costs rise, *New York Times,* p. B3, Retrieved 11/18/05, from ABI/INFORM (ProQuest) database, August 27.

Ricci, J. (2004). Manhattan's hottest property, *UMassMagOnline,* Retrieved 6/18/05, from the World Wide Web: http://umassmag.com/Spring_2004/Manhattan_s_Hottest_Property_657.html, September.

Rich, M. (2004). All's fair in love and listings, *New York Times,* p. F1, Retrieved 11/18/05, from ABI/INFORM (ProQuest) database, February 19.

Rich, M. (2005). Average Manhattan apartment remains over $1 million, *New York Times,* p. B3, Retrieved 5/13/05, from ABI/INFORM (ProQuest) database, January 3.

Richter, P. (1990). From high rise, Manhattan takes a steep downturn, *Houston Chronicle,* p. 6, Retrieved 7/23/05, from ABI/INFORM (ProQuest) database, July 1.

Rohatyn, F. (1985). Lessons of the '75 fiscal crisis, *New York Times,* p. A19, Retrieved 11/18/05, from ProQuest Historical database, June 10.

Shanahan, E. (1974). 2 realty groups agree to end dictating of fees, *New York Times,* p. 47, Retrieved 11/18/05, from ProQuest Historical database, November 19.

EXHIBIT 2: NEW YORK CITY'S LARGEST RESIDENTIAL REAL-ESTATE BROKERAGES, 1997-2001

Company	*Year*	*Property Sales: NYC (in millions of $)*	*Number of Units Sold in NYC*	*Number of Units Rented in NYC*	*Number of Agents in NYC*
Ashforth Warburg Associates	1997	N/A	N/A	N/A	N/A
1998	N/A	N/A	N/A	N/A	
1999	408	395	71	N/A	
2000	480	342	101	76	
2001	567	433	89	81	
Bellmarc Realty	1997	N/A	N/A	N/A	N/A
1998	633	2,423	908	233	
1999	882	2,666	982	243	
2000	969	2,237	727	223	
2001	896	1,955	428	217	
Brown Harris Stevens -[1]	1997	N/A	N/A	N/A	N/A
1998	850	N/A	N/A	140	
1999	1,320	1,000	N/A	N/A	
2000	1,860	1,200	N/A	156	
Terra Holdings	2001	3,179	2,442	3,627	527
Charles H. Greenthal Group	1997	400	800	250	80
1998	750	975	275	85	
1999	700	1,070	350	85	
2000	896	1,145	374	65	
2001	275	982	350	65	

Coldwell Banker Hunt Kennedy	1997	300	598	95	84
1998	387	671	99	105	
1999	477	687	390	129	
2000	540	710	836	130	
2001	517	879	602	139	
The Corcoran Group	1997	925	1,897	654	280
1998	1,230	2,248	706	400	
1999	2,000	2,968	1,367	480	
2000	2,200	3,241	1,825	650	
2001	2,400	N/A	1,517	670	
Douglas Elliman[2]	1997	1,560	4,116	2,713	600
1998	1,869	4,177	2,831	600	
1999	2,200	4,679	2,910	720	
Insignia Douglas Elliman	2000	2,800	3,400	2,495	720
2001	2,500	3,000	2,200	720	
Gumley Haft Kleier Inc.	1997	157	164	220	42
1998	239	289	292	42	
1999	287	364	194	45	
2000	330	403	205	44	
2001	352	415	218	41	
Halstead Property Co.[3]	1997	560	1,120	875	250
1998	685	1,160	890	265	
1999	1,048	1,568	1,425	295	
2000	1,345	1,595	1,554	295	
Prudential/ MLBKaye International Realty Inc.	1997	250	1,140	400	110
1998	N/A	N/A	N/A	N/A	

1999	N/A	N/A	N/A	N/A	
2000	550	1,000	N/A	100	
2001	650	1,000	N/A	150	
Sotheby's International Realty	1997	N/A	N/A	N/A	N/A
1998	N/A	N/A	N/A	N/A	
1999	N/A	N/A	N/A	N/A	
2000	1,100	N/A	N/A	100	
2001	1,100	N/A	N/A	100	
William B. May Co.	1997	384	1,329	482	N/A
1998	452	1,620	562	140	
1999	574	1,912	605	150	
2000	712	2,153	744	150	
2001	707	2,003	651	160	

[1] Brown Harris Stevens belonged to a private partnership, Terra Holdings.

[2] In 1999, Insignia acquired Douglas Elliman.

[3] It was acquired in 2001 by Terra Holdings.

N/A Not available.

Data are reported for those firms who agreed to participate in annual surveys conducted by *Crain's New York Business*. Some firms (e.g., Stribling & Associates Ltd.) declined to provide information; others (e.g., Sunshine Group Ltd. and Fillmore Real Estate Agency) did not provide enough consistent information.

REFERENCES

Chen A. (2001). NYC's Largest Residential Real Estate Brokerages, *Crain's New York Business, 2001 Book of Lists 16* (52), p. 52, Retrieved 7/13/05, from EbscoHost database.

Cullen, J. F. & Lopez, D. (1999). NYC's Largest Residential Real Estate Brokerages, *Crain's New York Business, 1999 Book of Lists 14* (52), p. 80, Retrieved 7/13/05, from EbscoHost database.

Lopez, D. (2000). NYC's Largest Residential Real Estate Brokerages, *Crain's New York Business, 2000 Book of Lists 15* (52), p. 50, Retrieved 7/13/05, from EbscoHost database.

NYC's Largest Residential Real Estate Brokerages (2002). *Crain's New York Business*, Retrieved 7/13/05, from the World Wide Web: http://www.newyorkbusiness.com, March 11.

Rodrigues, J. H. (2001). NYC's Largest Residential Real Estate Brokerages, *Crain's New York Business 17* (53), Retrieved 5/12/05, from EbscoHost database, December 31.

EXHIBIT 3: THE CORCORAN GROUP: A COMPANY PROFILE

Business Summary

The Corcoran Group is a residential real estate brokerage company headquartered in NYC. It operates 46 offices and employs 2,600 sales associates who work in Manhattan, Brooklyn, and Long Island, New York as well as in Palm Beach and Delray Beach, Florida. The most recent company-released financial information reveals that its closed sales volume in 2004 was $9 billion (up from $5 billion in 2003, $4 billion in 2002 and $2 billion in 2001).

The Corcoran Group's mission statement reads as follows:

"The Corcoran Group is dedicated to creating exceptional real estate experiences for our customers and communities through the passionate delivery of truly remarkable service. We pledge to promote a fun, fulfilling and respectful environment, one that is open to change and innovation, providing personal growth opportunities for all."

The Corcoran Group has developed a reputation for selling high-end, luxury properties to Hollywood movie stars, famous musicians, successful businessmen and other celebrities. It was responsible, for example, for handling one of the largest real estate transactions in the history of NYC. In 2003, Robby Browne, a Corcoran sales associate, sold a $43 million condominium in one of the twin 80-story skyscrapers in the Time Warner Center to British financier, David Martinez. The transaction was complex because it involved putting together apartments on two different floors and changing the appearance of the building. A team approach was required with Pamela Liebman, The

Corcoran Group's CEO, handling the tough negotiations between lawyers and developers.

The company's structure is comprised of 6 divisions (three of which reflect the geographic scope of the firm and three of which reflect the diverse services provided to clients):

(a) In the Manhattan/Brooklyn division, associates are responsible for the sale and rental of apartments and townhouses.

(b) In the Hamptons/North Folk/Shelter Island division, associates are engaged in the sale and rental of homes and the sale of land.

(c) In the Florida division, associates sell land, sell/rent houses and condominiums and sell/rent commercial properties.

(d) Corcoran Relocation and Client Services: relocation specialists work with corporations to find housing for employees and their families, for members of entire departments and for foreign nationals.

(e) Corcoran Marketing Group: Founded in 1996, this division is responsible for taking properties from pre-development to sales or leasing. The group's vice presidents, directors and project managers work together to convert commercial/industrial space to for-sale housing and to complete bulk sales for sponsors and investors.

(f) Corcoran Group Brooklyn Development: In-house experts study the latest real estate trends, act as developers for its investors, and provide professional consulting services.

Pamela Liebman has been the Corcoran Group's President and Chief Executive Officer since 2000. She oversees the day-to-day operations of the company and provides guidance to the firm's 55 managers and 2,600 employees. She joined the Corcoran group in 1985 as a broker. Soon after, she became the director of the brokerage firm's first downtown office. Under her management, the office grew from 12 agents to 70 agents. Liebman became a partner in 1990 and played a crucial role in developing the brokerage firm's marketing division. She worked with developers to market new properties from inception and generated a sales volume of over $1 billion. Liebman also negotiated the deal in which NRT Incorporated acquired the Corcoran Group in 2001. She grew up in Staten Island, a borough of NYC. She received her bachelor's degree from the University of Massachusetts (Amherst) and studied at the European Business School in London.

Firm Ownership

The Corcoran Group is a subsidiary of NRT Incorporated. NRT is the largest residential real estate brokerage company in the U. S. It has more than 1,000 offices and employs 62,000 sales associates who work in 35 major metropolitan areas, Its acquisition of Sotheby's International Realty from Sotheby's Holdings in 2004 enabled NRT to enter the U.K residential real estate market. In addition to the Corcoran Group, NRT owns Coldwell Banker, ERA and Century 21. In 2004, it posted $204 billion in closed sales volume (up from $167 billion in 2003).

NRT Incorporated is a subsidiary of the Cendant Corporation. Cendant is a large diversified company that owns and operates: (a) hotel franchises (including Days Inn, Ramada Inn and Super 8 brands); (b) vehicle services (Avis and Budget Rent a Car); (c) travel distribution services (including CheapTickets.com and

Orbitz) and (d) real estate services (through NRT Incorporated). In 2004, it had 87,000 employees. Its revenues were $19.79 billion and its net income was $2.08 billion. Cendant's board of directors recently voted to spin off the corporation's business units into four separate, publicly traded entities. The Cendant's name will cease to exist and its long-time CEO, Henry Silverman, will run only the travel distribution company.

Recent Acquisitions

Under Barbara Corcoran's leadership, The Corcoran Group, made a few, select acquisitions. Its preferred method of expansion was to open new offices on its own in Tribeca, Harlem, and Brooklyn:

* In 1996, it acquired Towne Properties, Incorporated, a boutique agency specializing in corporate relocation. It thus gained access to such companies as Citibank and Union Carbide who needed to find housing for their managers and employees.
* In 1998, it acquired a half-interest in Brooklyn Landmark Realty Incorporated. Because clients found Manhattan prices too high, The Corcoran Group had been referring young couples who needed room to raise their families to other agencies in Brooklyn. Now, the firm could better serve the neighborhoods of Brooklyn Heights, Cobble Hill and Park Slope.

NRT Incorporated acquired several companies in its efforts to move The Corcoran Group into new markets. The operations of the acquired companies were merged and placed under the management of Pamela Liebman, the CEO of The Corcoran Group. The strategy was intended to help the firm build lifelong relationships with its clients. Managers wanted to address client needs as a client began his/her life in New York (and rented a first apartment), went on to build a successful career in advertising, insurance or investment banking (and purchased an apartment), and finally made the decision to retire (and bought a summer house). The National Association of Realtors reported that second-home market accounted for approximately $50 billion a year.

* In June 2002, NRT acquired the Sunshine Group (A NYC luxury residential real estate brokerage firm with 14 branches in Palm Beach, Florida and Las Vegas, Nevada). In June 2005, NRT merged the Sunshine Group's operations into The Corcoran Group.
* In June, 2004, NRT acquired Citi Habitats, the largest residential rental brokerage firm in New York City. It also acquired Citi Habitats' affiliates (a loft and fine home sales unit, a concierge service, a move-in solutions service and a wall installation and removal service).
* Florida was an attractive market because a large number of New Yorkers either owned or rented homes along the coast for use in the winter and/or during their retirement years. Others sought investment opportunities. In October, 2003, NRT acquired Paulette Koch Real Estate in Palm Beach, Florida. In July 2004, it acquired McCann Coyner Clarke Real Estate Incorporated in Palm Beach, Florida and in September 2005, it acquired Allmon, Tiernan & Ely, Incorporated in Delray Beach, Florida.
* The Hamptons in Long Island, New York were another attractive vacation spot for affluent Manhattanites. Some real estate brokers believed

that many families decided to leave Manhattan after 9/11, making Long Island their primary residence. In October 2003, NRT acquired Cook Pony Farm Real Estate, Incorporated (a 50 year old firm with 100 offices) and in March 2004, it acquired Dayton/Halstead LLC (a 98 year old firm with 3 offices).

Industry Characteristics

According to a recent GAO report, there were 98,000 active brokerage firms and 1.9 active brokers (individuals who generally manage their own offices) and agents (salespeople who work for licensed brokers) in the US residential real estate industry in 2004. Real estate brokers usually have provided a full ranges of services to clients, including marketing a seller's home, assisting a buyer's search, holding open houses for sellers, showing homes to buyers, preparing offers and negotiating prices, and coordinating closings. Customers rely on the specialized knowledge of brokers and agents who are familiar with tax laws, zoning codes and local market conditions. For most people, buying or selling a home represents a major financial decision.

Pricing — in the form of broker commissions — has not been a significant competitive factor in the industry. Brokers typically charge clients a fee of between 5 to 7 percent of the amount for which an apartment or home was sold. The commission, paid by the seller, represents the costs associated with marketing, selling, and taking a house through settlement. To avoid charges of price-fixing, brokers in most states are required to write in listing agreements that "real estate sales commissions are negotiable." Clients, however, may have little incentive to ask an agent to lower his/her fees.

In a booming housing market, agents reason that the same amount of work is required to sell an expensive home ($500,000) as it is to sell a less expensive home ($200,000). If the seller of the more expensive home agrees to a 6% commission, $30,000 will be collected. If the seller of the less expensive home negotiates a commission of only 3%, the resulting draw is $6,000 compared to $12,000 (at the usual percentage of 6%). An agent might agree to lower the commission on the more expense home, since he/she will still collect a relatively fat commission. It is also likely that the agent will work harder to sell the less expensive home with the 6% commission than the less expensive home with the 3% commission. The seller who has negotiated a lower commission runs the risk that the agent will bring fewer potential buyers to the home.

The commission generated from a sale often gets split four ways. A home sold for $400,000 at a 6% commission generates $24,000. 3% (or $12,000) goes to the firm that listed the property. This amount then gets shared between the listing firm and the listing agent (the person who put the house on the market). In a 50-50 split, the listing agent gets $6,000 and the firm gets $6,000. Sometimes top producing agents demand a more favorable split (getting 80% with 20% going to the firm. The remaining commission of 3% (the other $12,000) goes to the agent who sold the house which is shared with the firm he or she represents. The split again could range from 50-50 to 80-20. If the listing and selling agents are the same, the brokerage firm will received the entire 6% commission (part of which it keeps to cover expenses and show a profit and part of which it uses to compensate the agent).

A renter pays a broker's commission of between one month's rent to 15% of the first year's rent for an apartment in Manhattan. The commission also gets shared between the brokers and their firms. Proof of sufficient income (a salary of sometimes 42-53 times the monthly rent) is often required of tenants. Landlords might ask for a two month's security deposit along with the first month's rent. Young people often need their parents to co-sign the lease and act as guarantors.

The commission structure in the industry may change in the future. By posting listings online and communicating with buyers and sellers by e-mail, the Internet has enabled some firms to lower their costs. Full service discount brokerages (who conduct open houses, negotiate prices, and assist with closings) may charge commissions of 3% to 4.5% and offer rebates to buyers. Limited service discount brokers (who offer fewer services and who may not list a property on multiple listing services) also offer lower commission rates or flat fees for their services. Nonetheless, only 2% of all real estate brokerage transactions in 2003 were completed by nontraditional brokers.

Major Competitors

Overview

The Corcoran Group's key competitors are Prudential Douglas Elliman and Terra Holdings' Brown Harris Stevens. In 2004, The Corcoran Group had 2,600 sales people and $9 billion in closed sales volume while Prudential Douglas Elliman had 2,838 sales people and $10 billion in closed sales volume. Terra Holdings had fewer than 1,000 sales people and $8 billion in closed sales volume which would make its sales people, on average, the most productive of the three (using the metric of closed sales volume generated by sales person).

Competitor Snapshots

The predecessor to Brown Harris Stevens was founded in 1873 when Charles S. Brown opened a real estate appraisal business in lower Manhattan. In 1901, Brown went into partnership with Douglas Robinson (the brother-in-law of president Theodore Roosevelt). In 1922, the firm merged with Harris, Vought & Company. Colonel Duncan Harris was president of the firm between 1938 and 1951. In 1965, Harry Helmsley purchased the firm which he owned for the next 10 years. In 1995, a group of private investors consisting of David Burris, Kent Swig, Arthur Zeckendorf and William Zeckendorf acquired Brown Harris Stevens and named its holding company, Terra Holdings. The investors acquired Feathered Nest in 1998 and Halstead Property Company in 2001.

In 1911, Douglas Elliman started a brokerage firm in a basement store on Madison Avenue. He became known for renting and selling apartments to famous people, including Elihu Root, a Nobel Prize winner. After Elliman died in 1972, the brokerage changed hands several times. In 1999, Insignia Financial Group, led by Andrew Farkas (whose grandfather founded the now defunct Alexander's retail chain), bought Douglas Elliman. Farkas wanted to create a real estate supermarket that would serve the needs of both residential and commercial clients. In 2003, Dorothy Herman (founder and CEO of Prudential Long Island Realty) and her financial partner, Howard Lorber (president of New Valley Corporation and owner of Nathan's hot dogs) acquired Douglas Elliman for $71 million. The firm was renamed Prudential Douglas Elliman. Herman wanted to be the number one broker of luxury homes "from the top of Manhattan to the sandy beaches of Montauk."

The Fight for Market Share

Corcoran and its competitors raced against time to expand their market shares in Long Island and Brooklyn by gobbling up pre-existing firms.

A day after The Corcoran Group acquired Cook Pony Farm Real Estate in East Hampton, New York, in January 2004, Terra Holdings' Halstead Property Company acquired William S. Ross Real Estate (a 9 year old firm based in Brooklyn Heights with a Cobble Hill branch). Terra Holdings' Brown Harris Stevens purchased Dunemere Associates Real Estate (a 20 year old firm with five offices in East Hampton). In July 2004, it formed a joint venture with Resort Properties (a 26 year old agency with one office in West Hampton Beach, Long Island) and Hahn Realty (a 20 year old firm with two offices on the North Folk, Long Island). Finally, it bought William B. May's Brooklyn operations.

Prudential Long Island Realty's followed a reverse growth pattern. It was already a large firm with offices in Nassau, Suffolk, East Hampton and South Fork when it entered the Manhattan real estate market with the purchase of Douglas Elliman. In 2004, it acquired the brokerage division of Goodstein Realty (a 77 year old firm with a main office in Manhattan and three branch offices in Nassau County). It also made its first entry into Brooklyn by acquiring Marilyn A. Donahue Real Estate (with one office in Brooklyn Heights and one office in Cobble Hill). In 2005, it acquired three additional real estate agencies in Long Island.

Other Competitive Tactics

The three rival firms tried to attract the best talent. This often meant making employment offers to sales associates currently working for competitors. Prudential Douglas Elliman attracted Jacky Teplitsky, who was a vice president and top performing broker at The Corcoran Group (her staff was responsible for more than $50 million in sales in 2003). Prudential Douglas Elliman also lured away Corcoran's chief technology officer, Charles Olson (he was credited with making the Corcoran web-site user friendly). Prudential Douglas Elliman made Robert McFarland, a vice President at Brown Harris Stevens, its senior managing director for its property management division. In retaliation, Brown Harris Stevens hired Janice Negrin, who had been a managing director and head of compliance at Prudential Douglas Elliman. The Corcoran Group took four of Alice Mason's top brokers, including Deborah Grubman (whose clients included Tommy Hilfiger and Tommy Mottola). Each firm accused the other of offering attractive splits and signing bonuses to bring over its top performers.

As real estate firms in NYC grew larger, managers set up arrangements enabling brokers in the same firm to work in pairs or groups. According to Scott Durkin, who had once been The Corcoran Group's chief operating officer, the firm had 2,000 small businesses under its umbrella. Reid Price, specializing in real estate in Chelsea, Tribeca and Clinton, for example, teamed up with Gigi Madl to form the Price-Madl Group (a sub-brand within The Corcoran Group). Dorothy Herman, CEO of Prudential Douglas Elliman, believed this arrangement attracted top producers; they could work almost as independent agents without bearing the costs of advertising and other administrative expenses. There was, however, an inherent risk. Michael Shvo joined Douglas Elliman in 1998. He was so successful in sales that he was able to form a group with a staff of 27. When he had a falling out with the owners of the brokerage firm, he struck out on his own, taking with him about a dozen associates.

REFERENCES

www.brownharrisstevens.com
www.cendant.com
www.cocoran.com
www.gao.gov/cgi-bin/getrpt?GAO-05-947
www.nrtinc.com
www.swigequities.com
www.therealdeal.net

DISCUSSION QUESTIONS

1. Describe the industry conditions in the residential real estate market. What are the challenges facing brokerage firms and what might be the critical factors for success?
2. History shows that residential brokerage firms compete on the basis of non-price factors. What might these non-price factors be? Does Barbara Corcoran demonstrate an understanding of these non-price factors? Explain.
3. In her years as primary owner of The Corcoran Group, Barbara Corcoran overcame many major obstacles that could have ruined her career and derailed her company. List all of the obstacles, organize them into distinct categories, and rank them in terms of which obstacles were most difficult to overcome and which obstacles were least difficult to overcome.
4. You read in the chapter how Barbara Corcoran dealt with the possibility of bankruptcy when sales slowed after the stock market crash of 1987. Did she do a good job? What were the positive and negative consequences, if any, of her actions? Did she have any other alternatives? What would you have done if you were in her position? Is your solution to the problem better than hers? If so, why?
5. Bruni, Gherardi and Poggio (2004) combined and summarized the best-known patterns of female entrepreneurship in the literature. They identified 7 "ideal-typical" profiles of women entrepreneurs:

a. the "aimless" young women who establish a business essentially as an alternative to unemployment.

b. the "success-oriented" women for whom entrepreneurship is a long-term career strategy and not a more or less random or obligatory choice.

c. the "strongly success-oriented" women, usually without children, who see entrepreneurship as a means for achieving greater professional fulfillment or for overcoming career obstacles found in the organizations for which they previously worked.

d. the "dualists" or women with substantial work experience interested in reconciling work and family responsibilities and seeking an arrangement which gives them flexibility.

e. the "return workers" or women who had quit their previous jobs to look after their families and are motivated mainly by economic considerations or by a desire to seek self-fulfillment outside of the home.

f. the "traditionalists" or women with family backgrounds for whom owning/running a business is a longstanding tradition.

g. the "radicals" or women who start their own businesses to make a statement and to promote the interests of women in society.

Which type of entrepreneur is Barbara Corcoran? Justify your choice by referring to information in the chapter.

6. Using this case study, analyze how hard work and tenacity contributed to or compensated for a lack of financing? What leadership lessons can be derived?

7. New research suggests that women are just as likely as men to suffer a "midlife crisis" (broadly defined as "a stressful or turbulent psychological transition that occurs most often in the late 40's and early 50's"). Do you think that Barbara Corcoran experienced such a transition? If so, when? What might have been the triggering event(s) ?

8. The general public has a negative impression of real estate agents. A Harris Interactive Poll conducted in 2004 found that real estate agents ranked lowest of all professions (below accountants, stockbrokers and journalists) in terms of prestige (Rich, 2005). An online survey carried out by Penn Schoen & Berland Associates in 2004 found that 78 percent of the brokers and 69 percent of the buyers polled agreed with the statement: "Most people don't trust real estate brokers or expect much from them" (Brozan, 2004). Do you think these negative perceptions are justified? Why or why not? What, if anything, should real estate agents do to improve their image?

12
Vickie Buyniski Gluckman and United Medical Resources, Inc.

Rebecca J. White
Fred M. Beasley

ABSTRACT

United Medical Resources (UMR), founded by Vickie Buyniski Gluckman, is one of the largest and most successful third-party administrators of employer-sponsored health plans in the U.S. UMR creates customized solutions for companies that choose to self-insure their employee health benefits.

The case traces Gluckman's business from its conception to its current state. Besides focusing on how technology is used in the business, the case conveys Gluckman's thoughts for prospective female entrepreneurs and discusses the possibility of transferring the company's business outside the U.S.

INTRODUCTION

As she drove back into Cincinnati, Vickie Buyniski Gluckman saw the large yellow arches of the I-471 bridge spanning the Ohio River. She was crossing the river from Northern Kentucky, home of the Greater Cincinnati regional airport, where she had just returned from an out-of-town board meeting. As she drove she was reminded of the tremendous growth that was being experienced in this tri-state region of southwestern Ohio, northern Kentucky and southeastern Indiana. The recent Procter and Gamble acquisition of Gillette had just made Cincinnati, OH home to more Fortune 500 companies than Boston. In Northern Kentucky, home to their share of large companies such as Toyota Manufacturing International and Fidelity Investments, tremendous economic development and growth in upscale retail and residential properties were making the southern side of the river extremely desirable. She was filled with gratitude that this tri-state region had turned out to be the perfect location for the company, United Medical Resources (UMR), that she created in 1983.

Before founding UMR, Gluckman's experience included seven years of designing and managing healthcare utilization review programs and she had an extensive background in data processing and analysis. Her work administering utilization review for Federal Medicare and Medicaid, and state Workers Compensation programs led her to the idea that cost containment would also work for the private self-funded market. UMR exceeded their customer's expectations in that first year and has gone on to become one of the largest and most successful third party administrators (TPAs) in the country. TPAs provide administrative and management services to companies that self-fund their employees' healthcare costs.

It was Sunday afternoon and tomorrow Gluckman was planning to use the bulk of the day to prepare for two significant events that would occur in the coming week. She and her strategic planning team would leave on Thursday for the annual UMR top management retreat and strategic planning meeting. During these four days, the group would take a hard look at where UMR has been and where the company should be headed. This kind of meeting was always invigorating, stimulating and intellectually challenging. Vickie loved this kind of opportunity and was always well prepared for these retreats which had been so rewarding and critical to the success of UMR. But first, on Tuesday, she would be the luncheon keynote speaker for the Greater Cincinnati Venture Association. This group of investors and entrepreneurs met monthly to hear brief presentations from seasoned entrepreneurs who could share their stories of success. When she accepted this invitation she knew that preparing to tell her story to the venture association would help her get ready for the retreat.

THIRD PARTY ADMINISTRATORS IN THE U.S. HEALTHCARE INDUSTRY

Healthcare costs in the U.S. have been increasing at the rate of 7 to 14 percent per year during the past several years. They now comprise more than 13 percent of the U.S. GDP. Employment-based healthcare coverage has existed in the U.S. for more than 50 years. Today, more than half of all Americans and nearly 3 out of 4 employees in the U.S. have healthcare coverage through their employer. In an effort to cut healthcare costs, organizations have increased the practice of outsourcing human resource activities. Industry analysts estimate that companies spent $24 billion in 2004 outsourcing human resource activities. Increasingly, companies see that other organizations can deliver some of their human resource services more efficiently than they can. One important aspect of human resource outsourcing is the outsourcing of health benefits administration.

An important difference in the healthcare benefits provided by small and large companies in the U.S. is that smaller companies are much more likely to buy health insurance policies from insurers, while larger companies are more likely to self-fund the employees' healthcare costs. According to the Agency for Healthcare Research and Quality, while only 13% of establishments with less than 100 employees self-fund, nearly 78% of establishments with more than 500 employees do so. A self-funded (or self-insured) employer, rather than paying premiums to an insurance company is their own "insurance company" — paying their own claims, administrative costs, and creating safeguards against high dollar claims. The popularity of self-fund plans grew in the 1980s because self-funded plans are exempted from state regulations. That is, while all employer-sponsored health care coverage is subject to federal regulations (e.g., minimum benefit requirements and the establishment of an internal review process for appeals of denied claims), the Employment Retirement Income Security Act of 1974 (ERISA) releases self-funded plans from state regulations.

The term "third party administrator" (TPA) is used to describe an assortment of firms that provide benefits administration and management services to companies that self-fund their employees' healthcare costs. A TPA processes and pays claims on behalf of the employer, and *helps to ensure that the company complies with government regulations*. According to Fred Hunt, President of the Society of Professional Benefit Administrators, "TPAs typically have an ongoing, long-term relationship that resembles that between an employer and their independent CPA or law firms." About 66% of U.S. workers with non-federal health benefits are in plans that use a TPA. For the most part, the approximately 400 TPAs that exist are relatively small, privately-held companies. Many of the firms were started by the people who still run them. However, other entities such as insurance companies, consulting firms, and lawyers also perform TPA services.

Most TPAs provide a set of services to their clients. TPAs differentiate themselves by the type of services or the type of clients in which they specialize. According to a survey by *Employee Benefit Plan Review* in 2005, the most common services provided by TPAs were COBRA administration (89% of respondents), data management and reporting (83%), pre-certification (78%), managed care plans (72%), and prescription drug cards (72%). Typically, TPAs charge a fee that covers all the administrative services they provide. However, others are paid based on a commission or offer a menu of possible services and set a fee for each of the services. Fees for a client are typically determined based on a number of criteria, including the client's number of employees, the demographic profile of the employees, and the past claims volume of those employees.

According to *Employee Benefit Plan Review and* Fred Hunt at the Society of Professional Benefit Administrators, the TPA industry is undergoing consolidation. Mergers and acquisitions, typically involving smaller TPAs, have been occurring for two main reasons. First, smaller TPAs have more difficulty affording the information technology and the skilled people needed to manage the information systems that are necessary to provide effective services today. These technological implementation costs have forced many smaller TPAs to sell the business, merge with a larger TPA, or exit the industry entirely. Second, many TPAs were created in the late 70s, and the owners of these companies, nearing retirement age, are increasingly more motivated to sell their businesses.

VICKIE BUYNISKI GLUCKMAN AND HER COMPANY

Vickie Buyniski Gluckman was raised in a hard-working, blue-collar home in Dayton Ohio. She became an entrepreneur at an early age. At the age of ten, Gluckman walked door-to-door selling greeting cards and handmade Barbie Doll clothes. In high school, her entrepreneurial interests grew when she became involved in Junior Achievement. During this time Vickie saw both of her parents experience the loss of jobs in large corporate organizations and then find themselves required to take inadequate replacement jobs. She decided then that there was less risk in putting her future into her own hands than in the hands of an organization owned by someone else. She remarked about this time in her life, "I decided that creating my own business would be the best way to achieve financial independence and make a better life for myself." Due to her family's financial condition, Gluckman skipped college and entered the workforce immediately after high school.

While the director of two medical review organizations in the late 1970s and early 1980s, she became aware that there was waste and inefficiency in the management of healthcare in the U.S. She thought that the information contained in medical claims could be used to help control healthcare costs. She saw evidence that there were differences in the practices and treatment patterns of doctors and hospitals, and differences in the healthcare consumption of consumers with comparable medical conditions. "From my first experiences with the U.S. healthcare system, I believed that American consumers did not have a vested interest in healthcare, and this created waste, high costs, and changed the quality of people's lives."

She became convinced that she could provide services which would help companies and consumers become more efficient purchasers of health care. She said, "My background led me to a business concept that combined the latest technology for claims processing and reporting, cost management, and a more fair, flat fee structure with something new in the insurance industry – personalized service."

Illustrative of her strong work ethic, determination and "take charge" personality, Gluckman started her company at an early age. She had been thinking about her business concept for some time when the opportunity to capture her first client presented itself. As the Director of two not-for-profit medical review boards in Cincinnati, Ohio, Ms. Gluckman "competed" with a similar board in Cleveland. Because of her success in Cincinnati, she was invited to provide assistance to the Cleveland Health Care Coalition. The VP of Human Resources at Stouffer's Corporation was the Chair of that Coalition. Stouffer's, a business unit of Nestle, Inc. started in Cleveland OH, has six divisions. It was through the relationship she developed with him that Gluckman was afforded the opportunity to impress other key leaders in the organization. Initially, Stouffer's offered her a job. However, as they discussed her passion for reducing waste in the U.S. healthcare system, her strong desire to start her own business emerged. Stouffer's decided to support her new venture instead. Thus, Vickie began UMR with a couple of employees and a single customer, Stouffer's Corporation. According to Gluckman, "I approached Stouffer's with a plan to save them over $1 million in their healthcare costs. It was a risk for Stouffer's, but they believed in the concept and recognized my passion."

EARLY CHALLENGES FOR UMR

From the beginning, Gluckman realized that information technology would play a key role in the company's ability to manage claims. She also realized that it would be difficult for her young firm to obtain financing to purchase the kind of technology that she would need. So, she negotiated an arrangement with her first client, Stouffer's, in which UMR would use Stouffer's mainframe computer via a remote connection. Stouffer's purchased the software for the claims administration system and leased it back to UMR.

The company grew rapidly in the first 10 years, solely by word-of-mouth. UMR provided clients with something that they had not seen before, the concept of cost-management. According to Evie Poe, UMR's Chief Operating Officer, "Vickie drilled down into the medical claims information to find what was really driving costs, and she developed in-depth analyses of what clients could do to reduce their costs."

In the early 1990s, for a brief period of time, Gluckman decided to not take any more business. Company growth had been so rapid that she feared she would be unable to maintain the company's high level of customer service if more clients were added. As Gluckman said, "you can't take on more customers unless you can continue your commitment to your current ones."

The rapid growth also strained UMR's relationship with its initial client, Stouffer's, particularly in the operation and management of the claims administration system. At the time Gluckman felt it had become necessary to move the system to UMR and this required the company to ramp up its infrastructure, purchasing other systems and hiring

IT people which UMR had not employed before. UMR faced the task of both serving their customers and at the same time constructing an IT department.

In the early years, Gluckman also faced the challenges of establishing credibility in the industry, establishing a business location, earning the confidence of re-insurers, developing and enhancing service and capabilities, staying current on changing regulations affecting the industry, hiring employees that shared her strong customer service orientation, and building an effective management team.

From the beginning, having a strong management team has been a key element in the success of UMR. In the early years when the company was small, Gluckman recruited a team of people with diverse skills who were willing to work hard and do whatever had to be done to turn UMR into a sustainable company. Her earliest management team recruits were extremely passionate, loyal and were able to thrive on building a new venture. Later, as the company grew and matured, Gluckman had to also formalize the top management team. This change in leadership was sometimes quite painful as the organization "outgrew" some of her long time dedicated employees. However, Gluckman has found that her current top management team – all four from large corporate backgrounds with very specialized experience in marketing, operations, technology and finance – are critical to the success of UMR today and into the future.

Gluckman also found that her social and professional network was important to her success. In retrospect, she found that volunteering in community groups helped her establish a strong reputation as someone who could be trusted and who would deliver on promises made. In fact, as the Director of two not-for-profit organizations she was afforded many opportunities to serve on local, regional and even national boards. Like the Stouffer's relationship, she has found many customers through this work. However, she acknowledges that the main reason she decided to volunteer initially was because she was young and new to the Cincinnati region and wanted to meet people. She has also always had a strong desire to "give back" to her community, especially to organizations like Junior Achievement, that had provided her with opportunities as a young woman interested in entrepreneurship.

While there is an abundance of government and grant programs to help early stage entrepreneurs, especially in health care cost containment, Vickie chose not to pursue any of them. In essence, the costs associated with working with government programs (e.g. reporting requirements, strategic redirection, etc.) led her to find alternative strategies for growth.

Finally, Gluckman faced additional challenges as a female entrepreneur. Reflecting back on the early years, she says, "With two children, I quickly had to learn the delicate balance of raising a family and running a business." As a result of her experiences as a working mother, her company was one of the first in Cincinnati to offer flex hours and job sharing to employees. This was important for a company in which 8 out of 10 employees were and still are women and 10 percent of the female employees could be out on maternity leave at any given time.

UMR TODAY

Today, UMR is a nationally known third party administrator of self-funded medical, dental, prescription drug, disability, and flexible benefits plans.

With close to 400 employees and revenues over $30 million in 2004, UMR manages over $1.7 billion in healthcare services for clients. UMR has received much recognition, including being named one of America's Top Women-Owned Companies by Working Woman magazine.

Currently, UMR administers more than 1400 healthcare plans for about 130 organizations that have, on average, about 1000 employees. UMR's largest client has 17,000 employees, but it also has many clients with fewer than 250 employees. While all of UMR's clients are headquartered in the U.S., most in the eastern half of the country, many clients have employees that live and work in other countries around the world. UMR routinely manages the claims of these international employees as well. As indicated in Exhibit 1, the company processed $1.7 billion in healthcare claims in 2004. The company processed 3.5 million claims in 2004 and expects to process 4.7 million claims by 2008.

Exhibit 1: Claims Processing at UMR (2004)

Medical Claims	$1,536,500,139
Dental Claims	$ 58,765,749
Vision Claims	$ 1,332,550
Disability Claims	$ 4,008,150
Prescriptions Claims	$ 96,181,550
Flexible Spending	$ 13,794,573
	$1,710,582,711

The company has experienced continuous revenue growth since it was founded. Recently revenues have grown at UMR without any increases in the number of employees, in part due to technological advancements that have increased efficiency. As an example, five years ago more than 90% of healthcare claims processed by UMR were handled by a UMR employee, while today 50% are auto-adjudicated (i.e., processed without a human). Exhibit 2 shows the historical revenues of UMR. Profit margins during these years have ranged from 4-17 percent, averaging 8-10 percent in the last 5 years.

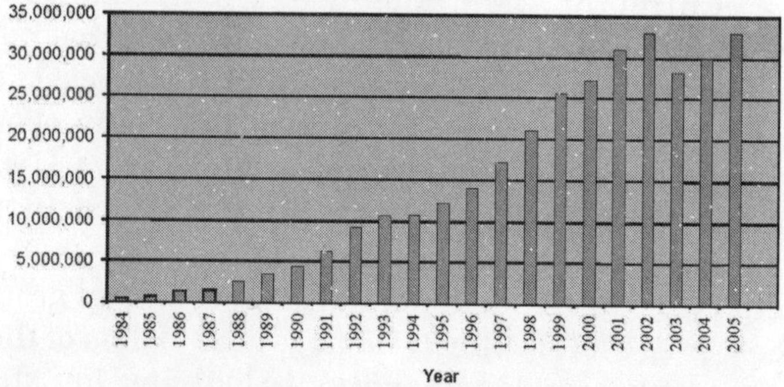

Exhibit 2: Historical Revenues at UMR

UMR'S EXTERNAL ENVIRONMENT

As mentioned above, about two-thirds of all employee benefit plans in the U.S are administered by some form of a TPA. Companies have found that TPAs can deliver health benefits administration more efficiently than they can. Fred Hunt, president of the Society of Professional Benefit Administrators, believes that the future for TPAs is quite bright. Increasing regulations and court decisions in the area of healthcare will only strengthen the need of companies for the specialized expertise provided by TPAs.

The approximately 400 TPAs are typically small-privately-held firms. In the past, there were relatively low barriers to entry into the TPA industry, but increasingly, TPAs must make a significant investment in information technology in order to remain viable competitors. Hence, today many smaller TPAs are either merging with other firms or exiting the industry.

TPAs compete and attempt to differentiate themselves by the types of services or the type of clients in which they specialize. UMR considers its target customer to be an employer with 500 or more employees who seeks a benefits administrator that will act as a "partner" and who desires full-service medical and utilization management services. UMR establishes relationships with partners, such as provider networks, to better enable it to contain its' customers healthcare costs.

Many large insurance companies offer Administrative Services Only (ASO) contracts to large organizations in which they act as a TPA. Because UMR also focuses its efforts on larger organizations (i.e., greater than 500 employees) it considers these large insurance companies (e.g., CIGNA, Aetna, United Healthcare, Anthem, and Humana) to be its primary competitors. The strengths of the large insurance carriers are their "deeper pockets" which allows them to more readily adopt expensive new technologies and their direct provider contracts with hospitals and physicians that allow them to offer deeper discounts on medical services. UMR, smaller and more nimble, considers its flexibility and personalized service to be strengths that these insurance companies cannot easily match. UMR exploits its strengths by targeting market niches in which customers want to actively engage their employees in their healthcare decisions (e.g., hospitals), and want services that are customized to fit their specific needs and specific workforce.

Apart from competition, another important aspect of UMR's external environment is the ever-changing regulatory environment. The regulatory environment can be viewed as both a threat and an opportunity for

TPAs. Most recently, HIPAA regulations regarding privacy and the electronic submission of information have affected TPAs. For example, a HIPAA privacy requirement, which took effect in April 2003, prohibits firms from disclosing health information without authorization. If a company has a self-funded plan it is required to establish policies and procedures for safeguarding privacy, issue a notice of privacy practices to its employees, appoint a privacy officer, and train employees regarding the new privacy regulation. On the other hand, an important part of the services provided by a TPA is the insight and assistance given to clients about their adherence to government requirements. Each new regulation is an opportunity for TPAs to further justify the need for their services.

INFORMATION TECHNOLOGY AT UMR

Capturing, assembling and sharing information has been critical to the mission and operation of UMR since its inception. From the early years when Gluckman negotiated the arrangement with her first client, Stouffer's, to use their mainframe computer via a remote connection, the handling of information and the hardware and software necessary to process information has been a key consideration. Today, one of the greatest challenges for UMR is the use of a "legacy technology" – older technology that has been modified over the years to support the growth and expansion of the company.

The company processes 3.5 million healthcare claims a year and handles an additional 1.5 million phone calls. Claims come to UMR from a number of sources including the mail, from direct access to customers and from a number of outside firms (e.g., Web MD, and DDC). UMR sends out more than 7 million documents annually, including checks, letters, and statements explaining benefits. The company also transmits a large number of monthly, quarterly, annual and ad hoc reports to clients. These inflows and outflows, essentially a highly specialized service assembly line, require an advanced technological capability.

The IT department at UMR, the third largest department in the company, employs about 45 people, each having an average of 12 years experience in the field. According to Charlie Shaskus, Chief Information Officer at UMR, the mission of the IT department is to "provide the tools and the systems to enable the account representatives and benefits administrators to meet company goals." Eighty percent of IT resources at UMR go to maintenance of existing systems. IT expenses at UMR have averaged from 19 to 24 percent of the company's gross revenues. Shaskus says that over the last 5 years or so the IT department has performed 300 additional maintenance tasks with the same number of employees. This increased efficiency has allowed profit margins at UMR to grow.

At UMR, technology involves more than a claims processing system and an informational website for its clients. UMR uses technology to provide timely information so that a client's employees can access their personal information any time, so that nurses at UMR can promote better health among a client's employees, and so that account executives at UMR can help employers manage the cost and performance of their plans.

Advances in technology have brought about tremendous change and opportunities for businesses of all kinds. Perhaps the most important change in information technology for UMR and other TPAs in the last few years has been growth in the use of the internet. UMR now communicates with customers 24 hours a day. A client's employees (as well as the spouses and dependents of employees) can use portals on UMR's website to access information about their healthcare plans and benefits including detailed claims and eligibility status information. In addition, the internet has allowed UMR to be more responsive to its clients. Moreover, the growth of the internet has provided greater efficiencies and cost savings to UMR, like it has to other organizations.

A number of forces in the external environment will affect information technology at UMR in the future. Potential legislative changes are always a source of uncertainty for TPAs. Recently, HIPAA regulations in the area of privacy of medical information forced UMR to examine its systems to determine which needed to be more secure. New regulations can often be a financial burden for a TPA, but they also are a barrier for organizations wanting to enter the industry. Changing demographics in the U.S. may also affect information technology at UMR. For example, the growth of the Hispanic population in the U.S. has caused UMR to provide bilingual customer service representatives and may in the future require changes in the company's website.

The cost of IT labor in the U.S. is also becoming problematic for UMR. Currently, some non-critical IT functions at UMR are outsourced overseas. For example, a UMR partner in India scans and keys in claims that cannot be optically scanned. One concern UMR has is the effect of increased outsourcing on the personalized service that they provide to clients. But, UMR expects that continued efforts to lower healthcare costs will increase the scope and amount of off-shoring in the future.

THE SUCCESS OF UMR

The success of the company has been due to a number of factors. First, UMR is selective in their choice of clients. The company does not take every possible client that they can find. Companies that are "bottom-line driven" typically are not the type of client that fits well with UMR, according to Joseph Gulley, UMR's Chief Financial Officer. UMR is willing to lose a "wrong" customer. UMR seeks partners that share its philosophy about healthcare management. From the beginning, Gluckman says, "The concept of UMR was to get consumers - our clients — involved in understanding and maximizing their purchasing power." UMR seeks partners that desire the product benefits — emphasis on strategic cost management and personalized service – that it provides. When UMR finds a customer that desires those benefits, it strives to develop a long-term relationship with the organization. The average customer has been with UMR for more than eight years.

UMR is also selective when it comes to the type of employee that best fits with the company. UMR seeks employees who are self-motivated, willing to speak their minds and who are customer-focused. CFO Gulley believes that it is the culture of the company that makes it successful. This corporate culture, established from the beginning by Gluckman, allows employees the ability, according to Gulley, "to fail, to learn, and to grow".

UMR has been successful, in short, because they are a customer-driven company. UMR excels in two areas that provide benefits to their customers — strategic cost management and personalized service. Strategic cost management is the most important issue a company faces in managing its health plans. UMR engages in strategic cost management by providing a number of services designed to manage client's healthcare costs. For example utilization management services at UMR authorize or deny healthcare benefits to a client's employees, and case management services evaluate the provision of services and care to employees experiencing a catastrophic illness.

Another key to UMR's success has been its personalized service. For example, UMR maintains a team of dedicated employees (account executive, customer support manager and benefits administrator) in order to provide responsive customer service. Each UMR benefits administrator participates in four weeks of in-depth training. After integration onto a dedicated customer team, benefits administrators continue to be regularly evaluated on key measures of customer service.

THE UMR CULTURE

There is a strong feminine influence at UMR that appears to directly contribute to the success of the company. Approximately 80 percent of the employees at UMR are female. Company executives feel that having a female founder and a large number of women in the organization has contributed to its culture. For example, UMR employees often speak with customers and family members when they are at a stressful and emotional moment in their lives, when they are having health problems. Executives at UMR conjecture that perhaps women are more compassionate and empathetic when they are taking these phone calls.

It is no accident that employees and customers find the atmosphere at UMR nurturing and supportive. Gluckman has invested significant thought, time and money intro creating a work environment where employees can be comfortable and ultimately more productive. Gluckman describes her philosophy in the following manner.

People want to enjoy their work. There is a reason people love to go home. That is the feeling I try to replicate at UMR. In fact, I want my employees to love coming to work as much or more than being in their own home. The UMR team is known in our industry for good old fashioned hard work, continual thirst for knowledge, commitment to excellence, unsurpassed customer service, and dedication to ethics. ***This is a treasured reputation*** *with the strength of our associates behind it. Within the company we are a family with great energy to achieve, to grow and to provide compassionate commitment to the health of our customers.*

At UMR Gluckman has used philosophies such as Feng Shui, an ancient Chinese tradition of placement and design that guides human beings in living harmoniously with their environments, to guide the UMR workspace. When asked how she would describe the goals she seeks with workspace design, Gluckman describes an "uncluttered, warm, inviting and convenient" environment that she believes translates into uncluttered minds and ultimately more patience and better customer service. She encourages the use of warm colors and fabrics, expressive and calming displays of artwork, inviting spaces, and conveniences such as having employees' dry cleaning picked up and delivered to work.

Gluckman has also created a family-oriented workplace that includes flex hours and other family-supportive policies. Employees are encouraged to share their stories about personal achievements and family activities at work. For example, in one recent publication of *The Core*, the company newsletter, weddings, births, and other special events or awards in the lives of company employers were discussed, along with a story about an employee who had just completed her cave diving certification and a story about sons and daughters of employees in military service. These stories were interspersed with quotes from employees who had recently won quality awards for their ability to handle "difficult situations with patience and understanding".

Gluckman goes beyond encouraging open communication in the company. She expects everyone to contribute at the highest level and encourages personal growth and development in a "safe" environment. Gluckman believes strongly in empowering her employees and has decided they should be referred to as associates because it "conveys our professional image and emphasizes that we are all associated in the daily success of UMR."

Evidence of the strong, nurturing open culture is demonstrated at all levels of the organization from the receptionist to the top management team. From the office décor to the meetings of the top management team, there are examples of a caring environment with open communication. Quotes from several UMR associates illustrate:

"It was during the first few weeks at UMR that I was invited to an important meeting of directors and Vickie. As the discussions progressed, Vickie turned to me and said, 'You have a responsibility at this table to share your intelligence.' I gave my opinion and Vickie listened, even though it was contrary to what others were saying. We formed a committee to research both sides of the issue and my opinion proved successful.

I come to work every day because I feel I can make

a difference here. In my department we are always focused on doing the right thing for everyone involved. Anyone who works hard and show they want to make a difference will be given the opportunity to do it. Management always pushes you to do more – to challenge you. Our environment here fosters creative thinking."

STRATEGIC PLANNING AT UMR

The company's mission statement and core values (see Exhibit 3) drive the planning process and the day-to-day activities at UMR. Strategic planning has been important at UMR since the inception of the company. While the basic principles on which the company was founded have never wavered, Gluckman has not been afraid to make strategic changes when necessary. For example, the early expansion strategy was based on growth through franchising - replicating the small shop concept that had worked so well in the early stages. Providing more flexibility in a creative, entrepreneurial environment to only a few customers had been the basis of their success and the company aimed to re-create that strategy in a variety of locations. Moreover, the strategy included a location physically near customers. So, when UMR began to acquire additional customers disbursed throughout the region, the decision was made to open two additional locations – one Northwest of the city in 1991 and another in Northern Kentucky in 1993. However, it soon became apparent that the franchising concept would not work because the necessary information technology was too expensive to replicate. So, in 1998, the franchising for growth strategy was abandoned and all operations were consolidated at the new and current location. Today UMR customers are located throughout the US.

Since 1998 UMR has based their growth strategy on the belief that "the growth and profitability potential for UMR is unlimited as long as we focus on superior quality, claims turnaround, 'world class' customer service, and managing customer's healthcare cost. Essential to meeting these goals is continued realization that we need the right people, processes and technology."

Exhibit 3: UMR's Mission Statement and Core Values

Mission Statement

We will provide world class administration of employer health benefit plans and related services.

We will partner with customers and their advisors to provide customized solutions basedon data and experience to minimize risk, control cost, and promote long-term health at the employer and member level. Our services will be offered to a variety of selected markets and industries allowing us to continually grow without compromising service.

Our belief is that healthy people create happy families and are productive employees.

Core Values

We are the company

We go the extra mile

We keep positive, collaborative relationships

We are proactive

We bend and grow

We are responsible for our own careers

We are highly ethical

We are organized and efficient

We continually learn

We empower individuals

We believe and support each other.

For the past 8 years, UMR has had a group 20-25 people involved in the company's strategic planning process. Gluckman decided that the large number of people was necessary. "We're not a large company, but we're not a small company anymore either. I needed to engage more people, give more managerial strength to the organization, as well as thinking out a new strategy. This bottom-up approach has proven to be effective because, as Evie Poe notes, "You really get the buy-in from people who are going to have to implement plans and projects."

Two outcomes from the most recent strategic planning process were: 1) the realization that to create a long-term competitive advantage the company would need to develop new products, and 2) that, although advanced technology was extremely important to the business, the core focus of UMR's strategy should be superior customer service. One important breakthrough from this planning process was the new UMR product – UMRmD.

UMRmD

UMRmD is a new product developed by UMR, designed to control a client's healthcare costs. The product combines advanced technology with disease and compliance management skills. It targets a population of individuals that are predicted to use the highest amount of a client's healthcare dollars in the future. Gluckman explains, "With the launch of our newest solution, UMRmD, we don't wait for people to get sick with chronic diseases. UMRmD uses powerful information to forecast and proactively reduce healthcare costs in the future. We have specific information at our fingertips that enables us to alert members of a potential health risk on how to reduce that risk from becoming a reality. We strive to support healthcare providers in affecting and ultimately changing the behavior that contributes to future disease. This proactive outreach not only improves members' health, but it reduces significant, future healthcare costs and risks for employers."

The UMRmD product, which grew out of the strategic planning process at UMR, was the result of a partnership between UMR and two other vendors (MD Hawkeye and DXCG). UMR adapted the software of these two companies to fit its needs. UMR is believed to be the first TPA to develop such a product internally. The product, using predictive modeling, looks at claims data and the health risk assessment scores of individuals to identify those individuals that are likely to produce higher than average healthcare costs in the future. Health risk assessments can identify health risk factors that don't show up in claims data, such as weight problems and a history of smoking. Once they are pinpointed, UMR's health management services group, composed of about 35 nurses, reaches out to these high-risk individuals. The nurses act as patient advocates, giving information, support, and guidance, so that these high-risk individuals can make behavioral changes and have more confidence in their choices. As a result, the individuals are healthier and more productive, and clients contain future healthcare costs and at the same time show their employees that they care about their health.

Exhibit 4 shows a sample page of output from the UMRmD product. The exhibit emphasizes the compliance management capabilities of UMRmD. Specifically, it identifies those diabetic individuals who have failed to take an annual test recommended for diabetics. The healthcare expenses of these individuals are presented.

Exhibit 4: Sample Page from UMRmD

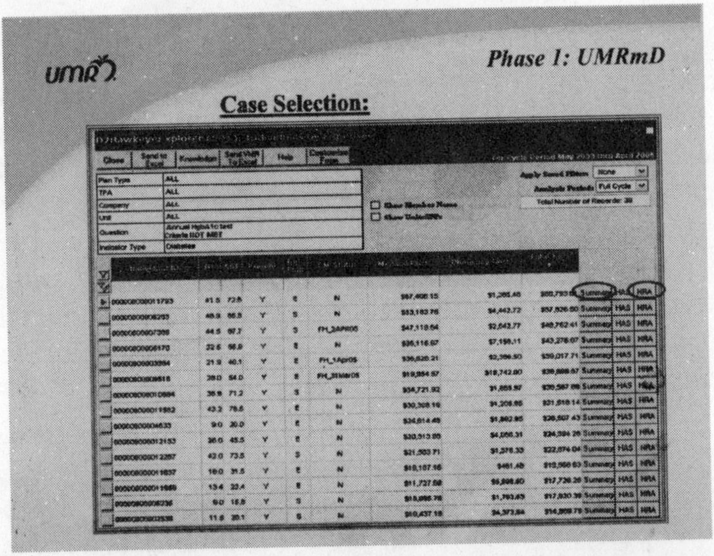

In addition to identifying employees who are at risk for high healthcare claims expenses, UMR also detects employees with chronic conditions that require coordinated care. Disease management is important because chronic medical conditions account for a majority of the money spent on healthcare. Says Gluckman, "We know that 20 percent of the members in a healthcare plan contribute 80-90 percent of an employer's healthcare cost. We also know that several chronic diseases which can be controlled by lifestyle changes make up over 50 percent of that employer's costs. Our new service UMRmD is designed to focus on those individuals."

THE POTENTIAL FOR INTERNATIONAL EXPANSION BY UMR

Concerns about healthcare costs are not unique to the U.S. There are three broad models for funding healthcare globally – government funded, private and some combination of the two. While much of the world provides socialized, or government funded health care to their citizens, in many countries, private health insurance supplements public financing. Today, many countries are committed to providing publicly-funded healthcare, but are increasingly becoming concerned that private funds may also be necessary to supplement publicly-funded healthcare. Consequently, since the late 1980s, many countries have begun to incorporate elements of competition, privatization, and managed care into their national health programs in an effort to contain costs.

According to the World Health Organization, thirty-nine countries in the world have private health insurance that exceeds 5 percent of total health expenditures. Most often, private health insurance is voluntary but in a few countries, Switzerland for example, citizens are required to purchase private health insurance. While private health insurance is most prevalent in South American countries (for e.g. in Uruguay, 60 percent of the population has private health insurance) it is also found in countries in Africa (for e.g., South Africa, Namibia, and Zimbabwe), the Middle East (for e.g., Bahrain, Lebanon, Morocco) and Asia (for e.g., Indonesia and the Philippines). Exhibit 5 provides a list of the top countries in terms of the percent of health expenditures accounted for by private health insurance coverage.

It is these countries in which healthcare is more likely to be privately funded that are more attractive to TPAs that are considering expanding outside the U.S. According to Gluckman, "if a private health system exists in a country then there is a need for company like UMR." She added that the key to success would be understanding the overseas market that you would be entering – its regulatory system, its healthcare system, its culture and its demographics.

Exhibit 5 :Countries with Private Health Insurance Expenditures over 10% of Total Health Expenditures

Africa	North America
Mali	Canada
Morocco	United States
Namibia	
South Africa	**Asia**
Zimbabwe	Philippines
South America	Slovenia
Argentina	**Europe**
Brazil	
Chile	France
Columbia	Netherlands
Paraguay	Switzerland
Uruguay	

Since the mid-1990s there has been an influx of U.S.-based managed care organizations into other countries, particularly South America, due to increased privatization in these countries and slower growth rate for managed care plans in the U.S. Several UMR competitors have expanded their operations globally. For example, CIGNA has managed-care operations in Brazil, Chile, Argentina, and Mexico, and United Healthcare is involved in healthcare administration services operations in Hong Kong, India, Malaysia, the Philippines, Portugal, and South Africa.

One important competitor of UMR that has expanded internationally is Aetna. Aetna markets healthcare services in 16 countries including Mexico, Taiwan, Brazil, Argentina and Columbia. "Aetna is now serving customers in every large-scale Latin American market," says Frederick C. Copeland Jr., the president of Aetna International, Inc., and Aetna is the leading health insurer in Mexico and Brazil. Aetna has expanded internationally by using subsidiaries in foreign countries, by engaging in joint ventures with foreign insurers (for e.g., with Sul America Seguros, the largest insurance company in Brazil), and by purchasing ownership interests in local in-country health insurance organizations (for e.g., Cruz Blanca in Columbia). By engaging in alliances with local organizations, Aetna is able to more easily adapt to the specific regulatory and cultural characteristics that they face in each country.

Aetna sees an opportunity in international expansion. Economic growth and growth in the middle class in Latin America presents insurance companies with more families with incomes large enough to purchase private health insurance. The removal of trade barriers has also hastened the international expansion of insurance companies.

Although UMR has no current plans to expand overseas they are concerned about healthcare costs in other countries. UMR administers the healthcare plans for a number of clients that have employees working and living outside of the U.S. Nationally, the number of employees sent by multinational corporations to work abroad is increasing. One concern of firms that have employees in other countries is that they continue to maintain an attractive benefits package so that they can attract and retain the best employees. Large companies typically have a number of healthcare plans worldwide. UMR administers these plans and handles international claims.

THE FUTURE FOR UMR

The current state of healthcare financing in the

U.S. and around the world is uncertain and changing. This environment provides both tremendous challenge and opportunity for entrepreneurs. In general, the role of TPAs in healthcare management is likely to grow in the future especially in areas such as the administration of health savings accounts in employee benefit plans.

Executives at UMR are confident that even with the most radical transformation of the healthcare system in the U.S., there will continue to be a need for companies like UMR to process and pay healthcare claims. This is especially true since one of the most important problems companies face today is managing the costs of their health plans. With cost management as a distinctive competency the company is well positioned for the future.

UMR will have a continued need to expand the services that they provide, to keep their technology up to date, and to respond to legislative changes. According to CFO Gulley, the biggest challenge facing UMR in the years ahead is to compete effectively with insurance carriers who are able to obtain network discounts and thus can price services lower than UMR. As the company moves forward, Gluckman sees the need for UMR to engage in more "mass customization" of its services in order to effectively compete with the large insurance carriers and their inherent cost advantage. In the future, information technology will only grow in importance for UMR. Clients will make greater use of the internet to receive information and self-service. Clients will make decisions based on more information and TPAs like UMR will make increased use of business intelligence and will expand their data warehousing capabilities.

CONCLUSION AND QUESTIONS

As Vickie reflected upon her upcoming speech to the young entrepreneurs at the GCVA meeting she was reminded of something her father once said, "At the root of most successful projects is a large measure of enthusiasm. This often comes from individuals who have committed to the idea that they are going to make it happen, no matter what. These are the ones I call Champions." She thought this quote went a long way in summarizing her thoughts about advice she might offer to any budding entrepreneur. She decided she would like to tell them that "Women and men can build successful, well-run businesses based on three guiding principles: 1) Love and be passionate about what you do – My first client not only recognized that my business model could save their health plan significant costs, but they also believed in my passion; 2) Be honest with yourself – play to your strengths, and hire good people to make up for your weaknesses; and 3) Work hard, work smart."

She recalled that the most important business lesson she ever learned as an entrepreneur was to trust her employees to do the right thing. It is often very difficult for entrepreneurs to "let go" and allow others to make decisions. Moreover, it is important to hold others accountable, but to also reward them for their performance.

Ms. Gluckman also noted that one of her most painful lessons was learning how to deal with employees when the business outgrew their abilities. She knew it was important to both the company and the employee to terminate the relationship, but she also clearly recalled the pain of that process.

Her support network had also been valuable. She

had become a part of both formal and informal networks that had contributed to her success. Her spouse, her customers and literally everyone with whom she had worked had taught her many valuable lessons and provided support and encouragement along the way.

As she considered her upcoming strategic exercise, Gluckman knew the future could never be predicted. However, at the top management retreat she also knew that her management team must make some strategic decisions that would shape the coming years of UMR. The group needed to review the key success factors for TPAs and examine the strengths and weaknesses of the company. Strong leadership, a family culture, an undisputed value proposition and market opportunity had provided unparalleled growth for UMR. However, operating with older "legacy" technology in an industry driven by cost reductions and dominated by large insurance carriers who were increasingly controlling the landscape required a smart and nimble strategy. The team would likely consider four options for the future of UMR.

1. Stay the course and build on the UMRmD product.
2. Invest in new technology.
3. Consider expansion – including exploring whether the UMR value proposition would work outside of the United States.
4. Prepare to take one of many offers to sell UMR to a competitor.

KEY QUESTIONS

1. How did Victoria Buyniski Gluckman's career and personal life shape her choice to start a new company? What influences do you see?

2. What is a TPA? Describe the customer, industry, and environment in which UMR operates. (You may want to conduct a SWOT analysis and a Porters Five Forces Analysis.)
3. How important is technology at UMR? Where did the first technology come from? How has technology evolved at UMR? What role has technology played in strategy?
4. What is the current strategy at UMR? How would you describe the company culture and how has the culture been influenced by Ms. Gluckman? How has the culture influenced strategy at UMR?
5. What strategy would you recommend to Ms. Gluckman and the UMR team?
    1. Stay the Course and build on the UMRmD product.
    2. Invest in New Technology.
    3. Consider Expansion – including exploring whether the UMR value proposition would work outside of the United States.
    4. Prepare to take one of the many offers to sell UMR to a competitor.

13
Costa Rica: The Two Vecosa Cases

Steven F. Freeman

ABSTRACT

These cases focus on two broad marketing strategy decisions for a young Costa Rican woman trying to establish a vegetable processing business in her home country. In Vecosa (A) there is a question of exploring the market segment to initially pursue, retail or institutional sales, but it is a rich case on an interesting, easy-to-understand new venture that can be used to illustrate how to:

(1) evaluate a new venture opportunity,

(2) analyze a marketing problem,

(3) research a new venture,

(4) make an entrepreneurial decision, and

(5) how an entrepreneurial situation differs from that of a large, established firm.

The question of Vecosa (B) is how to deal with a powerful anticipated competitor. Dole is about to enter a market that Vecosa is also poised to enter. Should the owners try to beat Dole to the punch, or should they wait and follow?

The cases also illustrate general aspects of entrepreneurial life and the particular opportunities and challenges of initiating a new venture in a developing country (and for a young woman). Set in Costa Rica, the cases present a familiar context for developing world students; for students in North America and Europe, the case helps present a picture of life and business in the developing world.

VECOSA (A)

In April 1998, Marcela Solano and her husband Carlos Diones of Costa Rica were ready to startup a pre-cut fresh vegetable business that they had conceived of two years earlier. Although they had already invested in machinery and infrastructure, they still needed to figure who to try to sell to and how to do it.

ORIGINS OF THE BUSINESS

In 1994, upon completing her "bachillerato" in Food Technology, Marcela began to work for her family business. After a short time there, she ventured out to work for *Comercializadora Carlson*, a supplier of prepared food for the airline industry. While working at *Carlson in 1996*, Marcela noted the lack of any suppliers of pre-cut fresh vegetables in the region.

Carlos finished his MBA education in 1992 and decided to startup his own construction company. Carlos, who now had some experience as an entrepreneur, agreed with Marcela that this looked like a good opportunity. Once she decided she was going to pursue it, Marcela set out to get the proper training: she traveled to the US to get professional training in food preparation -a M.S. from the University of California-Davis, which had a highly regarded program. There she learned about production and packaging; organic farming; produce processing, selection, and preservation; and the most current technologies to provide safe, hygienic processing and vacuum sealing to maintain freshness. She also took a course in entrepreneurship. Once she completed her degree,

Marcela was ready to come home and initiate operations. Investment in the enterprise would come from Carlos' construction company, which had excess cash at this time. They named the new business Vegetales Cortados, S.A.—*Vecosa* for short.

THE US PRE-CUT FRESH VEGETABLE INDUSTRY

At the time, the US pre-cut fresh vegetable industry was by far the largest in the world. The first pre-cut vegetable provider had been operating in the US for more than 25 years. The industry's first clients were restaurants and hotels, which appreciated the benefits listed in Tables 1 and la.

Table 1. Benefits of buying pre-cut vegetables:

* Portion Control and standardization
* Reduction in receipt of raw materials
* Minimization of waste
* Constant supply, quality, and price
* Reduction in storage space
* Reduced training costs

Table 1(a). Hidden costs of using (unprocessed) whole vegetables:

* Preparation at the workstation
* Raw material management (ordering, receiving, inspection, storage)
* Work injuries
* Employee training and support
* Waste removal
* Supervision and control of quality
* Cleaning
* Washing and storage of finished products
* Raw material perishing

Over time, a supermarket retail market developed. By 1998, 70 percent of total US sales were retail, while 30 percent were to institutions - principally schools and hospitals, in addition to restaurants and hotels.

Consumption of pre-cut fresh vegetables in the United States had been increasing at an annual rate of 25 percent, and continued increases were expected. Although the products were now widely accepted, total consumption was still less than a quarter of projected market saturation. In 1997, the American market surpassed $1.8 billion*. in annual sales ($7* per capita). Most producers had entered the market within the past 10 years.

Institutional sales growth was due to two important trends: First, large companies that bought foods sought increasing savings and efficiency in production. Second, "outsourcing" of non- strategic activities was an important business trend. Both tendencies contributed to the growth of this segment. McDonald's, Taco Bell and other fast food chains were the largest buyers, but there was also a great variety and number of institutional clients.

The principal *retail* buyers were educated women workers. Analysts attributed the growth of retail sales to three factors:

1. Increasing health awareness. Nutritionists had been recommending greater consumption of vegetables and fruits due to high nutritious value and low fat content. At the time, the US American Medical Association recommended .250 kg minimum daily consumption of vegetables. Many nutritionists suggest that number should be even higher.

2. Convenience : Using pre-cut vegetables was easier and it saved time. It had been becoming increasingly common among North American households that both spouses worked and had less time available for household tasks such as food preparation. This is the kind of product that would appeal to DINCs (dual incomes, no children), an increasingly important demographic group.

3. Retailer incentives : Pre-cut vegetables provided substantially higher profit margins than unprocessed produce.

At the time, the most important retail pre-cut vegetable product was prepared salads. By 1997, consumers could find a wide variety of pre-cut salads, including not only vegetables, but also complete packets that included dressing, croutons, and chopped bacon. Sales, growth rates, and market share of the principal companies are shown in Table 2.

Table 2. US Sales, growth, and market share of prepared salad products

Business	*1997 sales ($ Millions)**	*Change from 1996*	*Market share*
Fresh Express Farms	188	+97%	31.4%
DOLE	127	+150%	21.3%
Ready Pac	67	+111%	11.2%
Supermarket labels	46	+24^	7.7%
Salad Time	35	+285	5.8%
Others	135	+42%	22.6%
Total	598	+87%	100.0%

*The average price per salad pound was US$1.65.

Although prepared salads accounted for a third of pre-cut vegetable sales, other products were also successful, especially those considered difficult or unappealing to prepare, such as garlic, onions, broccoli, potatoes, and carrots.

THE FRESH-CUT VEGETABLE INDUSTRY OF COSTA RICA

The purchase of pre-cut fresh vegetables was not common in Costa Rica in 1998. Most potential clients, both retail and institutional, were unaware of the product, although there was indication of the emergence of markets similar to those of industrialized countries. (Competitors in both of these emerging market segments are identified in Appendix 1.)

Most restaurants and hotels were still family-run companies that cut vegetables manually, without applying any modern processing. The first fresh-cut vegetable provider, *Empecasa,* had been in the market for fifteen years, serving then-new fast-food chains, and growing as they grew. It was a simple, manual cutting company that did not utilize any of the new technologies that Vecosa would employ.

Retail sales of pre-cut fresh vegetables were minimal. There were few producers, none of which had attractive or high quality products. The suppliers of the industry were agricultural product wholesalers that bought directly from the producers, but because the products were not an important revenue source, they were not actively managed, and supplies were erratic.

Automercado, the country's largest supermarket chain, had their own brand, but neither they nor anyone else actively promoted the product. The line of products available was limited and sales were slow so supermarkets did not provide much shelf space; because there was little shelf space and promotion, sales remained low; and so, prepared salads, which were so successful in the

United States, were still hardly available at all in Costa Rica.

Market study. In 1997, Marcela sought to determine the viability of the project. She conducted a market study in which she tried to identify the potential clients, the quantity and type of vegetables they purchased, and from whom they purchased them. She was particularly interested in sales data on the five vegetables with the highest sales volume in the United States: lettuce, cabbage, carrots, onions, and peppers. She separated these potential clients into four groups: fast-food chains, big restaurants, hotels, and supermarkets.

She found, however, the subjects of her study were unwilling to divulge data related to the business. To overcome this reluctance, Marcela pretended to be a government official. Using this ruse, she was able to get data on monthly sales data from at least one branch of the supermarket, hotel or restaurant chain. She used this information to extrapolate annual consumption (Appendix 2), trying to take into account seasonal variation and relative volume of the particular branch.

BEGINNING OF VECOSA

The couple set up shop in an industrial zone ten kilometers from the capital, where they installed their processing equipment, refrigeration chamber, and offices.

The core of the production process consisted of washing, perforation and storage operations. The Diones thought that to excel in the market, the company should use the advanced technologies that Marcella learned in the US - hygienic washing, and vacuum-packing, which would help to maintain freshness and to increase product-life. No existing competitor could offer these features. Therefore, they imported from the United States specialized washing and vacuum- packing machines, as well as specialized machines to cut garlic and potatoes.

THE MARKET DECISION

At this point, the couple had to choose a course to follow. The two broad possibilities they considered were selling to institutions and selling directly to customers through supermarkets. Whatever market segment was to be chosen, the production process would not change substantially. The key operational difference between an institutional and retail strategy would be in packaging, promotions, logistics, sales, and variable costs associated with scale.

Marcela calculated cash outlay for the first year of approximately $350,000 regardless of market segment - although more money in the institutional segment would go to capital investment (Appendix 3) whereas selling to retail clients would require higher promotional expenses (Appendix 4: Annual Fixed Costs). To implement either strategy, they planned to hire salesmen to visit the potential clients and convince them of the value of Vecosa products. But despite their optimism over the future of pre-cut vegetables, the Diones had a hard time figuring out how to get started.

The institutional market. The Diones observed that the institutional market was already established and growing. Costa Rica was enjoying a boom in tourism, and the government projected significant continued increases. Nevertheless, Marcela was concerned that, due to the competitive pressures, she could not expect to receive from institutions a price commensurate with the superior quality of her product. She lamented that price seemed to be the key factor by which suppliers were chosen and that the price-competition was ruthless.

Doing business with the hotels and restaurants could also be unpleasant in other ways. For example, the hotels would ask for orders with only one-day notice or less than one-day notice. This was partly due to the nature of their business (i.e. to take care of big groups of tourists that arrived unexpectedly), but it was also partly due to the power that the buyers could exert over suppliers. Because they didn't need to schedule their orders in advance, the hotels didn't do it. This led to instability and uncertainty for suppliers; but that wasn't the hotels' problem.

In spite of these considerations, doing business in the institutional segment provided certain advantages: the distribution points were relatively few, the distances were short (in the capital region), purchase orders were large, and the clients focused on a few products. And despite purchasing irregularities, hotel demand could be predicted based on seasonal variation, local celebrations, and special events.

Servicing the institutional segment would require that Vecosa have a constant supply on hand, establish good distribution capabilities, develop the flexibility to adapt to restrictions, and capability to provide special cuts or meet special demands. For example, one of the fast food chains demanded that supplier's use cooled trucks to transport the product - which would cost an additional $25,000. Another would require specialized cutting machinery that cost $15,000.

The retail market. Marcela felt generally more attracted to the retail option-in particular the higher potential prices, freedom from ruthless price competition, and the opportunity to produce premium products that would utilize her special capabilities in hygienic preparation, selection, processing, and vacuum-packing. Selling in the stores could also allow a more systematic scheduling of orders. Marcela thought that the retail segment, being in an earlier stage of development than the institutional segment, had more potential. She could open up the market not only in Costa Rica, but also throughout Central America. As in the US, Costa Rican women and other Central American women were increasingly entering the labor market, and had less time to dedicate to household chores.

Despite these positive sentiments, some doubt persisted about the potential of development of the segment. Although the habits of consumption of the United States strongly influenced Costa Rica, some very successful US products, such as the frozen foods, never obtained more than a marginal penetration anywhere in Central America.

Marcela also recognized that retail sales would require additional skills and expenditures. First, the company would have to developing attractive packaging, which would also permit the product to maintain freshness. This was risky, however, because attractive packaging was known to backfire in this market. (Many Costa Ricans consumers believed that packaging increased the sale price to them, and so resisted anything beyond a plastic bag.) Second, it would be necessary to maintain sophisticated systems of distribution and information. Most important, Vecosa would have to educate consumers about the benefits of their product, and build a brand awareness to differentiate Vecosa from that of the competition, all of which would probably require substantial investments in promotions and advertising. Marcella estimated she would have to spend at least $40,000 just to pay for the beginnings of a limited marketing campaign.

CASE PREPARATION QUESTIONS

To whom should Marcella try to sell her product

to and how can she do it? How should she go about making the decision?

Also be prepared to discuss: (1) whether or not this a good business opportunity, and (2) how to *research* a new venture opportunity and Marcella's research.

General Comments: Few consumers know any brand name – rather the products are perceived as generic. Competition in the segment occurs at level of buyer in the supermarket, more than at level of end user. The average price per kilogram of a product found in the market was US$1.75 with a margin to the distributor of 25% (25% of the price that the final consumer pays), and gross margins to the producer of 50% (50% of the price that the final consumer pays) – or more.

NOTE ON RESEARCH METHODS

I met Marcela through a colleague, Carlos' former professor, whom Carlos had consulted regarding Vecosa. I interviewed my colleague, and then with the aid of a research assistant, met and interviewed Marcela. All discussions and interviews were conducted in Spanish, and the interview was taped. We toured the Vecosa facility with Marcela, and took detailed notes. Upon writing a draft of the case, we held an additional discussion with Marcela to clarifying remaining questions we had at that point. All the names have been disguised, but everything else is accurate to the best of my knowledge and abilities. Marcela spoke to two classes in which the case was assigned.

VECOSA B

A year after initiating operations, Vecosa had developed a niche selling pre-cut vegetables to four-

and five-star hotels in Costa Rica's central valley (the capital region). They also had some sales to fast-food restaurant chains but they had, for the moment at least, abandoned their efforts to penetrate local restaurants and supermarkets.

The couple had decided to focus mainly on the hotels because that was where they were able to make the sale. The salesman they hired failed to make even a single sale, and so Marcela took up the sales effort herself. The first person she was able to convince to give her firm a chance was the Canadian chef from an international hotel who was already very familiar with the product, and happy to find such a service locally. As it turned out, several chefs working in the international hotel chains had come from Europe and the United States, were familiar with this type of product, and were happy to give Marcela business. Marcela, at that time, had no competitor in the high quality hotel market segment.

Although price was still important in this segment, by maintaining a good relationship with the hotel purchasing managers, so long as Vecosa maintained competitive prices, they were at least somewhat protected from the competition.

VECOSA IN 2000

The company had grown in some of its functions, but in others it remained just as it had been at the beginning. The production area had started with a single person. Now, it had ten employees, although Marcela continued to supervise production. The company began processing 150 kg of vegetables per day. Presently it processed 800 kg daily – still well below capacity.

PRODUCTS

Vecosa produced 22 products. The ten top-sellers were onions, cauliflower, broccoli, chayote, lettuce, mixes for meat dishes, potatoes, hemstitch, green cabbage, and carrots. In addition, if the different cuts were considered (peeled, in squares, grated, etc.) the total number of products reached to 37. This product expansion had made the scheduling production more complex.

The company contracted for product transport, but Marcela continued to manage distribution, and handle sales. For one thing, they couldn't afford a salesman, for another, Marcela liked to get out of the facility and meet the clients.

According to Marcela's estimates, Vecosa had a 15% total market share (institutional and retail). The most important competitor, *Corteve*, had approximately 60% total market share. She considered these numbers very approximate because of the difficulty in obtaining information. She wasn't sure how much information her competitors even kept.

A NEW QUESTION

Although her business was growing and becoming increasingly secure, Marcela lamented that many of her clients still did not appreciate Vecosa's standards of production, cleanliness, and quality and the value they added to the product. She was bitter about losing one client because a farmer in the public market offered him a price savings of ten colones (less than US $.04) per kg.

Aside from the increase in the line of products, which complicated production scheduling, Marcela was frustrated by hotel ordering practices asking for deliveries with only one day notice. Finally, the margins in this segment had not been even less than what she estimated — gross margins typically only about 25% of sales price.

Given this situation, Marcela was reconsidering entering the supermarkets with her own brand of pre-cut vegetables. She estimated that gross margins in the retail sector could still reach 50-60% and felt there could be a large potential market. For the moment, Dole had not yet entered the market, but its future entry already had been announced in products such as lettuces, broccoli and cut carrots. Marcela had to make a decision: Should she enter the retail market immediately, prior to the entrance of Dole, or should she wait and see what happens?

QUESTIONS FOR DISCUSSION

The case is around a young Costa Rican woman trying to establish a vegetable processing business in her home country.

In Case Vecosa (A)

1. Which market segment should be initially pursued, retail or institutional sales? Your discussion should have inputs on (a) evaluate a new venture opportunity, (b) research a new venture, (c) analyze a marketing problem, (d) make an entrepreneurial decision, and (e) how an entrepreneurial situation differs from that of a large, established firm.
2. Dole is about to enter a market that Vecosa is also poised to enter. Should the owners try to beat Dole to the punch, or should they wait and follow?

APPENDICES

Appendix 1. Analysis of the Existing Competitor

A: Sales of supermarkets

Producer	*Product Line*	*Strengths*	*Weaknesses**	*Other comments*
Cortasa	Vegetables simply packed Exotic dwarf vegetables	Best known and best distributed (carried in all stores)	No clear market positioning Unattractive packagingShort shelf-life	Packing consists of a styrofoam plate and a plastic or mesh cover No uniformity in product or packagingNot vacuum packed
Vege-todo	Exotic dwarf vegetables	Good placement in upper and middle-class supermarkets	Unsophisticated packagingShort shelf-life	Packing consists of a styrofoam plate and plastic or mesh cover
Dole	All types of fruits and vegetablesInternational-style prepared salads and fruits	Known brand and company Deep pocketsManagement, production, marketing and logistic capabilities Vertically integrated	Limited relationship with local producers Flexibility	Although DOLE not yet had entered the market, its entrance was expected imminently
Revesa	Cut & packed greens and vegetablesReady-to-make "picadillo" (a popular local accompaniment)	Good presence on Automercado supermarket shelves	No brand name Customers do not know the product	Store brand for Automercado Packing consists of a styrofoam plate and a plastic or mesh cover

Corteve	All types of pre-cut vegetables Ready-to-mix with recipes for "olla de carne" (a popular local food)	Broad Product Line Widest distribution	No clear market positioning Unattractive packaging Short shelf-life	Packing consists of a styrofoam plate and a plastic or mesh cover

Marcella felt that higher value-added products such as prepared salad mixes could command prices as high or higher than those found in the US, and estimated that average prices for the full complement of products that Vocasa would produce would be about US$2.50 per kg.

Producer	*Product Line*	*Strengths*	*Weaknesses*
Corteve	All types of fresh vegetables	Wide portfolio of clients Production Plants	Change in management. Similar processing of all vegetables (Not the recommended practice)
Empecasa	In addition to fresh vegetables, they also sell prepared foods	Most established firm in the market Good portfolio of clients (fast-food chains) Low Prices Good relations with suppliers	Unsophisticated production: manual Machinery Poor presentation of product Short product-life
Comagrico	Could not get information	Very low prices	Very low quality Completely manual systems

General Comments: Prices are highly competitive. Chefs usually make the purchases. Know ledgeable chefs like broader product lines, longer product life, and greater variability of cuts.

Appendix 2. Estimation of Institutional Consumption.

A. Hotels

Very Large Hotels (5)	3,405,600
Large Hotels (12)	1,034,064
Mid-size Hotels (5)	87,720
Total (Kilograms)	**4,527,384**

B. Restaurants

Total annual consumption (kg) of onions, peppers, lettuce, carrots, and cabbage

Pizza Buena	1,345,182	Adole	85,413
Aros Dorados	523,755	Fenicia	32,328
KIKOS	517,962	Princesa del Oriente	31,287
Super Pollo	275,880	Nuevo Oriente	10,140
Hamburbuena	144,000	Bonerosa	9,882
Lalos	141,186	Arcos	6,657
Pollos al Carbón	129,693	Ambus	6,135
Cucharaditas	107,484	Others	265,563
Total annual consumption all restaurants: 3,632,547 Kg			

The average price per kilogram of a product for institutional sales was US$1.05

Appendix 3: Summary of initial capital investment (in US$)

Initial Capital Investment	*Retail*	*Institutional*
a) Plant	$12,400	$12,400
b) Large packaging machinery and refrigeration units	77,400	77,400
c) Smaller equipment	2,200	2,200
d) Office equipment and supplies	800	800
e) Licenses	5,200	5,200
f) Truck	38,000	38,000
g) Working capital	22,000	22,000
h) Refrigerated truck		25,000
i) Specialized machinery		15,000
Total capital investment	**158,000**	**198,000**

Appendix 4: Projected Fixed and Variable Costs (in US$ per year)

Marcela estimated *variable costs* of production, packaging, and delivery to average about $.55 for institutional sales (typically these costs are about 50 percent of sales price, but Vecosa's costs are higher than those of competitors due to advanced processing).

She estimated variable costs of produce, packaging, and delivery in the retail segment to be considerably higher — $.62 per kg — due to higher packaging and delivery costs.

Marcela estimated *annual fixed costs* as per the table below:

Annual Fixed Costs	*Retail*	*Institutional*
Depreciation (25% of Investment)	34,000	*44,000
Costs of Vehicles and distribution	15,000	15,000
Administrative salaries and costs	22,000	22,000
Salesmen salaries & associated sales expense	50,000	50,000
Maintenance costs	7,200	7,200
Employee Benefits	26,500	26,500
Utilities & Other Fixed Costs	12,000	12,000
Retail Promotional Expenses	*40,000	0
Financial Costs (15% of Investment Capital)	30,000	30,000
Total Projected Fixed Costs	236,700	206,700
Fixed Cash costs (Fixed Costs – Depreciation)	202,700	162,700

Differences in investment in fixed costs depending on market segment are due to the following: Marcela estimated that selling in the retail segment would require additional expected annual expenditures of $40,000 for marketing, promotions, and packaging – most of which would need to be spent before revenues would come in. On the other side, institutional sales would require additional depreciation for additional investment in a refrigerated truck and specialized machinery. (See Appendix 3)

Appendix 5: Demographics for Costa Rica and Central America[1]

	Costa Rica	*Elsewhere in Central America*
Inhabitants	4,000,000	28,000,000
Percentage of the population with college degrees	7%	3.5%
Percentage of college graduates who are female	48.5%	43%
Percentage of the population that eat fresh vegetables daily	50%	50%
Annual population growth rate	2,5%	3,5%
Principal socio-cultural influence	(1) USA (2) Europe	(1) USA (2) Mexico
Real income trends	Stable	Increasing
Consumption of meat	Declining	Stable
Average number of people per household	3.2	4.7

14

MOKKA: 20 Years of Tradition

Fredy Valenzuela
Victor Nocetti

ABSTRACT

This case shows the story of Martha Pfeil and her incursion in the business world. Together with two friends, she created CAFE MOKKA - a store recognized for selling the best sandwiches in Santiago, Chile's capital city. For more than 20 years she has been running this business and has been able to generate delighted customers who have been the main source of publicity for attracting new ones. This has not happened without any difficulty. The implementation of new technologies and getting a balance between her personal and business lives have been very difficult issues that she has had to deal with.

MOKKA: "THE STORY BEGINS"

The history of "MOKKA" could not be more domestic. It all started when Martha Pfeil's husband got an offer for a store of 28 squared meters inside a new mall called "Parque Arauco" that was built in Santiago, Chile's capital city. That was the first mall opened in Santiago, so it was unclear if it would be a good investment. Would people visit the mall? Would people use it for shopping? or would they use it just for spending time during the weekend? Despite of all these questions, Marta's husband considered this business an excellent opportunity for her wife, who has always shown interest in running something of her own.

Chile is a long and narrow strip of earth located in South America. It is well known for being the main world producer of copper, producing good wine and delicious fruits and having one of the most stable economical and political situation in Latin America. The amount of natural resources owned is huge. Current Chilean population is 15 million people and Martha Pfeil is one of them. She is forty eight years old and she's got three children. She is the typical Chilean woman who takes care of her family, and she is very happy about it, but she constantly thought she would be even happier if she complemented her family life with an activity done outside her home. When her husband offered her the possibility of leasing a store at the mall, she immediately thought in her girl friend with whom she had had a very close relationship and talked several times about running a business together. They did not have any background on market studies, gastronomic issues or business experience at all, but they did have an anthropology education and a sound business sense. Besides, they have always been active, open minded, enthusiastic, highly-committed toward achieving their goals, reasonably optimistic and the most important of all, they are very conscious of their weaknesses and that they have to consult experts in those topics they do not manage should they want to be successful.

When they got the offer they were not sure about what type of business to establish in that store. They wanted to choose something new but at the same time they did not want to take too much risk. They figured out that selling food would be the easiest way of doing business and also it would be the low-risked choice because 'every people have to eat' and, particularly in Santiago, so many people work very far from home. Hence, they look for a convenient place to have food, one that offers them both high quality food and reasonable prices.

THE SANDWICH MARKET IN SANTIAGO, CHILE

The traditional sandwich that is sold in Chile is the 'Miga Sandwich'. By 1982 there were only three stores that excelled for the production of high quality sandwiches in Santiago, Chile. One of them was called 'La Novia' ('the bride'). This store was a very old one located in the center of the city, very far from the mall, so in opinion of Martha it was not a real threat. The other store that offered a high quality sandwich was 'Coppellia'. This store was located much closer to the Mall, however the main product it used to sell was ice cream. Sandwiches were a very small part of the business, situation that changed years later when they opened several stores in other malls. The last store was "Café Paula". This store was facing serious problems in its image. Customers were not happy with the service this store was offering them. '*We are not getting value for money*', as some of them mentioned.

THE MOKKA SANDWICH

Based on all the information they gathered, Martha and her friend came up with the idea of selling sandwiches, but high quality ones. But what is a high quality sandwich made of? They did several tests with different types of bread, toppings, and they even checked the characteristics of those toppings (i.e. thickness of the ham, etc.). After all these tests they came up with the idea of a thick and fresh sandwich. *'Every body gained some extra kilos after all these tests but it was well worth it,'* she argued.

BRANDING

The second decision they had to make was relative to the brand name of the store. They knew this was a very important decision because it would be the way their customers would both remember the store and recommend it to their relatives and friends. During a brain storming session Martha, who had became the heart of the business, came up with the name of 'Weimar', which had a very important meaning for her because of emotional family reasons. In spite of the arguments given by Martha on favor of this brand name, her business partner did not like the name because she considered that 'Weimar' was too difficult for Chileans to pronounce. This decision was mainly based on the fact that the mother tongue in Chile is Spanish and only a low percent speak English as a second language, and even though 'Weimar' was the mix of two words, Chilean customers would think it was an English word and they could be afraid of pronunciating it, which would negatively affect the number of customers who would do business with them. After this rejection Martha came up with another alternative name. *'What about MOKKA? but with two 'k' with the aim of giving the brand name the strength it requires for being successful', she said.* Marta's business partner liked this brand name very much and so they came up to an agreement on this matter. Nowadays and looking backward they still think this name truly reflects the spirit of the business they are running.

THE FIRST MONTHS OF OPERATION

MOKKA opened business in April 1982 and during the first year Martha and her business partners faced several difficulties due to the lack of business experience, which lead to the need of constant improvisation to solve the problems they used to have every day. They had never had a business before, nor they knew how to schedule production process. This meant, for them, that during the first two months they had too many sandwiches left in inventory by the end of the day. Martha had the goal of selling high quality products so all the unsold products were thrown away to the garbage, causing some cash flows problems. They wanted to reduce inventory but they had no idea how many customers to expect each day so it was almost impossible to plan in advance. As Parque Arauco was the first Mall in Santiago, it made even more difficult to predict customers' behavior, which in turn did not allow them to have more precise sales forecast. There was lot of improvisation that fortunately worked very well for them, but also there was a lot of creativity that helped to come out of some troubles they faced and that made very enjoyable going to work to the store every day. When Martha looks back and thinks about the reasons for choosing entering to this business she realizes how wrong she and her partner were. At the beginning, they had the perception that this was a business very easy to manage, but now with more experience she is conscious of all those variables that they did not take into account at that time. Despite of all these difficulties they were very committed to turn the negative situations around and to improve MOKKA's bottom line.

In terms of the way they operated their business, they began to make sandwiches in Marta's house from where they distributed them to the stores. By that time, there were only eight people working at the starting company: two people for preparing the sandwiches and four assistants that served the local. They had a blender and a coffee machine. It was crazy thinking of having a cashier! ... just improvisation!

THE BUSINESS STARTS TO GROW

In time, the business started to grow, which was happening not only for Marta's sense of the business, but also for their analysis of what was happening in their business and in the economy in general. In doing this analysis they gathered data that allowed them to know and learn what was happening in their store (i.e. customer behavior, sales per product, etc.), in the environment (i.e. number of people who visit the mall, number of competitors, weaknesses and strengths of the competition, etc.) and their feeling regarding the more convenient locations for other MOKKA stores. This was reinforced by the fact that many people used to ring them to offer them space in other buildings for establishing new MOKKA's branches. A non-written policy was that Martha and her partner always have to study any new potential location to determine if it was suitable for MOKKA. Variables such as number of people who visit the building or mall, level of income of those people, number of existent suppliers offering a similar product, among others, were considered in their analysis. In this way they came up with the idea of opening a second store in Plaza Lyon. The new store gave them valuable information about the importance of location and the fact that there is no recipe that works exactly the same way every where. For some reasons, which they did not know, customers walked on the other side of the street and they did not cross to Plaza Lyon, so they did not have too many customers entering to the store. To solve this problem they decided to offer a lunch menu as a strategy for attracting new customers. This worked fine and very soon the store started to be fulfilled every day. In spite of this success, the amount of work that meant running that store was so different to the other stores, and there were too much effort put into it that they decided to sell it. It did not take long to sell it off.

ENTERING TO A NEW MARKET

The same policy used to open in Plaza Lyon, helped to increase the number of MOKKA's branches in Santiago covering different geographical sectors (west, east, south and north) and during the year 2000 they opened their first branch out of Santiago in a city called Viña del Mar. The branch in Viña del Mar demanded more work for Martha and her business partners. It was the first time it took them so long to get profits. Several reasons caused this situation. First of all, this store was inside the first mall built in Viña del Mar and people from this city behaved totally different than those from Santiago. Secondly, not many people were accustomed to go to the mall. This lack of customers led to a high turn over in the stores that were inside of the mall, so it was not very clear the target segment of the mall as a whole. Over the time the right mix of stores was found, which led to an increase in the number of visitors and a more steady flow of customers to MOKKA. Beside this situation, MOKKA brand name was not known in Viña del Mar, so customers had no idea about the quality of the product it was offering. In terms of production, they had very high costs because of the lack of economy of scale (all fixed costs have to be allocated to only one branch, not like in Santiago where there are more branches). In addition, Martha wanted to keep the same quality of the sandwiches made in Santiago, which was a very relevant issue, but the distance between the two cities did difficult to control it. In Santiago was much easier because they have only one production unit for all stores. In Viña del Mar, instead they had to open a new production facility. To get this task done well, she sent the most experienced people in making the sandwiches in Santiago to Viña del Mar. She also visited, on a regular basis, the store in Viña del Mar to make sure that every thing was been doing as expected. Martha has a directive-oriented style of management, and she likes to know everything. She knew this was positive because she could control the quality of the products offered to her customers, and knowing that she could not be every where, she had to rely on other professionals, what was not something easy to be accepted. This issue became more important as long as the business kept growing. Through experience and knowledge, acquired by running the business, she started to learn about the weaknesses of the business, where she needed to put more emphases and spend more energies. The business had a "history" so it was easier to determine which issues were the most relevant.

THE INCORPORATION OF NEW TECHNOLOGY

Regarding the incorporation of new technology, this has been one of the most difficult aspects they have had to deal with. The reason for this is the fact that the business operates during all day, so any technological innovation and the correspondent training of employees had to be done without disturbing the level of attention given to MOKKA's customers. Time was a critical factor, but there also was the logical resistance of people to change and innovations in the way of doing business in MOKKA, after being in the market for several years without having a high employee turn over. A good example of this problematic issue was MOKKA's introduction of the new computational system. Due to the increase in demand, they had to go from manual receipts to the use of a computational system, and also to implement procedures and control measurements. One of the issues that they had to deal with was how to train employees in the use of this new technology. This matter was very relevant because Martha was very concerned about the quality of the service they were offering to their customers, so employees had to follow a very strict schedule during the day, in order that they did participate in any training. To solve this problem, Martha got the services of an external company, which offered on-site training. By doing so, employees learnt the use of this new technology but at the same time the quality of the service did not go down. In terms of the implementation of control systems they had even more difficulties because the supplier of the software, which was outstanding on theory, did not have apt personnel to support the implementation of this system in MOKKA stores. Because of this they had several problems, such as errors on times, changes on technicians, etc, which delayed the perfect functioning of this control tool.

In terms of web site design, an institutional web site was developed. It was more fashion than anything else!...*because every business has it.* Martha and her business partner did not consider that having a web site would lead to an increase in MOKKA sales, therefore it would not have a great impact on the business bottom line. In their opinions the business' key success factors are *location* and *quality of the product.*

THE GENDER FACTOR

After 20 years of running MOKKA, Martha

considered that the greatest challenge she has faced has been not losing her female qualities and getting a balance between her personal and business life, which means achieving success in her business, but also having a happy and lovely family. This goal was very difficult to achieve because in Chile men do not help much to their wives in household related matters, such as cleaning and taking care of the children. Besides her children were very important for her and she wanted to be close to them. She was very concerned about all the negative information that youngsters can get nowadays regarding drugs and other negative temptations. For these reasons, Martha wanted to personally raise her children in order to provide them the right information so they would become excellent persons and professionals.

In terms of the advantages and disadvantages for being a woman, in her opinion, this has not been a negative issue, but rather has been a 'plus' in some cases.

'In the Chilean business world there are many more men than women so for women it is easier to get the initial attention that it is required to enter to the business world and from then it is up to women to demonstrate how much they are worth. Women have to have faith in themselves. They do not have to have fear of having fear, because fear provides the consciousness in the business world. They also have to work harder than men, they have to be committed to their jobs and they should fall in love with their businesses, they should know it like they know their loved ones for good and worst'. Martha commented.

In her opinion, the only problem that women are facing today is caused by some legal issues, which forced businesses to pay child care for a period of two years, making more costly hiring a woman for the risk of pregnancy. This situation instead of helping women in the labor market is reducing the chances for them to being hired.

MOKKA´S CURRENT SITUATION

From an ownership point of view, MOKKA has only one owner, Martha Pfeil. Her partner left the business after only one year of running the business because she could not cope with the pressure of spending so much time in the business and leaving her family behind. In terms of the business itself, MOKKA is stronger than ever and even though it continues having that domestic and personal accent that would explain, in part, the recipe of its success, this brand name is being associated to an important chain, very well organized and very professional. Today MOKKA has 15 stores along the Chilean cities of Santiago and Viña del Mar, and despite of having more stores, they still do not forget the first store they had because this was very special to them and also because they do not have it any more. The lease of that store finished and the owner did not want to renew it to MOKKA. Nowadays it has 140 employees, has one and half million customers per year (4,000 customers per day), and sells 200 thousand crumb sandwiches (58 thousand are made of avocado) and 330 thousand coffees per year. Regarding the items they used for preparing these products, every year they purchase approximately 140 thousand eggs, 50 thousand kilos of fruits, 36 thousand liters of ice cream, 30 thousand liters of milk, 22.4 thousand kilos of chicken, 9 thousand of ham and 5.4 thousand kilos of grain coffee.

The sandwiches are no longer prepared in Martha's house nor distributed in Martha's van, as it was common until 1992. But there are things that have not changed at all, such as the hegemony of the product. In her opinion that period of time was very intense but very rich in family experiences. They spent 10 years preparing the sandwiches at home, which was very demanding, because every time the phone rang every body used to scream out loud "sandwich", and because the stores used to work from Monday to Sunday. So there was no day for relaxing. However this was compensated by the fact that somehow the family life was not affected by Martha's job. Despite of the convenience of preparing the sandwiches at home for family matter, to improve business efficiency they purchased a house that served both as a factory and a main center of delivery. This house is right in front of one of its most important suppliers which allow MOKKA's customers to receive the same sandwich in any of the MOKKA's branches. One of the things that has not changed is the fact that Martha has been taking care of the people who prepare the sandwiches (these people have been working for several years with Martha) and any difference to the standard established by Martha was immediately corrected by her. By doing so she has maintained one of the key success factors of the business.

In term of the waitresses they had a low turn over, compared to other stores, due to the high "tips" they got every day. Apart from that, Martha tried all the time to make them believe in what they are selling. Martha personally explained to them the characteristics of products, asked them to taste their products and the products of the competition so they could see the difference in quality and would be able to explain customers all this. In addition Martha visits all stores very often and talks to employees about the quality of the service they are offering. She asks them for customers' complaints and also for suggestions in how to improve the level of service. With all this for the past 20 years Martha has been able to maintain the service quality she wants, but also she has maintained very satisfied and motivated employees who are committed to MOKKA. Regarding those employees who do not behave in the way Martha expects, and were also, negatively affecting MOKKA's atmosphere, Martha talks to them to let them know what she expects from them and if they continue behaving in the same way they are fired.

The location is also strategic. Every day 4 deliveries are done to the ten sale-centers located in different areas of Santiago, which allows decreasing transportation times of both raw materials and finished products. One of the company's policies is to never sell a sandwich that was made the previous day, since it affects negatively the brand name. This implies that MOKKA has to be provisioning its locals as they run out of stock, and has to have very close relationships with its suppliers, which are essential for the good operation of the business as a whole.

Martha recognizes that the temptation to lower quality is very big and it tends to occur more than it is desired. In order to keep quality it is necessary to increase prices, something that they do once or twice a year. They constantly test, in different places, the quality and the price of their products. The latter has been done every day for the past 20 years, because they have tried to make sure that they sell high-valued products. All this effort trying to control the quality of their sandwiches has paid off because nowadays they do not have to spend too much resources in advertising their brand name for attracting new customers. The main means of promotion has been the "word of mouth" of delighted customers, who have become committed and loyal customer to "MOKKA".

TO GROW OR TO SELL, THAT IS THE QUESTION

MOKKA's business has had excellent results during these twenty years. Now Martha is planning to expand the business by attacking new markets or just by franchising it. She has already spent some time analyzing different markets that can be attacked by Mokka and also the best way to do so. She would like to enter to the major Chilean cities, such as, Concepcion and Rancagua. However, the distance between the cities where Café Mokka already has a branch and those potential markets is too big, which might lead them to lose control over the quality of the product offered in those potential new markets. After spending some time thinking about the most suitable solution, and when it seemed that she has made up her mind, she received an excellent offer to sell her business. In financial terms, this offer is very attractive and would allow her to live very confortable for some time or to begin a new business. So, she has the possibility of continuing ahead with their initial plan or to take advantage of this excellent financial opportunity, but that would imply to leave a business of a lifetime. What is the most convenient alternative for her? She is not sure.

QUESTIONS FOR DISCUSSION

1. Management and new entrepreneurial ventures:

Please analyse the concepts of efficiency and efficacy of Cafe Mokka throughout the years. Also discuss the importance of environment in supporting and leading to failure of certain entrepreneurial ventures.

2. Marketing mix and value creation:

What are the "value added" factors that differentiate Cafe Mokka from other similar businesses. From a strategic point of view it would be interesting to consider Cafe Mokka's scope and the competitiveness factors that create its advantage in the market. Also discuss how Martha Pfeil has struggled over the years to maintain and improve them.

3. The conflict between management roles and family roles:

One of the main issues deals with how Martha reaches a healthy equilibrium in her life spending time with her family and the time she devotes to cafe Mokka. Getting involved too much in running the business would undoubtedly lessen the time devoted to family, so how one should proceed? Should someone involve the family in the business? What issues become then relevant?

4. The evolution of a firm:

How has Cafe Mokka has evolved? What changes have been implemented and why? Have those changes been positive or negative and why? Taking cue from some data from the environment analyse how the market changes and how well cafe Mokka did?

5. Dealing with Strategic Decisions:

The decision that Martha is going to make regarding selling her business is an important issue. She has the possibility of either expanding the business to other main Chilean cities or selling the business. What factors should she consider in arriving at her decision?

15
Conclusion: Women, Technology and Entrepreneurship

Charla Griffy-Brown
Vinnie Jauhari

This book demonstrates that the face of entrepreneurship is changing globally. While the popular image still tends to be the risk-taking male, in many instances it is actually women who are starting successful, thriving businesses across the globe. Furthermore, while the image of women entrepreneurs is skewed toward businesses that do not involve technology, the entrepreneurs in this book use technology to create new businesses and to work "smarter". That is, women use technology, particularly information technology to assist in achieving a wide range of strategic and operational objectives from marketing, to the operational underpinnings of the business or simply to strategically embrace a new business opportunity.

THEORETICAL FRAMEWORK

In order to move beyond the quantitative comparison of women owned businesses globally, this book provides insight into actual businesses and the specific issues faced by the entrepreneurs who started them. This book contributes to the literature on women on entrepreneurs in several ways. Firstly, it explores the role of technology in businesses started by women. Quite simply, the question was: does technology play a role in women's entrepreneurial activity? In these cases we were interested in seeing if we could observe women owned businesses even in emerging economies that leverage technology to create wealth. O'Connell(1999), Yin(1994), Miles and Huberman (1994), Strauss and Corbin (1998) have explored the deployment of technology usage and the role played by technology is ushering the change in business.

The book uses the case study approach to get a rich insight into entrepreneurial experience for women from various geographies. These entrepreneurial initiatives have occurred across numerous industry sectors. Those cases have been selected which demonstrate success in the start up experience. Research has indicated that the success rates for new business start ups irrespective of the gender is less that 10%. Therefore the collection of these case studies has a special significance as it has lessons for future entrepreneurs and also implications for policy makers. There are steps which could be initiated which could ensure a better entrepreneurial experience for women in particular.

The different case studies give a perspective on the following dimensions :

1. A brief background of the business and the Role of Technology in the Business.
2. Motivation for setting up the business (opportunity/necessity based).
3. Characteristics of the entrepreneur which contributed to success of the venture.
4. Role of Gender

5. Growth strategies adopted by businesses.
6. Major challenges encountered by the entrepreneur and were they overcome.
7. Competitive analysis for the firm and challenges therein.
8. Financial analysis and viability of the business wherever it was possible. This also included perspective on how initial start up happened.
9. Any cultural factors which were impediments or responsible for success of the venture.
10. Sustainability of business in the long run.

The case study technique has been deployed in the book. The power of case research is that it enables us to test 'in vivo' the assumptions explored in theory to see what role they actually play in successful business start-ups. These cases provide an opportunity to look at the stories behind the business creation in order to identify what elements might be common across national boundaries. It also provides an avenue for testing commonly held theoretical assumptions to see if these assumptions are valid, particularly as they are perpetuated across quantitative research in the area of women and entrepreneurship. The research questions were: "Are there common themes across national boundaries related to these entrepreneurial success stories?" and "Do commonly held theoretical assumptions hold true across these cases?"

In this regard, most of the discourse on women entrepreneurs assumes that women entrepreneurship is "unusual" or "not typical". Helen Ahl (2004) suggests that embedded in research on women and entrepreneurship are discursive practices that lead to the reproduction of the idea that women and men entrepreneurs are fundamentally different. She points to several discursive practices and assumptions in research that produce this result:

* Entrepreneurship is discussed as male gendered, but thought of as neutral;
* Men and women are assumed to be essentially different as entrepreneurs.

Several research strategies that perpetuate the assumption that men and women are essentially different include:

1. Stressing small differences between men and women while ignoring similarities or large overlaps.
2. When finding similarities between men and women proclaiming women entrepreneurs to be exceptions from "regular" women.
3. Molding an alternative, feminine entrepreneurship model such as the "good mother".

Interestingly, the methodological preferences for building this discourse are surveys and statistical analyses (quantitative research) that look for differences and theories that concentrate on the individual or the individual firm. According to Ahl's work, the discourse is perpetuated by a writing and publishing system, including a blind review process, which shares the basic assumptions and reinforces the theoretical and methodological preferences. In addition, institutional support, research financing and the academic career system further enables this discourse and it is even perpetuated in the training of entrepreneurship researchers which then continues to reinforce this discourse.

This collection of cases is an attempt to dramatically depart from this mold. In order to breakaway from this discourse and truly test these fundamental assumptions and methodologies, this book brings together a collection of global qualitative research, which when analyzed collectively and qualitatively allows us to test whether men and women are fundamentally different as entrepreneurs. By looking at the institutional and cultural values in which each of these ventures are embedded it further allows us to diminish the "gendered" approach by allowing the entrepreneur themselves to reveal how this is constructed in their own culture, if in fact they perceived gender to be an issue at all in their venture.

The methodology used in analyzing these peer reviewed cases was established qualitative research methodology based on the work of Yin (1994), Miles and Huberman (1994) and Strauss and Corbin (1994).

ANALYSIS OF THE CASE STUDIES FEATURING IN THE BOOK

Fourteen cases were examined documenting successful women entrepreneurs in India, China, The United Arab Emirates, Singapore, Great Britain, the United States, Canada, Chile, Costa Rica, and Slovenia. The types of enterprises explored in the cases range from bio-technology, software, real estate, online education, manufacturing, retailing, food processing, natural products, water purifying systems the development of non-government organizations, and services.

The following paragraphs summarise the key observations on the key dimensions covered in the various case studies featured in the book:

1. A brief background of the Business and Role of Technology:

In terms of technology, the businesses range in the use of technology from deployment of primary technology to the establishment of sophisticated online enterprises. The use of technology is categorized according to the role it plays in the organization. For example if technology supports operational functions only, then it is classified as operational. If the firm deploys technology which drives the growth of business or used as a business model such as inline business then it is classified as strategic. In most instances, companies that use technology as central to their business models, also use technology operationally as well.

The businesses have been classified as high- tech or low-tech depending on the deployment of technology. However, the reverse is not true. Some companies are either low-tech or do not use technology at all. This was also noted. The table below also classifies the domain of the business in terms of high tech, medium tech or low technology. In addition, most businesses in the 21st century are evolving in their use of technology, particularly information technology, along a trajectory as described by Ross (2003). In order to not just take a snapshot of how technology is being used, but to see if its use is changing over time, the cases were analyzed for descriptions of this as the enterprise evolved. In this way, the role of technology in each of the cases was examined to see if it remained static or if the use of technology changed over-time ie dynamic.

The deployment of technology and area of business is documented in Table1.

Table 1. Technology and its use in the case studies

Case Study	*Nature of Deployment of Technology*	*Trajectory of Change*	*Nature of Business*	*Nature of Business*
The Biotech Industry: The Case of Kiran Mazumdar Shaw	Strategic	Dynamic	High Tech	Biotechnology, India
The Case of Shahnaz Hussain: A Perspective of Global Products from India	Operational	Dynamic	High Tech	Cosmetics,Chemicals, India
Women Entrepreneurship in India – A Case of Lijjat Papad	Operational	Static	High Tech	Food Products, India
Social Entrepreneurship : A Case Study of Divya Thangadurai	Operational	Dynamic	Low Tech	Handicrafts, India (Social Entrepreneurship initiative)
SEWA: Creating Women Entrepreneurs	Operational	Dynamic	Low Tech	Handicrafts , India (Social Entrepreneruship)
Women Entrepreneurship in Asia: A Singaporean Case Study	Operational	Dynamic	High Tech	Electronics, Singapore
A Case Study of DOBA, Voted the Best and "Coolest" Private Educational Institution in Slovenia	Operational and strategic both	Dynamic	High Tech	Online Education, Slovenia

Tejari.com – 'The Middle East Online Marketplace' Under the Leadership of Sheika Lubna Al Qasimi	Operational	Dynamic	High Tech	B2B online business, UAE
Sustainable Entrepreneurship- The Case of the Body Shop	Operational	Dynamic	High Tech	Cosmetics Chemicals and Retailing,UK
Barbara Corcoran's Successful Career in Real Estate: A Story of Resourcefulness, Marketing Prowess and Creativity	Operational	Dynamic	Medium Tech	Real estate, US
Vickie Buyniski Gluckman and United Medical Resources, Inc.	Operational	Dynamic	High Tech	Health Care, US
Costa Rica: The Two Vecosa Cases	Operational	Dynamic	Medium Tech	Food Retailing, Costa Rica
MOKKA: 20 Years of Tradition	Operational	Dynamic	Medium Tech	Restaurant Retailing

The analysis of table 1 indicates that the spectrum of entrepreneurial initiatives indicate that majority of the businesses are in high tech areas characterized by a rapid change in business environment and technology change. The area of businesses is also quite diverse ranging from biotechnology to real estate, social entrepreneurship, food, restaurants.

All of the cases used some form of technology to enhance their operations and facilitate growth. The strategic deployment of technology is however very limited. However, the use varied tremendously from low-tech handicraft making to sophisticated biotechnology processes and software development. In addition, the evolution of the use of technology was changing over time for the majority of the enterprises. Looking at the cases, we see that this is primarily driven by the competitive environment and the marketplace, particularly in services. While these conclusions cannot be generalized, they do suggest that global enterprise development whether by men or women spans the gamut in terms of the use of technology and that in almost all cases the use of technology is not static for successful enterprises.

2. Motivation for setting up the business (opportunity/necessity based):

The motivation for setting up a business can be based on identification of opportunity or fulfillment of a necessity. Longenecker, Moore and Petty(2000) have elaborated on the concept of opportunity based entrepreneurship. Opportunity based entrepreneurship is characterized by along term horizon, deployment of strategy, broad education, deployment of sophisticated financial and marketing strategy, rational approach and willingness to delegate.

A necessity based entrepreneurship is a venture which is an alternative to a job and may not address a strategic gap in the market. There is a risk in terms of ease of replication of business as well as the business falling in the "me too category"(lack of a distinctive offering to the market). There is a need to move over to opportunity based entrepreneurship rather than necessity based entrepreneurship. This is in line with the Global Entrepreneurship Monitor Framework as well.

The numerous case studies are opportunity based rather than necessity . This means that there is an evidence of long term planning, sophisticated business processes and ability to delegate as well. For example, Biocon used sophisticated business processes to target the value chain and also fostered international alliances to source technology. Similarly the Cocaran Real Estate example illustrates the deployment of sophisticated strategy to address the market need. The Body Shop case gives an insight into passion for indigenous knowledge and converting the same into products. This was coupled with a passion for issues which affected the community at large, This gave a phenomenal presence for the firm in the market. In m any cases, the need /passion for achievement has been the underlying motivation for initiation of the business. The social entrepreneurship case studies illustrate the concern for community issues which led to an intervention which addressed number of concerns such as women empowerment, education, credit for poor, sustainable livelihoods etc. Even if the firm was founded as a necessity, the pragmatic implementation and hard work went ensured its success.

3. Characteristics of the entrepreneur which contributed to success of the venture:

The characteristics of an entrepreneur play an important role in the success of the venture. Four common themes were identified across all of the cases:

1. Persistence and Perseverance.
2. Leadership.
3. Purpose and Idealism (including internal values).
4. Business Skills.
5. Social Networks (people and community).

The above themes were mentioned throughout the case studies in the description of the venture as well as the lessons learned. Persistence and perseverance was identified in all of the cases as an essential element of success and embodied in the entrepreneur as she adapted to the changing circumstances of the venture. It was also discussed with respect to business skills required to surmount obstacles and challenges faced in developing the business. Leadership was discussed in terms of setting a vision for the company, motivating employees and even developing relationships with key stakeholders including clients. This theme was also discussed in terms of a having and developing a strong social network to support the business. Purpose and idealism were discussed in terms of the values that under girded the venture and the passion that drove the entrepreneur to take the business risk in the first place

The persistence of Olivia for her initiatives to set up Hyflux, Kiran Majumdar in case of Biocon, Shahnaz Hussain for her venture and in all other case studies as well clearly bring out the importance of a strong passion for , never say die attitude and to go on even in face of adversity is a common thread all along.

The entrepreneur in almost all the case studies took on various roles as manager and leader and often served as an inspiration with their commitment and passion. The "never die attitude" helped in surmounting even difficult situations. The entrepreneur displayed lot of courage and maturity in dealing with start up problems and even gender aspects were eventually overcome in all the cases. There was a systematic approach adopted in the creation of enterprise and everything did not center around one person as is normally the case in most start up operations. In this case, the tasks were delegated a systematic approach to creation of an effective supply base and forward integration through a effective distribution channel is also very much evident. The marketing element has been a strength in almost every single case study which has featured in the book.

4. Role of Gender:

Interestingly, the barriers and challenges for the entrepreneurs varied across the national boundaries and were either business obstacles or social/cultural and institutional obstacles. These challenges were also not discussed as a function of gender alone but were constructed within a specific social and cultural context. In fact, all of the themes identified as common across the cases were not gender constructed but rather constructed as essential for successful entrepreneurs. In this regard, the prevailing theory indicating that men and women are fundamentally different does not hold true in the cases in this book.

In fact, the entrepreneurial activities are not gender constructed. In all of the cases, gender plays a minimal role in the development of the enterprise. When explicit barriers and challenges were described that were gender based, it is interesting that these were socially and culturally constructed and the entrepreneurs consistently spoke of them this way in their own voice. In some cases, institutional barriers were described. However, these institutional barriers, such as finding financial support, were also described as socially and culturally constructed. In some instances the institutional barriers were actually transcended in creative ways, such as sourcing capital internationally. Many of the issues mentioned as challenges were mentioned as challenges that all entrepreneurs face in the same way that many of the reasons for success identified earlier were more universal than gender constructed. What follows is an analysis of how gender was constructed in each of the cases followed by a look at the role technology played in each of the cases.

In the case of Biocon, gender was constructed primarily in the descriptions of the Kiran Shah's being the first woman Brew Master and being the only female in her graduating class. After that, gender did not play a central role in the enterprise development. The case does discuss the initial reluctance that some people had in working for a woman which was discussed in the context of culture. However, the statistics presented in terms of the low employee turnover suggest that this problem was easily overcome and was not an institutional issue.

In the case of Lijjat Pappad, Sandhi and SEWA actual focus on enterprises primarily concerned with women's issues or assisting women in business. Ironically, by addressing the issues of women in business directly, these cases also show in their own enterprise development that gender was not an issue. That is, the enterprises and the entrepreneurs do not describe encountering difficulties in creating successful enterprises because they were women. It is difficult to ascertain from these cases whether this is because of the fact that they were directly addressing women's issues and had institutional support, or if this was just the social and cultural realities of the business environment. Regardless, these successful enterprises, created by and for women, do not describe gender as a central element to either the difficulties they encountered or their success.

The MOKKA case also does not present gender as central to the success or difficulties encountered by the business. The challenges of work-life balance are described as the initial lack of experience. Similarly, the Vecosa does not present gender as a central issue or even mention gender as playing any significant role in the successful development of the enterprise.

Gender is openly discussed as a challenge in the UMR case as well as the Corcoran case, both US based businesses. Here again, the gender issues appear to be socially and culturally constructed. In the Corcoran case, the construction of gender seems to be even highly culturally and socially localized. That is, in this case, the difficulties related to gender were that women were not being taken seriously in the Real Estate market specifically in Manhattan. The construction of this bias was institutionalized in office leasing, commercial sales and realty management and construction. The entrepreneur herself discussed her perceptions that the predominance of men in real estate in this market came from the same social strata and were both wealthy and well connected. It is important to point out that again, gender played a role in the challenges faced by the entrepreneur, these issues were not central to the success of the organization. Instead, the ability to creatively market the business and bridge financial gaps played a key role. In addition, the larger issues of persistence, leadership, business skill, and strong sense of purpose played a key role in the success of the organization.

In the UMR case, gender is described as intrinsic to the culture of the company and the predominant female employee base. In this case alone, the culture of the company, which is described as "feminine" is represented as one element that is important for the success of the company. In this description, however, the description of the company as an exemplary place to work includes predominantly non-gender based attributes, such as "open communication", "challenging employees to do more", "listening to dissenting points of view", "acknowledging good service" and "celebrating personal achievements." The primary elements for success in this enterprise are identified as perseverance and leadership.

The DOBA case discusses gender from the perspective of the work-life balance which is mentioned through-out as a key value for the enterprise. However, in the enterprise development, gender is not mentioned as an element of significant challenge or playing a key role in success. In the Hyflux case, gender does not appear to play a role at all as either an impediment or a factor in success.

The case of Tejari does address the role of gender in the development of the company. The description is culturally and socially constructed. In fact, this case devotes a section to explaining the social and cultural construction of women in the UAE. The success of the company is not described as related to gender. The entrepreneur describes feeling "extra pressure" on herself because of being a woman in a senior position. While she felt that most of what she was experiencing was universal "dealing with the egos of male colleagues" and "gender conflict", she also felt this was particularly acute in a society "where women in employment is a relatively new concept."

Interestingly, in all of these cases, even those that explicitly describe gender as playing a role in the enterprise, none of the cases place gender as a ***central role*** in enterprise development. It is not cast as a critical impediment or .a key factor in the success of the business.

5.Growth strategies of the business and possible reasons for success:

The initial start up challenges include the access to capital and limited resources in almost all the case studies. Almost all the firms had a humble beginning and started with small initial capital. As the firms tasted success, they expanded and grew to larger organizations. Different firms have demonstrated different routes for growth. Some of them have deployed technology to reach out to wider markets while as some like SEWA have opted for geographical expansion coupled with widening of the gamut of operations. Body Shop deployed franchising as a technique for expansion coupled with opening of their own stores. However during the last days of Anita Roddick, the firm was acquired by L'Oreal,

The emergence of Biocon with international alliances and technology tie ups is a sterling example of technology acumen and business pragmatism to put resources together for expansion. Biocon has deployed various value drivers for complete value chain to offer drug development to clinical testing facilities. At Biocon for instance, the organisation structure was flat coupled with intensive communication, low attrition rate and an open culture which fostered team work. The entrepreneurial firm despite moving on to a large firm status, retained the nimbleness of a small firm. The firm deployed a pragmatic financial strategy to manage the operations of the firm.

Shahnaz Hussain's venture also saw a global expansion strategy as a means of growth. It deployed franchising as well as their own stores. The firm not only manufactured cosmetics but also grew its operations in value added services such as salons which cased on the product brand name. So it has been a combination of manufacturing as well as retail operations. Lijjat Pappad operations grew as it capitalized on the skills of rural women and also adopted a meticulous approach to offer a product which has a mass appeal. Also linked with the commercial operation was an element of social empowerment. The catapulting of a small set up into Rs 3000 million(1USD=INR40) deploying 42,000 women with 62 branches. Such a huge network with primarily women and managing sophisticated marketing, sales propmotion, exports and advertising is a case in point.

In case of Sandhi in India, access to markets, capital, efficient supply chain , ongoing support to the prospective entrepreneurs have been the key drivers for growth of the firm. So it has been more about operational excellence that has led to the growth of the firm.

The case study of Hyflux at Singapore demonstrates the success of the firm which was listed at Singapore stock exchange. The deployment of proprietory Kristal membranes for water treatment and third party membranes provided a distinct competitive advantage. It also utilized the strategic partnerships with key players in the market. The joint venture with

Chinese entrepreneurs helped its business grow.

In case of Tejari.com, it is the lowering of the procurement costs and global trade which helped the business to grow. It is also a case of operational excellence coupled with an excellent team culture which led the organization to grow.

The Body Shop grew by deploying franchising as a means for growth and also through setting up their own stores. While adopting this strategy, the firm also associated with issues that affected the community such as environmental concerns, cruelty to animals which won them several loyal customers and partners.

Cocaran's case study highlights a pragmatic business strategy also deploying an effective use of technology to reach out to customers and also provide better experience factors to help them make effective decisions. This was coupled with distinct organization culture characterized with open communication, supportive environment and making work a relaxed and fun place to work.

United Medical Resources as a case clearly indicates towards the strong management team with diversified team, personal and social networks as key driver to success of the firm.

The case studies around Costa Rica - The Vecosa Cases and Mokka demonstrate the success of start up operations deploying fair amount of technology in managing their operations but at the cross roads to decide which strategy would be more useful for future growth.

To sum up, the cases range from successful global firms to regional firms and have deployed a combination of strategies to be successful. A pragmatic strategy coupled with good management practices, open communication, excellent team work, strategic alliances, networks - personal and professional have all been contributors to the growth and success of these firms.

6. Major challenges encountered by the entrepreneur and were they overcome:

The challenges which the entrepreneurs faced across all case studies are as below:

a. All the ventures began with limited capital investment, The firms started in a small way with little geographic reach and eventually expanded through leveraging networks, partnerships and strategic alliances. The case of Body Shop, Biocon, Shahnaz Hussain, Tejari.com, Hyflux are good examples of successful firms which expanded globally by incremental increases in their investments in their initial years. What is quite evident across all cases is that none of the cases involved deployment of venture capital and it was primarily family support that helped these entrepreneurs to start up their operations. All the firms have been financially viable and infact have been profitable. The financial data wherever possible has been included in various case studies. Many of the firms have global operations. This clearly indicates that a combination of effective business strategy coupled with ability to raise capital to manage the operations of the firm effectively.

b. The strategy was not pre-conceptualised but it evolved as the business grew. The lessons that one learns is that the entrepreneurs added to their product / service offering as the business evolved. The brand creation was backed by a strong commitment to making the venture successful. The entrepreneurs understood the value drivers and then carved a niche for themselves despite a competitive market. Even in case of the social entrepreneurship endeavours such as SEWA and Sandhi, the entrepreneurs assessed the market gap, addressed the same matched by seamless operations which helped them being successful.

c. There have been also challenges around the creation of brand and business expansion. The severe competition and an established market created lot of challenges coupled with sometimes challenges around being a woman entrepreneur which were eventually overcome. In case of Mokka for example, the challenge was to build up the brand and choose an appropriate name that would generate interest for selling sandwiches. They faced issues in managing operations-scheduling of production process, inventory management, later when the brand was established the challenge was to identify new areas for expansion. Also, as the entrepreneur mentions subsequently - the greatest challenge she faced was not losing her female qualities and getting a balance between personal and business life.

d. Normally building a strong team and finding the right people is challenging. In many cases the entrepreneur was able to find atleast few reliable people who could be a part of the core operation. The environment has been to build a trusted team of people and there has been an environment of trust and collaboration in almost all the cases. The professional set of people managing their roles effectively has been one common thread for almost all the enterprises.

e. Marketing spends for expansion:

Despite being there in the markets which heavily depend upon the advertising spends for success, the firms featured in the book sustained themselves by focusing on the customer needs and addressing the gaps in the market. For example, in case of SEWA the social impact that the firm had was so large that it could support from customers, vendors, communities where it has been operating. Similarly, in case of Body Shop, where advertising and endorsement by celebrities has been a norm, the firm by focusing on community issues and involving women as franchisors and supplier of ingredients created a huge fan following which more than made upon dollar spendings on advertising. Similary for Corcoran, despite the fiercely competititive real estate market coupled with market recession, the entrepreneur with her deft approach to handling customer expectations, led to creation of a successful firm.

7. Competitive analysis for the firm and challenges therein:

Most of the businesses faced tough competition. The competition has been with big established brand names. Therefore, the creation of these successful ventures in this kind of a scenario has been really creditable. The key has been to identify a gap in the market and then position the product to address the market needs. Most of the case studies in the sample have been opportunity based ventures rather than necessity based ventures. When a venture gets created to offer a distinctive offering, the chances of being successful are far higher. The case of Mokka is illustrative of this. Even though the product offering was elementary yet the entrepreneur identified a gap in the market and offered "value for money" proposition. The case of Body Shop with distinctiveness of being a humane firm along with using natural ingredients was a contributor to the success of the firm. Similarly, the management acumen with intelligent deployment of technology in Corcoran's case is another insight into success in a tough realty market .

The case of Lijjat Pappad's success with indigenous formula for manufacturing and SEWA's social reach and impact was able to compete with a tough competition.

8. Cultural factors which influenced the women in business:

There are numerous factors which can be deduced from the case studies which point out at the cultural dimensions affecting the women entrepreneurs. In case of India, for example, though by law men and women have an equal status yet the social conditions are such that it is tougher to have equality in areas which have a pronounced poverty or illiteracy. In light of the socio-economic conditions, social entrepreneurship is a very powerful tool to bring dignity to lives of hundreds of women as in case of SEWA or Sandhi. So an entrepreneurship intervention in this case addresses number of areas such as women empowerment, illiteracy, employment, child care, healthcare, etc., among other aspects.

In UAE for example, women's roles are positioned in the context of the family (Kemp). In the case study, Linzi Kemp quotes (ArabNet, 2002) "The family is the basis of society which shall be responsible for protecting the childhood and motherhood. Sheikha Lubna in an interview with Suhaili (2002) talked about the dichotomy of a culture that does not accept women's capability in employment along side home management. In the context of the need for national workforce to expand to replace non–nationals, Sheikha calls for males to recognize the possibility of a dual role for females and that men need to adapt in light of this.

For example in Chile, in case of Mokka, Martha indicates that in Chilean business world, there are many more men than women. So, for women it is easier to get the attention that is required to enter into the business world and it is upto the women to demonstrate how much are they worth. Women have to work harder than men. But deploying women in a business can also lead to some issues. Legal policies force businesses to pay child care for a period of two years making more costly hiring a woman. This defies the conventional logic of an entrepreneur very educated and suave to create a successful enterprise. Herein comes a social commitment, address a market need and bring in the community together to address the community needs.

The Barbara Corcoran case does indicate about the attitude of some male professionals to women. There is an indication at some point where she felt that the predominance of men in real estate made Barbara feel like an outsider. Yet it did not let Corcoran let the financial and cultural gap bother her. In case of United Medical Resources, Vickie felt that women and men can build successful well run businesses on three guiding principles:

1. Love and be passionate about what you do.
2. Be honest with yourself - play your strengths and hire good people to make up for your weaknesses.
3. Work hard, work smart.

9. Sustainability of business in the long run

All the firms covered in the case study are an intriguing example of successful firms despite challenges which they faced in the initial start up and growth phases. The financial data for most firms which has been documented in the case studies indicate that the firms have managed the financial aspects very well and the businesses are sustainable as a business model rather than dependence on grants. Many of them are at a verge of big expansion plans or exploring possoibilities of tie ups. The sale of Body Shop to L'Oreal is a testimony of the value created by the firm. However, it is also to be seen that these firms become acquirers of other brands and influence their operations.

SUMMING UP

This collection of cases does not obviate the statistics and quantitative lessons regarding women and entrepreneurship, but extends it. The commonalities sought are in the areas of success (what makes them successful). The barriers and challenges throughout the cases are primarily embedded in the local context. While this approach does throw into question the fundamental assumption that women entrepreneurs are fundamentally different, it does not eliminate the reality that there are very real barriers to women entrepreneurs. Through an exploration of each social, cultural and institutional context, these cases help explain not only what the barriers are but how they play out and whether these barriers are gender based or a mix of gender, culture and institutional challenges. In some cases, the difficulties experienced are the same as that experienced by any entrepreneur, but may be magnified depending on the local, social and cultural context.

In terms of technology, these cases demonstrated that technology plays a role, but a dynamic changing role. In each case, the use of technology evolved over time. For sure, in each case technology played a role depending on the venture and the type of learning that each entrepreneur puts into their organization as they respond to the market and its inherent challenges. In a few cases, a very low-tech start was developing into leveraging more and more advanced technology to achieve growth.

This collection of cases demonstrates that women are entrepreneurial regardless of culture or socio-economic level or language. It is hoped that this book provides tools for doing just this for women considering entrepreneurial activity. In addition, it is hoped that to this book contributes to the literature on women and entrepreneurship by addressing some of the assumptions in this discourse through offering qualitative data that questions some of these central tenants and provides a broader sociological and cultural framework for analysis. It is also hoped that this collection of cases provides a powerful set of tools for students and academics to use in exploring this area from a very practical perspective in the business classroom. Ultimately, it is hoped that policy makers will take note of the rich array of opportunities that exist for socio-economic development by supporting women entrepreneurs in ways that are consistent with indigenous social and cultural values.

AREAS FOR FUTURE RESEARCH

Future research could also deploy quantitative analysis across various countries on how leadership characteristics are correlated with success. It could also be about exploring relationships with various environmental and business factors. There could be more detailed studies across very specific sectors and document the success of women entrepreneurs in that sector globally. There could also be research on detailed analysis of select entrepreneurs,

The role of technology and technology-based women entrepreneurship can also be another area of future work.

REFERENCES

Ahl, H. (2004). *The Scientific Reproduction of Gender Inequality: A Discourse Analysis of Research Texts on Women's Entrepreneurship.* Copenhagen Business School Press. Books International Inc., Herndon, Virginia.

Griffy-Brown, C. & Chun, M. *"Aligning Business Strategies and IS Resource Utilization: A Resource-Based View of Establishing Dynamic Capabilities in Japanese SMEs"*, Journal of Global Information Technology Management, 10(3), 2007.

Miles, M. and Huberman, A. (1994). *Qualitative Data Analysis,* Second Edition. Thousand Oaks, CA: Sage Publications, Inc.

Ross, J. W. (2003) *"Creating a Strategic IT Architecture Competency: Learning in Stages,"* MIS Quarterly Executive, 2003, 2(1), 31-43.

Strauss, A. and Corbin, J. (1998). *Basics of Qualitative Research: Techniques and Procedures for Developing Grounded Theory* (2nd ed.), Thousand Oaks: Sage Publications, Inc.

Yin, R.K. (1994). *Case Study Research: Design and Methods,* Thousand Oaks, CA: Sage Publications, Inc.